Current Perspectives in Psychology

Divorce

Causes and Consequences

**Alison Clarke-Stewart
and Cornelia Brentano**

YALE UNIVERSITY PRESS   NEW HAVEN AND LONDON

The Library of Congress has cataloged the hardcover edition as follows:

Clarke-Stewart, Alison, 1943–
Divorce: causes and consequences / Alison Clarke-Stewart and Cornelia Brentano.
p. cm. — (Current perspectives in psychology)
Includes bibliographical references and index.
ISBN-13: 978-0-300-11044-9 (alk. paper)

1. Divorce—Psychological aspects.   2. Children of divorced parents—Psychology.
3. Child custody.   I. Brentano, Cornelia.   II. Title.   III. Series.
HQ814.C55 2006
306.89—dc22
2005018881

A catalogue record for this book is available from the British Library.

The paper in this book meets the guidelines for permanence and durability of
the Committee on Production Guidelines for Book Longevity of the
Council on Library Resources.

ISBN: 978-0-300-12593-1 (pbk. : alk. paper)

10 9 8 7 6 5 4 3

In memory of my academic father, William Kessen,
and happy days at Yale.
AC-S
To my mother, Katharina Lehnen, with much gratitude
for all her support.
CB

Contents

Series Foreword

Current Perspectives in Psychology presents the latest discoveries and developments across the spectrum of the psychological and behavioral sciences. The series explores such important topics as learning, intelligence, trauma, stress, brain development and behavior, anxiety, interpersonal relationships, education, child rearing, divorce and marital discord, and child, adolescent, and adult development. Each book focuses on critical advances in research, theory, methods, and applications and is designed to be accessible and informative to nonspecialists and specialists alike.

This book focuses on divorce and its precursors, causes, and consequences. Among the topics explored are history and trends in divorce, theories of divorce, characteristics that place individuals at risk for divorce, the processes and consequences of divorce, custody issues, child rearing, single parenting, postdivorce adjustment of children and adults, remarriage, and stepfamilies. The authors cover the latest research on each of these topics to convey the multiple effects of divorce. In addition to presenting research, the authors suggest national policies, based on empirical findings, that would support couples before divorce and promote parent and child adjustment after divorce.

Drs. Clarke-Stewart and Brentano have provided an authoritative book on the topic by showing the many influences on adult and child adjustment after divorce. They have underscored the connections of marriage and divorce with many other topics, including employment and income, personality characteristics of one's partner, religious affiliation, and patterns of interaction among couples and how these all can converge to place families at risk for divorce. The authors weave theory, research, and examples in a way that provides information useful for individuals, families, and policymakers interested in overcoming the effects of divorce and improving family functioning. The book provides a model for integrating multiple areas of research in such a way as to disseminate the results to a broad readership.

Alan E. Kazdin
Series Editor

Preface

Every book has a history, and this one is no exception. We have long been interested in the topic of divorce, having studied it, taught it, lived through it, and survived it. It was against this backdrop that we received a request from Alan Kazdin to contribute a volume to the Yale University Press series Current Perspectives in Psychology. We recognized that the invitation provided us with an opportunity to share our thoughts, our knowledge, and, of course, our experience with a wider audience. We viewed our task as providing a balanced review of a conflicted and contentious field. Instead of taking sides in the divorce wars, we tried to be honest brokers of the divorce literature. Our goal was to present the good, the bad, and the ugly as fairly and judiciously as possible. To meet this goal we reviewed hundreds, perhaps thousands, of research reports, chapters, and books. We were comprehensive in our scope but did not dismiss inconsistencies, avoid controversies, or dodge unanswered questions. We hope we have achieved a reasonable and reasoned synthesis of what we know for sure, what we believe to be true, and what we still need to know about this socially and politically charged issue in the early twenty-first century. To enliven our presentation and to provide a more human face to the topic of divorce, we inserted "personal stories" gathered from students enrolled in our course, "The Impacts of Divorce," at the University of California at Irvine. To convey the real-life consequences of divorce for children and young adults, we share excerpts from the students' autobiographies of their parents' divorces, in which they describe in their own words how divorce affected them and their parents. We have written our book to appeal to a wide audience—parents and teachers as well as clinicians and researchers. And we hope that our synthesis will provoke a healthy debate about this important topic and stimulate laypeople and professionals to think seriously about this issue and try to find more humane ways of helping children and parents deal with the difficult transitions of separation, divorce, and remarriage.

1

The Social Context of Divorce

A Brief History of Divorce

Today's media coverage of divorce often gives the impression that divorce is a new and modern phenomenon. But this is not so. Divorce has been around as long as bad marriages; however, the ways we do divorce have changed.

Early History

In the beginning, divorce was a personal decision determined by individuals, not by religion or the law. With the rise of Christianity, however, the Church began to control marriage and divorce.[1] Jesus' oft-quoted response to the question, "Is it lawful to divorce one's wife for any cause?" became the cornerstone of every Christian marriage ceremony: "What God hath joined together, let no man put asunder. Whosoever divorces his wife, except for unchastity, and marries another, commits adultery." Adultery, of course, had been forbidden since Moses received the seventh commandment, "Thou shalt not commit adultery." But this strict position was new. In the Roman Empire, divorce was common. Jesus' words therefore led to a conflict between the Church and the state. The solution attempted by the Roman government was to outlaw marriage between Christians and non-

Christians. But this did not solve the problem, and the ensuing struggle between state and Church lasted for centuries.

As the Church grew in numbers and power, marriage became exclusively a religious sacrament, and by the thirteenth century, the Church controlled divorce in Western Europe. For the following eight centuries the Church remained the victor in the battle between Church and state, and yielding to the command of the Church, the state issued stringent laws controlling divorce. This was the Dark Ages for couples who wanted to divorce.

Then in the early sixteenth century, something happened that reopened the divorce debate. Henry VIII, king of England formed his own church, the Church of England—in order to get a divorce. In 1527, Henry announced his desire to divorce his wife, Catherine of Aragón. He had fallen in love with Anne Boleyn, one of Catherine's ladies-in-waiting. In order to divorce Catherine, Henry needed permission from the Pope, who refused to give it. In response, Henry dissolved his ties to the papacy, secured control of the clergy, and compelled them in 1532 to acknowledge him as head of the Church of England. The following year, he married Anne Boleyn and crowned her queen. Only two years later, Henry charged Anne Boleyn with incest and adultery and had her executed. In short succession Henry married wives three through six, alternately divorcing or executing them after they did not bear him sons or he had tired of them. Henry's ruthlessness illustrates a somber fact: regardless of prevailing laws and despite the teachings of the Church, people have always been willing to go to extreme lengths to rid themselves of undesired spouses.

The Roman Catholic Church continued to forbid divorce, and the Church of England and other Protestant denominations allowed it only in rare cases. Yet the door to divorce had been opened a crack. In the sixteenth and seventeenth centuries in England, it was possible for a man to get a divorce on economic grounds. For example, a man could divorce a barren wife in order to marry a mistress who had born him a bastard son, thus allowing him to give the son his inheritance. Nonetheless, Christianity's stance was still too strict for many people. Gradually, in Britain and Europe and in the American colonies, the control of marriage and divorce decisions drifted away from the Church and the state into the hands of local authorities.

By the eighteenth century, this shift of power to local authorities led to substantial differences in the ease of getting a divorce in different geographic locations. This was the beginning of so-called "migratory" divorces. In the eighteenth and nineteenth centuries, couples from England would go up to Scotland, for instance, stay forty days to satisfy the residency requirement, and get a Scottish divorce; just as, in the United States not so long ago, people would travel from New York to Reno or Mexico for a divorce.

Divorce: An American Tradition

In the American colonies, local authorities had different views and different laws governing divorce. In the southern colonies there was no divorce, but in the north there were some options. In Massachusetts, for example, a magistrate could issue a divorce on the grounds of adultery, bigamy, desertion, or impotence. These more liberal divorce laws had been established in the northern colonies through pragmatic necessity. Confining people in loveless or childless marriages imposed hardships in the new colonies, which were struggling to survive and grow. Any concessions in divorce laws were implemented primarily for practical reasons.

After the American Revolution, in the 1780s and 1790s, many states established divorce laws, and divorce became a civil proceeding in the court rather than a state proceeding requiring action by the legislature. The grounds for divorce were continually extended. For example, physical cruelty and misconduct that "permanently destroys the happiness of the petitioner and defeats the purpose of the marriage relation" became legal grounds for divorce. In Rhode Island, "gross misbehavior" and "wickedness in violation of the marriage covenant" were sufficient grounds for divorce. In Pennsylvania, a wife could get a divorce if her husband turned her out of the house, subjected her to "cruel and barbarous treatment endangering her life," or "imposed indignities to her person to render her condition intolerable or her life burdensome." The length of time to get a divorce was shortened, and women began to be accepted as divorce petitioners. Still, no one was advocating divorce. People continued to be concerned about how to preserve the family and protect morality. The hope was that liberalizing the grounds for divorce would decrease immoral acts such as bigamy and infidelity, which tough divorce laws were encouraging.

The Civil War provided a brief hiatus during which few had the luxury of thinking about divorce. Then, right after the war, in 1866, the number of divorces granted increased sharply. This illustrates another trend. Throughout history, the number of divorces tends to drop during a war and sharply increase immediately after. During a war, many couples live apart and, in addition, are too preoccupied with survival to entertain thoughts of divorce. The grueling experience of war changes people. Women become breadwinners and heads of households; they hold down jobs that before were men's work—and they manage. Men confront issues of life and death, experience comradery and conflict— and they survive. After the war ends, the men return and the situation changes. A hasty marriage undertaken for sentimental or economic reasons at the beginning of the war comes to haunt a couple at its end. When soldiers come home and couples confront the consequences of their hasty decision or their lengthy separation, the divorce rate climbs. Men's wartime transformation and women's newly gained independence make it difficult for both spouses to fall back into the roles they held or anticipated before the war, and so, reunited couples often find it impossible to continue their marriage.

Not surprisingly, hard on the heels of the increase in divorce rates after war, comes a political backlash. As part of a general move toward conservatism after the chaos of the Civil War, the "liberal" divorce laws were repealed. For the first time, some states instituted waiting periods: a six-month waiting period for divorce and a two-year waiting period for remarriage. The misconduct clause was eliminated, and churches made a more active effort to stop divorces by prohibiting ministers from remarrying divorcees.

Regional differences persisted. The West was the most liberal, and the South continued to be the most restrictive. Historian Carey McWilliams wrote that California's divorce rate was the highest in the world during the gold rush, and that "divorces were naturally looked upon with favor and were freely granted."[2] Women were tremendously scarce in the West, and divorce afforded them alternative options— new husbands—and men the chance to get a woman. Thus migratory divorces continued. As time passed, though, would-be divorcers had to travel farther and farther west to get their marriages dissolved because as each state was inundated by an influx of people seeking divorce, its outraged citizens passed stricter divorce laws. In Indiana, for example, citizens complained that they were "overrun by a flock of petulant, libidinous, ill-fitting husbands and wives . . . with no better cause of divorce than their own depraved appetites." So the Indiana legislature tightened the laws, and would-be divorcers had to keep moving west— until they reached Nevada.

Into the Twentieth Century: "Social Conditions Cause Divorce"

Although they had to travel farther, would-be divorcers did not give up, and divorce rates continued to climb in the twentieth century. The divorce rate in 1910 was an alarming one out of every ten marriages. By this time, sociologists had recognized divorce as a major social problem and expressed their concern. They joined the cry of alarm that the clergy had raised earlier, but unlike the churchmen, they suggested that the solution to the problem was not to keep people together in unhappy marriages, but to prevent unwise marriages. Divorce was evil, but a bad family was worse. They did not believe, as churches did, that divorce was the result of immorality, but suggested that it was the result of economic and social conditions. Men were leaving home to work in factories; couples were moving away from their parents to live in cities. Industrialization, urbanization, and women's suffrage were causing the divorce rate to escalate. Families needed time to adjust to the new lifestyles of the modern era, and then, the sociologists speculated, the divorce rate would decline and families would be better than ever, egalitarian and harmonious.

To support families' adjustment, the sociologists had several proposals for reform. Family conditions should be improved by means of welfare payments, pensions, public health services, female labor laws, and compulsory education for the poor. The government should exert more control over marriage, forbidding marriage for unfit couples who did not meet physical and mental prerequisites and giving instruction and education to the to-be-marrieds. Even though education and welfare increased, the national divorce rate did not decrease. Instead, it continued to climb.

Social Changes and Rising Divorce Rates

In the 1920s and 1930s, psychologists and psychiatrists came up with a different explanation for the rise in divorce rates and also a new set of proposals. Divorce and family disintegration were caused neither by immorality, as the Church had suggested, nor by economic and social conditions, as sociologists suggested, but by psychological problems. Marital disharmony was simply the result of psychologically unhealthy individuals in conflict-laden situations. Mental-health professionals saw divorce as a medical problem, a mental illness. Sigmund Freud suggested that divorce was the result of conflict that was inherent in the passion of close relationships in any family. It was worse if a person had grown up in a psychologically unhealthy family and was playing out neuroses developed in childhood. American psychologists cited research showing that delinquency, suicide, crime, insanity, and bad attitudes toward marriage were common among divorced individuals.

These psychological experts, like the sociologists in the previous two decades, had suggestions for reform: the law should provide "therapy," judges should be parental and supportive, and petitioners should have mandatory psychological counseling. The government should set up a "Court for Domestic Relations" or a "Family Court," with "Divorce Proctors" to investigate facts, make recommendations to the court, and try to dissuade couples from divorce. In California, in 1939, a Conciliation Court was established with the purpose of helping couples reconcile or reach amicable settlements, but participation was voluntary, not mandatory, and the idea did not spread. Judges and lawyers were not trained in counseling; their priority remained order and control, not therapy. Although the Great Depression tempered the divorce rate for a while, it did not decline significantly.

One reform that did stick was a further liberalization of divorce proceedings. The broad term "mental cruelty" was instituted as a new legal reason for divorce. This reform was based on the belief that acts may occur in a marriage that "humiliate, annoy, and endanger life as much as physical cruelty." Mental cruelty became *the* major grounds for divorce, replacing desertion and adultery.

During the 1940s, the divorce rate continued to rise, and all the experts—ministers, sociologists, and psychologists—continued to wail. As the divorce rate grew higher and the grounds for divorce became more liberal, their cries grew louder. But even though grounds for divorce were becoming more liberal, they were still not liberal enough to serve every couple that wanted a divorce. So the disparity grew between what the law allowed and what people were actually doing. People lied and fought as they tried to prove that their spouse had inflicted mental cruelty.

Then came World War II, and thoughts of divorce were once again suppressed as people focused on their survival, not the quality of their relationships. But after the war, the divorce rate surged. In 1946, the annual divorce rate in the United States reached a high of about twenty-four divorces for every thousand married women younger than forty-five. This was twice as high as the divorce rate recorded in 1930. Despite the persistent increase in the divorce rate, most states still required the plaintiff to prove at least one legislatively recognized ground. This reflected the traditional "fault-based" view of divorce that the "innocent and injured" spouse should be able to obtain relief from the spouse who had done "a wrong." Typical grounds were adultery, desertion, habitual drunkenness, conviction of a felony, impotence (carried over by many state legislatures from annulment law), and, most commonly used by divorcing parties, "cruel and inhuman treatment."

After the postwar boom in divorces, the divorce rate began to drop, most markedly in the 1950s. Sociologist Andrew Cherlin suggests that the stability of the middle-class, single-earner family of the 1950s was a consequence of the disruptions of the Great Depression and World War II, the existence of a postwar economic boom, and the persistence of an ideology of domesticity.[3] For a short time, people savored their peaceful and prosperous suburban lifestyles. After this interlude, however, divorces increased once again in a continuation of the long-term trend, this time fueled by rising expectations of emotional satisfaction in marriage and women's increased economic independence. Although the divorce rate dipped briefly in the 1950s, it never again dropped to the levels seen before the two world wars.

The legal grounds for divorce continued to shift. By the 1950s, most state legislatures had recognized one or more "no-fault" grounds for divorce such as insanity, incompatibility, or a substantial period during which the spouses had lived "separate and apart." But because the law operates on the assumption that stable marriages are in the best interests of the state, the courts interpreted these "no-fault" provisions narrowly and required proof that there were grounds for divorce—even when both spouses agreed that they wanted a divorce. As a result, divorce trials were filled with charges and countercharges. Moreover, the courts required that the plaintiff (the person who filed for the divorce) be without fault. Thus, would-be divorcers found themselves navigating through archaic laws and intricate qualifying factors that did not fit the reality of their lives or society.

For example, a plaintiff could be denied a divorce if he or she were guilty of any of the following:

> *Condonation:* Forgiving the defendant for the behavior that provided grounds for divorce. For example, if a wife forgave her husband for cheating, she would not be entitled to a divorce.
>
> *Recrimination:* Bringing a countercharge against the accuser. A plaintiff who had himself or herself been guilty of behavior that was grounds for divorce was not entitled to the help of a court. That meant that if both husband and wife had cheated, neither could get a divorce. The result of this practice was that if both parties wanted a divorce so badly that each provided grounds, neither could terminate the marriage.
>
> *Connivance:* Setting up a situation so that the other spouse committed a wrong. For example, if a wife refused to have sex with her husband and he eventually cheated on her, then his cheating could be blamed on her actions, and she, as the plaintiff would not be entitled to a divorce.
>
> *Collusion:* Conspiring together to provide evidence of grounds for a divorce. A plaintiff who had colluded with the defendant to provide evidence of grounds for divorce could then not be granted a divorce.

It is easy to see how such fault-based statutes could complicate legal proceedings and raise the financial ante as each side tried to prove his or her case. However, the realities of divorce litigation in practice were actually quite different from the legal requirements. For example, although it was technically illegal for husband and wife to collude, collusion was quite common. Advertisements were explicit: "Divorces quietly, any cause, manufactured adultery a specialty," and the tabloids featured headlines like "I was the Unknown Blonde in 100 New York Divorces."

In addition, trial judges and lawyers, pressed by a society that wanted divorce on demand while maintaining publicly the ideal of "'til death do us part," operated a legal system that permitted spouses to terminate their marriages without proving grounds if both parties wanted the divorce. This "consensual-perjurious divorce" was obtained by having the plaintiff lie about grounds without objection from the defendant and having the judge accept their story without probing. Thus, despite the strict laws, the divorce rate continued to climb.

The legal grounds for divorce also continued to differ from state to state. The difficulty of obtaining a divorce in the more populous eastern states led to a tremendous increase in migratory divorces to so-called divorce havens or divorce mills. For instance, a six-week gambling sojourn in Reno, Nevada, would really be a cover for a divorce. Many considered this system of migratory divorces to discriminate against the poor, who could not afford to take up residence in another state or travel to a foreign country in order to get a divorce. This was another incentive for divorce reform.

Divorce Reforms

As divorce became less stigmatizing and as serial marriages became more common, the burden on lawyers and judges to maintain a fictional fault-based divorce system grew even greater. This all changed in the 1960s. The roaring social changes of the period reanimated stagnant divorce reforms and triggered a sharp increase in the divorce rate.

First, economic circumstances improved widely. In general, divorce rates rise when people have more money and can better afford to live separately. The improvement in economic circumstances was especially important for women. Women became able to support themselves financially and so were able to leave their husbands (or be left by their husbands). More generous welfare payments during this time allowed poor women to live by themselves, and this, combined with the availability of legal aid, increased divorce in low-income families.

As women entered the workforce, they found that they could make more demands and that more demands were made of them. The Women's Movement encouraged women to be more assertive and independent at home and at work, where they demanded equality and power. It gave women higher status, and, it turns out, when women have higher status, divorce rates are higher. When women no longer depend on men for status and income, they are less likely to stay in unsatisfying marriages.

But the Women's Movement was only one contributor to the increase in the divorce rate from the 1960s through the 1980s. Changes in personal values throughout society also made a difference. All institutions, not just marriage, were being questioned. People were searching for meaning and fulfillment, and with this search came a change in attitudes toward marriage and divorce. People became less tolerant of marital unhappiness. In a study conducted in 1962, researchers found that half of young mothers they interviewed agreed with the statement "When there are children in the family, parents should stay together even if they don't get along." But when the same women were interviewed in 1985, less than one-fifth agreed with the statement.[4]

The dramatic social changes of the 1960s culminated in a divorce reform movement that swept America and Britain in the 1970s. This reform was inspired by a rather unlikely figure: the Archbishop of Canterbury. He recognized that existing procedures were encouraging perjury and collusion and that adversarial procedures were stigmatizing individuals and making negotiations about child custody and support difficult. To remove the immorality—the lies and perjury—from divorce proceedings, the Archbishop proposed a single, no-fault ground that required a judge to grant a divorce if a marriage was "irretrievably broken." This proposal was accepted by a study commission in California, and in 1969, with Governor Ronald Reagan's signature on the

Family Law Act, California became the first state to adopt "no-fault divorce."

Under the no-fault divorce law, one spouse can dissolve the marriage without proving any grounds for divorce and without obtaining the partner's consent. Decrees of "dissolution" (the new, more neutral word for divorce) are granted on the basis of "irreconcilable differences." This qualifies as no fault because it takes two to have irreconcilable differences, so the breakdown of the marriage is no one person's fault. This law eliminated the double standard for men and women and helped remove the morality issue from divorce. As a result of the Family Law Act, divorce became more straightforward and honest and less contentious.

The California Family Law Act bolstered the efforts of divorce reformers who were trying to implement uniform marriage and divorce laws across the United States. The resulting Uniform Marriage and Divorce Act turned out to be, in some ways, more progressive than even the California act. This act made marital conduct irrelevant to the court's decisions about custody, support, and property. It did not use the term "irreconcilable differences"; instead, marriage was said to be, simply, "irretrievably broken." Although not all fifty states accepted this act, it served as a prototype for reform in many of them. As a result, divorce procedures throughout the United States have become more lenient and informal, less punitive and restrictive. No-fault reasons recognized by the states include "incompatibility," "irreconcilable differences," and "irremediable breakdown of the marriage." Some states, however, require a couple to separate physically for months or even years before they can obtain a no-fault divorce.

Many states have retained traditional fault grounds in addition to no-fault or separation-based provisions. Fault-based grounds include cruelty (the most common ground for fault-based divorce), adultery, desertion for a specified length of time, confinement in prison, and impotence that was not disclosed before marriage. Fault-based grounds can be used to circumvent the period of separation required for a no-fault divorce. Furthermore, in some states the faultless spouse may be entitled to a larger financial settlement. In states that offer only no-fault divorce, one spouse cannot prevent the divorce; such

an objection is regarded as further evidence of an irreconcilable difference.

Divorce Today

Today, divorce is quicker, easier, and relatively consistent across states.
All states have some form of no-fault divorce, although there are still
regional differences in settlements and custody. Not only has the law
changed to "no fault," social attitudes toward divorce have also gotten
away from the "fault" notion. Divorce proceedings have become more
honest, simpler, and less contentious, realizing the goal of divorce reformers. We have come full circle. Divorce is once again a personal decision. It is possible for anyone who wants a divorce to get one, without
getting approval from the Church, the legislature, or even the spouse.
But divorce procedures are still complex, and most people do not take
divorce lightly, especially when children are involved. And the fallout
from the divorce experience is still of concern to the church, the state,
and the experts.

Currently, there is once again a strong backlash against liberal divorce laws. Various conservative would-be reformers and grass-roots
organizers—most of them religiously motivated—are trying to repeal
the no-fault divorce law and return to fault-based grounds for divorce.
There are attempts to institute waiting periods for divorce and to establish "covenant contracts" that would supplement or supersede a
state's existing divorce laws, with the specific goal being to constrain
the possibility of divorce. These efforts are driven by the conviction
that liberal divorce laws are the cause of increased marital breakdown
and are imperiling family life. Although it is true that the rate of divorce has increased in states that have reformed their laws, no clear
causal evidence indicates that the laws by themselves are responsible
for increasing divorce. Conversely, history has clearly shown that strict
divorce laws by themselves do not cause happy marriages and that unhappy spouses seek a way out of their relationships whether or not divorce is available. It is doubtful, in fact, that most people are aware that
divorce laws were liberalized more than thirty-five years ago.

A review of the history of divorce makes it clear that the high divorce rate is due to complex social, cultural, demographic, and eco-

nomic changes that were the *cause* of divorce-law reform, not its *consequence*. Ironically, among these changes is a stronger belief in the emotional value of marriage, which more readily disposes unhappily married spouses to divorce in order to seek more suitable relationships and happier lives. It is reasonable to assume that most marriages these days eventually dissolve not only because of the greater acceptance of divorce but because of the greater expectation that a marriage should be fulfilling, not just functional. Divorce sanctions the ending of a dysfunctional relationship and offers individuals a chance to find healthier relationships. Some observers have commented that divorce is indeed a necessary mechanism for rectifying marital mistakes and for improving the overall quality of life.[5]

Divorce Statistics

Governmental agencies, such as the U.S. Census Bureau and the National Center for Health Statistics, regularly take the nation's pulse, reporting vital statistics on marriages, births, deaths, and divorces. The compilation of these nationwide statistics in the United States began in 1887–88, when the National Office of Vital Statistics prepared estimates for the years 1867 to 1886. Since 1944, marriage and divorce statistics have been collected and published annually.[6] The standard way of calculating the frequency of divorce is the "crude rate," that is, the number of divorces per one thousand people. The drawback of the crude rate is that the "population" sweeps up everyone in the country, including children and those who will never marry and are therefore not at risk for divorce. Nevertheless, there is no better index. The most accurate way of assessing the divorce rate would be to collect data on all marriages and follow them until they end in divorce or death; but this process is not feasible. What agency could collect data on every single marriage over the course of years and decades, and who would bear the cost of such an undertaking?

The crude rate of divorce shows that after the enactment of the no-fault divorce law in 1969, the number of divorces rose to an all-time high of just over five divorces for every thousand people in the United States in 1979–81.[7] Since then the tide has turned, and the number of divorces has steadily declined. By 2002, the rate was four divorces per

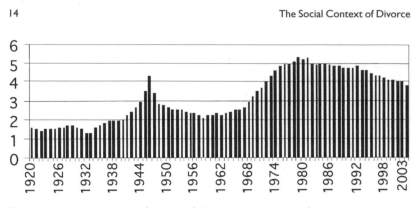

Figure 1-1. Divorce rate in the United States per 1,000 population, 1920 to 2003.

thousand people. In contrast to popular myth, the divorce rate is not still rising; it has been declining over the past two decades.[8] In part, the downtrend in divorce rates is a result of increased rates of cohabitation; the split of cohabitating couples does not add to the divorce rate. However, marriages also are becoming more stable. A recent analysis from a national sample of nearly eleven thousand women in the National Survey of Family Growth indicates that U.S. marriages contracted after 1980 are becoming more stable, not less.[9] Figure 1-1 shows the current downtrend in the number of divorces. In 2003, the most recent reporting of complete annual divorce statistics, the rate had dropped to 3.8 divorces per thousand people.[10] This represents a 33 percent drop from the all-time high and is the lowest it has been in more than thirty years. It is even lower than at some earlier periods in the twentieth century *before* the implementation of no-fault divorce law.

The ratio of marriage and divorce rates has been stable at about 50 percent for the past thirty years, indicating that, during this time, for every two marriages there has been one divorce. This ratio can be a bit misleading, however, because most marriages do not end in the same year that they began. The divorces in any given year end marriages that began at any time earlier. Thus the ratio of marriages and divorces in any given year is based on two very different populations. How does one then arrive at a risk ratio for divorce? Projections of the divorce risk are computed by demographers on the basis of detailed analyses of population demographics, including divorce rates by birth cohort, age, and lifespan projections. Such projections are subject to change if societal conditions change. According to a special report by the U.S. Census Bureau, if current population trends continue, about 40 percent of first marriages in the youngest cohort may eventually end in divorce; if divorce trends return to the pattern of divorce during the period 1975 to 1980, however, 50 percent of first marriages may eventually end in divorce.[11]

Just as divorce laws differ geographically, so do divorce rates. Western and southern states tend to have higher divorce rates than northeastern and midwestern states. For example, in 1995, when the national divorce rate was four and a half for every thousand people, Massachusetts had a divorce rate of only two for every thousand people.[12] Such regional differences are attributed to greater residential mobility in the areas with higher divorce rates, less social integration, and fewer community supports. These factors may explain why Nevada was the state with the highest divorce rate—eight divorces per thousand people.[13] Marriage rates also differ by region. Utah has the highest proportion of married couple households in the country (63 percent), with Idaho (59 percent) and Iowa (55 percent) following. In contrast, only 23 percent of households in the District of Columbia are maintained by married couples.[14] Incidentally, Nevada garnered one more top score as the state with the nation's highest marriage rate, an amazing eighty-eight marriages per thousand people.[15] This unusual statistic reflects, however, migratory marriages and divorces, not the marital patterns of the state's own residents.

The special report by the U.S. Census Bureau revealed a number of population trends in marriages and divorces.[16] Comparing the second half of the twentieth century with the first half, census takers observed the following trends:

- The likelihood of marrying dropped slightly, from 97 to 90 percent.
- People married at older ages; the proportion of people married by the age of twenty-five dropped from 68 to 49 percent for men and from 84 to 63 percent for women.

■ People spent less time married—because of delays in marriage and increases in rates of divorce and cohabitation.[17]

■ Marriages were shorter. The likelihood of a couple reaching a tenth anniversary dropped from 90 to 73 percent, of reaching a twentieth anniversary from 81 to 56 percent, and of reaching a thirtieth anniversary from 70 to 55 percent.

Over the past few decades, however, this last trend has reversed. Although marriages today do not last as long as they did one hundred years ago, they last longer than they did twenty or thirty years ago. In 1975, the median duration for first marriages was six and a half years; in 1995, it was eight years.[18] The increase in duration is even greater for remarriages.[19] Today, about one-fifth of men and women have been divorced. The percentage is highest among men in their forties and fifties (35 percent) and women in their forties (37 percent). Marriages are more likely to be permanent if couples are older; women who marry before the age of eighteen have twice the risk of divorce as women who marry after the age of twenty-five.[20]

The "Seven-Year Itch": When Is Divorce Most Likely?

As popular myth has it, spouses are most likely to stray after they have been together seven years. Today's couples are more impatient. As we see in Figure 1-2, the risk of divorce starts as soon as the ink on the marriage license dries. Although the number of divorces within the first year of marriage is lower than in later years, this is because there is a legal waiting period between filing divorce papers and the actual divorce decree. The number of divorces peaks only two and a half years after marriage; most divorces occur within ten years.[21] In 2002, the Centers for Disease Control and Prevention released a report about marriage, divorce, and remarriage trends based on a nationally representative sample of women fifteen to forty-four years of age. The data indicated that, after only three years, 12 percent of marriages had ended in either separation or divorce.[22] After five years, 20 percent of all first marriages had ended; after ten years, 33 percent; and after fifteen years, 43 per-

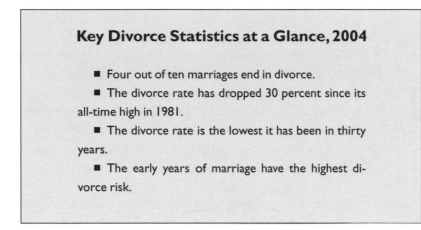

Key Divorce Statistics at a Glance, 2004

- Four out of ten marriages end in divorce.
- The divorce rate has dropped 30 percent since its all-time high in 1981.
- The divorce rate is the lowest it has been in thirty years.
- The early years of marriage have the highest divorce risk.

cent. The risk for marital disruption is greatest in the first years of marriage and noticeably levels off after the fifth year. Thus, the risk for divorce decreases with the length of the marriage.

Marriage and Divorce around the World

Although it is sometimes tempting to think of divorce as an American phenomenon, divorce is in fact present in nearly all countries in the world and has been common in most tribal societies. The status of divorce in other nations varies according to the prevailing religious beliefs and social traditions. Nonetheless, provisions for divorce or separation do exist universally, and since the 1950s, the divorce rate has increased in all industrialized nations. Divorce has increased even in countries where religious and legal impediments are strongest. In Europe's southern countries such as Italy, Spain, and Portugal, where social norms are heavily influenced by the Catholic Church, public demand for divorce resulted in changes in the law in the 1970s and early 1980s that made divorce possible.[23] Ireland, which remained most staunchly opposed to divorce for religious reasons, bent to public and political pressures and made divorce available for the first time in February 1997. Social data clearly indicated that marital breakdown was widespread and that the lack of legal solutions forced many families into unbearable living conditions. The Irish example illustrates a

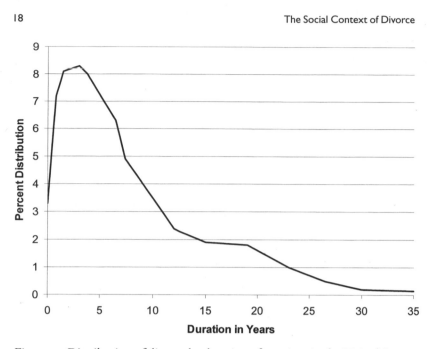

Figure 1-2. Distribution of divorce by duration of marriage in the United States, 1990. Source: Clarke, 1995.

long-standing truism: even if divorce is illegal—and the divorce rate is zero—the absence of divorce does not lead to a higher rate of happy marriages or functional families. These divorce reforms also illustrate the historical trend of increasingly permitting legal provisions to deal with the reality of marital breakdown—even in societies where political life and social traditions have been strongly shaped by religious proscriptions.

The United Nations reports that the trends in other countries parallel those observed in the United States. Globally, the initiation of marriage is delayed. Most people still marry but they marry later in life, especially women. The composition of the family continues to diversify. In developed countries, marriages are increasingly preceded by a period of cohabitation, and remarriage after divorce is increasingly delayed or absent. For example, in the United Kingdom, the age at which people get married for the first time has risen from twenty-six years for men and twenty-three years for women in 1961 to thirty-one and twenty-eight years, respectively.[24] Although there are differences among

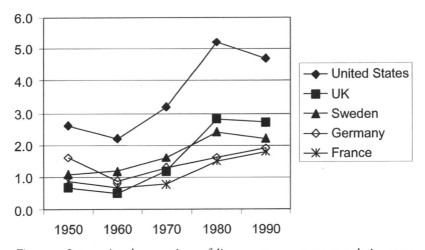

Figure 1-3. International comparison of divorce rates, per 1,000 population: 1950 to 1990. Source: U.N. Yearbooks, 1992.

countries, in general, this trend is consistent for all nations of the European Union. The increase in premarital cohabitation, higher levels of education, especially for women, and greater participation in the workforce all contribute to these changes.

Figure 1-3 compares divorce trends of some European countries with that of the United States. The most striking difference in this and other comparisons is that the U.S. divorce rate is much higher than in any other country in the industrialized world. For example, in 1994, the U.S. rate of 4.6 per thousand compared with 2.6 in Canada and 1.3 in Japan. Beyond the higher rate, the overall pattern is essentially the same. Like the United States, the European countries experienced a dip in their divorce rates (most pronounced in Germany) after World War II. The rise in divorce rates that began in the 1970s is another common feature. In light of the present-day clamor in the United States for a tightening of divorce reforms, it should be noted that not all countries had divorce reforms that were as extreme as those in the United States; nevertheless, the number of divorces increased uniformly during the 1970s and began leveling off in the 1980s. Even countries that had divorce provisions for generations, like France and Germany, followed the same trend. Moreover, these countries that had divorce provisions for a long time, boast the lowest divorce rates of the countries shown. Both the commonalities and the divergences in divorce trends, in the absence of identical laws, suggest that the shifts in trends are influenced by forces other than legal divorce reforms.

Another universal fact is that the elaborate marriage ceremonies that are common to many cultures are no guarantee for a happy or lasting marriage. Even in very traditional societies where weddings are well-defined social events conducted with considerable formality, marital breakdown occurs. Elaborate ceremonies are perfectly compatible with high divorce rates—the United States being a prime example. Thus, neither prohibitions nor restrictions against divorce, nor highly formalized wedding ceremonies, offer protection against marital breakdown. In the end, the success of every marriage begins and ends with the individual couple.

Theoretical Perspectives

To understand and explain the complexities of the divorce process, psychologists have ventured a variety of theories. In addition, psychological models developed to explain human relationships and psychological functioning more broadly have been adapted to explain the causes and consequences of divorce. These may be helpful ways to think about what divorce means.

Social Exchange Theory

The social exchange theory of divorce focuses on the period preceding the divorce, in which people evaluate their relationship in terms of costs and benefits. How good the marriage is depends on the person's satisfaction with his or her share of the rewards and costs. Rewards include love, support, companionship, emotional security, social status and connections, and sexual relations, as well as property, financial resources, and assistance with daily tasks; costs may include extra work and responsibilities, annoying habits, or limited individual choices and freedoms. This theory assumes that people behave in ways that maximize their benefits and limit their costs, although these motives may not be explicit or rational. When people feel that the rewards of the relationship are equitable and the costs have been equally distributed, the relationship is stabilized and strengthened; an unequal exchange pushes the relationship toward dissolution.[25] The decision to divorce is shaped by the resources of the spouse and the rewards of the relationship compared with alternative attractions outside the marriage—a new love interest, a sense of freedom, more independence, or potential for self-actualization. If alternative attractions outweigh the rewards of the relationship, the barriers to ending the relationship decrease.[26] Marriage stability also depends on the level of outcomes an individual believes he or she deserves.[27] Exchange theory provides a stark contrast with romantic notions about love, marriage, and family; however, it has been a useful framework for analyzing a couple's risk of divorce.[28]

Process Models of Divorce

Several theories have originated from the idea that divorce is a complex psychological and social process rather than a single event. Two theories illustrate these approaches.

Bohannon's Six Stations of Divorce

Paul Bohannon suggested that individuals must work through six parallel stages to complete the divorce process.[29]

> *Emotional divorce.* This first stage involves decreasing emotional investment in the marriage. Emotional bonds and communication are replaced with alienating behaviors and withdrawal from the relationship. This may lead to decreased conflict as one of the spouses loses interest in solving problems and invests energy in planning an exit strategy.
>
> *Legal divorce.* This stage involves the legal steps of filing for a divorce and developing legal agreements, property settlements, child custody decisions, and so on. If both partners agree on everything, the process can be, if not easy, fairly straightforward. Any disagreements, however, are likely to complicate and lengthen this process and increase its emotional and financial costs.

Economic divorce. This involves the practical steps by which the spouses dissolve their existing economic unit and create two economic units. Many details usually need to be negotiated, and the process of splitting property, household goods, and personal items—in addition to finding one or two new residences, relocating, and reestablishing separate households—is challenging.

Coparental divorce. Coparental divorce involves drawing up a detailed plan for child custody with specifications for custody type and details of child contact with each parent. Establishing a functioning coparenting relationship is often full of friction as parents attempt to maximize their opportunities to be with their children (or to be free of them).

Community divorce. Divorce affects the couple's social relationships and social status outside the family as well as splitting up the family. The stresses of the divorce experience may place higher demands on the couple's social network. Friends may withdraw because they feel awkward taking sides or disapprove of the change or feel threatened by their newly single friends. New friendships are gained, too, as individuals leave their familiar networks and enter new ones.

Psychic divorce. The "psychic divorce" refers to regaining psychological autonomy through emotional separation from the former spouse. It involves developing insights into one's own contributions to the breakdown of the marriage and provides a basis for personal growth.

This theory is useful for describing the multiple and different issues and processes that are involved in a divorce. Clearly, a divorcing couple goes through many steps before signing the piece of paper, and the ripples of the divorce are felt by the community as well as the couple.

Wiseman's View of Divorce as a Crisis and Mourning Process
In contrast to Bohannon, who included many different domains of life, Reva Wiseman focused on the internal emotional and psychologi-

cal dimensions of divorce and based her view of divorce on crisis theory and Elisabeth Kübler-Ross's description of the mourning process.[30] Wiseman proposed five stages of divorce: denial, loss and depression, anger and ambivalence, reorientation of lifestyle and identity,
and acceptance and integration.[31]

Denial is the stage before marital problems are con-
sciously acknowledged, when conflictual issues are ignored
or attributed to external causes. Some marriages are maintained through denial for many years. Sooner or later, however, the precarious balance is broken and the couple shifts
into a state of crisis.

Loss and depression follow once a crisis has set in and the
spouses are forced to acknowledge that the marriage has serious problems. Anxiety and grief reactions are triggered by
the imminent losses and loneliness.

Anger and ambivalence are experienced during the next
stage, when interactions between spouses sometimes turn
vindictive, punitive, or even violent. At the same time,
spouses may feel fearful about the future and vacillate between holding on to the marriage and taking the plunge
into the unknown. This is a period of emotional purging,
which eventually culminates in the decision to separate.

Reorientation of lifestyle and identity follows separation
and the recognition of being a single person once again.
This is a time of facing the reality of the divorce and redefining who one is outside of marriage, deciding how to
live one's life, and musing about what relationships to
choose in the future. The transformational nature of this
phase makes individuals vulnerable. To combat loneliness
and anxiety, they may indiscriminately enter into sexual relations with new partners without emotional investment,
or they may avoid social contacts altogether. The identity
crisis of this phase also offers the opportunity for a constructive redefinition of the self and movement toward personal growth.

Acceptance and integration reflect the final resolution of divorce, as the divorced person accepts himself or herself, with nothing to prove and no need to be defensive. Anger is replaced by acceptance of self, the past, and others. Having worked through each preceding stage, the person is willing to invest in a new emotional relationship.

This theory of divorce as a process of crisis and mourning takes us inside the divorcing person's head and illustrates the complex and shifting emotions that accompany divorce. It shows that the process of divorce extends deeply into the psyche.

Family Systems Theory

The family systems theory focuses on the family context in which the couple is embedded; it is based on the premise that marriage and divorce can best be understood in the context of family relationships. Just as when a couple marries, more than a couple marries, when a couple divorces, more than a couple divorces. Family systems theorists view the family as a social system composed of dynamic and interdependent relationships such that every member of the family system is influenced by the actions of other members and by the quality of interactions between the other members. Appropriate boundaries between family members as well as closeness of family members are central issues. The family systems perspective interprets psychological functioning—or dysfunctioning—as a reflection of family processes. This perspective is useful for understanding interactions among spouses and their children and the reciprocal influences of these interactions on the psychological functioning of family members. Thus divorce could be a product of dysfunctional relationships across the entire family, and it could also be a cause of impaired functioning in children after the divorce.

Risk and Resilience

In risk and resilience theory, "risk" refers to the presence of difficult, challenging, or adverse circumstances; "resilience" refers to positive adaptation in the face of these risks.[32] A discussion of divorce in terms of risk and resilience focuses on the risks divorce creates—downward mobility, social rejection, household chaos, battling parents, neglectful parenting—and the ability of individuals, particularly children, to adapt to these circumstances. Researchers studying risk and resilience have shown that some children who experience adversity develop without significant problems while others falter and fail, and they have searched for factors associated with the successful children's resilience.[33] Resilience is not strictly an individual trait, they have discovered; it is also a function of supportive factors in the environment.[34] More resilient children have strong individual qualities (high intelligence, self-esteem, social competence, and an easy temperament), but they also are protected by supportive relationships with their family, teachers, and peers and by economic resources and helpful community services.[35] These protective factors moderate the potentially harmful effects of adverse circumstances and events, such as those brought on by divorce. Protective factors act as immunizations; they do not enhance children's health per se but provide protection when the child is exposed to "pathogens."[36] When children are exposed to multiple pathogens, researchers have found, the combined risks increase the likelihood of poor outcomes.[37] Divorce researchers have increasingly employed the risk and resiliency perspective as a useful framework for understanding the long-term consequences of parental divorce on children's development, the ability of individual children to cope with divorce, and the familial and extrafamilial factors associated with adolescent well-being in different family structures.[38]

Attachment Theory

Another psychological theory that has been applied to divorce is attachment theory. Seminal work on attachment by British psychiatrist John Bowlby in the 1960s defined attachment as a close emotional bond between an infant and his or her primary caregiver—typically, the mother.[39] In the 1970s, psychologist Mary Ainsworth classified attachments into different types: *Securely* attached infants use their mother as a base from which to explore the environment; they are easily comforted by her and not overly distressed by brief separations; *in-*

secure infants are either avoidant—they engage in little interaction with the mother and avoid contact after a brief separation—or ambivalent—they cling to the mother one moment and then push her away the next.[40] Ainsworth and Bowlby speculated that these different attachment styles give rise to different mental models that are stable over time and influence later relationships; a secure attachment provides an important basis for later secure emotional relationships.

In the 1980s, the concept of attachment was extended to adult relationships.[41] In adults, attachment refers to a strong emotional bond between two people that motivates them to engage in behavior that maintains their relationship. There are differences between adult attachment and infant attachment, of course: adult romantic relationships are reciprocal and contain a sexual component; therefore, the motivation for proximity-seeking can be either to offer comfort or to engage in sexual activity.[42] Still, it makes sense to think of these adult relationships as parallel to those in infancy and to look for secure and insecure types, just as Bowlby and Ainsworth did with babies. Doing so, researchers have found that about 50 to 60 percent of adults are classified as securely attached.[43] Like secure infants, these adults use their romantic partner as a base for comfort and security. They see themselves as valued and worthy of others' concern, support, and affection; they describe their partner as reliable, accessible, and well-intentioned. Secure individuals easily develop closeness with others, feel comfortable depending on others and having others depend on them, and are rarely concerned about rejection or abandonment. They actively seek out intimacy and support in close relationships and score high on both autonomy and intimacy.[44] Their relationships are characterized by frequent positive affect, trust, commitment, and satisfaction.[45]

The 25 to 30 percent of adults who display insecure-avoidant or dismissing attachments deemphasize the importance of attachments, presumably because they have been rejected in the past. Avoidant adults say that they are uncomfortable trusting and depending on others and they tend to be skeptical in relationships, maintain emotional distance, and avoid intimacy.[46] Often they describe significant others as being unreliable or overly demanding of commitment. An additional 15 percent or so are classified as insecure-preoccupied or ambivalent in their attachment style. They react with hypersensitivity to nuances of the relationship based on prior inconsistent attachment experiences and vacillate between high levels of attachment-seeking behaviors and angry rejection of the attachment figure. These adults often feel misunderstood and underappreciated and describe their partner as undependable and uncommitted. They fear abandonment and express concern that their partner is reluctant to get as close as they would like. These fears lead to a preoccupation with attachment needs and make them especially vigilant in their attempts to be close to their partner. Although insecure attachment represents a risk factor for healthy development, it may allow an adult to tolerate the loss of a relationship and feel comfortable without a significant relationship for an extended period.[47]

The application of attachment theory to divorce has aided our understanding of divorce. For one thing, studies of divorce risk have indicated that an insecure attachment style raises the risk of divorce and remarriage.[48] Attachment styles have also been used to explain coping and adjustment processes in separating couples.[49] In addition, attachment theory helps us understand the emotional processes divorcing couples go through. Alan Sroufe, an attachment theorist, explains the strongly negative emotions that ensue during marital separation as a normal response to the loss of an important attachment figure. From this perspective, anger, vengefulness, and depression are part of a normal developmental course in divorcing couples. The threat that results from the impending loss explains the paradoxical approach-avoidance behavior that separating couples often engage in: although their commitment to the relationship has ended, spouses' attachment system is threatened by the loss, and this often triggers brief attempts at reconciliation to restore a sense of security.[50] Mental-health or legal professionals can use an understanding of the normal range of emotional reactions to separation to curb their urge to pathologize divorcing individuals; they can use such knowledge to focus interventions on helping couples overcome their negative emotional reactions. Finally, attachment theory is helpful for understanding children's reactions to divorce. When a parent—an attachment figure for the child—disappears from the child's daily life, it is normal for the child to experience grief and longing, and it behooves divorcing parents and judges to make arrangements that minimize this suffering by maximizing the child's contact with both parents, at least during the period immediately after the separation.

In sum, divorce is a complex phenomenon that must be viewed in its demographic, social, psychological, economic, and legal contexts. This overview of the history of divorce, current and international trends in divorce, and theoretical approaches to divorce helps us understand and interpret what follows: an up-to-date summary of research on the psychological causes and consequences of divorce.

2

At Risk for Divorce

Despite the efforts of theorists to organize our knowledge of divorce, there is no simple explanation for why people divorce: divorce is not caused by a single factor; it cannot be predicted on the day the couple ties the knot. Many causes on multiple levels—social, historical, cultural, demographic, and individual—interact to bring about the demise of a family.

Sociocultural Factors

Current trends in marriage and divorce are the result of decades of social change. Numerous historical and social factors have contributed to the way we view marriage and divorce today.

Changes in the Role of Family

Knowing about the profound changes that have occurred in our concepts of marriage and family is important for understanding divorce. The definition of "family" has evolved over time. One definition in 1934 defined a family as "a relationship of indeterminate duration existing between parents and children."[1] In 1971: "The family is a group of persons united by ties of marriage, blood, or adoption; constituting

Traditional Functions of Marriage

- Procreation
- Sexual gratification
- Regulation of sexual relations
- Regulation of lines of descent
- Care of children
- Division of labor
- Economic production and consumption

a household; interacting and communicating with each other in their respective social roles of husband and wife, mother and father, son and daughter, brother and sister, and creating and maintaining a common culture."[2] And in 1990: "Family includes cohabiting groups of some duration composed of persons in intimate relationships based on biology, law, custom, or choice and usually economically interdependent."[3]

In these definitions we see that the notion of "family" has become looser and broader as major social changes during the past century have transformed the structure and functions of marriage and family in Western civilization.[4] Public institutions now perform many of the tasks that were once the domain of the family. Education, economic production, religion, and recreation have become specialized realms serviced by institutions outside the home: education is provided by state or private schools; religious instruction is taken care of in houses of worship; employment typically occurs away from home, rarely on the family farm or at the kitchen table—although today it sometimes occurs in front of the family computer. Recreational activities are plentiful outside the home; to access or enjoy them does not require family participation. Even procreation is not limited to traditional family relationships. The tremendous surge in single parenting by choice and alternative methods of reproduction such as parenthood via a surrogate challenge the proposition that a traditional marriage and family are necessary for having children.

The family is still responsible for the socialization and care of children, but even in this capacity, the availability of child care, after-school programs, and extracurricular activities and the influence of peers, mass media, and, increasingly, the Internet have diluted the role of the family. Moreover, improved economic conditions, more and better education, and the availability of birth control have resulted in smaller families. The average number of children in a family fell from seven in 1800 to two in 1990, and this reduced family size has decreased the length of time between the births of the oldest and the youngest children, that is, has decreased the number of years of child rearing. At the same time, people's longevity has increased. Today, husbands and wives potentially have about as many years together after the children leave home as before, and this places demands of a different sort on their relationship. A marriage has to be solid and satisfying enough to endure beyond the activities of bearing and raising children.

Given these changes in families it is not surprising that the primary purpose of marriage today seems to be the satisfaction of personal needs for affection and emotional support. Several observers have suggested that a decline in commitment to marriage as a bond for life may be contributing to the high level of divorce.[5] It appears that the primary motivation for marriage is personal happiness. A greater emphasis is now placed on mutual feelings of love and fulfillment than on obligation to marriage vows and children, and marriages are supposed to be based on romantic love and free choice, not duty and dynasty.

As the definition of family has evolved, variations in the composition and functioning of the family have emerged. Figure 2-1 illustrates the current diversity of households in the United States. Before the 1960s, most households were composed of two parents, some children, and sometimes extended family members, but today's households may be quite different. The number of unmarried-couple households increased sevenfold between 1970 and 1994, and between 1990 and 2000, households composed of two or more unrelated people increased faster than family households.[6] Cohabitation among elderly couples increased because, for economic reasons, they chose to cohabit rather than remarry. Homosexual couples, including those with children, were more likely to live openly together. Today, approximately one-third of families with children younger than eighteen are single-parent families, and their numbers are projected to increase. One of the reasons for the increase in single-parent families is that people are

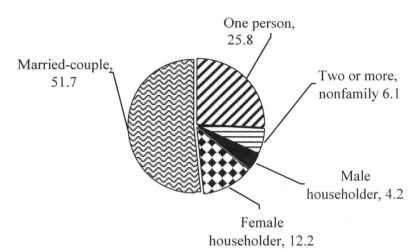

Figure 2-1. Households by type in the United States, 2000. Source: Simmons and O'Neill, 2001.

less content to stay in loveless, unsatisfying marriages and more willing to consider divorce.

Changes in Economic Contributions

Another reason for the upsurge in single-parent families may be the change in the relative economic roles of men and women. The contributions of husbands and wives to the household income have increasingly converged and deviated from the traditional division of breadwinner and homemaker. By 1990, wives were contributing 30 to 40 percent of household incomes.[7] It has been suggested that as women became more integrated into the workforce and, therefore, potentially more financially independent, the likelihood they would marry decreased and their risk of divorce increased.[8] Recent evidence contradicts this notion, however. For one thing, it appears that women's higher earnings actually increase their value as potential spouses and thereby their probability of getting married.[9] For another, several large studies have contested the notion that women's economic independence increases the risk of divorce.

In one study, Liana Sayer and Suzanne Bianchi investigated the underlying mechanisms involved in the link between wives' economic independence and heightened divorce risk.[10] Using data from a longitudinal study of more than three thousand women who participated in the National Survey of Families and Households, they found that it was not economic independence by itself that led to divorce. Marital satisfaction and commitment were better predictors of marital dissolution than measures of economic independence. Any positive association between a wife's contribution to family income and divorce disappeared after the quality of the marriage was taken into account. The authors concluded that wives' economic independence may aid the escape from a bad marriage, but having money doesn't mean that women are on the lookout for greener pastures. The economic independence idea is based on the notion that marital stability is promoted when men and women have complementary roles in the family and specialize in different household tasks.[11] As Sayer and Bianchi point out, however, there is also ample evidence that when men and women are alike in their ages, values, and levels of education, they are more likely to stay married. Hence, it would be reasonable to assume that greater similarity in roles and functions would improve spousal relations by giving husband and wife more common ground and a shared understanding of challenges and achievements.[12]

In a second study that supports the idea that women's working is good for marriage, a researcher compared two birth cohorts: women born between 1944 and 1954 and women born between 1957 and 1964.[13] Although, in the older cohort, women's working had a detrimental effect on marital stability, this effect decreased over time, and among the younger cohort, women's work was beneficial to marital stability. In a third study, researchers found that women's earnings were a protective factor for marital stability if the husband had lower earnings than the wife.[14] The author of a recent review of the literature documenting the economic context of American families in the 1990s concluded that economic advantage due to both spouses' earnings was associated with greater marital happiness and less likelihood of divorce.[15]

These newer findings suggest that, in recent cohorts, spouses value the increased economic resources derived from dual earnings. Along with having more egalitarian gender ideologies, today's men may appreciate the relief of not being the sole breadwinner. Surveys indicate that the majority of Americans today (more than 75 percent) endorse women's participation in the labor force.[16] It thus appears that men may willingly forego their solo role of "bringing home the bacon" and increasingly enjoy eating the jointly earned filet mignon. In sum, women's economic independence, by itself, does not explain divorce.

Increases in Work and Family Demands

The flip side of women's increased involvement in work and money-making is their decreased availability for household tasks. This is another possible contributor to divorce. Women feel caught in the middle, burdened by increased demands from both work and family. To investigate whether changes in work and family demands have affected marital quality, researchers Stacy Rogers and Paul Amato compared two generations of married couples.[17] The first cohort of eleven hundred couples had married between 1964 and 1980; a younger cohort of three hundred couples had married between 1981 and 1997. The younger cohort did report more marital discord than the older cohort, and this was explained by greater conflict related to balancing increased demands from work and family. In particular, couples in the younger cohort who thought that household work was unfairly distributed—because husbands did less of it—reported greater marital discord. Husbands in this younger cohort contributed to household work more than husbands in the older cohort, but it was still not enough, because demands—and expectations for helping husbands—have risen. If younger husbands did not take on a greater share of household duties than their older compatriots, marital conflict would have been even greater in the contemporary cohort.

Demographic Factors

In addition to these sociocultural factors involving changes in family functions, economic and work roles, and work and family demands, demographic factors affect the chances that a marriage will end in divorce. Researchers have found that demographic characteristics such as age, race, and religion influence whether marriages stay together or fall apart. A recent comprehensive report by the Centers for Disease Control and Prevention and the National Center for Health Statistics provides divorce rate estimates based on personal interviews conducted with approximately 11,000 women (including 6,483 European American, 2,446 African American, and 1,553 Latina women).[18] Table 2-1

Table 2-1. Probability of first divorce by duration of marriage and selected characteristics

	Probability of Divorce		
	After 5 Years	After 10 Years	After 15 Years
Total divorces	20%	33%	43%
Race/ethnicity			
European American	20%	32%	42%
African American	28%	47%	55%
Latino	17%	34%	42%
Asian	10%	20%	23%
Age at marriage			
Younger than 18	29%	48%	59%
18–19	24%	40%	49%
20–24	17%	29%	36%
25 and older	15%	24%	35%
Education			
Less than high school	24%	42%	51%
High school	22%	36%	45%
More than high school	17%	29%	38%
Religious affiliation			
Any	19%	32%	41%
None	27%	46%	56%
Family of origin			
Intact two-parent	17%	29%	38%
Other	26%	43%	52%
Ever had forced sex			
No	17%	30%	39%
Yes	34%	53%	63%
Had children at time of marriage			
None	18%	31%	40%
One or more wanted	27%	45%	55%
One or more unwanted	31%	54%	63%
Ever had anxiety disorder			
Never	19%	31%	39%
Ever	24%	42%	55%

Source: Bramlett and Mosher, 2002.

shows the probability of a first divorce by the length of marriage and other selected characteristics such as age, education, and the presence of children.

Marrying, and Divorcing, Young

Being young at the time of marriage is one of the primary predictors of divorce reported in this and other studies.[19] It has consistently been shown that marriage at an early age increases the risk of divorce. As indicated in Figure 2-2, women who are younger than eighteen when they marry have twice the risk of a failed marriage as women who are twenty-five years or older when they marry (48 percent versus 24 percent). Younger age also leads to short-lived unmarried cohabitations.

People who marry young are still developing and likely to change in unanticipated directions. They are less likely to have completed high school; they are more likely to be expecting a baby. When women take on parental responsibilities at this age, they are less likely to pursue their education and more likely to have more children. In turn, this limits the couple's employment opportunities, leading to lower income, lower occupational status, and a higher probability of being poor. Young couples rarely have the independent means to support

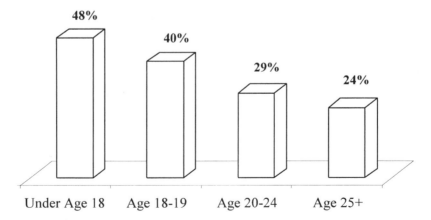

Figure 2-2. Probability that a first marriage will end in divorce within ten years, by age at the time of marriage: United States, 1995. Source: Bramlett and Mosher, 2002.

Personal Story: Marrying Young

My parents graduated together as "high school sweethearts." Shortly after, they married. They were young, naive, and in love (or so they thought). Unfortunately, they had no plans for the future. They got married because they didn't want to go on living at home, they weren't brave enough to live alone, and their families wouldn't let them just live together. The morning after the wedding, my father put his feet up on the easy chair to watch sports, something he had never done before. It was as if he was trying to fit into the role his father played, because he was unsure of what a "married man" was supposed to do. Because they were so young, neither of them had a lot going for them. My mom got pregnant right away and my dad had to give up his dream of going to law school because he needed to work to support them. He felt cheated and resentful. Four years later, they had three little girls. My mom looks back now in disbelief, realizing that they never discussed anything important. They didn't discuss how many kids they wanted, and birth control was never even mentioned. The marriage and the children just happened. I think they put a whole lot more thought in their divorce ten years later.

themselves, and early childbearing is likely to confine them to a difficult economic path.

People who marry young are also likely to do so for all the wrong reasons. For example, adolescents who suffer from emotional problems are more likely to marry young.[20] They may marry to escape an unhappy home, or they may view marriage naively and romantically with a focus on physical expressions of togetherness. They are less likely than more mature couples to fully understand the meaning of marriage with its implications for a long-term social, emotional, and material commitment. They are likely to be psychologically immature and not well equipped to prevent and solve problems. In sum, the "package" of lower economic resources, less education, higher occur-

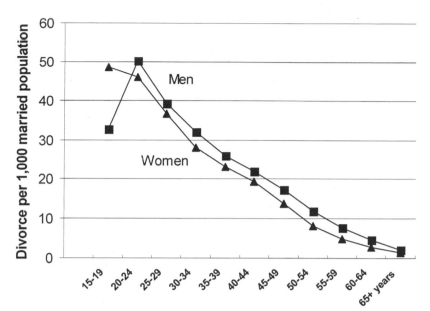

Figure 2-3. Census data for age-specific divorce rates in the United States, 1990.
Source: Clarke, 1995.

rence of premarital pregnancy, and increased emotional immaturity
contributes to the higher risk of divorce for couples who marry young.

Not only is marrying young related to a higher probability of divorce, but individuals get divorced when they are relatively young. Divorce is more likely when men and women are in their twenties and
thirties than when they are in their forties and fifties. In 1990, almost
two-thirds of divorcing men and three-quarters of divorcing women
were younger than forty. Figure 2-3 shows that the risk of divorce is
highest for men when they are between twenty and twenty-four years
old and for women when they are between fifteen and nineteen years
old.[21]

Education, Employment, Economics

Education, employment, and economic resources also influence marriage and divorce decisions. A college education can be helpful: men
and women with at least a bachelor's degree are more likely to marry

and less likely to separate than those who have only a high school degree or some college classes.[22] Employment is also a good idea for men: employed men are more likely to marry and stay married than unemployed men, and the higher their earnings, the greater the probability they will do so.[23] These earnings are critical: when men are under economic pressure, they are more hostile and less warm and supportive toward their wives.[24] With less money, they and their wives are less happy and more likely to divorce.[25] Earning fifty thousand dollars a year compared with earning less than twenty-five thousand dollars, for example, is associated with a 30 percent decrease in divorce. Having more economic resources acts as a protective factor for the marriage; and more affluent people also stand to lose more if they divorce, thus their level of affluence raises a barrier to divorce. In sum, couples with low socioeconomic status—lower education, occupational status, and income—are at a higher risk for divorce than those with higher socioeconomic status.[26]

Race, Ethnicity, and Divorce

Marital and divorce patterns also vary by race and ethnicity. African American men and women are less likely to marry or remarry than individuals in other ethnic groups.[27] In one recent study, 62 percent of African American men and 58 percent of African American women in their twenties had never married, compared with only 45 percent of European American and Latino men and 31 percent of European American and Latina women.[28] They are less satisfied with their marriages and more likely to divorce.[29] African American women today are more likely to divorce and to do it sooner than women in other ethnic groups. By the date of their ten-year anniversary, almost half of African American women's marriages have dissolved, whereas only about one-third of the marriages of European American and Latina women and one-fifth of the marriages of Asian American women have met this fate.[30] It is projected that 80 percent of African American children will live with a single parent compared with 36 percent of European American children.[31]

The differences between African Americans and other ethnic groups are due to long-standing cultural patterns, such as a greater reliance on extended kin during worsening economic conditions.[32] Additional reasons include a smaller pool of "marriageable" African American men; that is, those who are educated, employed, earning a reasonable wage, and not incarcerated.[33] Differences in attitudes toward marriage do not appear to be a reason; African Americans' attitudes toward marriage are similar to those of European Americans.[34] However, African American men, unlike European American men, report lower levels of marital satisfaction if they have to do a lot of housework.[35]

Interracial marriages are more likely to disrupt than marriages in which both spouses are the same race and ethnicity.[36] Interracial marriages have a 10 percent higher chance of failure in the first ten years than same-race marriages (41 percent versus 31 percent).

Community Characteristics

Research has also shown that community characteristics are related to the success or failure of a marriage. To some extent, the ethnic and racial differences we have discussed may be due to these community characteristics. People who live in neighborhoods with high levels of poverty are more likely to divorce—whether they are African American or European American.[37] Community poverty amplifies individual risk factors and reduces positive opportunities. The increased number of stressors associated with living in a poor community undermines marital relations. The causal link, however, is not simply one direction: divorce leads to poverty as well as the reverse. In poor communities, early marriage is more common as well, which may also contribute to the higher divorce rate.

In addition to poverty, marriage market conditions raise the probability of divorce. Divorce is higher in geographic areas with large numbers of attractive potential partners.[38] It is also higher in communities with more never-married women and in central cities.[39] It appears that a high availability of women in the workplace increases the probability that men will find a pleasing alternative to their current spouses. The Internet may change all this. A 2004 survey by *Elle* magazine revealed that one-quarter of divorced women blamed the Internet for their divorce.[40] The Internet offers both men and women access to a global community of attractive alternative playmates (and potential spouses).

Religion and Divorce

Being religious has traditionally been viewed as a barrier to divorce.[41] All religions provide their members with guidance on matters of marriage and divorce; however, religions vary considerably in the strictness of their practices.[42] No religion encourages divorce, but whereas Roman Catholicism continues to forbid divorce, Jewish and Protestant rules permit it. The influence of the Catholic Church on family life has declined since the 1960s, but it still appears to influence its members' divorce decisions: Catholic women are less likely to divorce than non-Catholics.[43]

A recent review of ninety-four studies focused on the links between religion and marriage indicates that greater religiousness facilitates marital functioning and decreases the risk of divorce—although the effects are quite small.[44] Adults who are affiliated with a religion are also less likely to engage in premarital sex, more likely to marry someone if they move in together, and more likely to see marriage as a lifetime commitment.[45] Results of a recent study using data on 4,587 couples who participated in the National Survey of Families and Households (NSFH) indicate that frequency of religious attendance has the greatest positive effect on marital stability. If both spouses regularly attend church together, they have a lower rate of divorce than if they attend church alone, rarely, or not at all.[46] It has been suggested that frequent joint church attendance reduces the risk of divorce through an internalization of norms and a reduction of marital problem behaviors.[47] Regular interactions with the church community may enhance "couple identity"[48] and reinforce shared beliefs in the value of marriage. Affiliation with a church may also provide a support group and guidance in times of need. Furthermore, embeddedness in a cohesive group that endorses marriage may raise the barriers against divorce.

On the other hand, religion does not guarantee a happy marriage. A longitudinal study of about one thousand married people offered little support for the idea that religious activity improves marital

The Top Ten Risk Factors for Divorce*

1. Young age: Marrying before the age of twenty-five.

2. Low income: Earning less than twenty-five thousand dollars per year.

3. Race: Being African American or marrying someone of another race.

4. Rape: Having been raped.

5. Religion: Having no religious affiliation.

6. Children: Having children at the time of the marriage or having unwanted children.

7. Divorced parents: Having divorced parents.

8. Education: Having less than a college degree.

9. Work status: Being unemployed.

10. Poor communication: Nagging, stonewalling, escalating conflicts.

*For the first ten years of marriage.

relations. Although increases in religiosity slightly decreased the probability of divorce being considered, there was no evidence that religious activity enhanced marital happiness or decreased conflict and problems commonly thought to cause divorce.[49] Moreover, in the NSFH study, the effect of religious affiliation disappeared when other demographic characteristics such as education and income were controlled.[50] Religious activity does not under any circumstance buffer against divorce. In fact, if only one spouse attends church, the risk of divorce is greater than for couples who both do not attend church.[51] This is because fundamental differences between spouses lead to conflict and increase the divorce risk. Not surprisingly, interfaith marriages have consistently been shown to have a greater divorce risk than marriages in which couples share a faith.[52]

Children's Influence on Divorce Risk

The presence of children is a double-edged sword for marriage. Some evidence indicates that couples with children are slightly less likely to divorce than childless couples.[53] Given that approximately 60 percent of divorcing couples have children, however, the presence of children is clearly not an insurmountable barrier to marital breakup.[54] The arrival of children, in fact, is a stressor that leads to a decline in marital satisfaction for most couples.[55] Having children before a marriage, as we have mentioned, is also linked to a higher probability of divorce.[56] By the date of their ten-year anniversary, half of all couples who have a child at the time they get married are divorced, compared with only one-third who did not start the marriage with a child. Even having a child within the first seven months of the marriage was associated with a higher divorce risk than if the child was conceived during the marriage. In part this may be due to hurried marriage decisions; a premarital pregnancy may compel individuals into marriage who otherwise might not have married. In addition, couples who have not had an opportunity to adjust to their roles as spouses before taking on the role of parents are less prepared for the challenges of parenthood and more stressed by them.

Individual and Relationship Factors

In addition to the sociocultural and demographic causes of divorce that we have discussed, individual and relationship factors are also associated with increased divorce risk. A troubled background, a difficult personality, specific stressors, and substance abuse all contribute to the likelihood of divorce.

A Troubled Background

The path to divorce is a long and winding one that can begin even in childhood. When children witness their parents' dysfunctional relationship in their early years, their learning of important relationship skills is limited, and their ability to form committed and trusting relationships is undermined.[57] In one study, adults who were experiencing marital discord in their own marriages reported that their parents also exhibited marital discord.[58] The parental behaviors that were most likely to predict problems in the offspring's marriage included being jealous, domineering, critical, and moody; getting angry easily; and not talking to the spouse. Conflict with parents in the adult years is another family factor that can destabilize a marital relationship by adding a salient stressor and depriving each spouse of important social support.[59] Growing up in a divorced family also increases a person's divorce risk.[60] In one two-generational study, parental divorce doubled the odds that offspring would see their own marriages end in divorce—presumably because these individuals held a comparatively weak commitment to the norm of lifelong marriage.[61]

Adverse personal experiences may also increase divorce risk. Marital dissolution is more likely for a woman who has been forced to have sex at some time in her life before she was married.[62] Childhood sexual abuse has also been identified as a risk factor for later divorce in women.[63] It is likely that the experience of such a severe violation heightens a woman's vulnerability to relational insults and increases her vigilance in monitoring and responding to perceived slights.

Risky Marital Interactions

When divorce researchers ask couples what caused their divorce, the couples seldom say it's because their parents didn't get along, they were too young when they got married, or they didn't have enough education. Instead, they talk about their spouse's annoying habits or destructive behaviors and how their interactions deteriorated into screaming matches or days without speaking. Wives, especially, focus on marital problems. In one study, researchers found that the particular marital problems that predicted divorce up to twelve years later included the spouse's jealousy, moodiness, anger, and irritating habits; foolish spending, drinking, and drug use; and, last but certainly not least, infidelity.[64] In another study, women complained about their husband's personality, authority, money management, drinking, sex problems, lack of support, time with "the boys"—and both spouses complained about infidelity.[65] Women also complained specifically about their husbands' lack of support for their careers—a new reason for divorce that has appeared since women became more involved in the workforce.[66] These problems do not always lead to divorce, of course. In a study of couples who were still married, many couples said that they had disagreements over sex and money and that they did not feel satisfied with their relationship: wives were dissatisfied with the time they spent together with their husbands, and husbands claimed that their marriages were unsociable and they felt lonely.[67] These problems made the couples think about divorce, but they were still together at the time of the study.

Another cause of divorce is perceived inequities in the division of labor in the home. As we have already mentioned, the increased demands of work and family that accompanied the rise in women's participation in the workforce contributed to a higher divorce rate; the same issues lead to divorce on the small stage of the individual family. The results of a recent study indicate that, among dual-earner couples, perceived unfairness in the division of household labor is associated with more marital unhappiness for both husbands and wives and, for women, with a higher risk of divorce. The researchers suggest that perceptions of an unfair division of household labor not only decrease women's marital quality but also lead to role strain that makes them more likely to end unsatisfying marriages.[68]

More important than whether the husband takes out the garbage or the wife does the laundry, though, is whether he or she gets involved in an extramarital affair. Having an affair is the ultimate insult to a marriage and one of the most common and consistent causes of divorce.[69] An extramarital relationship may be a symptom of an unhappy relationship and provide the proverbial "last straw" in the decision to divorce, or it may be the cause of the marital breakdown. Even happy relationships can be ended by a casual, meaningless one-night stand. The sense of betrayal, hurt, and mistrust when the infidelity is discovered undermines the marriage and results in a so-called "accidental" or "useless" divorce.[70] The realization of a spouse's infidelity can be so profoundly humiliating and hurtful that it not only raises the possibility of divorce but leads to major depression and anxiety, which further destroys the marriage.[71] In contrast, when a couple maintains a high level of commitment, spouses do less mutual monitoring, feel less trapped in their marriage, and experience more satisfaction in their relationship.[72]

Communication Hazards

In the end, the major reason for marital breakdown in as many as half of all divorces is conflict between the spouses.[73] All couples have conflicts—about how much time to spend alone with friends, how money is spent, or who picks up the children from child care—but some couples work through their problems better than others do. Over the past two decades we have learned a lot about the communication patterns that lead a couple to the brink of divorce. John Gottman studies the processes that destroy or strengthen relationships. Central to his work is the observation that distressed and nondistressed couples manage their conflicts differently. He divides couples into "regulated" and "nonregulated" types. Regulated couples manage their conflicts in a way that facilitates problem solving and does not damage their relationship.[74] The communication of nonregulated couples, however, is not constructive; it does not support problem solving but instead escalates tensions and increases the couple's distress. Not surprisingly, nonregulated couples take longer to rebound from a conflict and are less likely to achieve a solution to their problem, which leads to reoccurrence of the conflict and continuation of their "serial argument."[75]

Gottman finds that *how couples argue* is more closely related to marital instability than *what they argue about*. Conflicts and the expression of anger do not need to be destructive forces but can actually strengthen the marriage over time. Contempt, criticism, belligerence, and defensiveness, however, are harmful.[76] If the partners use a "negative startup" when they argue—responding in ways that escalate the conflict—the risk of divorce is increased. Frequent negative startups in which the wife responds with a belligerent comment to the husband's neutral or negative remark pose a particular risk. In this "female demand/male-withdrawal" pattern, the wife expresses a negative demand and the husband reacts with defensiveness, withdrawal, or passive inaction, which, in turn, escalates the wife's demands and negativity.[77] Marriages are less likely to survive when wives complain to their husbands about their dissatisfactions and husbands, in turn, show little understanding and empathy for these concerns but instead escalate conflicts into major fights.[78] Marriages are more likely to last if wives use a softer startup and husbands accept influence from their wives and deescalate conflict.[79]

Is There a Divorce-Prone Personality?

But maybe there are divorce-prone personalities that even the softest responses and the most controlled retorts cannot save from the divorce bin. The view that individual psychopathology is a major contributor to divorce risk has a long tradition.[80] And indeed, when researchers have compared couples who stay together with those who divorce, they have found that divorcers have some personality traits in common. There is not complete overlap in the results of different studies, as noted in a recent review of more than one hundred studies on the quality and stability of marriages;[81] nevertheless, research does converge on certain personality characteristics as risk factors for divorce: neuroticism and hostility in both husbands and wives; an inability to control impulses, especially in husbands; lack of conscientiousness; limited perseverance; and a propensity to get angry.[82] In the Terman Life Cycle Study, which followed individuals from childhood through old age, more disagreeable individuals—those who were angry, vain, egotistical, and lacking in sympathy and tenderness—were at higher risk for early divorce.[83] In fact, to some extent, these characteristics explained why couples who married young often ended up divorced: individuals who married at younger ages were less conscientious, less persevering, and more vain and egotistic than those who married later.[84]

Competitiveness is another personality characteristic linked to relationship problems. A hypercompetitive person needs to be right all the time, shows little understanding and appreciation of the partner's needs, has limited ability to see the partner's perspective, and feels little empathy. Competitive people admit that they have difficulty communicating, that they inflict pain on their partners, and that they have more conflict in their relationships than uncompetitive individuals.[85]

Marital dissatisfaction has also consistently been linked to psychiatric disorders such as generalized anxiety disorder, depression, and panic.[86] Recent government data show that women who have, at any time in their lives, suffered from generalized anxiety disorder are more likely to be divorced than women who have never suffered from anxiety.[87] Paralleling this finding, as we mentioned in the last chapter, attachment theory suggests that people who have not developed an emotionally secure attachment in infancy may be at risk for divorce. People with an anxious, insecure, avoidant attachment style are more likely to have serial marriages, and those with an insecure attachment style are also more likely to marry a previously married person in their first marriage.[88]

Is Biology Destiny?

The focus on personality characteristics as contributors to divorce risk has generated a discussion about whether divorce originates in a person's genetic makeup. Are people who divorce doomed by their DNA? Several recent studies have shown that genes do influence divorce risk—through their influence on inherited psychological qualities, such as personality.[89] Further support for the gene-divorce link comes from a recent longitudinal study of two thousand female twins.[90] Among identical twins, alcohol consumption patterns were associated with co-twin divorce: women who later divorced drank more than women who stayed married. This suggests that the concordance in marital patterns is due to biological factors that influence drinking as well as those that affect personality.

Other biological factors are also important: in a recent study of nearly two thousand men, testosterone levels were higher in divorced men than in married men.[91] Testosterone levels fell during marriage and rose in the years surrounding a divorce. The researchers suggested that these raised testosterone levels around the time of divorce explain, in part, the increase in wife battering at that time because increased testosterone levels have been consistently linked to aggressive, dominating, or antisocial behavior in men.

Another study found that stress hormones measured in newlyweds foreshadowed divorce.[92] Neuroendocrine function was assessed in ninety couples during their first year of marriage and was found to be related to marital satisfaction and divorce ten years later. Epinephrine and norepinephrine levels were higher in couples who divorced compared with those who remained married. Thus it appears that biological variables can contribute to marital quality and divorce risk. However, before we conclude that biology is, indeed, destiny, we need more research on how these biological factors push people toward divorce.

Alcohol and Divorce

Nobody likes a drunk, and a drunken spouse can be especially intolerable—not to mention argumentative and abusive. Numerous studies have documented an association between divorce and alcohol consumption, demonstrating that people who drink more are more likely to divorce.[93] Divorced people have the highest alcohol consumption levels in our society; married people have the lowest; and although alcoholics are just as likely as others in the general population to marry, they are at least four times more likely to separate or divorce.[94] The link between alcohol and divorce can even be seen at the national level: in a recent study of eight nations, those with the highest consumption of alcohol had the highest divorce rates.[95] Heavy drinking tends to decline with age, but among people who divorce, it increases.[96] Men are especially likely to report that their alcohol abuse, along with their drug and spousal abuse, contributed to their divorce.[97] It is somewhat difficult to disentangle the drunken chicken from the egg here, though. It is not clear whether stressors encountered during the marriage contribute to alcoholism, individual characteristics that existed before the marriage contribute to both alcoholism and marital instability, or alcohol consumption directly leads to divorce. Whichever the causal direction(s), those who want to stay married would be well advised to limit their drinking.

Stress

Finally, the risk of divorce is heightened by stressful experiences.[98] Parents of severely ill children—such as children with a congenital heart disease, cerebral palsy, or blindness—are one group that is at risk for divorce.[99] Unemployed men are another. Higher unemployment rates are associated with higher divorce rates in the United States and in other countries.[100] Stressors like these increase spouses' individual needs while simultaneously reducing their capacity to meet family demands. Prolonged stress and exhaustion lead to frustration and conflict, and because individuals' psychological resources are diminished, these conflicts may escalate into blaming and withdrawal from the relationship. Ineffective coping strategies, like increased alcohol consumption, amplify problems further.

Summary

Divorce has no single cause. Many factors contribute to divorce, including societal changes, economic conditions, ethnic and community characteristics, and individual and relationship qualities—and these factors are interlinked. Societal changes have reduced legal, moral, and social restrictions against divorce. Sociocultural changes have broadened our definitions of "family," and people have become more accepting of nontraditional families. The functions of marriage have changed dramatically: couples have fewer children, many of the needs that were traditionally met by the family are now fulfilled by external institutions, and the focus of family life has shifted from economic production and interdependence to emotional fulfillment. The lives of contemporary families are more complex than in earlier times. Typically, both spouses now work outside the home, and the simultaneous demands of work and household increase strain, especially for women. Demographic factors such as ethnic background, age at the time of marriage, socioeconomic status, religiousness, and the presence of children can also contribute to a couple's divorce risk, as do individual and relationship factors. For example, youthful marriage or a family history of divorce or abuse increases a person's divorce risk. Certain personality factors and behaviors such as alcohol abuse or poor communication skills destabilize a couple's relationship. For example, impulsiveness and neuroticism, combined with poor communication skills, may diminish marital quality and pave the way for divorce.

Underlying many of these divorce risk factors is stress—the stress of getting married too young and being too inexperienced; the stress of being overwhelmed with the responsibilities of having children, especially children with problems or children born before the marriage; the stress of being uneducated, poor, and living in a poor community. All these stressors undermine individuals' well-being, place greater importance on effective communication skills, and jeopardize relationships. The decision to divorce is especially likely if one or both spouses feel that alternative attractions, such as individual freedom or a new and better partner, await them. Thus, a key to preventing divorce and stabilizing marriage would be for couples to recognize and address the stressors in their lives; engage in active problem solving to prevent, resolve, or minimize stressors; and practice effective communication and coping skills.

3

A Marriage Ends

Divorce is not a single event that happens on the day that the divorce decree is issued: it is a long, drawn-out process. The initial decision-making process can take months or even years, and even when the divorce decision has finally been made, the progression of divorce may not be quick. Couples often separate, then reconcile, then separate again. They may end up litigating and sometimes, after years have passed, relitigating. Throughout this process, important practical decisions need to be made and actions taken that initiate and advance the process and lead to the rebuilding of separate and functional lives.

Deciding

"To stay or not to stay" is the key question in the decision-making stage. The divorce process begins slowly, with occasional realizations of dissatisfactions with the marriage; evolves gradually into increasing ruminations about perceived slights and alternative options; and then proceeds to the first serious and consistent thoughts of ending the relationship and rebuilding a separate life. From a social exchange perspective (see Chapter 1), the divorce decision involves a cost-benefit analysis of the pros and cons of leaving the marriage. The unhappy spouse considers the barriers to divorce—for example, religious restrictions, obligations to children, the financial costs and consequences

Personal Story: Making the Decision to Leave

From the beginning, my parents experienced numerous marital conflicts. These mostly revolved around their conflicting personalities and their inability or unwillingness to compromise. My father entertained the notion of divorce even in the first few years of their marriage. My mother never did, despite their disagreements. As the years went by, and the conflicts didn't lessen, my father began more and more to weigh the pros and cons of staying in the marriage. Sometimes he actually sat down with pencil and paper to list things out. Especially when he and my mom were experiencing intense conflict, he felt the desire to be "free." Eventually, he contacted a lawyer, without my mom's knowledge, to see what he needed to do to gain that freedom.

of divorce, and social pressures to stay married. These barriers are weighed against the alternative attractions outside the marriage—for example, a more peaceful life, a better partner, or greater individual freedom. If the alternative attractions outweigh the perceived benefits of the marriage and the costs of divorce, the spouse may decide to end the marriage. The extent to which this analysis is a conscious and rational process differs for different individuals. In addition, for some people, the process is fairly quick; for others it takes years or even decades. It is not uncommon for significant problems to exist in a marriage long before a divorce.[1] Often, individuals vacillate in their decision making for years, chalking up one more violation, another broken promise, until, with the discovery of infidelity or a final violent episode, they arrive at a clear decision.

Seldom do both spouses reach the point of no return simultaneously; in most cases one spouse wants to end the marriage more than the other does.[2] Although women, on average, are economically more dependent on marriage than men, researchers have consistently found that women are more likely to initiate a divorce than men.[3] Regardless of how divorce "initiation" is defined—whether it means "who wanted to leave the marriage first" or "who actually filed for divorce"—women are more likely to be the initiators.[4] Women also find more problems with their marriages and are more likely to have been dissatisfied for longer than their husbands.[5] Although men are less likely to initiate divorce directly, clinical observers have noted that men may work on terminating their marriage indirectly by acting in ways that sabotage the relationship.[6] For example, a man may carry on an affair, thereby forcing his wife to be the one who ends the marriage. It is thought that this frees the husband from the responsibility and guilt of having terminated the marriage.

There may be an alternative explanation, however. Men tend to be less in tune with their marital relationship than women. They are less sensitive to the needs of their partner and less aware of problems in the relationship. When a wife raises an issue, it is common for men not to "get" it. They may not understand what their wife wants, may feel attacked, and in response, resist, or in defense, escalate the conflict.[7] In an effort to regain their sense of control, after wives' repeated complaints, men may withdraw from the relationship into other activities, such as hanging out with friends, staying longer at work, or having an affair. These actions are not conducive to problem solving; indeed, they add new problems and escalate existing ones. Thus, men's actions may be less the consequence of a conscious or unconscious effort to sabotage the marriage than a symptom of their inability to deal adequately with marital problems.

As one or both spouses move toward divorce, and as the emotional, economic, and social consequences of divorce become palpable, it is common for there to be increased emotional ambiguity. Anger and ambivalence alternate much of the time.[8] Couples may engage in an approach-avoidance dance, one moment clinging to the familiar routines of the marriage, and the next moment recalling all that is wrong with their marriage and pursuing their escape from it. This ambivalence often increases after separating. Whereas initially any dissatisfactions in the marriage may have been countered with denial, after the problems of the marriage are acknowledged, anxiety and depression often follow as a reaction to the approaching loss of the relationship.[9] Both spouses are faced with fending for themselves, with unfamiliar and painful loneliness, and with increased uncertainties about whether the

Personal Story: Withdrawing from the Relationship

Two weeks after my brother was born, Mom had severe medical complications. The ambulance took her to the hospital. She almost died. When she called home to ask my dad to bring the baby to her, he was nowhere to be found. Later she found out that he was out playing music with his friends. She was deeply hurt. Mom said, "When I was so ill, I desperately needed him to be there for me but he didn't care enough about me to give up his buddies for one evening." As the months went by, Mom continued to have medical problems. It was difficult for her to care for my brother and me by herself because there was always the chance that she would faint at any moment. Her illness and the problems in her marriage made her extremely depressed. She wanted the marriage to work, because of her religious beliefs and because she had children, so she kept hoping and working on the relationship. But after a year of this, she became desperate. She threatened my dad with divorce. She really did not want a divorce, but at this point it seemed to be the only way to get my dad to try harder at the marriage. Her threats made no impression on him. Finally, in a fit of anger, she told him to leave. Then, with incredulity, she watched him calmly pack and leave never to return to our family.

alternatives are truly as attractive as they have imagined. Not surprisingly, separated couples frequently reconcile and move back together.[10] If relationship dynamics do not change and old problems remain unresolved, however, couples eventually separate for good. Failed reconciliation attempts amplify existing anger, which in turn strengthens the resolve to separate.

Separating: Reactions

The couple finally decides they are going to separate and get a divorce—and they mean it. One or the other spouse packs up his or her belongings—at least one suitcase—and leaves the premises. The door slams. "I'll see you in court," he or she shouts—or whispers. Now, the couple is faced with the consequences of their decision. The period immediately after the actual physical separation is usually a crisis characterized by high levels of distress.[11] In fact, for most people, the period immediately before and after the separation is more stressful than when the divorce becomes final.

Loneliness may be the greatest challenge during the separation period.[12] Living alone comes as a shock, even if the marriage was terrible and the person is glad to be out of it. Separated people often report a profound sense of loneliness and emptiness that goes beyond missing having a warm body to sleep beside and represents a deeper need for a sense of belonging and groundedness. About six months after the separation, people report that the painful intensity of their loneliness diminishes, but its frequency does not.[13] If friends and family disapprove of the breakup, feelings of loneliness are amplified.[14]

Other common reactions in the aftermath of separation include anger, anxiety, guilt, and depression.[15] Depression is more intense in people who have recently separated than in those who are actually divorced.[16] Depression is often accompanied by dysfunctional behavior such as alcohol abuse.[17] Adverse alcohol-related health effects tend to occur in the immediate period around separation, especially if the person lacks social support.[18] Separation is also linked to physical symptoms. In one study, in the first six months after separation, more than half of the participants reported that they had experienced physical problems—stomach upsets, body aches, fatigue, appetite loss, weight loss, headaches, and insomnia.[19] However, it is also the case that many people feel some relief when they have finally separated because the marriage is finally over and they can get on with their lives.[20]

Tasks of Separation

Whether the person reacts immediately with distress or relief, the separation is followed by increasing stress—especially for parents with children—as practical, legal, and emotional challenges arise. People cannot simply wallow in their grief or go on a shopping spree to mark their newfound freedom. Critical decisions about legal procedures, child custody, property and debt, spousal and child support, and housing and living arrangements must be made during the separation period. Couples face five major tasks during the process of separation and the transition to divorce:[21]

1. They must separate emotionally and psychologically from each other and establish separate identities.

2. If they have children, they must become single parents and begin to learn to coparent.

3. They must separate their finances and each establish an independent economic existence.

4. They must reorganize and reestablish their social networks.

5. They must carry out the legal steps required to divorce and to settle all financial matters and child custody.

These different tasks are overlapping in time and interrelated so that success or failure in one area may influence functioning in other areas.

Separating Psychologically

"Uncoupling" is a protracted process during which spouses gradually redefine themselves as single.[22] Marital separation and an impending divorce change the relationship between the spouses but do not automatically redefine it.[23] New boundaries must be established to permit the emergence of new identities that are separate from being a couple. Spouses must decrease their emotional investment in the marriage; end their intimate exchanges, including sexual relations; and accept the marriage's end. Despite the reality of the divorce decision, it is not uncommon for separating spouses to miss each other. Their continuing attachment, loneliness, and need for intimacy, however, do not negate their rational understanding that the marriage does not work.[24] Attempts to sustain intimate bonds in moments of loneliness, longing, or despair are counterproductive if the marriage is "irretrievably broken." They may raise hopes of reconciliation in one of the spouses— most likely the one who was less eager to divorce—revive old hurts and fuel further conflict, and delay people's ability to reorient and fully invest in new and separate lives. Continued attachment is also related to increased emotional and psychological distress and feelings of guilt.[25] Although emotional disengagement may engender feelings of loss, failure, and pain, detaching from the relationship is necessary for regaining psychological autonomy and establishing a new identity.[26]

Separation is a time to acknowledge that the marriage failed, grieve the loss, and begin to work out who one is or wants to be outside of marriage. Separation is a time for individuals to strive to understand their own contribution to the breakdown of their marriage. Accepting and processing the failure of the marital relationship should be used to redefine what to look for in a partner in the future and how to readjust one's own behavior. Gradually, anger should be replaced by an acceptance and integration of the divorce experience into one's identity, and energy should be reoriented toward the demands and opportunities of the new life.[27] It is often necessary to redefine one's values and goals as this new life begins.

Becoming Single Parents

If a couple has children, their adapting to the new demands of becoming single parents is a critical task of separation. Although parents' explicit intent is to end their spousal relationship, they need to recognize that their parenting relationship endures and that they continue to be related to each other because of their children. They need to try to avoid having their interpersonal disagreements spill over into their child rearing.[28] Parental interdependency during the separation period to some extent requires even more cooperation than during the marriage. Important decisions about child custody must be made, and the details of children's contact with each parent must be specified. Parents need to coordinate their schedules, transfer the children between them, and arrange the myriad details that pertain to the daily care of the children. They need to negotiate how they will do this, how they communicate with each other and make joint or autonomous decisions. One of the most difficult changes that parents must accept is the loss of some of their influence over their children—because they will not be able to control the type and quality of interactions between the children and the other parent.[29]

Just as they need to redefine the boundaries of their own relationship, after the separation parents need to renegotiate the boundaries of the entire family system. Divorced parents and the parent-child-parent triad typically benefit when boundaries are somewhat distant, formal, and dependable. Unpredictable ad hoc scheduling and lack of reliability in following through on arrangements are confusing and upsetting to children and violate the boundaries of the coparenting relationship.[30] Especially during the separation phase, when adjustment to the newness of circumstances is greatest, it is important that parents strive to be effective, authoritative, and consistent and both stay involved with their children.

Economic Adjustments

Grasping the complex challenges of and coming up with constructive solutions to the economic problems of divorce are key tasks of separation. These problems involve agreeing how to split up jointly held assets and liabilities and completing the legal actions that ratify such agreements. They include terminating joint contracts and obligations, such as insurance policies, pension plans, and tax responsibilities, and replacing them with individual ones. They include establishing two new households. They also include all the practical steps of splitting property, household goods, and personal items in addition to finding new housing and relocating. They may include finding work, typically for women who did not work during the marriage, or finding new work that pays more or is in a different location, closer to the new home. Because two households are more expensive and economically less efficient than a single household, both spouses frequently move into more affordable housing. With the termination of the joint household, parents' division of labor also ceases. This means that tasks previously tackled by two must be borne by one in each household, and because this is difficult, such tasks are frequently outsourced at an additional cost. For example, if both parents work full time they may need additional child-care or cleaning services to cope with the daily demands. In sum, economic adjustments are complex and costly, and it takes careful planning, sensible decision making, and realistic expectations to weather this task.

Social Consequences

The end of a marriage changes the couple's social relationships and social status beyond the nuclear family, and these changes must also be
dealt with in the separation period. Whereas marriage typically extends people's social networks—by incorporating extended family
and friends of both spouses as well providing opportunities for the
couple to form links with other married couples—divorce often has
the opposite effect. Friends and family, hearing about the separation,
react in unanticipated ways. Because boundaries between the separating spouses are still unclear, these individuals may find contact with
the divorcing person confusing, uncomfortable, and problematic. The
end of the marriage also calls the social status of the separated person
into question, and this ambiguity may be unsettling. Some people offer continued companionship and support, but others withdraw because they feel awkward, disapproving, or threatened. Losing friends
and even family during this time of need may be particularly painful
and embittering. The experience of unexpected tension and rejection
from family, friends, and colleagues heightens a sense of isolation, rejection, and loneliness in the newly separated individual. Separated individuals are also often uncomfortable around their married friends
because it makes their own loss more salient. Children experience similar changes in social networks, especially if the separation precipitates
a move to a new neighborhood and school. This poses the additional
task for parents of trying to maintain their children's prior friendships
and actively promoting the development of new friendships.

The Legal Process

The legal process of separation and divorce involves three main steps:
filing for divorce, making financial arrangements, and if children are
involved, deciding on child custody. If both partners agree on everything, the process is reasonably simple and straightforward. Given the
emotional nature of divorce, however, it is more likely that the legal
process is complicated, costly, and lengthy.

Filing for divorce. The first task is to file for divorce in family law
court. To do this, the divorcing couple must find out which court has

jurisdiction for their particular case and what its requirements are. Jurisdiction is tied to residency requirements, which vary across states. In most states, residency requirements range from three months to one year. Nevada has the shortest residency—only six weeks. In California, a person must have lived for at least six months in the state and at least three months in the particular county in which he or she intends to file. The original divorce petition can be filed in a number of ways. Many people hire a lawyer or paralegal service to write the petition and file it for them with the court, but it is also possible to file the petition in court oneself. Filing the petition involves a fee, which is paid to the court. Whoever files the petition, either husband or wife, is called the "petitioner"; the other spouse, who has to respond to the petition, is called the "respondent." The easiest and least costly process is when the couple agrees on all important matters; if not, a judge will make the decisions and the couple must abide by the court orders. If the initial filing is not contested by the other party, the divorce is granted at the end of the waiting period, which varies in most states from six to twelve months. Nevada's waiting period, again six weeks, is the shortest.

Financial arrangements. In the past, marital property laws were biased in favor of the husband, who held title to the couple's assets. Under English common law, wives were unable to hold and dispose of property until about 1850, when statutes were passed to protect the rights of married women. At present in the United States, most states use traditional laws that vest all property to the husband. To achieve equity, however, judges may use their discretion to make an "equitable distribution." In nine states, judges use the concept of "community property" to determine the division of possessions. Community property designates ownership of property or debt acquired during marriage, including all income earned during marriage and all property acquired with that income. Property owned before the marriage and any income from such property remains separate and apart. Inheritances or gifts specifically made to one spouse during the marriage or personal injury awards are also treated as separate property. Contractual agreements may also be made by the couple before the marriage (prenuptial) or during it (postnuptial) to allow them to maintain individual property.

Despite the fact that the idea of community property is intended to provide equitable treatment for both parties, it is not easy to divide the assets. Couples may not agree on what constitutes community property: after several years of marriage it is often difficult to prove who owned what before the marriage and to separate assets brought into the marriage from those acquired during the marriage. If there is disagreement, the process of discovering "who owns what" can itself become costly and time-consuming and may not always end equitably. It is also difficult to reach a fair division of property because of in-equities in what men and women want and need after divorce. Women often want to have the children and the house—because it is difficult to find a new more affordable place and because they want to maintain stability for the children—but both the house and the children mean a considerable financial burden and no possibility for financial gain. Meanwhile, the man's "deal" leaves him largely free of obligations (mortgage payments, real estate taxes, child care) and more able to earn income—but "homeless."

One obligation some men still have is to pay spousal and child support. Not so long ago, it was common for men to be ordered by the court to pay their ex-wife alimony 'til death did them part. Nowadays, spousal support is limited in amount and duration—if it is awarded at all.[31] Most support is ordered for a relatively short time—a few years—and there is a strong expectation that the supported spouse will be self-supporting after this transitional period. The no-fault divorce law basically eliminated permanent support for middle- and upper-class women; it certainly eliminated a level of support that would allow them to live in the style to which they were accustomed. If and how much spousal support is awarded depends on a number of factors. It is most likely for a husband to be ordered to pay spousal support when the couple had a high standard of living, the marriage was of long du-ration, the husband has a much greater earning capacity than the wife, the wife requires a period of time to become self-supporting, she has more needs than the husband (for example, the need to complete col-lege in order to become self-supporting), she has more responsibility for the children, and she is unable to work without adverse effects on the children.

Child custody. Decisions concerning child custody and visitation can be even more complicated than the financial arrangements. Both parents want to remain involved with their children, but neither one necessarily wants to bear the entire burden and responsibility of being the sole parent; everyone needs some time for himself or herself. Both parents want to have some control over their children's lives and want to be free of the other parent's interfering, but each would probably like some encouragement from the other parent for their efforts. Working out this delicate balance between cooperation and control is tricky. If parents can come to a decision about custody, the court will respect it. If they cannot, the judge steps in and makes a decision based on "the best interests of the child." (The issue of child custody is discussed in detail in Chapter 8.)

As this brief discussion implies, the legal road to divorce is not an easy or obvious one. Most people quickly realize that they are poorly prepared for the challenges of the legal process. They blindly hope that an experienced judge will see their perspective clearly, recognize their needs, and make an order that will settle affairs in their favor. The reality is quite different. The court is a world with its own authoritarian rules based on the "adversarial model" of adjudication, a concept derived from English law. This model presumes that it is best if the parties to a dispute openly present their different views to an impartial third party, the judge, who listens and eventually decides what should happen. It is presumed that fairness will result when both parties are allowed to examine the meaning and accuracy of each other's claims. Difficulties arise because the presentation of evidence demands very detailed and strict rules. Typically, attorneys know how to handle this; the client, however, is likely to get lost in the rules and the legal language. It is particularly difficult if one side has an advantage over the other—for example, if one side is represented by an attorney and the other is not, or if one side has a more skilled attorney than the other. When this happens, outcomes may be biased in favor of the advantaged party. This is a huge problem; any mistakes in the legal setting can have severe and long-lasting consequences—a fact that many going through divorce realize only belatedly. In one recent study, researchers found that although many participants entered the divorce process expecting a fair and reasonable experience and outcome, only 12 percent of them ended the process believing that they had a positive experience.[32] Instead, they felt a complete lack of power and control over the outcome. When people feel the legal process is unfair, more-over, the negative consequences spill over onto their views of the out-come. Perceived inequities in the court process lead people to be less satisfied with the final divorce decree and the child custody order.[33]

So should individuals hire a lawyer to help them navigate the shoals of divorce and get a better deal? Lawyers are not necessary for di-vorce. From a legal standpoint, it is possible for a couple to initiate and handle the entire process by themselves. But often lawyers are involved because spouses do not communicate well with each other, because the issues they are dealing with are complex, and because the legal pro-ceedings are intricate, involving legal forms and terms, detailed rules, and deadlines to observe. It seems easier to have a lawyer take care of things. Many people also feel angry and hurt or they are afraid that their children will be taken away; therefore, they feel a strong need for legal counsel. Unfortunately, the lawyer's role in divorce is ambiguous, and his or her training may be inappropriate for expediting the di-vorce. Only a small number of lawyers are family law specialists, and even those who are trained in family law may be programmed to argue for their client's position, right or wrong. It is not their job to be con-ciliatory, to negotiate, or to decide what is right or best. Their role is to win the case. This adversarial style can magnify ill will and increase hostility between husband and wife.

People assume that lawyers know what they're doing and how to handle divorce best. Still, not all lawyers are competent, and they can be careless at filling out forms and following procedures. They may leave some issues unresolved—like who will take care of the children, where the children will be educated, and whether there is life insurance to cover the children. They may also strike bargains with the opposing attorney or the judge that are convenient for them but turn out not to be so good for their client. In one study, fifty-three of the fifty-six women who dealt with lawyers during their divorce had strong com-plaints about them.[34] The most common complaints were that the lawyers had not informed them about the legal process; they had made mistakes that cost the women money, time, and grief; and, most telling, these women claimed, the lawyers were not interested in their problems. In another study, researchers found that lawyers' actions of-ten raised the emotional level of the divorce dispute.[35] These findings are disappointingly consistent with research done three decades ago. In a study of divorcing couples in the mid-1970s, researchers found that the majority of court clients were dissatisfied with the legal system; they found that their attorneys gave them advice to act in ways that reduced their chances of reconciliation and also encouraged them to lie or make trumped-up statements to the judge.[36]

An alternative to using a lawyer to fight a battle in the courtroom is to use a mediator. The goal of mediation is negotiation, not winning a battle. Mediators are trained to defuse conflicts and achieve win-win solutions (see Chapter 8). Some couples are able to resolve their differences with a mediator's help and avoid a courtroom scene. If going to court is unavoidable, however, would-be divorcers should prepare for the legal process. They should gather information about finding and working with a lawyer, about legal terms and legal documents that need to be filed, about their rights, about child custody and support rules, about what it's like to go to trial, and about alternative dispute resolution procedures. They should understand the motions their lawyers file and should help the lawyer prepare arguments and evidence. It is essential in going through the divisions of divorce that people have realistic expectations and make reasonable demands. They should think through their true needs from a long-term perspective and decide how these can be served by decisions about child custody, property, and spousal and child support. If each party's position is to grab as much as possible for themselves in the division of children and assets, a long legal and emotional battle is likely.

Summary

Divorce is a complex, drawn-out process. The decision to divorce may take years as individuals engage in cost-benefit analyses and vacillate between staying and leaving. Women are more likely than men to see problems in the marriage and to initiate the divorce. The period immediately after the actual physical separation is usually characterized by high levels of distress—more stress than the actual divorce. Loneliness and coping with living alone are key stressors, and physical and psychological health problems are common. Divorcing people must face a series of challenges and decisions pertaining to legal procedures, child custody, financial and living arrangements, spousal and child support, and single parenting and single life.

The psychological tasks of separation include accepting the fact that the marriage has failed and processing the loss. Parents are faced with the extra challenge of having to provide reassurance and care for their children at a time of turmoil. Moreover, they must establish a functioning coparenting relationship with the other parent. Divorcing individuals also experience changes in their social networks. They typically lose some of the friends they had as a couple and need to make efforts to rebuild their social network with new friends. The challenges of coping with the legal system arise when couples cannot agree on the postdivorce arrangements and decide to seek third-party help. Dealing with legal procedures adds complex demands that are costly in terms of finances, time, and emotions. In sum, the time leading up to the divorce decision and the actual separation are transitional periods in which spouses need to make important, life-altering decisions, manage the multifaceted challenges resulting from the decisions, and cope with the stresses of adjusting to single life and single parenting.

4

Adults in the Aftermath
of Divorce

After the legal wrangling is over and the divorce is final, after the initial pain and shock of the separation have dissipated, what is life like for di vorced adults? What happens to men and women emotionally and socially in the years after divorce? What are the economic consequences? How quickly and easily do individuals adjust to the divorce and to their new single life, and what factors either help or hinder their adjustment?

The Effects of Divorce
Downward Mobility

In 1985 a startling finding was published: a researcher had found that one year after divorce women's standard of living had dropped drastically— 73 percent—while the standard of living for men had increased—by 42 percent.[1] Consternation—and criticism—erupted. One criticism was that the researcher had interviewed only divorced men and women in California and her findings could not be generalized beyond the Golden State. Since then, a number of studies have been conducted using larger and more representative samples in states across the nation, including the National Longitudinal Survey of Labor Market Experience, the National Longitudinal Survey of Youth, and the National Public Opinion Research Center's General Social Surveys. Quite con-

sistently these studies show that women's per capita family income declines after divorce and is substantially lower than married women's—
not as much as 73 percent, but, on average, about 30 percent lower.[2]
The largest declines are for middle-class women and women whose
marriages have been of long duration.[3] Some of these studies also show
that men's per capita income or standard of living increases after divorce—by 28 to 48 percent.[4] This is because, after the divorce, children typically live with their mothers, so men have fewer "capita" to
feed. However, although divorced men's per capita income may increase and they typically do better than divorced women financially,
the family income of divorced men is still lower than that of married
men.[5] In the divorce, men lose their wife's income, and they often have
to pay her some support as well. Statistics for 1998 showed that in the
United States, the median family income was fifty-four thousand dollars for married couples, thirty-six thousand dollars for father-headed
families, and twenty-two thousand dollars for mother-headed families.[6] Thus, both mother- and father-headed single-parent households
have an economic disadvantage compared with two-parent families.[7]
As a consequence of this economic disadvantage and decline, divorced
individuals experience downward mobility that requires many to move
to less desirable housing. They move from residences they owned to
residences they rent, from single-family houses to apartments, from
upscale housing to dilapidated digs, and from "uptown" neighborhoods to the other side of the tracks.[8] Interestingly, the economic decline in divorced families starts even a few years before the divorce and
continues its downward tumble throughout the process of disruption.[9] The disadvantage lasts at least five years after the divorce.[10] Thus,
one of the clearest consequences of divorce is downward mobility.

Shifts in Social Networks

Divorce also causes dramatic changes in adults' social lives. First and
foremost, of course, the spouse is gone, leading to a decline in couple-
related activities. In addition, when the spouse goes, the spouse's family often goes as well, and contact with former in-laws decreases
sharply. In one study, the majority of respondents (66 percent) saw
their parents-in-law at least once a month before the divorce, but after

Personal Story: Facing Downward Mobility

Within a year after the divorce, the relief my mother first felt after she separated from my dad had worn off. Her new life was a burden. She could hardly pay her bills. She had been working in a series of dead-end jobs and she was exhausted. She was tired of moving (we had moved to six different houses within the year), and she was suffering from the stress of having to start over again and again and again. After ending a particularly bad relationship with a boyfriend, she decided it was time to move back to our old neighborhood. At this point my dad stopped paying child support. Then my mom was fired from her new job (for refusing her married boss's advances). Our phone was disconnected, the power was turned off, and there was nothing in the refrigerator. Times were brutal as Mom struggled to provide for us.

the divorce, many (42 percent) never saw them, and those who did stay in touch were likely to get together only occasionally.[11] This drop in interaction with in-laws is especially marked for men—presumably because they are less likely to have custody of their children and so less likely to visit the grandparents.[12] In another study, only 13 percent of the divorced women listed their ex-husband's parents as part of their social network—in contrast with 50 percent of married women.[13] They claimed that they had difficulty maintaining relationships with their former in-laws because it was hard for these former relatives not to take sides and to act as if "blood is thicker than water."

But it is not only in-laws who disappear; many divorced adults find that friends disappear as well—especially if the friendship had been formed during the marriage and was shared with the spouse.[14] On average, people lose three friends when they get a divorce.[15] Sometimes this is the divorced person's idea; sometimes it is the friend's. Divorced individuals are twice as likely as married people to break off relations with a close friend, and they are also more likely to feel excluded by their former pals.[16] They discover after the divorce that the social world is like Noah's ark—they are not accepted without their mate. Some friends withdraw from both husband and wife to avoid taking sides; others split into his and hers camps.[17] Often, married couples do not know how to incorporate a single friend into their couple activities.[18] They may feel threatened by the single person because he or she looms as a sexual threat or makes too many demands. At the same time, divorced individuals may isolate themselves from their friends because they feel that they no longer fit in, they are upset by seeing others' happiness, or they assume that others are critical of their behavior. Especially if the divorced person is embarrassed because of the ex-spouse's behavior, it is difficult to put on a happy face and socialize with the old gang as if nothing has happened. It is also difficult to socialize if seeing the old gang brings up painful memories of the way it used to be. Changes in lifestyle as a result of moving, taking a job, switching jobs, or having less money also interfere with established friendships.[19] Whatever the reason, divorced adults are more isolated and feel more lonely than married adults.[20] In one longitudinal study of the aftermath of separation and divorce, 43 percent of the participants expressed a desire for more friends.[21]

Having lost old friends, many divorced individuals lose no time trying to acquire new ones or renew friendships that existed before their marriage.[22] Most find new friendships in their neighborhoods, work settings, or formal organizations.[23] They are likely to make friendships with other single people rather than married couples.[24] They are also more likely to have friends with marital difficulties.[25] On average, in the first year after divorce, women make five new friends—compensating, in number, for the friends they have lost.[26]

More than simply making friends, divorced adults are interested in meeting people with whom they might become romantically involved. Most begin dating within the first year.[27] Dating is a significant milestone on the path of distancing oneself from the ex-spouse.[28] Casual sex, with multiple partners, is quite common—in fact, sex of any sort is more common than it is for married people.[29] Meeting people is difficult though; ask anyone who's been there. It is particularly difficult for women. Many divorcees avoid bars and singles groups because they feel too old and find the overt and competitive sexual nature of these places offensive. They have trouble dating because their resources are limited, they are burdened by work and child-care responsibilities, their self-esteem is wounded, they feel they have been out of the game too long, and they are afraid of being hurt.[30] Sometimes they are still carrying the torch for their former spouse, and this, too, is a barrier to dating.[31]

Role Changes

Divorce also brings with it radical changes in the roles adults play, particularly if husbands and wives have been following traditional gender roles in their marriage. Divorce catapults women who have been homemakers into the role of breadwinner, while men who were only "backup" parents find themselves in the front lines of child rearing— at least on the weekends.

The likelihood that women are employed more than doubles after a divorce. More than 80 percent of divorced mothers are employed, compared with fewer than 40 percent before the divorce, and women who were employed full time before the divorce work even more hours after it.[32] In one study, divorced women were interviewed about becoming their family's breadwinner.[33] These women were not high-income professionals but were filling jobs such as secretary and nurse. The ones who had held full-time jobs and contributed to family finances and decision making *before* the divorce reacted to their changed circumstances most calmly and became most invested in their occupations after the divorce. Women who had worked part time increased their work loads dramatically after the divorce, and even though they had never expected to be the primary breadwinner and they missed the time they used to have with their children, they were not distressed. Women from traditional marriages in which the husband was the only breadwinner, however, had a great deal of difficulty accepting their new role and worried a lot about their children. They felt angry and frustrated about their new work responsibilities, guilty about not being with their children, and ambivalent about their jobs. The greater the role change precipitated by divorce, apparently, the more difficult it is to accept.

Women and men who have custody of their children after divorce experience another role shift: they become single parents. They find themselves juggling housework and child care along with work and financial responsibilities. The household chores that used to be divided between two now fall to one alone. This single parent is responsible for more housekeeping and house management duties, more child care, and more cooking.[34] This role shift has some problematic consequences. As the parent struggles, household routines may break down.[35] The family skips more meals and eats out more often.[36] The parent experiences child-rearing stress and task overload.[37] The role of the single parent is challenging and exhausting—like being pecked to death by ducks, according to one sufferer.[38]

Of course, not all divorced parents have custody of their children, but the role of a parent without custody also reflects a dramatic shift from the role of the married parent. Noncustodial fathers typically have limited contact with their children immediately after the divorce, and contact diminishes even further as time goes by, especially with daughters.[39] According to the National Survey of Families and Households, three-quarters of divorced fathers see their children less than once a week, and of those who do, fewer than one-third have extended periods of time with them.[40] Noncustodial mothers have twice as much contact with their children as noncustodial dads; they are more likely to continue their traditional parenting role and arrange their living situation to facilitate visits from their children.[41] Nevertheless, they, too, have less involvement than custodial parents.

Figure 4-1 summarizes graphically the postdivorce changes individuals face.

Psychological Problems

Given the downward mobility, loss of old friends, role changes, and task overload of divorced adults, it is not surprising that they often have psychological problems. Many experience anger and anxiety, depression and loneliness.[42] Divorce creates emotional turmoil and sometimes even mental illness.[43]

One consistent finding across different studies, including studies of large samples followed prospectively from before the divorce and studies conducted in different countries, is that, on average, divorced adults are more distressed and depressed than married—or single—

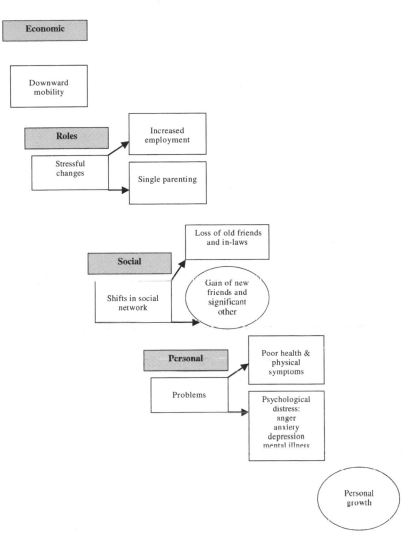

Figure 4-1. This figure summarizes economic changes, role changes, social changes, and personal changes after divorce. Most changes are negative and stressful (rectangles); some changes are positive (ovals).

adults.[44] Divorced mothers in one large, national British sample, for example, were almost 200 percent more likely to be depressed than married mothers.[45] In another study, one-quarter of the divorced women, who had been divorced, on average, for fourteen years, had a clinically significant problem with depression.[46] Other studies have also documented higher levels of psychiatric symptoms in divorced women compared with married women.[47] Suicide and suicide attempt rates are higher among divorced men and women in countries around the world.[48] For example, in a study in Australia, separated men were six times more likely to commit suicide than married men.[49] One-fifth of the women in a study in the United States thought about suicide after their marriages broke up.[50] Divorced women in Sweden were found to be at increased risk for violence, traffic injuries, and other accidents.[51] Divorced people also drink more alcohol and develop more addictions.[52] In one study in the United Kingdom, heavy drinking declined between the ages of twenty-three and thirty-three for the general population, but it increased among people who divorced during that age period.[53]

But are these psychological problems the result of divorce, or the cause? People with problems like drinking and depression are especially likely to divorce, as we saw in Chapter 2, and they are also less likely to marry in the first place.[54] Moreover, divorcing individuals often react to the separation with strong emotions such as anger and distress, as we discussed in Chapter 3. So is there evidence that divorce creates or exacerbates psychological problems that extend beyond the marriage or the immediate separation crisis, or are differences between married and divorced folks simply the result of "self selection" or short-term stress? A substantial amount of research exists on this question, involving large samples of participants. This research suggests that divorce does lead to problems beyond those that people had before the marriage ended or that they exhibited in the immediate crisis of separation.

One kind of evidence that divorce is responsible for psychological problems comes from studies in which researchers control statistically for individuals' personality problems. These studies show that this control does not eliminate the differences between divorced and married people's rates of distress and depression, suggesting that these psychological problems are a direct result of divorce.[55] A second kind of evidence comes from studies of people who have gone through divorce more than once. These studies show that when people get divorced for a second or third time they have even worse problems than people who have divorced only once—more anxiety, more depression, more severe distress.[56] In one study, for example, twice-divorced adults were more likely to attempt suicide (20 percent of the men and 40 percent of the women who had divorced twice tried suicide compared with 9 percent of the men and women who had divorced only once).[57] But the third and perhaps most convincing kind of evidence comes from studies in which individuals have been followed over time to see whether their problems increase and stay high after the divorce. These studies show that increases in problems like depression and drinking begin before divorce, rise sharply at the time of separation, and then, over the next few years, decrease somewhat but, on average, not to the same level as for married people.[58] In one example of this kind of research, investigators David Johnson and Jian Wu conducted a twelve-year-long study of a nationally representative sample of sixteen hundred people who, at the beginning of the study, were in intact marriages.[59] They found lasting effects of divorce on psychological distress for the 243 individuals who got divorced over the course of the study. This divorce effect was larger than the effect of selection. The researchers attributed the difference to the different social roles of divorced and married adults, with divorced people experiencing more social isolation, economic hardship, and child-care responsibilities. Another team of researchers examined the relation between divorce and distress in two hundred divorced mothers and three hundred married mothers.[60] For divorced mothers, stressful events and depressive symptoms increased significantly soon after the divorce (stressful events doubled, from three to six in the first year after the divorce) and then slightly diminished over the next three years— but not to the same levels reported by married women. Divorced women experienced significantly higher occurrences of nearly all stressful life events, including having a close friend move away, having a child involved with alcohol, moving to a different residence, and being physically attacked or sexually assaulted.[61] The same pattern appeared on a depression checklist that assessed how often in the past week they were bothered by such problems as crying easily, feeling trapped, blaming themselves, feeling blue, feeling worthless, and feeling hopeless about the future. Clearly, divorce has a direct effect on adults' mental health and well-being.

Physical Symptoms

The problems divorced adults experience may also show up in their physical well-being. Compared with married individuals, those who are divorced have more physical health problems and are likely to die earlier.[62] In a study of more than four hundred thousand initially healthy women in Sweden, divorced women (who had been single for at least five years) showed increased risks of mortality and lung cancer and, if they were poor, increased risk of heart disease.[63] In an American study, almost half of the divorced men and women reported health problems.[64] In another study, they reported weight loss, upset stomach, body aches, fatigue, appetite loss, headaches, and sleep problems.[65] Underlying these differences in physical health symptoms are physiological links between divorce and immune function.[66] Separated and divorced individuals have a lower level of the cells that resist tumors and bacteria and higher levels of the cells indicating susceptibility to viruses; in other words, their immune systems are not as effective in resisting disease as the immune systems of married individuals. The health behaviors of married and divorced people also differ: a recent study showed that divorced middle-aged women had higher risk profiles on cholesterol and body mass and were more likely to smoke and less likely to exercise than women in satisfying marriages.[67] In brief, there are links between divorce and physical well-being suggesting that divorce is a risk factor for poor physical as well as mental health.

Positive Consequences

Of course, not all consequences of divorce are negative. Some people also experience positive outcomes. As a result of divorce, individuals may develop new talents, attain new awareness, and learn from their past mistakes.[68] They may go back to school and improve their occupational status.[69] Divorce benefits these people, leading to more autonomy and personal growth, improved career opportunities, richer social lives, better parenting, and improved self-confidence (for women) and interpersonal skills (for men).[70] Some people report that their self-esteem is higher than it was when they were married because they have more control over their lives and have grown emotionally and discovered abilities and strengths they were unaware of.[71] In the Virginia Longitudinal Study of Divorce and Remarriage, a study that followed individuals for twenty-five years after their divorce, nearly one-fifth of the women grew more competent, well adjusted, and fulfilled after the divorce; they had high self-esteem, succeeded at work, were socially adept and good parents; they were less depressed and antisocial than average.[72] Although men were less likely than women to show this kind of "enhanced" consequence of divorce, some fathers were jolted by the divorce into realizing how much their children meant to them, and this was a positive consequence for them.

Adjusting to Divorce

People vary greatly in their reactions to divorce: for some individuals, divorce is a net benefit; for others, it leads to a temporary decrement in well-being; and for yet another group of people, divorce sets them on a downward trajectory from which they never recover fully.[73] Here, we discuss the kinds of things that affect how quickly and well adults adjust to divorce. These factors are summarized graphically in Figure 4-2.

Individual Qualities That Help

One quality that seems to affect adjustment to divorce is how old the person is at the time of the divorce. A number of researchers have found that older people are more distressed by divorce and have a harder time adjusting than younger people.[74] But the age trend may be more complicated than this. There is some evidence that for women divorce is easiest in their thirties and for men, in their forties. In one longitudinal study, years after the divorce, women who were in their thirties when they separated were happier, less lonely, more secure economically, and had made major improvements in their psychological functioning. Women who were older when they divorced were less likely to have an adequate income or a stable love relationship; half of them were clinically depressed, and all of them were lonely. Years after the divorce, men who were in their forties at the time of the divorce were secure financially and had remarried.[75] In another study, as well, men in their forties fared better than older or younger men because

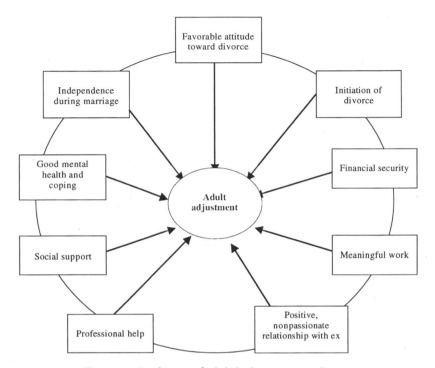

Figure 4-2. Predictors of adults' adjustment to divorce.

they were relatively free of the need to raise children, their careers were on the rise, and they had a wide selection of dating options.[76]

Personal qualities also make a difference in how well people adjust to divorce. Major problems accrue if the person has a mental illness or an antisocial personality (prone to lying, fighting, gambling, drinking, or shoplifting, for example).[77] In contrast, people adjust better if they have higher levels of education and better mental health.[78] They benefit from strong personality characteristics such as assertiveness, self-assurance, intelligence, creativity, social boldness, liberalism, self-sufficiency, ego strength, competence, sociability, and social maturity.[79] If they believe they will be able to adjust after divorce, they are more likely to do so.[80] If their image of themselves is of a masterful person—"I like myself as a person; I feel I can handle whatever comes along"—they will have a more positive experience after divorce.[81]

Men and women adjust better to divorce if they are effective copers in general—if they can reframe stressful situations in more manageable ways, use active strategies to master a situation, and have a problem-oriented coping style.[82] These strategies are better than not thinking about their problems, blaming themselves for the problems, engaging in fantasy, or looking for help from someone else.

Attitudes toward marriage, family, and divorce matter, too. Women adjust to divorce more easily if they are not heavily invested in their identity as wife and mother.[83] If their attitudes are androgynous rather than gender stereotyped, they are less distressed by divorce and experience more personal growth, self-esteem, and effectiveness.[84] For both men and women, it helps if their attitude toward divorce is more favorable.[85] People who believe that marriage is permanent and important and that divorce is immoral are most likely to feel stressed and depressed when they get divorced.[86] Roman Catholics, for example, have more adjustment difficulties than people of other religions or those who practice no religion at all.[87] Attitudes pave the way for people's adjustment to divorce, and those who are open to the possibility of divorce have less trouble dealing with their own.

Happy Marriage, Happy Divorce

Another predictor of how well individuals adjust after divorce is the quality of their marriage before divorce. In Johnson and Wu's twelve-year-long study of a nationally representative sample of sixteen hundred people who, at the beginning of the study, were in intact marriages, two patterns were clear.[88] For individuals who were in troubled marriages, distress was relatively high during the marriage, increased steeply just before the breakup, declined sharply with the relief of separation, then increased again and stayed high. For individuals in happy marriages, distress was relatively low during marriage, increased only slightly before disruption, increased sharply at disruption, then declined and in the end these individuals had improved psychological health. Thus, it appears that although there is a sensible mood swing during the early stages of separation so that people in bad marriages are happy to escape them and people in good marriages are distraught at their loss, having a poor marriage in the long run predicts poor adjustment to divorce and having a good marriage predicts a better outcome. Other researchers have also documented these effects of separation and divorce.[89] In one study, women from abusive marriages, who were physically or emotionally hurt or whose husbands were unfaithful, were more likely than women whose marriages were not abusive to be clinically depressed even many years later.[90] Men and women adjust to divorce best if they gradually grew apart during their marriage and the breakup was caused by disagreements over basic tasks and issues, such as arguments over money or neglect of household duties, rather than serious emotional problems like infidelity.[91] It also helps ease individuals' adjustment to divorce if they had separate interests, hobbies, and social activities while they were married.[92]

The Way the Marriage Ended

Not surprisingly, the people who initiate the divorce adjust more easily than those who do not want the marriage to end.[93] They are less distressed and depressed and more likely to think that the divorce was a good idea.[94] They even show better immune function.[95] In open-ended interviews, they are more likely to talk about growth, optimism, and social support opportunities, whereas noninitiators talk about being left, feeling vulnerable, and needing spiritual comfort.[96] Feeling guilty about the divorce also makes adjustment harder, especially for women.[97] In the long run, though, differences between initiators and noninitiators of divorce diminish: by the third year after divorce, in the Virginia Longitudinal study, the differences between the two groups were no longer significant.[98]

Another issue about how the marriage ended that predicts adjustment is how bad the divorce experience itself was. In fact, one can predict how difficult it will be for people to adjust to the divorce by just how negative their reaction to the separation is.[99] When people experience more negative events during the separation and life changes following divorce are more stressful, they have more psychological symptoms, both at the time and several years later.[100] Having poor legal representation during the divorce is also related to later depression.[101]

The Benefits of Social Support

After the divorce, especially if the experience is stressful, people whose friends and relatives offer them social support adjust better.[102] Social support from family and friends is related to better psychological adjustment and fewer health problems.[103] The kind of support that appears to be most helpful is socioemotional—companionship, listening, socializing—not giving money or material things.[104] People feel supported when they receive expressions of approval and acceptance, empathy and intimacy.[105] However, this raises a question: does social support actually promote better adjustment, or do people who are adjusting better (for other reasons) elicit or acknowledge higher levels of support from their friends? In one experimental study, individuals who were getting over a divorce were invited to join a social support seminar group. Social support among group members did increase over the course of the ten-week seminar; however, no improvement in divorce adjustment was observed.[106] It is apparently not so easy to help people adjust to the woes of divorce just by giving them some short-term sympathetic social contact with relative strangers. It may be that social support simply accompanies better adjustment; it may be that social support has to come naturally from friends and relatives.

A network of friends is the most likely natural source of support for people going through a divorce.[107] Friends are good for child care and chauffeuring, companionship and comfort. People who have more friends and a larger social network and who engage in more frequent interaction with their friends adjust better to divorce.[108] In one study of divorced mothers, in fact, the most consistent predictor of adjustment was how much socializing they did with their friends.[109] People who are socially isolated or who don't have much social activity after the divorce do not do so well.[110] However, social activity itself does not compensate for lack of emotional support and intimacy. What matters most is the quality of the social interaction. Psychological adjustment after divorce is better if the network is stable and contains good friends.[111] Having a slew of casual new acquaintances can be lonely and distressing.[112] It is also depressing if friends don't accept and approve of the divorce.[113] It helps if the social network contains others who are themselves divorced.[114] Not only are these divorce veterans more likely to approve of a divorce, but realizing that others have been through the same—or worse—experiences helps people put their own problems in perspective and aids them in overcoming their sense of being social outcasts. Associating with other divorced individuals works well as long as the person doesn't become isolated in a divorced world, which reinforces their sense of alienation.

A supportive family can offer help that eases the divorced individual's transition through divorce and facilitates their long-term adjustment.[115] Parents can often be counted on for practical assistance—for financial support, housing, and child care—and their presence is helpful in combating loneliness and isolation.[116] Approval and emotional support from parents are also helpful.[117] However, living in the same house and receiving advice from parents about what to do and how to do it is not.[118] In fact, it can be downright stressful. Women who move back home report interference and criticism from their parents.[119] Siblings can be more understanding and emotionally supportive than parents, although they are often busy, live far away, and may be estranged as a result of childhood rivalries.[120] Having contact, approval, and support from former in-laws—although infrequent—is another factor that predicts well-being and adjustment.[121]

The most important source of support after divorce, though, is having one close relationship with a good friend or a new partner. Divorced people who have a best friend, a confidant, someone who offers them social intimacy, feel less depressed and anxious and adjust better to the divorce.[122] They are less stressed than if they have only a network of people with shared interests and values.[123] And even better than a best friend, is a new love interest.[124]

Dating is an important part of the divorce adjustment process for both men and women. It serves a socialization function in familiarizing divorced individuals with the customs and values of the singles world they have just joined. It helps them appraise their own strengths and weaknesses. It reduces their loneliness.[125] Divorced individuals who are dating are better adjusted than those who are not.[126] They are more likely to have accepted the fact that their marriage is over and they must move on, and they are less attached to their former spouse.[127] But just dating or sleeping around is not the solution. Promiscuity can cause problems—mental ones, as well as physical.[128] The benefits of dating come from dating someone steadily and romantically, someone who offers intimate emotional support.[129] When this leads to living together, the rewards are even greater. Divorced people who are cohabiting are happier than those who live alone, and those who remarry have improved psychological functioning, at least for a while.[130]

Professional Assistance

When a person is going through divorce and adjusting to being alone or to being in a new relationship, how useful is professional help? This is an important question for psychologists, but the answer is not clear. If one asks people who have received professional or paraprofessional assistance, the majority of them think that the assistance was helpful, whether it was a support group or a singles club, psychotherapy sessions, or a newsletter for divorced mothers.[131] But we can't just take the word of contented consumers; we need objective proof. When researchers have analyzed how well people are doing—for example, by assessing the number of depressive symptoms they have—and related this to whether or not they received professional help, they have found that people who receive therapy are not better and may even be worse than those who do not avail themselves of these services.[132] The negative findings from such correlational studies are misleading, however, because it is unlikely that therapy *causes* more problems; it is more likely that troubled individuals seek out therapy.

A better way to assess the helpfulness of professional guidance is to conduct a study with a control group or a comparison group that does not receive therapy. Researchers have studied a variety of programs in this way, including workshops and therapy focused on divorce adjustment issues, communication skills, coping strategies, financial planning, parenting issues, social support, dating, and the expression of feelings. A review of these programs suggests that the ones that last at least ten hours have generally had some success in reducing individuals' depression and overall symptoms of distress, and some programs have even been successful in reducing anxiety and self-doubt, decreasing adjustment difficulties, and improving self-esteem and empathy.[133] One successful program in Colorado offered people individual and group sessions designed to provide social support and to facilitate competence in parenting, career planning and employment, legal and financial issues, and housing and homemaking. Paraprofessional staff contacted participating individuals and helped them to design their own program and then regularly contacted them and worked to meet their needs for support and information. Even four years after the program, effects on participants' divorce adjustment and quality of life were still significant.

A more limited program in a small sample of recently divorced individuals followed a different approach: it focused on encouraging divorced individuals to forgive themselves and their ex-spouses for the divorce. This program was also successful in reducing participants' anger, anxiety, depression, and hostility.[134] The success of this program raises the question of whether it is generally helpful for divorced individuals to participate in religious activities—another possible source of professional counseling and help with forgiveness. Although, as we have already mentioned, holding a religious belief that divorce is immoral may make adjustment more difficult, participation in religious or church-sponsored activities may actually help divorced people recover from divorce. Being part of a religious community can offer social support, practical help, opportunities to meet other single adults, and a feeling of belonging, as well as pastoral counseling. In fact, researchers have found that church attendance is linked to better adjustment after divorce.[135] Again, caution is needed: it may be that better adjusted people are the ones who are able to pull themselves together to go to services. No researcher has randomly assigned some individuals to attend church and others to stay home and watch football.

The Importance of Money

The underlying cause of much of the anguish people experience after a divorce is not just the loss of the spouse, but, let's face it, the loss of the spouse's money. Money is a preoccupying concern for divorced men and women, regardless of their absolute income level—and for good reason. Two apart cannot live as cheaply as two together. How individuals adjust to the divorce is strongly linked to their economic situation.

First of all, the *level of income* is important: individuals with higher incomes adjust to divorce more easily, and a difference in adjustment is evident even years after the divorce;[136] conversely, having a low income is related to poorer divorce adjustment.[137] This is especially a problem when the income is so low it constitutes poverty. It is impossible for adults to adjust to divorce emotionally when their very survival and the survival of their children is at stake. Money may not guarantee a person's recovery from divorce, but having no money makes it nearly impossible. In fact, an association between poverty and mental-health problems, in general, is one of the most well-established findings in all of psychiatric epidemiology.[138]

Second and even more important for adjustment to divorce is the *drop in income* the person suffers.[139] When people feel that their economic situation has deteriorated since the divorce, they are more depressed and have more adjustment problems.[140] Why? Because loss of income leads to stressful changes—moving to a less desirable residence; having to move back home with parents; losing the familiar neighborhood; being unable to go to movies, restaurants, plays, or sports events because there is less discretionary income; worrying about having enough money for basic needs like food; losing the lifestyle and social network they enjoyed during marriage—and these changes lead to more anxiety and depression.[141] Drop in income is a risk factor in the postdivorce period.[142]

Third, the *source of income* is important for divorce adjustment. Having an independent income predicts adjustment more than the absolute level of income or its stability.[143] People adjust better when they can draw from private resources rather than being dependent on other people or the government.[144] In one study, when women owned or rented their own home without assistance from their ex-husbands, for example, their adjustment was better.[145] In another study, women who were not living in a house co-owned by their ex-husband had a better relationship with him.[146] Receiving money from the government is probably the worst for adults' adjustment: divorced parents who received a higher percentage of their income from public funds (welfare, food stamps) had worse social and emotional adjustment than parents whose equivalent incomes came from personal earning or private transfer payments (child support, friends, family, church).[147]

Fourth, the *security of the income* is also important.[148] In fact, feeling economically insecure is more detrimental for individuals' psychological well-being than simply having a low income.[149]

So is low income the reason that divorced people have more psychological and physical problems than married people? It is one reason, but not the only one. In several large, longitudinal studies, researchers have found that income level accounts for some of the differences between married and divorced adults—but not all of them.[150] Unfortunately, researchers have not analyzed how much of the effect of divorce is the result of these other income factors—income loss, source, and security; however, it is reasonable to expect that they would explain even more of the differences.

The Significance of Work

The importance of meaningful work as a stabilizing influence after divorce should not be underestimated.[151] People adjust to divorce better if they are employed and have more stable, satisfying, complex, and better-paying jobs.[152] When they get divorced, women with higher level jobs—professional or managerial—do not experience an increase in accidents, suicide, and addiction. They do not experience as much depression and anxiety as women with lower level jobs.[153] Work offers an opportunity for advancement—out of poverty and into a better way of life: among women living in poverty, those who are employed are most likely to move out of poverty following marital disruption.[154] Work is also a source of psychological support. It gets people out of the house, provides them with an important arena for success and satisfaction, and brings them into contact with other adults. Social support at work promotes divorced men's psychological well-being.[155] Being employed makes women feel less depressed and isolated than if they stay at home all day.[156] Career success also leads to improvement in divorced adults' self-esteem.[157] Work is a protector against divorce stress: in one study, divorce stressors such as large declines in income, loss of friends, and a move to a new neighborhood were related to poor adjustment only among individuals who were not employed.[158] Of course, there is a price to pay for working; it is not a panacea. Work, especially unskilled work, can be draining, frustrating, and stressful. Working parents often feel as if they are on a treadmill, unable to balance the demands of work with the burdens of home and child care, especially if they work many hours every week.[159] Nevertheless, having a satisfying and productive job generally benefits adults' adjustment to divorce.

Getting Along with the Ex

Another important factor in divorce adjustment is the kind of relationship the ex-spouses develop. After a couple divorces, their conflict does not necessarily disappear, although for most, it diminishes. Researchers have found that a few years after the divorce, most divorced couples are no longer *intensely* angry at each other;[160] however, at least half are still *somewhat* angry.[161] Individuals who started out with more intense hostility tend to continue to have higher levels of conflict.[162] In one study, half of the participants (parents selected from divorce court records) continued to be angry with each other three years after the divorce; they were characterized on the basis of in-depth interviews as either "fiery foes" or "angry associates."[163] They continued their strife over the children, over money, over new relationships, over old problems, over new problems—indeed, over anything. They were unable to detach themselves from their former spouse. Frequently, their hostilities escalated into protracted legal battles.

At its most extreme, conflict involves violence. Studies consistently find that if the wife is abused during the marriage, the abuse is likely to continue after the couple separates.[164] For example, in one national study of violence against women in Canada, 39 percent of 437,000 women with previous violent relationships reported violence after separation, and for 30 percent of them the violence was more severe after separation than before. For these women, concern for safety was so fundamental it established the context in which they carried out their daily lives. Fear permeated their entire experience.[165] In another study, a similar statistic was obtained from the men's point of view: 40 percent of the divorced men reported threatening or using physical violence against their former spouse after separation.[166] They used violence—as part of their masculine identity—to regain their position of authority over their wives. Even men who had not been physically abusive during marriage could become so during the separation if they had a strong male gender-role identity.[167]

When couples have a violent or acrimonious relationship, they have more trouble adjusting to the divorce. If they cannot communicate openly and neutrally in a rational manner, they have problems. Women whose communication style was angry and raging were found in one study to be more anxious than women who could discuss issues with their ex-husband in a practical, businesslike style.[168] And years after the divorce, women in another study who had persistent strong negative feelings about their former spouse were more likely to be clinically depressed.[169] Cooperating couples are generally more satisfied with their lives and have better psychological well-being than those with a negative relationship.[170]

Nevertheless, the relationship between the former spouses can be too close. A continued preoccupation with the ex-spouse can be just as detrimental to healthy adjustment as the failure to establish a cooperative relationship. It is important to set boundaries that clearly define the former partner as a friend or coparent, but not as a spouse or lover. Failure to do so is a major source of conflict after divorce and an impediment to a cooperative relationship.[171] It is quite common for ex-spouses to have contact with each other after the divorce.[172] This contact is usually fine. In fact, in one study, two years after separation, couples who had more frequent interaction had better mental health and less psychological distress.[173] But continued passionate, romantic attachment to the ex-spouse may be detrimental for adjustment. When such an attachment continues, the individual is less likely to develop a rich social life and a new intimate relationship and has impaired emotional well-being.[174] One researcher compared three types of relationships between former spouses:

    1. *Friendship:* the person liked and got along with the ex-spouse; for example, he or she agreed with the statements: "My ex is there as a friend"; "We get along now"; "I like my ex."

    2. *Hostility:* the person disliked and got upset with the ex; for example, agreeing with the statements: "I dislike my ex"; "I want to forget my ex exists"; "I get upset when I see my ex."

    3. *Preoccupation:* the person had obsessional thoughts

about missing the ex; for example, he or she agreed with the statements: "I feel like part of me is missing"; "I miss my ex"; "I can't stop thinking about my ex"; "I miss the home life we shared."

The sample consisted of middle-aged divorced couples who had been divorced for one year. Those who turned out to have the best emotional well-being were the ones who were not preoccupied with their ex-spouse; this was more important than being either friends or foes.[175]

Clearly, after the divorce is final, it's best for people to move on psychologically, not to continue ruminating and wishing, living in the past. In fact, it has been suggested that hostility after divorce is evidence of a prolonged attachment.[176] Being angry is a way to stay involved and preserve the intensity of the marital relationship.[177] As a participant in one study put it, "The divorce war keeps me going."[178] For healthy adjustment, adults need to declare a cease-fire and end the war, whatever form it takes.

His and Hers Divorces

Who Is Hit Harder?

Although both men and women experience negative outcomes after divorce and gender differences are not always found in every study, a few differences appear consistently enough to suggest that there are "his and hers" divorces.[179] These differences appear in a wide variety of studies in countries around the world.

One difference appears when men and women first separate. Men experience more serious problems during this period. Suffering more intensely from the emotional trauma of the separation, they are more likely than women to go off the deep end. They are more distressed than women,[180] have more suicidal thoughts,[181] and are more likely to commit suicide.[182] In one large study of suicide in Australia, for example, separated men were six times more likely to commit suicide than married men, whereas suicide rates were not significantly elevated for separated women. Men also decline more in their physical health, have more severe health problems, are more likely to be hospi-

Personal Story: His and Hers Divorce

Adjusting to life after the divorce was not extremely difficult for my mom. The pain of divorcing seemed like nothing compared to the pain she had felt during the marriage. Soon after the divorce, she began working more hours, trying to move up in the company. She started feeling some hope for the future and began viewing the divorce as a welcome relief. My dad took the divorce much harder. He found himself drinking, not just socially, but after work, at home, and sometimes from a stashed bottle in his car, as he tried to sedate himself from the negative emotions he was experiencing. He felt angry at himself for allowing things to turn out as they had, angry at himself for the immaturity he had displayed, and angry at my mom for not giving him "another chance." He felt overwhelming sadness and grief with the loss of his family. Most of all, he felt that he was a failure—a failure as a husband and as a father. He had physical symptoms like headaches and sleeplessness. He suffered from depression, which he thought would never end.

talized, and report more physical symptoms, such as weight loss, pains, loss of appetite, heart palpitations, shortness of breath, dizziness, and feeling weak all over.[183] In a study of forty-four thousand deaths in Sweden, separated and divorced men were found to have relatively higher mortality rates than separated and divorced women.[184] In the Virginia Longitudinal Study of Divorce and Remarriage, in the year after divorce, men were more likely than women to be in a group the researchers characterized as "defeated"—they had health problems, depression, low self-esteem, and engaged in antisocial behavior such as alcoholism or drug abuse.[185]

One reason that men have more extreme reactions to separation is that, as we have mentioned (in Chapter 3), women are more likely to have initiated the divorce. Women are twice as likely as men to make the final decision to separate and to file for divorce—even over their husbands' protests.[186] Women tend to be dissatisfied with their marriage and think about getting a divorce for a longer time than their husbands, and when the marriage ends, their feelings about the marriage and their spouse are more negative.[187] Thus, for women, separation often ends a long and painful process; for men, it comes as a shocking blow.

Although men have more of the *most severe* symptoms after divorce, however, women have more of the *less severe* problems, and these problems last longer.[188] In the years after the divorce, women experience higher levels of distress and depression than men.[189] Perhaps this is not the result of divorce; women report more depression than men even when they are married.[190] But the difference shows up in longitudinal research following individuals before and after they divorce: the effect of marital disruption on depression is more pronounced for women than for men.[191] Women report more psychological stress and less psychological satisfaction after they divorce.[192] They report more negative life events and more psychological symptoms, such as depression, moodiness, and feeling stressed and insecure.[193] In the long run, women may be distressed not so much by the divorce as by its consequences. In one study, men were observed to get over the negative emotional effects of the divorce, overcome the divorce "crisis," and resume a "normal" life in two years; for women it took about three years.[194]

But the picture is not all gloomy for women; women are more likely than men to report that they have experienced positive growth and a new sense of independence and self-confidence as a consequence of terminating their marriage.[195] They say that these changes are *good* things that happened since divorce, whereas men are more likely to say that nothing good has happened.[196] In the Virginia study, women were more likely than men to be in groups characterized by high competence and high self-esteem or self-sufficiency and social skill.[197] Two years after divorce, the majority of women (72 percent) in a Swedish study reported that they had experienced improved mental well-being since separation, compared with only 28 percent of men.[198] Similarly, in a study in California, ten years after divorce, 64 percent of women versus 16 percent of men reported that they had experienced psychological growth, including developing a better image of themselves, feeling more deeply in their relationships, increasing their capacity for sustained commitment to goals, and resolving the psychological disequilibrium brought on by the divorce.[199]

In brief, there is no simple answer to the question, Who is hit harder? Men are hit harder by the separation and respond more dramatically and immediately; women are hit harder by the divorce lifestyle and respond with more depression or with more positive growth.

Two Social Worlds

One reason for these differences between men and women is that males and females inhabit two different social worlds. One way that these social worlds differ is in the availability of close friends and confidants. While they are married, men are likely to have one primary confidant, one person on whom they depend for support and comfort—their wife; women, in contrast, have several girlfriends to provide emotional support.[200] Thus, after divorce, men lose their confidant, but women keep theirs; in fact, after divorce, women's relationships with their friends, especially single women friends, become closer and more intense.[201] Men's strong initial reaction to separation may, in part, be a reaction to this loss of a confidant. Divorced men are less likely than divorced women to have a close friend with whom they can talk over their feelings and frustrations.[202] Those fortunate ones who do have someone to talk to about the divorce have better mental health.[203] Women are better at maintaining old and intimate relationships, and they are more likely to stay in the same community after the divorce, whereas men are more likely to move and to suffer for it, especially if they move to another state.[204] In a recent analysis of data from many studies, researchers found that divorced women receive 38 percent more support from their families and 40 percent more support from their friends than men do.[205]

But although women have close confidants and supportive families, after divorce their social networks dwindle in *size* more than men's do.[206] The structure of men's lives provides access to "instant networks." They have more opportunities for social interactions because of contacts at work, and they are more likely to take on self-improve-

ment activities, like enrolling in continuing education classes or joining athletic clubs, which bring them into contact with groups of new
acquaintances. In one study, divorced men, on average, joined three to
four groups—sports, cultural, religious, and service groups—whereas
divorced women joined only two groups.[207] Developed to alleviate
loneliness, these groups provide a place in the wider community that
men did not seek while married. Most divorced women do not have
the luxury of joining such clubs. They have fewer opportunities for interaction because they have less money, less confidence, and less experience. Their social life focuses on their children and extended kin;
they are not as good at developing new and casual ties.[208] Men are
more likely than women to receive support from their social networks.[209] They are viewed as dinner party assets, not threats, and they
are assisted by "casserole ladies"—neighbors, friends, and relatives
who appear at the door, hot dinner in hand.[210] Men with larger social
networks also report better adjustment a year or two after divorce.[211]
For women, network size is not related to adjustment; it doesn't matter
how many clubs and casual acquaintances they have.[212] Women have
better psychological well-being if they have made more *close* friends
since they separated.[213]

Another difference in the social worlds of men and women after
divorce is that men engage in a flurry of dating and sexual activity.[214]
Compared with their ex-wives, men date significantly more often and
with more different partners.[215] They go to singles' bars (which divorced women generally dislike), pick up women at work, meet
women at health clubs. Divorced women have fewer potential partners
because they are more constrained by age and appearance, they have
fewer opportunities to meet new people, and they are more afraid of
being hurt or rejected.[216] Men who engage in a frenzy of social activity, however, are not happy; they are more distressed than men who do
less socializing.[217] Frantic socializing is not a good way to get over a divorce.

Instead, one of the most important ways to improve self-esteem
after divorce is to establish a satisfying, intimate relationship.[218] Here,
also, men and women differ. Divorced men are more likely than divorced women to develop such relationships. Men remarry sooner and
at higher rates.[219] They are more likely to receive support from new

lovers, according to an analysis of the results from a large number of studies.[220] They are more likely than women to think that the best thing that has happened to them since the divorce is forming a new relationship.[221]

Thus, in their recovery from divorce, women have the advantage of close friends and family, while men have the advantage of a new intimate. In both cases, having a confidant is a critical aid to adjustment.

She Has the Children

One of the most salient differences between men and women after divorce is that women are more likely to have custody of and contact with their children.[222] Although the proportion of children living with their fathers has increased over recent years, fewer than 12 percent of fathers are awarded physical custody of their children at the time of divorce.[223] Even when the "children" are adults who no longer live with their parents when the divorce occurs, divorced fathers see less of them after the divorce, while mothers see more.[224] This difference in who has the children could contribute both to both men's more severe initial reaction to separation and to women's longer lasting low-level distress.

The reason that men have an intense initial reaction to divorce may be related to losing their home and their children in the separation. Divorced fathers move a lot; if they don't have custody, they almost always move out of the family home.[225] It has been argued that men mourn the loss of their home and children more than the loss of their wives.[226] Even if men left the marriage willingly, this loss of house and children precipitates distress, anxiety, and depression.[227] In one study, three-quarters of the fathers interviewed said that missing their children was one of the worst results of divorce.[228] Losing contact with their children brings dads pain because they want to still be dads—as one dad said, "Divorcing my children wasn't part of the bargain."[229] Fathers who do not have custody of their children are likely to be dissatisfied with their custody arrangement and think that the divorce proceedings were unfair.[230] Half of them describe their current relationship with their ex-wife in terms of hostility, tension, and bitterness.[231] They feel excluded from their children's lives and irrelevant to their development.[232] Most of them feel frustrated and victimized, lost, and unsupported.[233] Compared with married fathers or fathers with custody, these men are more likely to go on drinking binges.[234] Over the long run, when the number of children living with the adult is taken into account, the increased mortality rate that was observed for divorced men compared with divorced women is reduced.[235]

In contrast to *losing* the children, *getting* the children offers company and support to the divorced parent and gives meaning and grounding to the adult's life. Having the children helps the parent get through the emotional crisis of the divorce. Thus, women are buffered by having the children and continuing to live in familiar surroundings.[236] However, having custody has its own costs. Women's adjustment to divorce may be prolonged because of their child-care and child-rearing responsibilities. Divorced mothers often find that there is not enough time for both children and work, let alone time for themselves. They experience task overload. Mothers who get custody often feel overwhelmed, trapped, and resentful.[237] Their children are always on their minds. Stay-at-home mothers feel imprisoned with Mister Rogers or the Wiggles; working mothers struggle to juggle child care and a job.[238] Having children is also related to slower progress up the occupational ladder for women and to reduced likelihood that they will move out of poverty.[239] Mothers who find custody a burden and single parenting stressful have more psychological problems.[240] When men get custody of the children, their adjustment is the same as that of custodial mothers. They, too, find that they must curtail social activities because of lack of time or feelings of social ostracism; they, too, experience problems with dating, taking business trips, and pursuing job possibilities.[241] They feel overloaded and isolated and suffer emotional distress just as mothers do.[242] If the children are grown up when the parents get divorced so neither one has to deal with these child-related stresses, the amount of depression does not differ for divorced mothers and fathers.[243]

He Has the Money

The other salient difference between men and women in the aftermath of divorce is that men almost always end up with more money than women. As we have already discussed, research consistently shows that the negative economic consequences of divorce are greater for women than for men.[244] Many divorced women find themselves suddenly thrown into economic disaster, not knowing how they will support themselves and their children, certainly unable to do so at the level at which they have been living. In one study of middle-class families, five years after the divorce one-third of the women were enmeshed in a daily fight for economic survival; only one-fifth were financially secure.[245] This was two decades ago. Today, the gap between men and women is closing, thanks to better education of women and stricter enforcement of child support laws; but still, women suffer greater economic hardship than men do.[246]

This discrepancy results from the fact that, in traditional marriages, women focus on their families and men on their careers. So, when they get divorced, women still have their children while men still have their careers. For men, work goes on uninterrupted (and in fact may increase as family demands diminish). Many women are not prepared to support themselves, even if they had a job to supplement the family income when they were married. They have no money of their own, no assets except what they get in the property settlement, no career, few job prospects (because they have no job history or an interrupted one), limited earning capacity (they get paid only 75 percent of the wages men get), and they are under time constraints because they are responsible for taking care of the children.[247] These divorced women must enter the labor market without skills, seniority, or time for retraining. Compared with men, they have more trouble getting money from banks and they are likely to lack credit, pensions, insurance, and higher education.[248] Their jobs are less stable and satisfying than men's.[249] The law does not require a man to cover his ex-wife's medical insurance, pay for his ex-wife's education to the same level as his own, or share his future earning power. Men are required to provide financial support for their wives (and children) if their incomes are higher, but this support is not enough to ameliorate women's divorce-induced economic decline. The payments themselves are not large enough, they are not paid regularly enough, and they do not apply to all women.[250] Child support payments amount to less than one-fifth of the income of divorced mothers and their children.[251]

Personal Story: No Longer the Corporate Wife

Before the divorce, my mom was a "corporate wife" and used to living well. Now, she no longer attends the Republican Convention, the Governor's Ball, or ritzy dinners. She doesn't fly in the company jet to vacations in Hawaii or Florida, doesn't get her nails done, and no longer shops at Bloomingdale's. As a matter of fact, she doesn't shop anywhere. While her life progressively disintegrated, life for my dad was great fun. He still had all the perks that came with being a top lawyer. He had a great job and an ample income. Now, he lives with his girlfriend at the beach while my mom struggles to make ends meet.

For many women, the financial hardships accompanying divorce become their overriding experience, determining their psychological well-being and dictating decisions about where to live, what to eat, and how to care for their children.[252] One researcher documented the struggle of sixty middle-class women thrust into the harsh aftermath of divorce.[253] These women got by—barely—by renting out spare rooms in their now-too-expensive homes, selling their jewelry and furniture, and searching for loose change in the carpet to buy a quart of milk. They were swamped with legal fees and couldn't afford to take their ex-husbands to court when they refused to pay support. Only one-fifth of the women had been working before the divorce; almost all of them began working soon after. But they had trouble getting more than a "pink-collar" job. Two years after the divorce, 85 percent had not recovered economically. They struggled with depression, despair, and debt.

The economic aftermath of divorce is especially hard on three groups of women. One group is older homemakers. Women who are divorced when they are older than fifty, after a lifetime of domestic duty, do more poorly than younger women in terms of both economic and psychological adjustment.[254] Older homemakers were promised by their husbands and society that his income was also "theirs." But, in the divorce, the court says that the husband's income is his and that the

Personal Story: Fourteen Years Later, He's Doing Well, She's Depressed

For the first few years after the divorce my mom did okay, but then the money she got from selling the house ran out. She found that she did not have the skills or the experience needed in the job market. Her standard of living dropped dramatically. I often came home from school and found her still in her pajamas, sitting in front of the TV, smoking, with all the windows and curtains closed. Today, she is single and alone. She still has severe depressions and terrible headaches. Her electricity is shut off because she cannot pay the bill. I pay it when I can, but I am going to school and can barely make it myself. She lives off noodles and macaroni that she cooks on the gas stove. For my father, adjusting to the divorce was difficult because he did not have a house and he did not have his daughter. But, in the long run, he adjusted much better than my mother because he had his business to keep him busy and to provide an income. Now, fourteen years after the divorce, my dad is doing well financially and emotionally. He has remarried and has a new family and lives in a beautiful house.

ex-wife must find a job to support herself. What can a fifty-year-old woman who has not worked for twenty or thirty years do? She can never get to a high level of employment starting at an age when many people are retiring. She may be required to begin work for the first time, and the best job she can find may be as a short-order cook or a file clerk. After the divorce, older women are usually more bitter, lonely, angry—and poor—than younger women.

The second group of women for whom divorce is especially hard is women from upper-income families—because the higher up they are, the farther they fall. The drop in the standard of living after divorce is greatest for women whose husbands made the most money. These formerly affluent women who depended on their husband's income must move down into a different social class. They may lose their housekeeper, drive an increasingly decrepit car, and live on generic-brand food. The less the husband contributed to the household income, the less he can take away.

The third group of women who suffer from divorce is mothers with children. These women have greater demands on their resources and less ability to meet them. Mothers with college-age children suffer because child support usually lasts only until the child is eighteen, not through college; and mothers of preschool children suffer because, if they work, they must find and pay for child care. Divorce has created a new poverty class in the United States: single moms and children. More than half of the poor families in this country are headed by single mothers.

Clearly, then, divorced men have more money than divorced women. This does not mean that they have enough money, though. Men also complain about money troubles after divorce. Two-thirds of the divorced fathers in one study felt that money was their most pressing problem.[255] Men are less satisfied than women with the financial and property settlements ordered by the court.[256] They have to shell out for the costs of the divorce, moving, getting a new car, new house, and new furniture; they are paying a portion of their income for child support—and they think it's too much.[257] Psychological adjustment for both men and women is affected by income loss and downward mobility after divorce.[258]

Adjusting to Divorce: How Long Does It Take?

Although these effects on divorcing adults may be extreme, they do not last forever. Most individuals adjust to their new circumstances—at least eventually. How long does it take them to get back to "normal" after the divorce? How long before the nerves stop jangling, the kids' beds are made every morning, and dinners are ready on time? This is an impossible question to answer because there is no single timeline to adjustment. In general, though, the first year or two after divorce is particularly difficult.[259] For most people, symptoms and distress do not decrease by the end of the first year or year and a half.[260] It takes two or three years before routines are back to normal and the adult has adjusted to his or her new lifestyle.[261] It is even longer before stress levels get back to normal. Stress diminishes after the first two years and by the end of the fourth year has typically tapered off to a level comparable to stress for married couples or for the divorced couple before they separated.[262] Psychological symptoms such as distress and depression are diminishing over this period from two to four years postdivorce as well.[263] By the end of the fourth year, psychosomatic symptoms have decreased, and alcohol abuse has declined. Most individuals are happier than they were during the anguish of separation; they see the divorce as a positive event in their lives and believe that things are better than they were during the marriage.[264]

But not everyone is happy or psychologically well adjusted even then, and although symptoms have decreased, they have not necessarily dropped back to predivorce levels or reached the level of married people.[265] In a number of studies, researchers have found that people's functioning does not improve as time passes after divorce, suggesting that there are continued effects of social isolation, lack of social support, economic hardship, and child-care overload.[266] In Johnson and Wu's twelve-year study, although distress decreased after separation, the decrease was not statistically significant.[267]

Moreover, averages hide individual differences in adjustment to divorce. For some individuals divorce is a crisis from which recovery is quite rapid, whereas for others it presents strains that are not easily overcome.[268] In one study in which researchers examined individual patterns of adjustment during the first three years after divorce, half of the sample improved while one-fourth got worse.[269]

In brief, then, adults struggle through the period after divorce. Their path to adjustment may be paved by help and support from friends and family, work and money, or it may be full of jagged rocks thrown up by disapproval, loneliness, poverty, and unemployment. Resentments against the ex-spouse may linger, stresses may continue. But for the fortunate ones, within three or four years, life returns to normal, and for the most fortunate, personal benefits are realized.

Long-Term Consequences

If not everyone is back to normal after a few years, do these individuals ever completely recover? Or are there still differences among divorced individuals ten, twenty, thirty years later? The answer to the last question is clearly, "yes." Even years after divorce, people have entirely different views, ranging from exuberantly positive—"Getting divorced has been one of the best things to have happened to me. It helped me grow stronger, wiser, and deeper"—to distressingly negative—"Divorce is worse than death."[270] Fortunately, positive reactions are more common than negative ones. When women in one study were interviewed a decade after divorce, three-quarters of them said that their life was better than it was a couple of years after divorce because they had experienced increases in personal power, succeeded in raising their children, found new partners, developed independence, achieved financial security, or completed their education.[271] A far smaller number, only about one-tenth of the sample, thought that their life was worse than it was at that painful time. These women had financial difficulties, child-rearing problems, bad relationships, and feelings of insecurity and loneliness. Experts in the field estimate that close to one-tenth of divorced individuals are unable to work through their anger and loss. They have high rates of litigation and relitigation, high degrees of anger and distrust, and are unable to focus on their children's needs or establish healthy relationships with other adults.[272]

Information about long-term consequences of divorce comes particularly from two longitudinal studies that have followed families for several decades after divorce. One of these, a study by Judith Wallerstein, began in 1971 with sixty middle-class families in northern California who were going through divorce and who volunteered to participate in the study in return for counseling.[273] Since then, the parents and children in the sample have been interviewed in depth every five years or so. Although this was not a "clinical" sample (they were not referred for therapy), a court-referred sample (the parents were not in litigation over custody), or an economically high-risk sample (the parents had middle-class incomes and occupations), two-thirds of the families did have some psychological problems before the study began (such as chronic depression or problems controlling rage). So this is not a "normal" sample, and it is certainly not representative of the diversity of families in this nation. Therefore, we must be careful about generalizing from its findings. It is useful, however, to examine the different patterns of adjustment the study revealed. Based on the

Personal Story: Scars That Will Never Heal

Eighteen years after the divorce, my mom fears that the deep scars it left will never heal. She still feels sad and resentful because she worked so hard to put my dad through school and she was left with nothing. She still feels angry that her parents helped pay for so many things and my dad never paid them back. She is bitter because my dad blames the divorce completely on her. She is sorry because she had many close friends on his side of the family and now they are gone. She is hurt because her parents tried to stay close to my dad's family, but my dad's family always snubs them. I believe that these issues will never be resolved and my mom will suffer from them forever.

clinical interviews she made ten years after the divorce, Wallerstein defined three different patterns, or profiles, of adjustment. The most common profile reflected divorce "survivors"; these people were scarred by the divorce but kept struggling to move on, sometimes slipping up, sometimes succeeding. A second profile reflected more successful adjustment. These people were able to resolve past issues, accept past mistakes, learn from them, change their behavior, and function more adaptively. They seized the crisis of divorce as an opportunity for achieving a higher level of personal growth and self-actualization. These were the divorce "winners." They were likely to be young women, pushed by the divorce to enter the workforce, get more education, and improve their standing in the workforce—and as a result, they gained confidence and success. The third group were divorce "losers." For these individuals divorce continued to occupy a central place in their emotions. They were still grappling with the aching consequences of the divorce many years later. They felt that life was unfair, disappointing, and lonely.

The other longitudinal study of divorced families was the Virginia Longitudinal Study of Divorce and Remarriage conducted by Mavis Hetherington. This study, too, revealed patterns of adjustment that paralleled and extended the three observed by Wallerstein.[274] The Virginia study began in 1973 with 144 couples, 72 of them divorced, each with a four-year-old child. As in Wallerstein's study, parents and children, who were European American and middle class, were interviewed and assessed at intervals over three decades; however, these families did not receive counseling. Using statistical methods of analysis, Hetherington identified six different patterns of adjustment. The most common pattern was labeled "good-enough" (42 percent of the sample). These individuals were average copers. Ten years after the divorce, they were living lives that looked like their lives before the divorce—same old problems, same old complaints. For them, divorce was like a speed bump in the road; it caused problems while they were going over it, but it failed to leave a lasting impression, positive or negative. A second group were the "competent loners." These individuals (15 percent of the women and 5 percent of the men in the sample) were well adjusted, self-sufficient, and socially skilled. They didn't need (or want) a partner. They were doing just fine on their own. In contrast, individuals in a third group, the "seekers" (13 percent of the sample), were eager to find new mates. They were anxious and depressed and needed someone to lean on. A fourth, small group of individuals (5 percent of the women and 10 percent of the men) were labeled "swingers"; ten years after divorce, they were still playing the field. Together, these four groups might be considered divorce "survivors." Like Wallerstein's survivors, they added up to about 70 percent of the sample. The remaining two groups were equivalent to Wallerstein's winners and losers. The winners, or "enhancers" (nearly 25 percent of the women and 15 percent of the men), fared well over time. They grew more competent, well adjusted, and fulfilled over the ten years after their divorce. The losers, or the "defeated" (10 percent of the women and 12 percent of the men), remained in despair—helpless, poor, depressed.

It is clear from these studies that the long-term consequences of divorce vary vastly for different individuals. Most people manage to survive; they end up in the same place they started, albeit with a different partner or on their own. A smaller number turn the divorce into a growth experience; they end up ahead, smiling and confident. The smallest number—at least among middle-class adults—are the people who are defeated by the divorce and never fully recover.

Summary

A host of effects ensue in the aftermath of divorce. Perhaps the clearest and most consistent is downward economic mobility. Adults' social lives are disrupted too, with fewer couple-related activities, diminished contact with former in-laws, and loss of shared friends. Roles change as divorced wives take on more responsibility in the workplace and their husbands more—or less—responsibility for child care. Not surprisingly, these lifestyle changes are often accompanied by a rise in psychological problems. Both men and women experience elevated rates of problems, including traffic accidents, substance abuse, and depression—above and beyond the troubles experienced before the breakup. Physical and health-related maladies—weight loss, sleep disturbances, fatigue, and lowered immune functioning—also rise after divorce.

Although both men and women suffer these negative effects, they suffer in somewhat different ways. Men more often have severe emotional reactions to the initial separation; women more often have less severe symptoms that last longer. The reason for this difference seems to be that men suffer the loss of daily contact with their children but retain their higher incomes, more established careers, larger social networks, and better remarriage potential; women retain custody of their children but have less money and resources and find the continuing burdens of single parenting stressful and demanding.

How quickly and how well adults adjust to divorce depend on a number of factors. Those who are younger, better educated, and psychologically strong have the best chance of a rapid recovery. Being open to divorce and less tied to traditional gender roles also eases adjustment. Being the initiator of the breakup makes it easier to manage the stress of divorce in the short run, but this is not a major factor for long-term adjustment. An independent and secure income is more important; individuals who suffer a large drop in income and its consequent changes in lifestyle are especially at risk for adjustment difficulties. Having a stable, satisfying, and well-paying job, likewise, is linked with better divorce outcomes because it leads to better economic circumstances and provides social support.

Social, emotional, and material support from friends, family, and co-workers is important in the process of adjusting to divorce; even one close relationship helps ease stress and strain. Dating can reduce isolation and loneliness, especially with a steady and supportive partner; casual dating is of limited help. If informal support systems are not available, professional programs such as workshops and therapy can reduce depression, raise self-esteem, and improve adjustment. Even after divorce, getting along with the former spouse is related to adjustment: couples who continue to be angry and in conflict have more psychological problems than couples who cooperate; however, being too close to and preoccupied with the former mate can interfere with long-term adjustment and prevent future planning.

Despite the litany of negative outcomes that characterize the aftermath of divorce, the good news is that three or four years after the divorce most people are back to "normal." These divorce "survivors" have resumed their lives and their predivorce levels of mental health. A small group of individuals continue to suffer loneliness, isolation, and economic hardship; they never fully recover from the loss of their marriage. In contrast, a somewhat larger group experiences personal growth, increased autonomy, heightened self-esteem, and more occupational success. Women are more likely than men to be the beneficiaries of these positive effects, but some divorced dads do gain a new appreciation for their children after divorce. Thus, the effects of divorce vary over time, across individuals, and between the sexes.

5

Effects of Divorce on Children

As we saw in Chapter 2, nearly half of the children born to married parents in this country go through a divorce experience before they are eighteen—about one million children each year.[1] For these children, even more than for their parents, divorce can be an extraordinarily difficult experience. For adults, a divorce may offer advantages—pursuit of a new career, a new hobby, a new spouse, or a new lover. For them, the divorce, although painful, can be a net gain. But children see no benefit in divorce. The end of their parents' marriage is a complete loss, turning their lives upside down. Reactions vary with age, but across the board, children experience feelings of confusion and betrayal as they watch their family fall apart and feel neglected while their parents struggle with their own problems. They just wish their parents would get back together and shape up. But, beyond these initial reactions, how much does divorce affect children in the long run? Do they suffer permanent psychological and physical problems? Do they have trouble in school? Are they "victims" of the breakup in the same way some adults are? This issue of how much and how divorce affects children's well-being has attracted a lot of attention from researchers. A computer search of books and articles in the database PsycINFO reveals more than four thousand on the topic of "children of divorce"—half of them in the past decade.

Differences between Children in Divorced and Nondivorced Families

The main goal of research on children of divorce has been to compare the functioning of these children with that of children in intact, two-parent families. These comparisons provide ample evidence that children from divorced families have more behavioral, emotional, health, and academic problems.[2] As we will see, the differences are not large and they are not necessarily permanent; nor are all children affected equally. But the differences are consistent across studies and statistically significant. Compared with children in intact families, children from divorced families are more likely to have conduct problems and show signs of psychological maladjustment; they have lower academic achievement, more social difficulties, and poorer self-esteem. Because so much research has been conducted in this area, researchers have been able to combine findings from multiple studies in meta-analyses, in which the results of separate studies are expressed in terms of a common "effect size" representing the difference between children in divorced and intact families. One of these meta-analyses, published by Paul Amato in 1991, combined the results of ninety-two studies in which researchers had compared the well-being of children living in divorced, single-parent families with that of children living in continuously intact families.[3] In 70 percent of these studies, children with divorced parents had lower levels of well-being than children in intact families. The largest differences were in the areas of aggressive conduct and poor social adjustment, although significant differences also indicated that children from divorced families did more poorly in school achievement and psychological adjustment.

These meta-analyses were updated by Amato in 2001 with results from sixty-seven new studies.[4] The new studies were more sophisticated than those in earlier decades; they included larger, more representative samples and national, longitudinal data sets such as the National Longitudinal Survey of Youth, the National Study of Families and Households, the High School and Beyond Study, and the British National Longitudinal Study.[5] The new studies also included smaller but more intensively studied longitudinal samples, and they included prospective studies—that is, studies that started before people even got divorced, which made it possible to control statistically for such factors as parents' predivorce income and children's predivorce behavior problems.[6] Despite these improvements in the available research, results from the 2001 meta-analyses were strikingly similar to those from 1991. As in the earlier meta-analyses, on average, children with divorced parents did significantly worse than children with continuously married parents in terms of academic achievement, self-esteem, popularity and peer relations, misbehavior, depression, and anxiety.

These meta-analyses focused on children' psychological well-being because this is what has been studied most frequently by psychologists. However, differences have also been found in children's physical health. Their parents rate them as being less healthy, and the children themselves report more physical symptoms.[7] A link with diabetes has been found: 40 percent of children with diabetes had gone through a divorce before the onset of the disease, compared with only 17 percent of a randomly selected comparison group from the same community.[8]

Researchers have also discovered that there are more subtle costs for children when they have to cope with their parents' divorce, costs that do not necessarily show up on standard tests of achievement, behavior, or health. These emotional costs include embarrassment, fear of abandonment, grief over loss, irrational hope of reconciliation, worry about their parents' well-being, anxiety about divided loyalties, and uncertainty about romantic relationships.[9] In the early years after their parents' divorce, all children feel sad and almost all feel angry, and these feelings do not disappear easily.[10] In one study of college students, researchers found that those who had experienced their parents' divorce reported distressing feelings, beliefs, and experiences. These were resilient young people and the divorce had occurred years earlier, but still they harbored painful feelings. They were functioning well enough to be attending college, and their scores on standardized measures of depression and anxiety were not elevated, but they struggled with inner fears, worries, and regrets. Three-quarters of them said that they felt they would have been a different person if their parents had not gotten divorced. Half said they worried about events like graduation or weddings when both of their parents would be present. Half said they missed not having their father around, they had a harder childhood than most people, or they wished they had grown up in a never-divorced family. One-quarter wondered whether their father really loved them, and one-fifth believed they were doomed to repeat their parents' problems. These students' responses were significantly different from those of students who grew up in always-married families.[11]

It is clear from this plethora of studies that divorce has some negative emotional, social, physical, and cognitive effects on some children. In this chapter we discuss these negative effects for children at different ages. In considering these negative consequences of divorce, however, it is important to keep in mind that many—in fact most—divorce "victims" are functioning well despite their earlier experiences and emotions.

Infants and Preschool Children React to the News

It is often assumed that divorce will not have a strong effect on babies who have not yet developed an emotional attachment to the parent they will be "losing." There need be little noticeable change in the infant's routine and little stress experienced by the infant after the divorce. Even if the infant is attached to the father and loses contact with him after the divorce, it should be possible for the infant to get over it, as long as the mother continues her nurturant care. Nevertheless, even infants are vulnerable because they are helpless; they survive and thrive at the whim of the environment. Infants may have a strong reaction to losing their father—*if* the mother herself is stressed. Two studies shed light on the plight of young children in divorced families. In one, infants in separated or divorced families who had regular overnight visits with their father were more insecure and disorganized in their attachment to their mothers than infants in a married comparison group; they also were more likely to be disorganized with their father—their behavior with both their parents was relatively inconsistent, disturbed, and disturbing.[12] In a second study, when very young children were given the opportunity to play with their mothers, those from separated or divorced families were less positive, affectionate, and engaged than children from married families.[13] Thus, both these studies suggest that divorce affects infants' and toddlers' emotional relationships with their mother—perhaps reflecting the mother's own emotional problems.

Children who are a little older are likely to find divorce bewilder-

Personal Story: Feeling Confused at Age Five

One day soon after my parents separated, my mom found me crying and she asked what was wrong. I asked her if she and my dad would get back together, to which she replied: "No, because we don't love each other any more." Then I asked: "Even if Daddy lost weight?" Clearly, at age five, I was confused about the reasons they were no longer together.

ing.[14] These preschool-age children don't understand what is going on. They don't know what the words "separation" and "divorce" mean. They don't understand why Daddy is leaving, why Mommy is crying. They are confused because they conceptualize a relationship only in terms of the person's physical presence.[15] For them, love is *being with* the person. At this age children are frightened when the parent leaves—afraid of being left alone, anxious about being abandoned.[16] If Daddy has left, who is to say that Mommy won't stop loving them and leave too? They are afraid about who will take care of them if Mommy does leave. Compared with older or younger children, these children are most distressed and upset, most vulnerable to feelings of loss and rejection. They have the most intense reaction to parents' separation of any age group.[17]

Researchers have tried to delve into these young children's thoughts and feelings about divorce using play therapy and storytelling. These methods illustrate the anxiety preschool children feel about their parents' divorce. In one study, when three- to five-year-olds from divorced families were observed in play, they frequently acted out themes about the loss of a parent—not loss as the result of divorce, but loss by death, disaster, and abandonment.[18] Clearly, these children were anxious about losing their parents. In another study of children this age, those whose parents had divorced at least two years earlier were asked to complete a story that began: "The mother is sitting on the couch. She is so sad because Uncle Fred has died. Show me and tell

Personal Story: Feeling Abandoned at Age Four

I was four years old when my parents divorced, and I felt confused and bewildered. I started sucking my thumb and withdrew from activities at school with other children. I was very fearful about being abandoned by my mother, and I did not understand why I was being forced to see my father. I felt I did not know him and was angry at him without understanding the reason. I remember only feeling really "safe" in my mother's presence. She was the only person I could trust.

me what happens next."[19] This story stem was enacted with a bear family dressed in human clothes. At the beginning of each story, the mother and father bears were placed in separate "houses" at opposite corners of the table. Despite the length of time that had elapsed since their parents' divorce and the fact that the story did not specifically mention divorce, many children acted out stories that related to divorce. Most striking, again, was the theme of father loss, enacted in dramatic instances of abandonment or parental death. As in the first study, it was clear that many of the preschoolers were anxious about the loss of their father. The children also incorporated many instances of family reunification, by moving the houses together or making the father join the mother and child. They were anxious—but hopeful.

The confusion these children feel has also been documented in psychological studies. In one study of preschool children from divorcing families, researchers found that the children lacked accurate information about divorce and what they did know was often inappropriate, frightening, and confusing.[20] They had apparently cobbled together information from firsthand experience, from direct and overheard conversations, and from what they saw on television: "Divorce is when Mom and Dad hate each other and your family is dead." "Divorce is when you pay lawyers a lot of money to wreck your family." "It's when your mom and dad can't stop pushing each other around and they kill your family." In their play and conversations, these children made it clear that they were concerned with making home safe from monsters, beasts, and baby kidnappers. They were sad about permanent damage to their parents' relationship and resented how the process had "ruined their parents' being friends any more." Lawyers were sometimes described as pirates, vampires, or wolves who scared children and stole from parents. Preschool children have more difficulty accepting the permanence of the divorce and giving up hope for reconciliation than older ones.[21]

Sometimes parents add to the young child's confusion by their own confusing behavior. Preschool children are easily confused when parents move in and out of the household. As we saw in Chapter 3, it is not uncommon for parents to separate and reconcile and separate again before they ultimately get a divorce. From the child's point of view, this is even more confusing than one break, and certainly it is more difficult for the parent to explain. This confusion adds to the children's general uncertainty about what is going on.

The stress of divorce may lead young children to regress to more immature kinds of behavior—a reaction to stress and a return to happier times.[22] It is not uncommon for children of this age to regress in their toilet habits. Their play behavior with peers is less mature; they stare at the other children instead of joining in the play. Even their fantasy play suffers: they treat a stick merely as a stick rather than pretending that it is a witch's broom or magic wand. They are whiny, act out, and have temper tantrums. They have nightmares about monsters. They become afraid of separating from their parents—although earlier they had separated easily. They suck their thumbs, cry for their cuddlies, cling to their mothers. They withdraw in fear and anxiety, whereas once they had been outgoing and sociable. They wet their beds and refuse to eat their vegetables. They are profoundly upset, anxious, and irritable. Some of the boys even act like girls. Parents report that the children have more behavior problems and teachers say that they are more dependent, can't concentrate on a task, and are generally maladjusted.[23]

Preschoolers may also feel guilty and responsible, as if the divorce is their fault.[24] They assume they caused the divorce or that they caused the conflict between their parents that led to the divorce.[25] They reason as follows: a person who doesn't like someone goes away;

Daddy went away, so Daddy doesn't like me, so it was my fault. They may act super good to bring Daddy back, or they may deny that Daddy has left. They make up stories about seeing Daddy or talking to him on the phone. If they do still see their father from time to time, they may feel torn in two: they miss their mother when they are with their father, and they miss their father when they are with their mother. Preschool children don't have a good sense of time, so a week is forever. They don't understand blood ties, so they think the departed parent may find another son or daughter to replace them. They are afraid that the parent will forget about them when they're gone. As one child put it, "When I'm with one parent, I always think the other one is dead." Children's reaction to a divorce is like their reaction to the death of a loved one. They experience stress, guilt, loneliness, and sadness. These feelings and diminished functioning can last a long time, and even years later there may be residual effects. For most children, however, the effects are relatively short-lived as they come to understand and accept the realities of their new family arrangements. As we will discuss, there is a wide range of individual differences in children's adjustment.

School-Age Children Understand But Still Suffer

School-age children (six- to eleven-year-olds) understand better what the words "separation" and "divorce" mean, but they may be just as shocked and just as worried as younger children. Understanding does not relieve their pain or anxiety. These older children, too, experience grief and sadness. They still long for their intact family and yearn for their lost parents. We sometimes act as if, because they are little, children's emotions are little too. Mothers typically underestimate how intense their children's feelings about the divorce are.[26] But this is a mistake. Children are losing a parent, a family, a home—and they have no control over any of it. It is not surprising that they feel upset, anxious, and powerless.[27]

Younger school-age children (six- to eight-year-olds) are more anxious and depressed than children from intact families.[28] They are particularly affected by the loss of their father, expressing longing for him and grieving openly, wishing they could spend more time with him and counting the days until they are together again.[29] Older school-age children (nine- to eleven-year-olds) are not as likely to express their grief and sadness. Their most common reaction is anger, as they blame one parent for the divorce and for the other parent's suffering and lash out, openly expressing their animosity and even hatred.[30] In one study, researchers looked at the letters children participating in divorce adjustment groups had written to their parents; they found that anger was the most common feeling expressed by nine- to eleven-year-olds.[31] In another study, children in this age group expressed anger about moving away from their friends and having less money for things they needed, anger about their parents' suffering and their own deteriorating relations with their parents, and anger about practical problems with custody such as being shuttled back and forth between two homes.[32]

Many children in this age group also ruminate about the divorce. Nine- to eleven-year-old children in one study were interviewed to find out how much they thought about the divorce.[33] For example, they were asked: "During the past month, how often did you think about the divorce when you didn't want to? How much did you have trouble doing other things like paying attention in class or falling asleep because you were thinking about the divorce?" Although a year had passed since the divorce, 40 percent of the children reported that they ruminated about the divorce at least once a day.

Not surprisingly, given that they can't keep their minds off the divorce, school-age children often have problems in school. Amato's meta-analyses showed clear differences in academic achievement between children in divorced families and children in continuously married families.[34] But children of divorce are not only likely to have lower grades, they have other problems as well. In one study conducted in collaboration with the National Association of School Psychologists, seven hundred children from first, third, and fifth grades in thirty-eight states were selected at random by their school psychologists, half of them from divorced families.[35] The children from divorced families performed worse on tests of reading, spelling, and math achievement. They received worse scores on fifteen out of sixteen classroom behavior ratings. They were less regular in their school attendance, less popular and socially competent, and more likely to be referred to a psychologist

Personal Story: A Month of "Stomach Flu"

My parents separated when I was in the fifth grade. In retrospect, when I try to picture my family and how we interacted before my parents split, I realize how miserable they were and how much they fought. But regardless of how unhappy they were, I did not want them to divorce. Years later, I came to realize that my parents' divorce was the best thing they could have done for our family. But at the time, I was devastated by the news that my parents were going to get a divorce. Not only was I terribly hurt, I was embarrassed. I had taken great pride in the fact that my parents were still together while all my friends' parents were divorced. My parents' separation was the most devastating event in my life. I remember getting sick after I was informed of my parents' plans. I was sick for weeks; all I did was sleep and vomit. In fact, I remember vomiting for about a month after my parents separated. My parents' explanation was that I kept getting the stomach flu.

or placed in special education. Compared with children from intact families, they were rated by teachers as being more aggressive and disobedient and lacking self-control. Divorced parents, in other studies, also report that their school-age children have more problem behaviors, such as temper outbursts, stealing, fighting, breaking things, and telling lies, and that they are less socially and academically competent.[36] Trained observers who watch children in classrooms, lunchrooms, and living rooms also see more of these antisocial behavior problems in children from divorced families.[37] Furthermore, these children may suffer from psychosomatic symptoms of stress—headaches, vomiting, dizziness, sleep problems, inability to concentrate.[38] Again, it is important to note that not all children have these negative reactions; these differences reflect group averages and include children whose parents have just divorced and children whose parents divorced years earlier.

Young Adolescents Are Anguished

With adolescence comes greater awareness of the parents' problems and greater understanding of the separation—but not necessarily less sorrow, sadness, or fear at the end of their parents' marriage. In Wallerstein's study, young adolescents (twelve- to fourteen-year-olds) were observed to react with the same kind of anguish as school-age children and to grieve for the loss of their family.[39] Sadness, shock, and disbelief were the most common feelings expressed at the time of the divorce in another study of young adolescents; they wanted their parents to get back together and were angry at one parent, but they were less likely to blame themselves for the separation and divorce than younger children.[40]

Early adolescence is a vulnerable time at best—a time of shaky self-esteem and autonomy issues. When their parents divorce, young adolescents often overreact with unrealistic anguish and anxiety. In their adolescent egocentrism they can see only their own needs and they feel that the world's eyes are on them. So they lash out at their parents, "How could you do this to *me*?" They are preoccupied with shame and embarrassment and more self-conscious than adolescents from intact families.[41] Rarely do they understand their parents' perspective. They express harsh moral judgments against their parents as they become aware of the adults' weaknesses and failures.[42]

To make matters worse, their parents often give these young adolescents added household and child-care responsibilities and urge them to take on odd jobs to make some extra money. Young adolescents often see themselves as having to mature faster because of divorce.[43] As a result, the entire divorce experience can lead young adolescents to have a sense of "false maturity." They identify with the custodial parent and take on the role of the departed parent: an adolescent son becomes the man around the house; an adolescent girl becomes the parent's confidant. Often, they have to listen as their parents unload their feelings of misery and frustration.[44] This early push for maturity comes with a high price tag. Being cast into a role for which they are not ready may lead young adolescents to be depressed. It is all too much for them. They cannot hide behind the confusion of the preschool child or erupt into the angry outbursts of the school-age child. They understand what is going on, but they are helpless to stop it. They are angry about their lack of control and may engage in risky behaviors, such as sex, drugs, and alcohol.[45] Looking for love and attention to cover their pain and loss, seeing their parents dating, and lacking strict parental supervision, these young adolescents can be thrust into premature sexual activity—just as they are entering puberty. The consequences of these risky behaviors may be substantial— early pregnancy, problems in school, trouble with the law. Remember, though, that we are talking about increases in the *likelihood* of these problems for children of divorce; not all young adolescents experience these difficulties.

Older Adolescents Get in Trouble

Older adolescents (fifteen- to eighteen-year-olds) may not experience their parents' divorce to be as earth shattering as it is for younger ones because their egos are more mature. They are more involved in their own activities, more independent of their parents. Nevertheless, even these older adolescents often have strong reactions when their parents divorce. They may feel abandoned, anxious, and depressed.[46] Their use of drugs and alcohol may increase. They may have problems sleeping and eating and focusing on their work or studies. They may have problems with interpersonal relationships. Older adolescents are preoccupied with issues of their own identity: this is the time when they try to figure out who they are. They need to develop a self-image as a unique person so that they can enter adulthood with self-confidence and a clear idea of their personal goals and values. When parents divorce, especially if the divorce is unexpected, adolescents' developing identity can be thrown into chaos and their self-confidence may be undermined.

Without a clear path to a mature identity, adolescents can find a variety of ways to get in trouble. One place they may get into trouble is in school. Studies show that adolescents from divorced families get lower grades, do more poorly on achievement tests, and have lower educational aspirations than adolescents in intact families.[47] In one longitudinal study in Iowa, children from divorced families were at least twice as likely as those from intact families to have academic difficulties—they got more Ds and Fs, had trouble keeping up with their classes, and had less sense of mastery in their academic subjects.[48] Perhaps even more important, adolescents from divorced families are twice as likely to drop out of school as those from intact families. In a study that has been ongoing for ten years and covers ten large survey data sets, the high school dropout risk for adolescents whose parents divorced when they were between twelve and twenty years of age was 27 percent, compared with 13 percent for children in intact families.[49] As this finding shows, the risk of dropping out of school is significantly greater for adolescents whose parents divorce, but still the majority—73 percent—are not dropouts.

Adolescents from divorced families may also get into trouble with other people. They are not as socially competent as adolescents from intact families, according to their teachers and their mothers.[50] Worse, they often have behavior problems. For one thing, they are more aggressive and antisocial.[51] Their mothers and teachers notice this and so do trained observers; the adolescents themselves also admit it.[52] They say that they have committed more delinquent acts—shoplifting, damaging school property, running away from home, getting drunk in a public place, fighting, stealing, being stopped or picked up by the police, hurting someone enough to need bandaging, telling lies about something important.[53] In the Iowa study, 17 percent of the boys and 8 percent of the girls from divorced families versus only 4 percent and 3 percent of the boys and girls from intact families admitted to having committed at least six delinquent acts in the previous year.[54] They were also more likely than adolescents from intact families to have sex—more than twice as likely if they were girls and four times as likely if they were boys. They were more likely to smoke and to use other drugs.[55] Not only do adolescents from divorced families have these "externalizing" problems, they may also have "internalizing" problems. They are more anxious, withdrawn, and depressed than adolescents in intact families.[56] They have less self-esteem.[57] They more often have a sense of despair, and they are twice as likely to feel hopeless (30 percent versus 14 percent) or to think of ending their lives (16 percent versus 8 percent) as adolescents whose parents are happily married.[58] It is a testament to the resilience of children that so many fare so well under adverse circumstances. The majority do not commit crimes, abuse substances, or think about suicide.

Young Adults Are Not Immune

Even when the "children" are young adults, no longer living at home, they are affected if their parents divorce. They are sad and concerned about the well-being of their parents, especially their mothers, for several years after the divorce; they believe that their fathers are happier than their mothers—in fact, happier than they were when the family was together—and this is upsetting.[59] They may feel the demand to "parent" their parents after the divorce, a stressful and depressing consequence of the divorce.[60] They may develop psychological symptoms and seek professional help for mental-health problems.[61] Even years later, these individuals whose parents divorced when they were young adults tend to be more depressed than others whose parents have not divorced.[62] They are more likely to break up with their live-in partner, and they are more likely to suffer economically—men are more likely to be unemployed, and both men and women are more likely to live in subsidized housing and to be on welfare.[63]

How Large Are Divorce Effects?

Clearly, then, children of all ages—from infancy to adulthood—may suffer when their parents divorce. Dozens of studies indicate that *on average,* children from divorced families are different from children whose parents stay married. But how big are these differences and how many children are affected? The differences are *statistically* significant, but are they large enough that we should be concerned about them? There are several ways of answering this question.

One way is to examine the "effect sizes" for all these studies. An effect size is the difference between the divorced group and the nondivorced group expressed in terms of their standard deviations. (The standard deviation is a measure of how spread out the scores in the group are; in a typical, normal distribution about one-third of the scores fall between the average score, or mean, and one standard deviation

Personal Story: Challenges for a College Student

My grades at college during the quarter when my parents split up were the worst I've ever gotten. I couldn't concentrate on schoolwork at all. I went to a lot of parties and drank to get drunk. When I was drunk, I did not have to worry about my parents' divorce. I had horrible insomnia and rarely got to sleep before three in the morning. When I did sleep I would have nightmares and wake up with my shoulders so tense they hurt. During finals week, I got strep throat and mononucleosis. I missed all my finals, flew home, and spent five weeks in bed. I lost twenty pounds and almost did not go back to school in winter quarter.

either above or below the mean). The effect size is useful because it puts the results from each study into equivalent units that can then be compared or combined. In Amato's meta-analysis of studies comparing children in divorced and nondivorced families, 177 effect sizes were calculated (for different measures, such as academic achievement and psychological adjustment in different studies, and different subgroups, such as boys and girls).[64] Of these effect sizes, 88 percent showed that children in divorced families were doing worse than children in intact families, and half of them were statistically significant. The average effect size across all the studies was 0.29. This means that children with divorced parents scored slightly more than one-fourth of a standard deviation lower than children with continuously married parents on assessments of their psychological well-being. For academic achievement, the average effect size was 0.26; for psychological adjustment (depression and anxiety), it was 0.31; and for conduct problems such as aggression, it was 0.33. Amato also fine-tuned these estimates by evaluating how good the methods used in different studies were. In more methodologically sophisticated studies—those with larger samples, randomly selected from sources like court records, including more and better measures of each area of functioning—effect sizes were smaller. When these factors were taken into account, the average effect size was reduced to 0.18, or about one-fifth of a standard deviation. Similar results were found in Amato's analysis of long-term effects of parent divorce in adulthood.[65] The average effect size was 0.21 (about one-fifth of a standard deviation), with the strongest effects being found for psychological adjustment (0.32), conduct (0.28), and educational attainment (0.28). These differences, which range from one-fifth to one-third of a standard deviation, are undoubtedly quite small in absolute terms. They are statistically significant—in fact, one would need more than one thousand additional studies in which there was no difference to make their results nonsignificant—but they are small.[66] In fact, in view of the initial reactions of sadness, despair, and anxiety that so many children express, it is perhaps surprising that so many children and adolescents do so well.

A second way to answer the question of how large the effects of divorce are is to examine the likelihood that children from divorced families have problems compared with children from intact families. The effect size is a measure of the average difference across all the children in the study. But, as we have suggested, divorce affects different people in different ways. So perhaps the effect size is not the most useful way to describe divorce effects. An alternative is to calculate "odds ratios," that is, the odds or likelihood that children from divorced families will have problems. A variety of studies in which odds ratios are available show that children from divorced families are twice to three times as likely as children from intact families to have problems.[67] In studies of nationally representative samples, children from divorced families are twice as likely to receive psychological help, to skip school or get suspended, to get in trouble with the police, to drop out of high school, to get pregnant as a teenager, to be out of work in their later teens and early twenties, to see their own marriages end in divorce, and to experience clinically significant psychological distress and depression in childhood and adulthood.[68] Other national studies indicate even higher odds: in The Netherlands, children were three times as likely to have clinical levels of externalizing problems.[69] In Sweden, children of single-parent families were more than twice as likely to suffer depression, to kill themselves, to drink to excess, or to get hooked on illegal drugs.[70] In the United States, they were three times as likely to be smokers.[71]

A third way of expressing the size of divorce effects is to calculate the proportion of children whose functioning is impaired. In Wallerstein's study, one-third of the children in the sample were doing poorly in terms of their overall functioning when they were assessed five, ten, or twenty-five years after the divorce.[72] These were not children from typical American families, however. Their parents were volunteers who sought psychological counseling in return for participating in the study. Wallerstein's estimates, therefore, may not apply to the general population. In another study, researchers found that one-third of the children whose parents had requested counseling for divorce issues were in the clinical range for behavior problems—the same as Wallerstein's estimate—compared with fewer than one-tenth of the children whose parents had not requested counseling.[73] Amato and Keith similarly found in their meta-analysis that effect sizes were larger in clinical studies than in community studies.[74] The proportion of children in more representative studies who have clinical or persistent problems into adolescence or adulthood turns out to range from one-fifth to one-third. These problems include behavior problems (one-third), adjustment problems (one-quarter), physical symptoms (one-quarter), poor social relationships (one-quarter), dropping out of high school (one-quarter to one-third), and having a baby before the age of twenty (just less than one-third).[75] In the Virginia Longitudinal Study of Divorce and Remarriage, Hetherington found that between one-fifth and one-quarter of the children whose parents divorced when they were preschoolers were struggling with emotional, social, academic, or behavior problems six years later; in adolescence, one-fifth of them were sullen, oppositional, angry, or tense; had drug, alcohol, or delinquency problems; or had gotten pregnant or attempted suicide. As young adults, one-fifth were troubled, impulsive, irresponsible, or depressed.[76] Thus, Wallerstein's estimates are at the high end of the continuum, but not wildly different. Perhaps an estimate of one-fifth to one-third seems like a high number. However, it must be compared with the number of children from continuously intact families who have similar levels of problematic functioning. Studies indicate that in these families about one-tenth to one-seventh of the children have such problems.[77]

A final way to estimate the size of the divorce effect is to compute the percentage of cases in the distributions for divorced and nondivorced groups that overlap. Data from the Marital Instability Over the Life Course study were used in such an analysis.[78] Measures of self-esteem, life satisfaction, psychiatric symptoms, and happiness in adulthood were combined to form a single index of psychological well-being. The overlap between adults whose parents had divorced and adults whose parents stayed together was 90 percent on this index. In other words, only 10 percent of the children from divorced families grew up to have more psychological problems than the children from intact families. The most substantial difference between the two groups appeared in the children's relationships with their fathers—for which the overlap was only 65 percent. Given that many of these children had had little or no contact with their dads after the divorce, it is not surprising that as adults 35 percent of them had more distant relationships with their fathers than the children from intact families.

What do these numbers mean in terms of how concerned we should be about the effects of divorce on children? A statement cosigned by most of the participants at a 1994 conference sponsored by the U.S. National Institute of Child Health and Human Development to evaluate knowledge about how children are affected by divorce cautioned that although divorce is a painful experience that increases children's psychological vulnerability, the long-term effects of divorce should not be exaggerated. The statement pointed out, as these numbers all indicate, that the *majority* of children appear to be developing within the normal range—without identifiable psychosocial scars or other adverse consequences—even when the process of marital dissolution was painful for them.[79] At least two-thirds of the children who experience their parents' divorce are able to adapt well to the situation.

Nevertheless, the effect of divorce, as demonstrated by these different size estimates, is not trivial. Divorce has a stronger effect on problem behavior and psychological distress than race, birth order, moving, having a new sibling, experiencing the illness or death of a significant family member, being ill, or having parents with little education.[80] It has a stronger effect on teen pregnancy than exposure to family violence in early childhood, low family income, and a low level of education.[81] The association is larger than the link between smoking and cancer.[82] This is not a problem we should blow out of proportion, but it is not a problem we should ignore. Instead, we should try to understand how we can reduce its negative impacts and predict which children will be adversely affected and in what ways. We will then be better able to help these children adjust to this life transition.

Do Problems Disappear with Time?

We have established that the effects of divorce are statistically significant but small and that divorce affects some children, but not all. Another question is how long these effects last. Are the effects permanent or transitory? Do the observed differences in distress and depression, aggression and academic failure reflect a temporary crisis to which children gradually adapt, or do they persist more or less indefinitely? Do differences diminish over the years immediately after the divorce, or does it take more time for children to get back to normal? If we just wait long enough, will all children recover from their parents' divorce? Generally, the results of research on these questions show that the story for children is the same as for their parents: some individuals experience brief decrements in well-being while others never recover fully; some differences diminish over the first couple of years after the divorce; others persist for a long time.[83] There is no single, simple answer to the question of how long divorce effects last.

Diminishing Differences; Continuing Concerns

In some ways, children get over divorce faster than their parents. Some improvement in children's behavior and distress is found even by the end of the first year or year and a half after the divorce. Behavior that is a reaction to the acute stress of the separation has usually diminished or disappeared. Children's fear, grief, shock, confusion, disbelief, and desire for parental reunion fade quickly.[84] These feelings of shock and upset have a relatively limited life span. Children's behavior problems, especially aggressive behavior, also drop sharply after the first year or so.[85] In a national study of school-aged children in The Netherlands, aggression was more than twice as frequent in the first year as it was in later years.[86] Amato's meta-analysis also showed that the effect of divorce on aggressive behavior problems was stronger in the first two years than later.[87]

One feeling that may not diminish over time, however, is anger. Ten years after the divorce, shock and sadness were at a low level in one study of adolescents, but anger at the parent who had left them continued into adulthood.[88] Another outcome that may not disappear over the years following divorce is impaired cognitive and social competence.[89] Effects on boys' academic achievement (grades and tests) did not diminish over the five years after divorce in one study, and deficits in test scores in math, science, reading, and social studies were actually worse three years after divorce than earlier in a study of nearly ten thousand high school students.[90] High-school dropout rates are equivalent for children whose parents divorced during the preceding five years compared with children whose parents divorced six or more years earlier.[91] Psychological problems such as anxiety and depression also may persist.[92] In Wallerstein's study, five and ten years after divorce, about one-third of the children who were preschoolers or school age when their parents divorced were still depressed and spoke wistfully of life in an intact family.[93] If they had problems in the early years after the divorce, they were likely to have problems ten years later, and if a change occurred it was downward.[94] In the study with the National Association of School Psychologists, students from divorced families were still doing worse on average than students from intact families when their mental health was evaluated six years after the divorce.[95]

Long-Term Consequences

Far from disappearing, then, some problems of divorce persist into adolescence and later life for some individuals. In her longitudinal study, Wallerstein found that when children whose parents had divorced reached adolescence, they expressed a new sense of powerlessness and a yearning for their father and they were afraid of disappointment in love relationships.[96] These emotional longings are sometimes expressed in early sexual activity and pregnancy.[97] In the Virginia Longitudinal Study of Divorce and Remarriage, girls whose parents divorced when they were young children reached puberty earlier, initiated sex earlier, had more sexual partners and pregnancies, and left home at younger ages.[98] At age fifteen, 65 percent of the early maturing girls in divorced families had had sex, compared with only 40 percent of early maturing girls in intact families. In nationally representative surveys, the risk of childbearing before age twenty is about 30 percent for adolescents from divorced families versus only 15 percent for adolescents in two-parent families.[99] Psychological problems have also been observed. In one fifteen-year longitudinal study in New Zealand, with a sample of approximately one thousand, adolescents whose parents had divorced when they were children were more likely to have a range of psychological problems, including conduct disorders and mood and anxiety disorders.[100] One-quarter of the adolescents whose parents divorced six years earlier had clinically significant mental disorders in another longitudinal study in the United States.[101] Adolescents from divorced families are also more likely to use drugs and alcohol and to have friends who do so.[102] They are more likely to commit delinquent acts and to be arrested and convicted of juvenile crimes. Even if they are not delinquents, adolescents whose parents divorced when they were younger are twice as likely to drop out of school as adolescents from intact families.[103]

The problems that are evident in adolescence may persist and even increase in adulthood.[104] A meta-analysis carried out by Paul Amato to integrate studies dealing with the long-term consequences of divorce when children from divorced families reach adulthood revealed that across thirty-seven studies and eighty-one thousand individuals, adults who had experienced their parents' divorce had lower levels of psychological well-being than adults whose parents were continuously married.[105] They have more symptoms such as depression, anxiety, paranoia, and narcissism than the adult children of nondivorced parents.[106] They are more likely to be troubled, impulsive, and irresponsible; more likely to be aggressive and commit crimes; more likely to abuse substances.[107] In the National Survey of Children, 40 percent of the young adults from disrupted families had received psychological help.[108]

Growing up in a divorced family can also hurt young people's hopes for educational and occupational success. For one thing, financial support for college is often lacking. The majority of divorced fa-

Personal Story: Still Struggling as a Young Woman

In my early adolescence, the lack of a consistent, everyday father figure in my life became a source of many problems. Because I felt deprived of a quality relationship with a man, I tried to satisfy this need by starting to date very young. I was desperate to please every boyfriend, and this often led to promiscuous behavior. I was anxious and seductive in my interactions with males. It seemed like no matter how hard I tried I could not make these relationships work. Just as with my dad—no matter how good I was, my father remained emotionally unavailable. I still feel a lot of anger that I did not deal with as a small child. As a young woman, now, I am continuously struggling with these issues trying to get my life together.

thers do not provide support for higher education.[109] Consequently, *on average,* adult children of divorce have lower levels of education, lower occupational status, and less likelihood of getting and keeping a steady job; they have lower incomes, fewer financial assets, and higher levels of economic hardship.[110]

Adults from divorced families may also have relationship problems. Growing up in a divorced family, they are not surprisingly less likely to trust people and more ambivalent about getting involved in romantic relationships.[111] When they have a romantic relationship, it is likely to be more insecure, conflicted, and unhappy than the relationships of adults from intact families.[112] In one study of seventeen- to twenty-six-year-olds whose parents were divorced, three-quarters reported insecure close relationships.[113] These problems in relationships, of course, can lead to problems getting married. In her longitudinal study, Wallerstein found that twenty-five years after their parents' divorce only 60 percent of the children, then ranging from their late twenties to their early forties, had married, compared with 84 percent in the general population.[114] The individuals who had not married, Wallerstein concluded, had no idea what a loving relationship should look like. They found that trying to live in day-to-day harmony with another person was like "becoming a dancer without ever having seen a dance." They held out for the perfect mate, and once they were convinced they had found him or her, they leaped into marriage and then were let down as their high romantic expectations gave way to bitter disillusionment. According to Wallerstein, the impact of the parents' divorce increases over time and rises to a crescendo in adulthood, hitting most cruelly as young adults go in search of love, sexual intimacy, and commitment. Their lack of a model of a man and a woman in a stable relationship and their memories of their parents' failure to sustain their marriage cripple their search, leading them to heartbreak and despair. They have a hard time even describing the kind of person they are looking for; many end up with unsuitable or troubled partners in relationships that are doomed from the start. Anxiety about relationships is a constant, damaging theme in the lives of these young adults. It is not surprising, then, that, as we saw in Chapter 2, adults whose parents divorced are more likely to get divorced themselves.[115] Parental divorce doubles the odds of offspring divorce.[116] Adults whose parents divorced when they were young have a weaker commitment to the norm of lifelong marriage than adults whose parents stayed together.[117] They are less satisfied with their marriages and less likely to have traditional marriages.[118]

Poor physical health has also been observed in adult children of divorce, especially those who felt most negative about the divorce.[119] Using an archival prospective design, researchers in the Terman Life Cycle Study studied associations between parent divorce in childhood and how long people lived.[120] On average, children from divorced families died four years earlier than those from intact families. Why? Several reasons have been suggested: men from divorced families obtained less education, engaged in fewer service activities, and were more likely to get divorced themselves; women smoked more and were more likely to get divorced.

In brief, a number of negative consequences of parental divorce linger into adulthood for some individuals—poor health, poor income, poor relationships, and poor psychological functioning. However, to reiterate: these negative consequences do not affect all individuals whose parents divorce. Most children of divorce adjust successfully to

Personal Story:
Two Positive Consequences of Divorce

There were two positive consequences of my parents' divorce for me: I discovered my own strength by living through this most difficult experience and surviving the loss of my father, and I developed a close bond with my mother from sharing the experience. She and I have become best friends.

the situation and go on to live healthy, productive lives. Moreover, some of them even experience positive consequences as the result of the divorce. In the Virginia study, Hetherington found that one group of girls became exceptionally competent as a result of dealing with the challenges of divorce and grew into truly outstanding young adults.[121] As we indicated before for their parents, although negative consequences for children of divorce are observed *on average*, they do not affect every individual, and, in fact, for some, the divorce gives a boost to personal growth and success. Figure 5-1 shows graphically the variety of effects that divorce may have on children.

Figure 5-1. Effects of divorce on children, arrayed from initial reactions in childhood at the bottom to long-term consequences in adulthood at the top.

Summary

Children react to their parents' divorce with strong emotions—grief, anger, anxiety, fear. They experience significant problems in their mental health, physical well-being, and academic achievement. Specific reactions and problems vary with the age of the child. For infants, the major risk is that their attachment to their parents will be disrupted. For preschoolers, confusion and regression to more immature kinds of behavior, temper tantrums, withdrawal, and fear are the likely outcomes. School-age children feel sadness and a sense of loss; they are anxious and angry; their school performance deteriorates; their conduct is poorer; and they have fewer friends. Adolescents, forced to grow up faster and assume more responsibility in the household, are likely to experience depression and experiment with risky behaviors in the form of sex and substance abuse; they are more likely to have problems with school and the law. Even children who are young adults when their parents divorce are not immune: they often experience sadness, depression, anxiety, difficulties in intimate relationships, and employment problems.

Many of these problems dissipate over time. Behavior problems drop to normal levels by two years after divorce. Other problems such as anger and academic deficiencies are more likely to persist. Even in adulthood, individuals who experienced their parents' divorce have more physical and mental-health problems and less educational and occupational success than adults who grew up in intact families; they even die at younger ages.

It is important to keep these divorce effects in perspective. Although the differences between children from divorced and intact families are consistent and statistically significant, they are not large. Children of divorce are two or three times more likely to have problems than children from intact families, but this still means that only one-fifth to one-third of them have persistent problems. In adulthood, the number may be as low as one-tenth. The consequences of divorce, in short, do not affect all children in the same way or to the same degree, but for a significant minority there may be long-lasting effects that persist through adulthood.

6

What Causes Children's Problems?

We have seen how some children suffer—in the short run and long term—when their parents divorce. But what causes their suffering? Is it because one parent disappears? Their income disappears? Or their custodial parent is too busy to take care of them? Is it all of the above? Participants at the conference sponsored by the U.S. National Institute of Child Health and Human Development agreed that "overall, most children of divorce experience dramatic declines in their economic circumstances; abandonment or fear of abandonment by one or both of their parents; the diminished capacity of both parents to attend meaningfully and constructively to their children's needs because they are preoccupied with their own distress; and diminished contact with many familiar sources of psychosocial support as well as familiar living settings. As a consequence, the experience of divorce is a psychosocial stressor as well as a significant life transition for most children, with long-term repercussions for many."[1] It seems, then, that there are multiple reasons for children's problems. Here we examine these various reasons—economic decline, parental abandonment, diminished parenting, and diminished contact with familiar support—to try to understand how they cause the problems described in Chapter 5.

Personal Story: No Warning

I remember the exact words my father uttered as tears welled up in his eyes: "Your mother and I have decided to get a divorce." Nothing more was said. No explanation was given. No questions were asked. My brother and I quietly retreated to our separate bedrooms. That night, after almost twenty years of marriage, my father gathered together his clothes and moved out of our house. My brother and I were in shock.

The Shock of Divorce

Perhaps the first cause of children's emotional reactions to divorce is that they are ill prepared for the news that their parents are separating. Many children get no warning that their family is falling apart. Parents rarely discuss with their children the problems in their marriage or the possibility of separating before the event occurs. Perhaps they believe they are "protecting" the children; perhaps they are just too involved in their own difficulties to think about how the separation will affect their youngsters. Whatever their reasoning—or lack of it—parents typically spring the news on their children as they head out the door. In Wallerstein's study, all the parents had trouble telling their children, and one-third of the children didn't know about the divorce beforehand; in another study, half of the children were told within a week of the separation (one-fifth, on the day of the separation).[2] Other research shows that as many as one-fifth of the children were not even told about the marital breakup.[3] Even many parents who were in a divorce adjustment program in which they were encouraged to talk to their children about what was happening found this too difficult and painful. They did not know what to say, and they typically believed that the children were too young to be told—even when their children were adolescents.[4] Children, unprepared for their parents' announcement, are stunned and shocked. They fear for their own futures. They

Personal Story: No Explanation

I remember walking alongside a white wooden fence on the way home from the grocery store with my mom when I was seven years old. I asked her why she and Dad were getting a divorce. She quickly replied, "It's none of your business, I'll tell you when you are older."

are not able to take their parents' perspective and admit that the separation might be a good idea.[5]

Besides breaking the news of their impending separation suddenly, parents often give children inadequate explanations when they do talk to them.[6] They do not explain how the marriage has fallen apart, how they are going to survive, or what will happen next. They are especially unlikely to give explanations to younger children.[7] This leaves the children unnecessarily unsure and afraid, just when they most need reassurance and information. They don't understand the divorce or why it is happening; they feel unsafe and confused.[8]

In general, children believe that divorce is bad and that it results in enduring emotional and behavioral problems for children.[9] They have negative stereotypes of children from divorced families: these children are "less fun to play with," "less smart," "less good," "less likely to be a friend."[10] Some children also believe that it is the child's fault that the parents divorced. In one study, one-third of the third- and fifth-graders who were read vignettes about divorced families thought that the children had caused the divorce—because the parents didn't want children, or the child did things wrong or wouldn't mind the parents so the parents got mad and took it out on each other, or the parents couldn't stand the child so they got a divorce.[11] According to parents in another study, one-fifth of the children blamed themselves for the divorce.[12] Not surprisingly, then, when children are told that their own parents are getting a divorce, they oppose it strongly.[13] The lack of preparation and negative expectation make the transition to the postdivorce family difficult. Children have more problems if they are confused about the separation, if their parents have kept them in the dark about the deteriorating state of their marriage, if they see no obvious reasons for the divorce, or if they fear abandonment.[14] Not knowing why events occur is related to higher psychological symptoms in children in general.[15]

Loss of Lifestyle

With the divorce, many children lose the lifestyle they have enjoyed. Their access to resources diminishes. When researchers examine incomes in families that get divorced compared with those that stay together, they find that intact families' incomes rise over time (on average, in the 1990s, from fifty-nine thousand to sixty-five thousand dollars), while divorced families' incomes decline (from fifty-six thousand to thirty-three thousand dollars).[16] Thus, divorced parents no longer have the same budget for their children's housing, wardrobe, vacations, and entertainment. Children almost inevitably lose material things—from cars to computers. This drop in their standard of living, moreover, means further pressures for children, such as moving to a less expensive home, changing schools, losing contact with friends in the neighborhood, having more limited college choices, and living with a parent who is preoccupied with financial problems.[17] When children were asked about the difficulties they experienced when their parents got divorced, nearly half of them mentioned moving: "I didn't want my parents to sell the house because it held so many memories. In my mind, I was born there, and I'll die there. For me, it's like a sacred house."[18] For some children, losing their home causes severe grief resembling the loss of a loved one.[19] The children also mentioned the drop in their family's income: "I have less things. Before, we had more money."[20] It is particularly difficult for children to deal with the loss of family income if they see their father living an affluent lifestyle while they live on food stamps with their mother.[21]

Along with having less income and moving to a new house, children whose parents divorce usually move to a poorer neighborhood where they have less access to community resources.[22] The longer parents reside in a community, the more likely they are to know about and take advantage of opportunities in the community for their children. With a move, they lose contact with familiar community facilities, programs, and people.[23] They are less likely to know which are the best schools, the best teachers, the best after-school programs. Moreover, because they are depressed from the divorce, they are less likely to develop ties to the new community. After divorce, children who live with their mothers also lose access to the community resources that were provided by their fathers, such as membership at a country club or connections that are important in landing a first job.

To what extent does the drop in their standard of living cause problems for children? In a number of nationally representative surveys, the income drop due to divorce, regardless of the family's initial income, accounted for as much as half of the higher risk of children dropping out of high school, becoming a teen mother, not having a job, or exhibiting behavior problems.[24]

Lack of Money

After divorce, some children not only experience a decline in their standard of living but are, in fact, downright poor; 27 percent of children living with their mothers and 12 percent of children living with their fathers are in poverty, compared with 5 percent of children living with both parents.[25] Lack of money limits children's quality of education because they can't afford to live in neighborhoods with better public schools or to go to private schools. They are likely to attend lower quality schools, schools with higher dropout rates and more student behavior problems.[26] Lack of income also is related to parents' poorer psychological adjustment, and it impairs parents' ability to control the children.[27]

The lack of economic resources, as one would expect, is one cause of children's problems after divorce. It is a reason that divorce leads to behavior problems; depressed mood; lower test scores in math, science, reading, and social studies; less self-esteem; and worse school performance.[28] The last is especially a problem for children living with their mothers because single moms have less money saved for college and fewer computers and books than single dads.[29] In the study by the National Association of School Psychologists, controlling for family income reduced the differences between children from divorced and intact families on classroom behavior ratings and mental-health measures, and it eliminated differences in academic achievement.[30] Across ten other studies, controlling for income reduced differences in school dropout rates from 6 to 3 percent.[31] Clearly, economic depression is another cause of divorce-related differences in children's well-being—but it is not the only one.[32]

Absence of One Parent—Usually Dad

Lack of contact with the noncustodial parent, usually the father, is another cause of children's problems. Fathers have little contact with their children after divorce, and this contact decreases over time.[33] The pattern of modest initial contact and a sharp drop-off over time is strikingly similar across studies.[34] According to the National Survey of Families and Household, nearly one-third of divorced fathers do not see their children, and only one-quarter see them as often as once a week.[35] Even though fathers report that they see their children more often than their ex-wives say they do, contact is still not frequent. In one study, three years after divorce, mothers said that fathers visited three times per month, whereas fathers claimed to visit three and a half times; mothers said that fathers spent just over four days with the child in a month, and fathers said it was almost six days.[36] Fathers disappear from their children's lives because they move, remarry or get involved in a new romantic relationship, lack financial resources, have strained relations with their former spouse, or experience psychological pain caused by their diminished parental identity and status.[37]

Mothers are not as likely as fathers to disappear after the divorce. Not only are they more likely to retain custody, but even when they do not have custody, they are more likely to have continuing contact with their children, by telephone and letter and through longer visits.[38] In one nationally representative sample of eleven- to sixteen-year-olds, 86 percent had seen their noncustodial mothers in the past year, compared with only 48 percent who had seen their noncustodial fathers.[39] Because of the rareness of their visits, fathers are less likely to spend "their" precious time with the child in routine parenting—mundane activities like shopping for shoes or onerous tasks like supervising homework. Only about one-third are involved in the children's school activities.[40] Only half have their children for overnight visits.[41] Instead, dads fill their time with entertainment—going to Disneyland, McDonald's, the movies.[42] This can leave children feeling empty and

Personal Story: Still Can't Call Him "Dad"

It has always been extremely painful knowing that I have a father who is alive and perfectly capable of acting like a parent, but who does not care about me. As a child, I was often depressed and acted out. As I grew older I had very low self-esteem. In junior high school, although I was successful academically, I felt like I belonged with the "loser crowd." Throughout my high school years, curiosity about what my father might be like was eating away at me. I also felt guilty for all that my mom had to go through for me. I compensated for that guilt by trying hard to make her proud of me, and I deprived myself of much of the fun of childhood and adolescence by devoting all my time to trying to become the best for her. Even when I was the best in something, it was not enough for me. I still felt inadequate. I never told my mom how I felt about my father for fear of hurting her. I got really good at holding my feelings inside: so good, in fact, that it became difficult to express myself even when I wanted to. After I graduated from high school, I decided that I finally needed to fill the emptiness in my life by finding out at least a little about my father. I was seventeen when I found his number and called to see if he would be willing to talk. After a long hesitation, he agreed. We met and spent the day together. He has called me regularly ever since. Today I am able to better understand what I was feeling all those years. Now I am able to say without guilt that the absence of my father caused me much pain. I no longer feel abandoned, but many of the scars still remain. I still have not been able to bring myself to call him "Dad."

emotionally disconnected from their fathers. Children agree that "the worst result of divorce" is that they miss their father.[43] As they get older, they perceive their father as less caring than adolescents and adults from intact families do.[44] As adolescents, one-third didn't feel close to their father or satisfied with the affection they received from him; they didn't feel that they were sharing ideas with him or doing things with him that they really enjoyed; when they were young adults, two-thirds of them felt this way.[45] Young adults in another study were not only less emotionally attached to their father, they were less willing to care for him if he experienced a major disability.[46]

It seems logical that divorce impairs father-child relationships. But is loss or lack of the father responsible for the other problems children of divorce experience? Children who lose their father through death have problems with psychological adjustment and self-esteem similar to those of children whose parents divorce, but they do not have problems with achievement and conduct and they do not have symptoms in adulthood.[47] Thus, father absence seems to be linked, in particular, to children's early psychological problems. This suggestion is supported by the finding that boys who have a closer relationship with their father before the separation are more trouble after the divorce when they lose their father.[48] In addition, boys whose fathers are less involved after divorce have more externalizing problems, and this appears to be a major reason for the difference between boys from divorced and intact families.[49]

Poor Parenting

Another reason for negative effects of divorce on children is the quality of parenting they receive after the divorce. Because divorcing parents are themselves often emotional wrecks, many children go "unparented" in the first year after the separation. During this period, it is natural that divorcing parents are distracted, involved with their own problems, suffering their own pain. Divorced mothers may be struggling to make ends meet, looking for work, or working two jobs or long hours.[50] Feeling overwhelmed with these burdens, these women may neglect or even abuse their children. At the same time as their children are seeking more attention and reassurance, these preoccupied parents have less to give them. They are often oblivious to their children's distress, unaware of how upset, angry, and unhappy they are.[51] Daily living may become more chaotic as household rules, routines, and discipline are thrown into disarray in many divorced families.[52] There are fewer bedtime stories, family meals, and play times. Children eat out more often and in more fast-food restaurants.[53] They are more often late for school or absent.[54] They get less help with home-

Personal Story: No More Family Time

Six months after the divorce my mom was still devastated. Dinner used to be family time with the four of us sitting around the dinner table—my mom, my dad, my brother, and me. Now my mom would look at my father's empty seat and cry. My brother and I did not understand, and we would say something insensitive like, "Are you going to cry again?" or "Where is Daddy?" We were the most important thing in Mom's life, but she was always so sad and tired.

work.[55] Their mothers are more irritable, unresponsive, erratic, and punitive; they have more trouble controlling their children, especially their sons.[56] They are less affectionate, make fewer demands for maturity, supervise less, and are less consistent in dispensing discipline.[57]

A couple of years after the divorce, parenting has improved but parents remain less authoritative, and problems controlling sons may remain high.[58] Moms tend to be too coercive, and (noncustodial) dads too permissive, uninvolved, and indulgent.[59] In one study, about one-quarter of divorced mothers were dysfunctional parents—twice as many as married mothers.[60] Even when the divorced household has restabilized, divorced mothers still confront more negative life events and their task overload continues. They report more child-rearing stress, are more hassled, and experience more negative life events than mothers in intact families.[61] Single mothers have to perform a time-juggling act every day. They must continually make decisions about how they allocate their time, and because unexpected events interfere with their carefully made plans, they seldom feel in control of their schedules.[62]

Divorced mothers are less likely to eat with their children than married mothers; they are more likely to leave their children unattended.[63] They are less responsive and less likely to reward their children with praise and privileges and help them with difficult tasks.[64] They are more negative.[65] They tend to provide less cognitive and so-

Personal Story: No Supervision

I had no supervision after the divorce. My mom was always off at work or out with friends. I took advantage of the situation and threw parties every weekend and had people over all the time. Everyone liked my house because my mom had no control. When my mom tried to regain some control, I got mad and went to live with my dad. He was never around either. He was either out or watching TV or working on the computer. So I had parties all the time at his house, too. He would be downstairs, and about twenty kids would be in the house, and he never even knew.

cial stimulation than parents in intact families; the children have fewer toys, books, and games, even when the family income is taken into consideration.[66] Divorced mothers are also less involved in children's school-related events.[67]

Adolescents in divorced families receive less supervision from their parents than adolescents in intact families.[68] One-quarter to one-third of adolescents in divorced families compared with one-tenth of adolescents in nondivorced families become disengaged from their families, spending as little time at home as possible and avoiding interactions, activities, and communication with family members.[69]

Because parents are distressed and distracted, children in divorced families have to assume more responsibility for their own care.[70] They may feel like no one is in charge and they have to bring themselves up.[71] Divorced mothers often expect children to assume caregiving roles for themselves and their younger siblings.[72] They give their children more power in family decision making and accelerate their independence. Adolescents from divorced families are more likely to make decisions without direct parental input.[73]

Some children in divorced families are forced to grow up too fast. They feel responsible not only for themselves but for the functioning of the parent. In a process of "parentification," children reverse roles

Personal Story: Taking Care of Everything

My brother, Billy, who was four, would cling to me and ask me where Daddy was and if Mommy was going away too. I held him and hugged him and told him everything was going to be okay. Mom couldn't be bothered with Billy or any of us, so we just kind of took care of ourselves. We had no money, no real home, no father to turn to when Mom got upset. She had to go to work to feed us and pay the rent. At one point we were so poor we had to go on food stamps. Because I was the oldest, she piled everything on me. I was only eleven, but I had to do all the cooking and clean the house every day. Mom was hardly ever there to take care of anything. She was working, going to court, going out with her friends, or complaining about Dad. She barely acknowledged all the work I was doing for her. Besides the housework, I also had to babysit for Billy and my younger sister Valerie after school. Before the divorce, I had been getting straight A's in school. But now, if either of my siblings was sick, I had to stay home and take care of them so Mom could work. And with all the other things I had to do, I didn't have time to do my homework. So who cared when my grades went from A's to D's and F's. Little Billy really needed a mother more than the rest of us, and I was all he was going to get. He even called me Mom sometimes. Anyway, making sure he was okay was more important to me than getting good grades. What really upset me, though, was when Mom yelled at me if the house was messy. And if anyone did anything wrong, of course it was my fault. I slowly began to realize that my mom couldn't even take care of herself. She needed me to take care of her too.

with the parent and take on responsibility for the emotional needs of the family. They are treated inappropriately—like grown-ups—when they are only children, becoming their parents' advisors and confidants.[74] They do more emotional and instrumental caregiving than their peers in nondivorced families.[75]

Thus research shows that in numerous ways children in divorced families experience poorer quality parenting than children in intact families. Research also demonstrates that this poor parenting creates problems for the children. First, poor parenting in divorced families is related to higher levels of problem behavior in children. For example, when they are loaded down with responsibilities, children have less self-worth and are more depressed.[76] If they think they are unfairly burdened with responsibilities that interfere with their other activities, adolescents may respond with resentment, rebellion, and noncompliance.[77] Second, when researchers statistically control for poor parenting in analyses of differences between children in divorced families and intact families, they find that the differences are smaller; this means that poor parenting is causing some of the difference.[78] Third, researchers find that poor parenting mediates (explains or accounts for) the problems in children from divorced families. In a study of preschool children, mothers' lack of support and use of negative control at dinnertime and during play explained children's behavior problems.[79] In a study of school-age children, lack of parental involvement (in school activities and with the child's friends) explained divorce effects on children's school performance.[80] And for adolescents, loss of parental time and supervision explained the gap in adolescents' detachment from the labor force and half of the higher school dropout rate observed among children in single-parent homes.[81] In the Iowa study, researchers examined the extent to which adolescent adjustment problems in divorced families could be explained by loss of family income, continued conflict between the parents, mothers' psychological problems after the divorce, fathers' continued involvement with the child, and mothers' parenting practices. They found that the quality of the mother's parenting offered the most consistent explanation.[82] It explained children's depression, conflict with siblings, involvement in delinquent behavior, affiliation with deviant peers, early sexual activity, and indirectly, through its effect on delinquency, children's school problems.[83] In fact, this study showed that the way by which family economic pressure increased adolescent problems was largely by creating stresses that reduced the quality of parenting. In brief, it is well documented that a major cause of problems for children from divorced families is that they receive less-adequate parenting.

Personal Story: The Battle Continues

Twenty years and seven months have passed since my parent's divorce, but to this day the battle between my parents continues. They never stopped fighting, not even during my father's three remarriages. He took the divorce as a personal war against him. He told my mother, "I am going to punish you for this for the rest of your life. I am going to make your life a living hell." And he has. The first step he took was to file for custody of us kids—just to upset my mother and make her life difficult. He didn't win and this made him even angrier. Then, on many occasions he would bring the police when he came to pick us up, claiming that my mother was causing problems. Or, he would not pick us up when he should have. I remember many days when we got dressed and packed so we would be ready when Daddy came (if we were not ready, he would raise hell). Then we sat there, waiting and waiting and eventually we would take off our little coats and—all a bit numb—unpack our bags. When Daddy did pick us up, he would spend the time tearing our mother apart. He also liked to play my sister and me against each other by taking one of us somewhere and saying that the other could not go. This was his way of punishing our mother through us, because she was the one who had to pick up the pieces when one of us came home crying.

Parents' Continued Fighting

Conflict between the parents seldom ends when they separate.[84] In fact, conflicts typically become more heated and uncompromising than they were during the marriage.[85] After the divorce, though, the battles become more focused on the children, as parents fight about child support, visitation, how the child is being disciplined, and how well the child is adjusting to divorce.[86] These fights often occur when fathers pick up or drop off the children.[87]

These conflicts clearly cause problems for children. For one thing, when parents are at war, children feel caught between them.[88] They align themselves with one parent and distance themselves from the other. Conflicts in which children are caught in the middle while parents denigrate each other or fight about the children are destructive to children's well-being.[89] Not only are children more distressed at the time, but also they may learn to exploit and mislead their parents and escape their watchful eye when they are older.[90] Even when children are not directly involved in their parents' conflicts, they may experience adverse effects through increased parental irritability and diminished monitoring.[91] Parental conflict explains many of the adjustment problems children have after divorce—especially externalizing problems.[92] When parental conflict was controlled statistically in one study, the relation between divorce and externalizing behavior in young men and women who had experienced divorce in their childhood or adolescence was no longer significant.[93]

Do Differences Precede the Divorce?

Children Have Problems before the Divorce

A study conducted in the 1980s alerted researchers to the possibility that the problems children exhibit after divorce might not be the result of divorce after all, but might have been there before the marriage broke up.[94] In this longitudinal study, boys from families in which parents subsequently divorced were more emotional and stubborn and less considerate of other children at age three, and they were more impulsive and aggressive at age seven, compared with children in families that did not divorce. This study was based on a very small sample of families. Since then, the results of the study have been replicated many times, confirming the finding that children and adolescents from to-be-divorced families have more emotional and behavior problems—including conduct disorders, antisocial behavior, difficulty with peers, depression, and academic and achievement problems—even *before* the divorce.[95] Divorced parents report that they had more problems with their children as long as twelve years prior to the divorce.[96] These differences predating divorce are not always observed, particularly when the comparison group that does not divorce consists of high-conflict families.[97] Nevertheless, there is substantial evidence that psychological problems for children in divorced families predate marital breakup and that the effects of divorce are, to some extent, predicted by these predisruption problems.

Are the problems we have described as "divorce effects" really the result of children living in an unhappy family, rather than a divorced family, then? When researchers in one nationally representative study of secondary school students controlled for predivorce differences in delinquent behavior (being unruly, damaging property, stealing, fighting, using weapons), differences in postdivorce delinquent behavior disappeared.[98] More commonly, however, researchers have found that controlling for predivorce differences reduces but does not eliminate divorce effects—because behavior problems and academic difficulties actually increase after the divorce.[99] So apparently *some* problems are the direct result of the divorce.

It has also been suggested that children's divorce-related problems might be genetic in origin. In one longitudinal study of a national sample, adolescent girls' delinquent behavior predicted both their own subsequent divorces and their children's behavior problems fourteen years later.[100] So maybe behavior problems are in the genes. However, it appears from this and a number of other studies that although genes may contribute, they are not the whole story. In that particular study, mothers' delinquent behavior explained much, but not all, of the relation between divorce and children's externalizing problems. In other studies, researchers have compared divorce problems for biological and adopted children or fraternal and identical twins and found that divorce predicted problems even after genetic resemblance was taken into account.[101]

Families Have Problems, Too

Many studies have documented the difficulties children face in their families before the divorce, difficulties that could account for the children's predivorce problems. Even years before divorce, there is more tension, conflict, and acrimony between the parents and more mutually hostile patterns of conflict resolution.[102] When they were assessed five years before their divorce, about half of to-be-divorced parents were highly conflicted.[103] In addition to tensions between the parents, there are tensions between the parents and children. Parents who are in conflict are not as good parents.[104] To-be-divorced parents are less supportive and less invested in their children: they have lower expectations, are less likely to do things and discuss school-related issues with their children, are less likely to attend school events.[105] Even years before divorce, they have parenting difficulties.[106] Controlling for predivorce family difficulties reduces the effect of divorce on children's psychological problems, just as controlling for predivorce child problems did.[107]

Marital Discord versus Marital Disruption

Knowing that parents who divorce have conflicts even before they separate raises a question: which is worse for the child, the conflict or the divorce?

First, one might ask, do parents protect their children from their arguments? Do children actually see and hear their married parents fighting or is it kept behind closed doors? One research team trained parents to report details of their private marital disputes.[108] Husbands and wives kept independent records of conflicts at home for fifteen consecutive days. For each episode, they indicated whether their children were present and close enough to see or hear the dispute. These records revealed that children were present for about one out of three disputes. The big surprise, though, was that when children were there, the parents' emotions were *more* negative and they were *more* apt to engage in verbal attacks and insults and less likely to talk calmly or display affection. So although parents may want to shield their children from marital disputes, their most negative conflicts may actually occur in front of them.

Not surprisingly, then, research consistently shows that marital conflict has bad consequences for children. Children and adolescents whose parents have frequent and intense conflicts and who resolve them in a hostile way have more emotional and behavior problems and less self-esteem than children in harmonious families.[109] They have more internalizing and externalizing problems and trouble with peers, do worse in school (grades, behavior problems, suspension, truancy, fights), get into more trouble with police, and overall have lower happiness and well-being.[110] In one study, researchers found that parents' marital discord was even related to their offspring's marital discord years later; when parents were jealous, moody, critical, domineering, and got angry easily, their offspring carried on the tradition in their own marital relationships.[111] When parents were violent, their offspring were also.[112] Children are most likely to have problems if conflicts are longer, more egregious, more physical, and left unresolved.[113] Conflicts centering on the child are also particularly destructive.[114]

The effects of adults' conflict on children can be demonstrated in experiments simulating what happens at home. In one experiment, preschool children were visibly distressed during an angry argument staged between two adults and they acted more aggressive after the argument.[115] In another experiment, children felt more intensely sad and fearful when they watched a videotape of a man and a woman arguing than when they saw a couple of kids arguing.[116] They were especially sad and scared when the argument involved physical conflict.

In brief, then, it is clear that parental conflict is detrimental to children's emotional well-being and behavior. But how does conflict compare with divorce? Both lead to similar problems—distress and depression, aggression and academic problems.[117] But which is worse, conflict or divorce? The answer seems to depend on the study. Conflict has been found to be worse for children's behavior problems, well-being, and achievement and for adults' life satisfaction.[118] However, divorce has been found to be worse for children's perceived competence, problem behavior, and psychological distress and for adults' marital and relationship instability, relationships with father, and educational attainment.[119] There is no clear pattern; both conflict and divorce are bad.

Another question that arises is whether marital conflict is the reason that divorce affects children negatively. The most recent studies indicate that conflict contributes to children's problems but is not the only cause. Researchers in the National Survey of Families and Households investigated whether parental conflict before divorce explains why children with divorced parents exhibit more academic and psychological difficulties than children with nondivorced parents. The results indicate that parental conflict is partly but by no means completely responsible for the association between divorce and child well-being.[120]

Conflict accounts for about 15 percent of the effect of divorce on children's well-being. In other studies, conflict did not account for increases in behavior problems in children or lower educational attainment of adolescents with divorced parents.[121]

Should Parents Stay Together "for the Sake of the Children"?

You may have heard the story about the elderly couple who came before the judge seeking a divorce. Alice was ninety; Henry was ninety-three. The judge was, to say the least, surprised. "Why are you petitioning for divorce at this age? Did you just discover that you're incompatible?" "Oh, no," they replied. "We've been miserable for years—but we had to wait until the children died." Often, unhappy parents ask whether it is better to stay together, even in an unharmonious marriage, "for the sake of the children." Of course few of them go to the lengths that Alice and Henry did. Judging by the current divorce rate, conventional wisdom is that it is better to divorce than to wait. Not many miserable couples spend their lifetime together or even until their children are grown. Who is "right," then—Alice and Henry or today's divorce-prone couples?

There is research that supports the view that children are better off if their parents divorce rather than staying married—*if* the parents are in conflict before the divorce. In one study of preschoolers, young children with parents who couldn't get along were less uncontrolled and antisocial if their parents got divorced than if they stayed married.[122] In the National Longitudinal Survey of Youth, also, children whose parents had frequent conflicts and then divorced did better than those whose parents stayed married (they gained only four points on an inventory of behavior problems while children whose parents stayed married increased by seven points over the six years between tests).[123] Children remaining in high-conflict families were more anxious and depressed than children whose conflicted parents divorced.[124] In the National Survey of Families and Households, divorce led to improved self-esteem for girls in conflicted families.[125] (There was no positive effect of terminating a conflicted marriage on behavior problems in this study, but divorce was less harmful for the children in high-conflict families than the children in low-conflict families). Finally, in a study of young adults whose high-conflict parents had (or had not) divorced over the previous twelve years, those whose parents divorced had higher levels of well-being than those whose parents stayed together.[126] The conclusion from these studies, then, is that if parents are in conflict, it is better for them to divorce than to stay together.

Three longitudinal studies that tracked parental conflict *after* the divorce show that there is more to the story, though. When divorce did not end the parents' conflict, offspring in divorced families had more problems than those in high-conflict families that stayed together; when divorce did end conflict, children in divorced families were better off than those in high-conflict, distressed marriages.[127] They were more socially responsible—dependable, honest, understanding, obedient, conforming to adult values, and getting along with others—and more cognitively productive—persistent, self-controlled, well organized, hard working, doing well in school, and seeking intellectual challenges—and had fewer externalizing and internalizing problems. Thus, terminating a conflicted marriage is beneficial for children if it ends their stress. If conflict is going to continue unabated, it is better for children to stay in an acrimonious two-parent household than to suffer the deprivations of a single-parent household on top of the conflict.

But what if the couple is not in overt conflict? What if they just drift apart, develop their own separate interests, experience "personal growth," or find someone else they like better? Is it better for the children if these couples divorce? The literature quite consistently answers this question in the negative. Multiple studies show that children in low-conflict families are worse off if their parents split up than if they stay together.[128] In the National Longitudinal Survey of Youth, children in low-conflict families in which parents divorced increased by four points on a behavior problems inventory, while children in low-conflict families that remained together did not increase at all.[129] In the National Survey of Families and Households, divorce affected children's behavior problems and self-esteem most when family conflict was low.[130] In the three longitudinal studies, boys did worse in low-conflict divorced families than low-conflict nondivorced families.[131] Divorce after a low-discord marriage is especially distressing to children because they see no obvious reason for it. For them, parental separation, besides being unwelcome, is unexpected and inexplicable. It sets in motion a series of stressful events that are all negative—declines in income, loss of contact with a parent, a move to a new neighborhood, neglectful parenting—with few or no compensating advantages.[132] Divorce in low-discord marriages leads to long-term decrements in children's adjustment and well-being even into adulthood.[133] It has negative effects on their psychological well-being, support networks, educational achievement, and marital instability.[134] In fact, it has even been suggested as the reason that there seem to be worse effects of divorce on children now than there were a decade ago when it was more likely that only high-discord marriages were terminated by divorce. Longitudinal evidence indicates that a majority of recent divorces are not preceded by an extended period of overt and intense marital conflict.[135] For this reason, divorce probably helps fewer children than it hurts.[136]

In brief, there is support for both our elderly couple, Alice and Henry, who waited until their children died before they filed for divorce, and for couples who end their miserable marriages: it depends on how they are miserable. If they are in frequent open conflict and their conflict declines with divorce, it is better to divorce than to stay together. If they can keep their unhappiness hidden from their children, it is better for the children if they stay together.

More Than One Cause

We have seen that when parents divorce there are multiple causes of their children's problems. These multiple causes of children's problems are presented graphically in Figure 6-1. It is not only diminished parenting or limited financial resources, moving to a worse neighborhood or losing contact with the noncustodial parent. All of these factor into the equation that leaves some children depressed or aggressive, academically or socially incompetent, in dead-end jobs, with little education, or facing the divorce server themselves. When Amato compared five different causes of divorce effects on children—absence of the noncustodial parent, adjustment of the custodial parent, parental conflict, economic hardship, and stressful life changes—he found that a

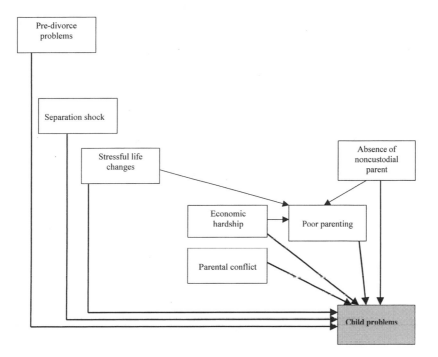

Figure 6-1. Causes of children's problems after divorce.

model combining all five accounted most fully for the research findings.[137]

Summary

There are many reasons for children's problems after divorce—emotional, social, and economic. Children are often emotionally unprepared for the divorce, and their parents provide inadequate explanations that make it harder for them to cope. Many lose the home and lifestyle they are accustomed to because of the economic decline precipitated by divorce. Loss of contact with the noncustodial parent—usually the father—is another source of problems. The quality of parents' care is likely to deteriorate after divorce, as single custodial mothers experience stress and depression themselves. In addition, some children are forced to take on more household responsibilities, leading to resentment and rebellion. Continued conflict between their parents is another source of problems for children, especially externalizing behaviors. Some children were troubled kids, living in hostile homes, even before the breakup, but divorce exacerbates their difficulties. A vexing question is whether unhappy parents should stay together "for the sake of the children." Just as divorce has negative effects on children's well-being, so does living in an intact family fraught with conflict. Although some experts suggest that divorce is the best solution if conflict is high in a marriage, this is true only if the parental conflict ends after divorce. If conflict is kept low or hidden, children are better off in an intact family even if the spouses have drifted apart. There is no single cause that explains why children suffer after divorce: many factors and multiple reasons operate together to cause children's adjustment problems after divorce.

7

What Helps Children Adjust?

Just as there are multiple causes of divorce problems, there are many things that help children adjust to their parents' divorce. The combination of these things can help children sail through the turbulent seas of divorce with ease, while the lack of them leaves children pitching and tossing. Some fortunate children recover from divorce in a few months or years, ending up basically the same children they were before the divorce, just a little older and wiser. Other children have enormous difficulty and end up in a sorry state as a consequence of the divorce and its aftermath. In recent years, researchers have studied the diverse responses children have to their parents' divorce and the factors that facilitate or impede their adjustment. In this chapter, we discuss how these factors influence how much children suffer and how quickly they rebound.

Qualities of the Child

Researchers have discovered that the characteristics and strengths that children possess when the divorce occurs help them adjust.

Does Being Older Help?

As we saw in Chapter 5, children react differently to divorce depending on their age at the time. But is age related to longer-term adjustment?

Results of studies of children's adjustment are somewhat inconsistent because researchers have not separated the age the child was at the time of the divorce from the time elapsed since the divorce.[1] Looking at the consequences in adolescence or adulthood reduces this problem, but even in these studies, the results are not completely consistent.

It might be expected that people who experienced the divorce when they were older would have an advantage. Children (especially young ones) are more vulnerable, they have less coping ability, and, if their parents divorce, they live more years of their life in a divorced family. Some researchers have found that when divorce occurs early, the children have more problems when they are adults than if the divorce occurs later. They have worse relationships with their noncustodial father and are more likely to perceive both their mother and father as less caring.[2] They do less well in the workplace and have less confidence about their chances of marrying successfully. They are more lonely, isolated, and worried.[3] They are more likely to get married or have a baby when they are still teenagers, they have lower levels of education (women only), and they are more likely to have smoking or drinking problems.[4] They are also more likely to divorce.[5] Other researchers have failed to find that age is related to whether children in divorced families finish high school, attend college, find and keep a steady job, become teen mothers, get arrested, abuse substances, or have mental-health problems.[6] It seems that age is most consistently related to relationship problems—with parents and partners. This is sensible, given that relationships with parents are formed in early childhood and relationships with romantic partners, to some extent, parallel them.[7]

Boys: Buffeted or Buffered?

In the 1980s, a number of influential studies suggested that divorce was worse for boys than for girls. In the Virginia study, for example, preschool boys from divorced families were more aggressive and less mature than girls.[8] Similarly, Wallerstein's study showed that boys were more likely than girls to be stressed and depressed.[9] In the study with the National Association of School Psychologists, boys with divorced parents had more behavior problems and lower academic achievement than girls.[10] There are a number of reasons that boys might have more problems than girls when their parents divorce: boys are more physiologically vulnerable to stress than girls are; parents and teachers are stricter with boys' outbursts; boys in divorced families, almost all of whom are in mother custody, have lost their male role model; and boys get less emotional support from their overstressed mothers who find that their demandingness, opposition, noisiness, and physicality make sons more exhausting and difficult to parent.[11]

Since these early studies, however, researchers have backed away from definitive statements that boys are worse off than girls when their parents divorce. Gender differences turn out to be less pronounced and less consistent than the early studies suggested. In more recent studies, a number of investigations have failed to find significant differences between boys and girls, and meta-analyses reveal that boys are not worse in terms of academic achievement or psychological adjustment.[12] In adulthood, no differences are found in long-term psychological well-being, and, in fact, men from divorced families are relatively more likely than women to graduate from college.[13]

Still, differences putting boys at a disadvantage lurk. Meta-analyses reveal that boys from divorced families are significantly worse in their social adjustment than girls: they have more problems with popularity, loneliness, cooperativeness, and parent-child relations.[14] Boys were also found to have more emotional and behavior problems, including delinquency (shoplifting, damaging property, being picked up by police, going to court), than girls in several large-scale studies of divorce.[15] Thus, even more recent research suggests that boys may suffer the effects of divorce more than girls do in terms of their social-emotional behavior.[16]

It has also been suggested that boys and girls are both affected by divorce but they just express it in different ways: boys are more likely to externalize their distress and girls to internalize it. There is some support for this idea. In letters children in divorce adjustment groups wrote to their parents, boys' themes were more angry, girls' were more anxious.[17] Boys were more likely than girls to have fights with their divorced mothers, and the size of the divorce effect on conduct problems was larger for boys than girls.[18] Supporting the suggestion, researchers in one study found that boys had more problems when it was the parent who did the reporting, whereas girls had worse symptoms when the children themselves were the reporters.[19] This is logical if parents are more aware of children's externalizing problems—because they hit them in the face—whereas children are more tuned to their own internalizing problems. In adulthood, young women from divorced families have more long-term anxiety, depression, and relationship difficulties.[20] Thus the suggestion that divorce affects boys and girls in different ways has some support—although there is a great deal of overlap: boys experience depression and girls act out.[21]

Another suggestion is that girls suffer more before the divorce and boys after it. There is also some support for this idea. Adolescent girls showed negative effects prior to separation whereas boys showed them after the divorce, in one study, and in a simulation of parents fighting, boys were more likely to exhibit aggression after the fight; girls were more likely to be distressed during it.[22]

In brief, the issue of how and how much gender buffers or buffets children as they confront the challenges created by their parents' divorce is not resolved. Researchers should continue to look for gender differences each time they investigate divorce and its aftermath.

Smart and Able to Look on the Bright Side

More important than gender are other personal qualities that give children the strength to help them through the divorce. Children who are psychologically healthy—happy and confident—adapt to the new challenges and stressful life experience brought on by the divorce more easily than children who have psychological problems.[23] In fact, they may even gain from the experience and become better at social problem solving later on.[24] Children who are highly intelligent also adapt to the divorce more easily.[25] Gifted children do not experience the academic difficulties that most children do after their parents divorce.[26] High intelligence buffers children from the negative effects of marital distress and divorce on academic achievement and also their relations with peers.[27] They may still have emotional problems; however, these problems are likely to be less severe.[28]

An easy temperament also helps children recover from their parents' divorce. In the Virginia study, temperament ratings were made by nurses when the children were infants. Later on, when their parents divorced, boys who had been rated as having a "difficult" temperament were likely to be more aggressive and insecure; children who were "easy" as infants were more adaptable.[29] In other studies as well, more easy-going children, or children who could control their emotions better, had fewer psychological problems after their parents divorced than children with difficult temperaments.[30] Being able to calm themselves down from emotional arousal or not getting aroused in the first place buffered these children against the negative effects of divorce.

Similarly, children adjust better to divorce if they have a more optimistic outlook: if they think more positively about events, don't blame themselves for things outside their control, try to think of ways to solve their problems and put them in a more positive light, are confident that they can deal with stressful demands and difficult emotions, and do not engage in wishful thinking.[31] These children have fewer psychological problems such as anxiety, anger, and depression in childhood, and, as young adults, are more secure in their romantic relationships.[32]

Conditions after the Divorce

It helps children adjust to their parents' divorce if they have an up-beat nature and a high level of intelligence, but what happens to them after the divorce is even more important. How quickly and completely children recover depends on how well the custodial parent adjusts, whether the noncustodial parent remains involved in their lives, whether the two parents get along, and whether there are other resources the child can draw upon.

Parents' Well-Being

We know that most parents suffer economic and emotional consequences after divorce and that these are two reasons that children in divorced families are worse off than children in intact families. But does the level of the parents' well-being after the divorce determine how well their children adjust? According to the statement cosigned by participants at the conference to evaluate what we know about how children are affected by divorce, the overall level of economic and psychological well-being of the custodial parent ranks as one of the most powerful predictors of children's adjustment after divorce.[33] What is the basis for this statement?

A number of studies indicate that children have fewer adjustment problems if their custodial parent (usually their mother) experiences minimal disruption of income after the divorce.[34] In one study, for example, all the children with serious psychological problems came from families who reported a 50 percent drop in income.[35] Other studies suggest that children's adjustment is better if the custodial parent has an income that he or she believes is adequate and if the family is not experiencing financial hardship.[36] However, having a high household income after the divorce does not necessarily aid children's adjustment; being rich is no guarantee of an easy recovery.[37]

Even more important than money is the custodial parent's psychological well-being. Children adjust better when the parent is in good mental health and has made a better recovery herself (or himself).[38] Children whose mothers are less depressed have higher levels of psychological well-being and fewer behavior problems when they are preschoolers; they are less emotionally disturbed and do better in school when they are of school age; and, in adolescence, they do better academically and emotionally.[39] Even children's physical health is related to their parent's: when the divorced parent is in good physical health and does not suffer from sleeplessness, lethargy, or feelings of helplessness, children also are in better health.[40]

In adolescence, at least, one reason that mothers' poor adjustment is related to children's problems seems to be that it leads children to worry about their parent. In a study of adolescent adjustment four years after separation, adolescents who were worried about their mother or felt that they needed to care for her had more adjustment problems than adolescents without these concerns.[41] In another study, when mothers made detailed disclosures to their adolescent daughters regarding financial concerns, negative feelings toward their ex-husband, job ups-and-downs, and personal issues, the girls worried more about their mother and, as a consequence, suffered more psychological distress.[42]

There is of course always the risk that mothers will be doing so well themselves—because they have a great new job and are moving up the career ladder, they are at long last completing their education, or they have a new lover—that they ignore their children.[43] In this case, children would not benefit from the parent's well-being; children only benefit if their mother functions adequately as a *parent*. This is why mothers' participation in adult-focused divorce adjustment programs, although it improves their own adjustment, is not typically related to improved child adjustment.[44] Most group interventions emphasize adult adjustment, ignoring parenting skills and family relationship issues—at the children's peril.

Parenting Quality

The quality of parenting that children receive after the divorce is probably the single most important aid to their adjustment. As we have discussed, after divorce, parents may be oblivious to their children's needs and their children may end up neglected and overburdened. When parents are loving and supportive, the contrast is profound. Perhaps it sounds trite, but research suggests that this is the key to children's well-being. Children do best when their parents are involved in their lives and have good child-rearing skills.[45]

One important child-rearing skill is appropriate supervision. The more attention and guidance parents provide, the better for children's adjustment. Children do best when their parents make sure that they have early and regular bedtimes, don't spend all their time watching TV, and get their homework done.[46] Supervision is especially related to deviance when the children reach adolescence. When it comes to reducing the likelihood that adolescents will act out, flunk out, cut class, or take drugs, the parent's continued monitoring and involvement in decision making play a highly important role.[47] They also help decrease the adolescent's distress and anxiety.

Another important child-rearing skill is "authoritative" discipline. Children and adolescents do better when their parents set firm but flexible limits, offer age-appropriate support, and explain the reasons for their rules rather than simply imposing them and meting out harsh punishments for infractions.[48] Authoritative discipline provides the child with consistency when everything else is changing; it fosters mutual trust and respect that make controlling the child easier.[49] Authoritative parenting remains important in adolescence as a counterweight to the dangers and temptations of the peer world and the risks of early maturing. When parents are too strict and "authoritarian"—or their children think they are—the children have more emotional and academic problems.[50]

A third critical parenting skill is nurturance. Children do better when their parents are loving and responsive, affectionate and accepting. These qualities buffer children from the stresses of divorce—stresses that include hearing relatives say bad things about one of their parents, having Dad miss a scheduled visit or turn up unexpectedly, and watching Mom and Dad argue or hit each other.[51] Maternal nurturance reduces children's fear of abandonment and promotes a sense of security. Children who have affectionate, loving relationships with their custodial parents have fewer psychological problems—less depression, impulsivity, and antisocial behavior. This has been demonstrated when children are evaluated soon after the divorce separation or years later, in studies of both young children and older ones.[52] The closeness of the relationship between parent and child is one of the strongest predictors of children's adjustment.[53] In one study, having a good relationship with their mother, in fact, completely buffered young male adolescents against the negative effects of divorce on cognitive achievement and externalizing behavior.[54]

The importance of good parenting has also been demonstrated in divorce adjustment programs for mothers and children. In one program, divorcing mothers were trained to reduce their coercive discipline and increase their positive parenting with their sons, who were in grades one to three. Both of these improvements—particularly the improvement in positive parenting—led to improvements in the boys' adjustment as reported by teachers, mothers, and the boys themselves.[55] In another program, increases in positive parenting led to improvements in children's mental health, compliance, and academic performance—and the benefits lasted for at least six years.[56] The results of these programs clearly indicate that parenting directly affects children's adjustment; the associations between good parenting and good adjustment are not just correlational.

Contact with Dad

As we know, children often lose contact with one of their parents— usually the father—after the divorce, and this is one of the reasons that they develop psychological problems. It would be reasonable to expect, therefore, that children who have more contact with the noncustodial parent after divorce would adjust better. Does contact with the non-custodial father help children's adjustment? To skip to the bottom line, the answer is "yes"—but it's not just any contact and it's not just how much contact.

One reason that researchers have even studied this question is that the answer has legal implications. It makes a difference for custody arrangements and visitation if children benefit from more contact with their fathers; it makes a difference in whether the custodial parent should be allowed to move away from the noncustodial parent to another state. Recently, the New York State Supreme Court referred to such "relocation" cases in which a divorced parent seeks to move away with the child and the other parent opposes that move as "one of the knottiest and most disturbing problems" courts face. The trend has been to permit such moves since the argument has been made that they are in the best interests of the child; that is, generally what is good for the custodial parent is good for the child.[57] One study in which researchers collected information about the effects of such moves, however, suggests that this conclusion may have been premature.[58] College students whose parents were divorced were divided into groups based on their parents' move-away status. On most child outcomes, the students whose parent did not move were significantly advantaged: they had more money for college; their parents got along better; they experienced less hostility, inner turmoil, and distress from the divorce; they were more satisfied with life and better adjusted. It was not important whether the mother moved with the child or the father moved and the child remained with the mother; it was the diminished contact between father and child rather than moving itself that mattered. Another study also supported the suggestion that diminished contact with Dad has negative effects, by comparing the amount of time children spent with their fathers before the divorce (on average, fifty-four hours every two weeks) and after the divorce (on average, twenty hours). Children who lost more time with their father were not as well adjusted, especially the seven- to thirteen-year-olds, who had developed a stronger relationship with their father before the divorce occurred than younger children had.[59]

So having less contact with Dad after divorce seems to be problematic for children, and children often yearn for more time with him. In one study of college students a decade after divorce, half of them wished that their nonresidential fathers had spent more time with them.[60] But does having more contact with Dad improve children's adjustment? Research indicates that more visits are not a guarantee of better adjustment. In meta-analyses of studies of contact with nonresidential fathers, the frequency of contact is not consistently related to child outcomes in general, and a recent literature review cited sixteen studies in which contact was positively associated with children's well-being and twenty in which it was not.[61] In the latter studies, the researchers had simply measured the frequency of visits. But the question of how important contact is may be more complicated:

- Perhaps having more contact is helpful only if the visits occur on a regular schedule, once or twice a week, for example. Some researchers have found that children have fewer adjustment problems if they have regular (not just frequent) visits with the noncustodial parent.[62]

- Perhaps contact is better if visits are longer. Researchers have found that children's self-esteem and school achievement are better the longer their visits are.[63]

- Undoubtedly, contact is better if children want it. Visitation is a two-way street. Researchers have observed that fathers visit more frequently and regularly when their children are not angry with them about the divorce, when they are happy about the visits and openly express their longing for more time together.[64] Visitation decreases when fathers perceive that visits are not going well, are not frequent enough, or are not long enough.[65]

- Contact is also better if the mother wants it. In an analysis of data from the National Survey of Families and

Households, researchers found that the children who were doing worst were those whose fathers visited frequently and whose mothers disapproved.[66] In general, it seems that if parents get along—and getting along includes agreeing about visitation—contact with the father benefits the child, but when parents are in conflict, children do not benefit and may even be harmed by more frequent contact.[67]

But probably most important is the *kind* of contact fathers and children have during their visits. What children need most from their fathers is meaningful contact with an emotionally involved parent. In the sixteen studies that reported that contact was positively associated with children's well-being, the researchers had gone beyond merely counting visits to measuring meaningful aspects of the parent's role.[68] As it turns out, noncustodial fathers often behave toward their children more as an adult friend or uncle than a parent.[69] Much of their time is spent joking and roughhousing, watching TV, seeing movies, going out to eat, or going to sports events. Fathers in intact families do the same things—but the tendency is exaggerated in divorced dads. When divorced fathers act more as parents rather than uncles, contact helps their children adjust to divorce. The experts who drafted the consensus statement on the effects of divorce agreed that parents not only need to spend adequate amounts of time with their children but need to be involved in a diverse array of activities with them, an array of activities that includes routine everyday interactions—getting breakfast together, cleaning up, going shopping, walking the dog, raking the yard, throwing a ball, doing homework, reading a bedtime story—and spending holidays together.[70]

Simply put, children adjust better when their fathers (or noncustodial mothers) are more involved in their lives—disciplining and dressing them, running errands for them, providing religious training, sharing holiday celebrations, and taking them for recreational activities.[71] Such involvement continues to be important as children get older. Adolescents feel more positive about visits with their father when they include more diverse activities and a higher level of involvement.[72] They are less likely to experience depression if they frequently

Personal Story: Lousy Father, Good Friend

After the divorce, my dad was one of those fathers who wanted to shove a lifetime of memories into a day of play. Often I would end up with a stomachache at the end of our time together. We developed an unusual relationship. He never attempted to be much of a "parent" figure to me. When I got older, we talked about politics, future goals, and the loves in both our lives. In other words, he was a really lousy father but a pretty good friend.

get advice from their father—about educational plans, employment goals, and personal problems.[73] In other words, after divorce, even though they may not live in the same house, it is best for the children if Dad remains a dad, providing meaningful contact and "full-service" parenting.

It is also advantageous if that full-service parenting is of high quality. When noncustodial fathers are authoritative and give their children emotional support and consistent, reasonable discipline, children have fewer psychological and behavioral problems and do better in school.[74] In fact, when the quality of the father's parenting is controlled statistically, this reduces or eliminates divorce effects on these child outcomes.[75] When fathers are good parents, their children develop or maintain closer relationships with them. Often, however, children of divorce lack a close relationship with their noncustodial father. In one study of five- to eighteen-year-olds, only about one-third had a good relationship with their noncustodial father.[76] Children who do maintain a good relationship are advantaged in many ways. They have fewer internalizing and externalizing problems in childhood, less depression and deviance in adolescence, and better psychosocial adjustment in young adulthood.[77] They do better in school and end up with higher occupational prestige, more assets, less marital instability, and less economic strain.[78] They are less depressed if they do not feel that they have "lost" their father.[79] They are more likely to

Personal Story: Empty Visits

My dad used to take me out for Disneyland trips—shopping, to the movies, restaurants—and I would always come home with something new and wonderful that he had bought for me. But looking back on those weekly visits, they were really empty, because my dad never really talked to me about anything important. We would only talk about surface things. After my mother and I moved to California, his phone calls and visits soon dwindled to nothing.

approve of their parents' divorce years later.[80] It is also important for children with a close relationship with the noncustodial parent to feel close to the custodial parent; otherwise, they feel like they are living with the wrong parent.[81]

Coparental Cooperation

As we saw in Chapter 6, continued conflict between parents is one of the causes of children's divorce problems. Numerous studies have shown that the more anger, hostility, and acrimony between the parents in the years after the divorce, the worse problems their children develop—problems with social interaction, self-esteem, cognitive competence, academic achievement, romantic relationships, aggression, and depression.[82] Even infants can suffer. When parents are in high conflict and the infant has overnight visits with the father, the infant is more likely to develop an insecure relationship with the mother.[83] It is especially detrimental when parents have a verbally and physically aggressive style of conflict resolution, particularly if it erupts into violence.[84]

So what can parents do to aid their children's adjustment? One thing is to keep their fights out of the children's view and not draw them into the middle of their conflicts. When they do this, children are less affected by their parents' conflicts.[85] Out of sight is out of mind for these youngsters. Not feeling caught in the middle of parents' conflict is one of the factors most powerfully associated with good adjustment in adolescence.[86]

Another thing parents can do is reduce the level of their fighting after the divorce. Research shows that reduction in conflict leads to improvements in children's mental health.[87] In one study, researchers divided children into three groups: (1) children in recently divorced families in which parents were in high conflict before separation and after, (2) children in recently divorced families in which conflict was high before separation but low after divorce, and (3) children in intact families. Adolescents from the first group had significantly more problems than those from the other two.[88] Parents in conflict is a little like parents smoking: it is bad for children, but the sooner parents stop it, the better.

A third thing, and the best, that parents can do is develop a cooperative coparenting strategy. According to Hetherington, the greatest gift a divorcing couple can bestow on their children is a respectful and cooperative parental relationship. About a quarter of divorced parents manage to become cooperative coparents.[89] They develop a relationship in which they talk over the children's problems, coordinate household rules and child-rearing practices, and adapt their schedules to fit their children's needs. The noncustodial parent supports the custodial parent's child rearing. If conflicts about coparenting arise, the parents resolve them peacefully. They forgive each other for their transgressions.[90] Children whose parents cooperate in these ways have fewer behavior problems, are more socially competent with their peers, and have more self-esteem.[91] Cooperating as coparents is even more important for children's well-being than whether the couple still has disagreements as ex-spouses.[92]

Limited Life Stress

Children's adjustment to their parents' divorce is also affected by how much stress the divorce brings with it. The more disruption and change, the less stability in their lives, the harder it is for children. If the child can stay in the same house or at least the same neighborhood, if the mother doesn't have to go to work for the first time or

Personal Story: Best Interests of the Children

When my parents divorced, they tried to do everything in the "best interests of the children." A friend had told my father that there are two
things you don't do to a woman. You don't threaten her for the children and you don't undermine her financially. My father took that advice and told my mother she could raise the kids but that he wanted a
part in it and that they would share the expenses. They developed a
way of dealing with each other respectfully, which made it easier on
both of them. Holidays were spent together at my mother's house—
including both sides of the family. My father would even bring his girlfriend. I didn't realize until much later that divorced parents often can't
stand each other.

double her work hours, if the father can remain nearby—these things
make the task of recovery easier. Researchers have examined how children's adjustment is related to the number of different stresses they are
put through after the divorce. Parents or children check off on a list
the negative life events they have experienced in the past year or the
events that have gotten worse since the divorce. The checklist can include difficulties that are a direct result of the divorce, such as relocation, litigation, and changes in custody arrangement, or more generic
difficulties that are, at most, only indirectly related to the divorce,
such as losing a friend or a pet, having a sick sibling, failing a class, being in a car accident, or hearing Mom or Dad talk about having serious money troubles. Either way, the more stresses checked off, the
more psychological problems the child has.[93] These problems include
acting out, having difficulty with schoolwork, being depressed, and
using drugs. The association between stresses and problems is strong,
pervasive across outcomes, and consistent across studies. In contrast,
stable positive events are related to children's reports of being well adjusted.[94]

Social Support

One final factor that helps children adjust to divorce is social support. A supportive social network can provide comfort and stability and let children know they are cared for and important; a supportive network can offer children advice, emotional support, positive feedback, and even opportunities for recreation. Children and adolescents who perceive that they have more social support available are less worried and anxious and have less difficulty adjusting to the divorce.[95] According to one study of some two thousand adolescents in grades seven, nine, and eleven, the positive effect of having support from neighbors, school, and peers ranks right up there with parental support.[96] These support systems buffer adolescents from family strain as they recover from their parents' divorce. For example, having a neighbor they could count on helped when parents didn't seem supportive; having a strong attachment to school lowered the risk that adolescents would engage in destructive externalizing behaviors; and having close friends helped adolescents feel good about themselves and less sad when parents were distracted. Other studies also confirm the importance of supportive friends. Friends were the source of support children and adolescents mentioned most frequently after divorce, and children were better adjusted when they were accepted and liked by peers and shared divorce-related concerns with friends.[97]

Another source of support after divorce is an adult mentor—the parent of a friend, a neighbor, coach, or scoutmaster. A mentor is a role model who gives advice, fosters skills, and makes the adolescent feel valued; having a mentor has also been observed to aid adolescents' adjustment to divorce.[98] Children who say that nonparental adults from the extended family or outside the family serve more support functions after the divorce have fewer psychological problems.[99] Children can also be helped when parents themselves have more social support—when they participate in social and professional support groups, are employed, or have help with child care from friends, neighbors, relatives, or paid daycare staff.[100]

Relatives also can provide support for children directly. Children who have close relationships with their grandparents, for example, have fewer adjustment problems.[101] In fact, social support from rela-

Personal Story: Support from Others

Fortunately I had my friends, my teachers, my grandparents, and my brother to help me through the whole crazy-making time after my parents' divorce. The most important people were my brother and a teacher I had in sixth and seventh grades. My brother was important because he was the only constant in my life; we shared every experience. My teacher was important because she took an interest in me and showed me compassion. My grandparents also offered consistent support. They gave my mother money for rent and food and paid for private schools for my brother and me; they were like second parents to us.

tives in the extended family may be one reason that researchers have discovered ethnic differences in children's adjustment to divorce. Generally, effects of divorce are less extreme for African American and Latino children, who typically have access to their extended families.[102] As an illustration, the risk of dropping out of school following parents' divorce is twice as high for European American children as for African American children.[103]

Support can also come from the larger community. In a study of college students in thirty-nine countries around the world, researchers found that those in cultures with collectivist (group) values and practices, like China, Colombia, Indonesia, and Nigeria, were less affected by divorce after high-conflict marriage than students in individualistic cultures like our own.[104] The extended social network in collectivist cultures may provide psychological and emotional support for children experiencing the trauma of divorce. Social support also may be the reason that children have fewer problems if they do not have to move to a new community after the divorce. Relocation increases the risk of social isolation for all concerned and limits the ability of friends and relatives to provide the social and emotional support needed during these stressful times.[105]

Support is especially helpful for children who experience high levels of stress after the divorce. In one study, when the aftermath of divorce was highly stressful, children who received high levels of support—from parents, grandparents, aunts and uncles, stepparents, teachers, school counselors, and mental-health professionals—reported fewer adjustment problems than children who did not receive support.[106] Apparently, support buffered their stress. For children who were not under so much stress, however, social support did not make a difference in how well they adjusted.

A final source of support for children going through divorce is professional help. Individual therapy sessions and school programs for children from divorced or divorcing families offer opportunities for children to talk about their experiences and learn skills that help them communicate effectively, express their anger constructively, and solve their personal problems. Unfortunately, research to evaluate the effectiveness of individual psychotherapy with children from divorced families is scarce.[107] In one study, though, children were enrolled in one of two treatments: a conventional form of play therapy or therapy based on a board game that gave them information about divorce and coping skills training.[108] After completing the therapy, children in both groups were significantly less anxious and depressed. This suggests that a variety of individual approaches may be helpful.

Most studies have focused on group therapy in schools.[109] School programs in these studies range from six to sixteen weekly sessions; most of them incorporate both educational and therapeutic activities as they attempt to teach children coping skills and give them emotional support. A primary benefit of these group programs compared with individual sessions is that they offer contact with other children who have had similar experiences. In fact, in one study, adding a skill-building component to a group-support program did not measurably increase its effectiveness.[110] Supportive peer groups help lessen children's feelings of isolation and loneliness, foster feelings of support and trust, and offer children opportunities to clarify divorce-related misconceptions.

In general, school programs have been moderately successful, chalking up improvements in children's abilities to deal with their feelings, cope with problems, behave appropriately, and do well in school.[111] The combination of counseling and peer support can lift children's spirits, raise their self-esteem, increase their adaptive social skills, and decrease their clinical symptoms.[112] Of course, not all programs succeed.[113] They seem to be more successful in alleviating children's distress than in eliminating conduct disorders at school.[114] One recent program for kindergarten and first-grade children, however, reported changes in classroom adjustment problems as well as diminished anxiety and fewer visits to the school health office even two years after the intervention.[115] Although not all children need it, professional help can be a buffer for children after divorce. It is most effective for children who have more stressors and more problems.[116]

Adjustment Factors Combined

As this abundance of research shows, children's adjustment after divorce is helped by many things—intelligence and an ability to roll with the punches, good mental health and parenting skills on the mother's part, meaningful contact with both mother and father, cooperation between the parents, limited life stress, and ample social support. These things are not all equal and independent; they act together, their effects cumulate, and some of them undoubtedly are more important than others.

Many people have asked which ones matter most. One attempt to weigh the different factors mathematically indicated that what helps children most are the things that most directly involve them—their relationships with both their parents, the fights they see erupt, and the social support they feel they have.[117] These factors were more than twice as important as factors farther removed from the child and the divorce—positive stable events, financial security, and social support received by the residential parent. Another way to try to figure out what is most important is to see which factors appear most consistently in different studies. Using this strategy, Robert Emery concluded that the most important factor for the child is having a good relationship with the residential parent, in which the two communicate about the divorce and the parent provides loving and consistent care.[118] Next in order of importance in his list were the manner in which parents express (and hide) their conflicts, the family's economic standing, and the child's contact and relationship with the nonresidential parent. These seem like reasonable suggestions, and the most important factor—a good relationship with the custodial parent—appears consistently using the two methods of weighing factors. However, other reviewers have concluded that attempts to estimate the relative contributions of different factors lead to conflicting results, futile controversies, and misleading conclusions—because statistics differ from sample to sample and vary across methods and analyses. Moreover, different factors are likely to come into play at different points in the life of the child and the divorce.[119] Researchers have not conducted a single, definitive study in which all these factors were assessed and compared, so we cannot lay out a map identifying all the various routes to optimal adjustment. However, the hints we have from the research literature are sufficient to illustrate the complexity of the issue.

First, there is evidence that the different factors are related to each other. External stresses are related to parents' abilities to cooperate and coparent; for example, parents cooperate more if they have more money.[120] In turn, parents' cooperation is related to how involved they are with the children; when there is more cooperation (and less conflict) between the parents, noncustodial fathers have more contact with the children.[121] Fathers also have more contact with their children if they have more money and higher education.[122] In addition, children's relations with both their parents tend to be connected; adolescents who feel closer to their noncustodial fathers also usually feel closer to their custodial mothers.[123] These associations suggest that there is an integrated "package" of factors that promotes adjustment, consisting of economic well-being and continued closeness and cooperation between parents and children.

Second, not only are these different factors related, but their effects are mediated by yet another factor—the quality of the custodial parent's parenting. That is, the way that parental conflict and cooperation and economic circumstances actually influence the child seems to be through their effect on the custodial parent's behavior. For example, in a study of recently divorced families, higher conflict between the parents led to mothers being more rejecting of their children, which, in turn, led to children having more internalizing and externalizing problems.[124] In two other studies, parental conflict was related to poor parenting by the mother (reflected in a poor mother-child relationship), which was then related to increased psychological problems for adolescents and children.[125] In addition, research shows that economic stress leads to poor parenting, which in turn leads to impaired psychological and academic functioning in children and adolescents—in general.[126] Thus it seems that effective parenting practices are the key to children's postdivorce adjustment.

Third, these factors are connected because one of them *moderates* the effect of another; that is, the effect of one depends on the level of the other. This is the case for conflict and contact; parental conflict moderates the effect of the child's contact with the father. As we discussed earlier, if parents are cooperative, more conflict with Dad is likely to improve the child's adjustment; if parents are in conflict, more contact may harm the child.

Finally, these adjustment factors are cumulative, that is, they sum together, so that children who are fortunate enough to experience *more* of them do better. For example, children who are intelligent *and* easygoing, *and* who have well-adjusted custodial mothers who provide them with effective discipline and care, *and* involved fathers who give them more than trips to Disneyland are likely to do better than children who have only one or two of these advantages. In one study, a comprehensive model that included the financial security of the family, the child's relationships with both parents, the level of conflict between the parents, and the social support the child had available explained more of children's adjustment than the individual components did.[127]

Hetherington and her associates suggested that children adjust to divorce best if the following conditions are met:[128]

- The children are less vulnerable to begin with; they have easy temperaments, are intelligent and socially mature, and have few behavior problems before their parents divorce.
- They experience less stress and socioeconomic disadvantage.
- They receive effective and conflict-free parenting from a custodial parent who is not distressed and depressed.

■ They have more contact with their noncustodial parent—as long as that parent is competent, supportive, authoritative, and not in conflict with the custodial parent.

These researchers concluded that all of these factors contribute to children's adjustment in complex and interrelated ways; our survey of the research literature leads us to the same conclusion. A graphic representation of the factors that lead to children's adjustment is presented in Figure 7-1.

Summary

Divorce can have negative effects on children, but many factors help them adjust. Qualities such as being smart and having an easy temperament and an optimistic outlook help children negotiate divorce more successfully. Being blessed with parents who are economically stable and psychologically healthy is also a great boon. These parents can provide better rearing environments—one of the most important aids to children's successful postdivorce adjustment. When parents are involved in their children's activities, express warmth and affection,

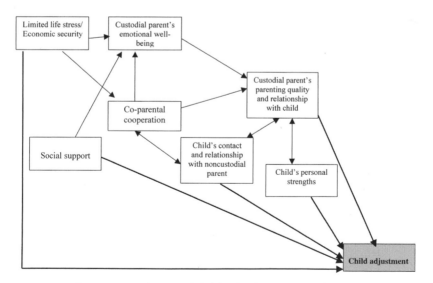

Figure 7-1. Predictors of children's adjustment to divorce.

and provide appropriate supervision and guidance as well as authoritative discipline, children are buffered from the adversities of divorce. Parenting programs can help the parents improve these parenting skills and thereby help their children as well. Another helpful factor is children's continuing contact with a noncustodial father, but regular contact of high quality and a positive father-child relationship matter more than the mere frequency of visits. Contact with Dad is more likely to have a positive effect if the parents get along. Parents shielding children from parental conflicts and developing a cooperative coparenting strategy help the children cope effectively. Children also find the adjustment to divorce easier if they experience fewer stressors, such as relocation, litigation, and changes in custody. A network of supportive neighbors, friends, relatives, classmates, and even an adult mentor can help ease children's transition through the divorce, and professionals can provide school programs, therapy, and advice to help them navigate the postdivorce terrain. These factors act together to ease children's challenging tasks. Only by appreciating the operation of multiple factors can we begin to understand children's postdivorce adjustment.

8

Child Custody and Child Support

Although the term "child custody" is widely used, it is not always well understood. It can refer to a variety of legal and practical arrangements, and, beyond that, its different notations may have different meanings in different settings. The concept has also undergone many changes over the past hundred years. An understanding of the history of child custody provides an important basis for interpreting the current custody situation.

Child Custody Background
What Is Child Custody?

Child custody refers to the legal and physical rights and responsibilities parents have with respect to their children. Having *legal* child custody means that the parent has the right to make all major decisions regarding the child's health, welfare, education, and religious training. Having *physical* custody gives the parent rights and responsibilities for the daily care and control of the child. In states that don't distinguish between physical and legal custody, the term custody encompasses both types of responsibilities. In practice, one may encounter different types of child custody that involve various combinations of legal and physical rights.

Sole legal custody grants one parent the right to legal custody. This "custodial" parent has the right to make all major decisions without regard to the other parent. That other parent, the "noncustodial" parent, typically has visitation rights, including overnight visits, vacations, and holidays.

Sole physical custody grants exclusive physical custody to one parent. Granting one parent both sole legal and physical custody is typically done only when the other parent has neglected or abused the child.

Joint legal custody grants legal custody rights to both parents equally. This means that parents need to inform and agree with each other before making major decisions for the child. Joint legal custody by itself may involve no greater time share than sole custody with visitation, but it may carry an important psychological meaning for parents.[1]

Joint physical custody grants physical custody rights to both parents. Parents who share physical custody typically also share legal custody; conversely, sharing legal custody does not necessarily entail shared physical custody. Joint physical custody does not require fifty-fifty time-sharing, but it does reflect substantial time with each parent. Parents with joint physical custody may have a parenting plan, a specific court order, or an informal arrangement that specifies the actual times the child will spend with each parent.

Split custody refers to "splitting" siblings between the parents and may entail any combination of physical and legal custody.

Bird's nest custody describes the least common situation, in which the children remain in the family home and the parents take turns moving between this "family residence" and their own places.

Deciding on a child custody arrangement is complex and challenging; it may be the most difficult part of the parents' separation, and the initial decision is seldom the last decision. Parents must decide if one parent will have sole legal responsibility for the child or if this responsibility will be shared. They must decide who the child is going to live with—mother, father, or both parents alternately. They must work out how often each parent will see the child, for how long, and on what schedule. When parents cannot agree on custody issues, they may take their dispute to court where a judge will decide the custody arrangement, based on his or her views of the child's best interests.

The Changing History of Child Custody

The notion of the "best interests of the child" was established early in the twentieth century following the suggestion that in custody cases the judge acts as *parens patriae,* a "prudent parent," who does what is best for the child. However, what constitutes the child's best interests has been subject to ideological changes over time. Until the mid-nineteenth century, fathers were unequivocally favored in custody decisions and mothers had virtually no rights. Under English law, upon which U.S. law is based, children and their mothers were viewed as a man's property. Given this presumption of paternal superiority, the mother was not even entitled to visitation or any other kind of contact with her children in the case of divorce. The paternal presumption lasted with minor concessions to mothers until the 1920s when it underwent a radical and complete change. The Industrial Revolution and increasing specialization in men's and women's roles in the family, with the father leaving the home to earn an income and the mother staying home to provide care for the children, may have initiated this change.[2] A concurrent powerful influence came from psychologists, who increasingly emphasized their belief that mothers were the natural and more nurturing parent because biology predisposed them to the parenting task. The role of the father was viewed as indirect.

During the 1950s and 1960s, John Bowlby described the mother's natural tendency to care for her offspring, with the father's sole purpose being to maintain and support the mother-child relationship.[3] Studies of the animal world advanced the argument that mothers were biologically superior to men in providing child care.[4] This sentiment was further strengthened by the commentaries of other notable psychologists. Bruno Bettelheim wrote, "infant care and child-rearing, . . . are not activities in which one should [engage] independently of physiology."[5] And still in the 1970s, Haim Ginott warned against the desire of "modern" fathers to engage in child care because "there is the danger that the baby may end up with two mothers, rather than with a mother and a father."[6] As a result, the allocation of custody rights shifted from a complete right of fathers to a sweeping preference for mothers. The new maternal preference was strengthened by the "tender years" doctrine, which held that children of "tender years"— usually younger than eight—should be raised by their mothers.

In the 1970s and 1980s, further significant reforms occurred. The first change came in 1969, when California enacted the first no-fault divorce law. Similar provisions were subsequently enacted in all states. A second major change was that most states discarded the "tender years" doctrine after a number of court decisions held that gender-based custody decisions were an unconstitutional violation of the equal protection clause of the Fourteenth Amendment of the Constitution.[7] Steadily, courts and the country moved away from the presumption that mothers are inevitably better parents. The courts began to demand evidence of the "best interests of the child," rather than automatically choosing mothers as custodial parents.[8] A third major change that revised the course of child custody proceedings was the requirement that all parents with disputes over child custody or visitation attempt mediation before a custody hearing. This became mandatory in California in 1981 and was subsequently adopted by most other states.[9] Mediation is a nonadversarial process in which a neutral person, typically a mental-health professional, tries to help parents settle their dispute.

Perhaps the most significant change was the shift to a preference for joint custody (at least joint legal custody) in many states, which meant that joint custody was ordered unless it was shown to be not in the child's best interests. This was a further attempt to reduce the effects of the adversarial system, which in earlier years had often led to perjury, falsification of evidence, and undue animosity between parents fighting to gain custody of their children.[10] The preference for joint custody was based on the presumption that it is important for children to have a continuing relationship with both parents.[11] At present, states differ in the extent to which they endorse joint custody.

Some have a presumption in favor of joint custody; others grant joint custody only if both parents agree to it. Under the Uniform Child Custody Jurisdiction Act judges are required to give "full faith and credit" to custody orders issued in other states and to enforce these decrees.

As this brief historical review should make clear, psychological and legal experts, despite their authoritative claims about the nature of parenting, the best interests of children, and proper allocation of parental rights, have varied dramatically in their recommendations about what is best for families. The only certain conclusion is that there is no basic, enduring, or universal "truth." What was once declared a "natural law" was eventually replaced with the opposite idea. Reflecting on these ideological swings cautions us not to simply continue the practice of dogmatic assertions but to find improved and sustainable ways of promoting children's and family's functioning after divorce.

What Determines the Child's Best Interests?

In most cases, child custody is settled in accordance with the parents' wishes.[12] The courts typically accept whatever parents have agreed upon. This process has been criticized because it does not necessarily ensure the children's best interests. Critics point out that this procedure may be especially harmful to children if violence exists in the family because agreement may have been coerced and the custody arrangement may prolong the child's exposure to violence. When parents cannot agree, judges consider many factors in trying to determine the best interests of the child. The following are the main ones:

> *The parent-child relationship.* To minimize the disruption children experience after divorce, it has been recommended that young children be placed with their "primary caretaker," that is, the parent who has provided most of the day-to-day care for the child.[13] Fathers have protested that this standard favors mothers. In response, it has been suggested that it provides an incentive for fathers to be more involved in their children's upbringing from the beginning.
> *Special needs of parents and children.* Special needs related

to parents' or children's mental and physical health are relevant only if they affect child rearing.

Parents' ability to provide adequately for the child. Concerns for adequate care—food, clothing, medical care, quality of schools—are considered; evidence of parental neglect or child abuse is also taken into account.

Continuity. To promote continuity—with the primary caregiver, the other parent, home, school, and community—courts may favor the parent who is more likely to stay in the same community and allow the nonresidential parent access to the child.

Lifestyle and conduct of parents. Parental conduct, including smoking, drug or alcohol use, criminal activity, and increasingly, domestic violence, may influence the determination of child custody. If neither parent is "fit" to have custody because of these problem behaviors, the court may award custody to a third party such as a relative or a foster parent. As social mores have changed, parents' sexual orientation has become less relevant to custody decisions unless it can be demonstrated that parents' activities would have a negative effect on the child. Several states, including Alaska, California, New Mexico, and Pennsylvania, have ruled that sexual orientation should not be assumed to have any effect on parenting ability. Even in those states, however, lesbian and gay parents may face difficulties in obtaining visitation and custody because personal biases can influence judges to invoke other reasons to deny custody or visitation without saying it has anything to do with sexual orientation.

Wishes of the child. Whether to consider the wishes of the child is controversial and varies from state to state. For example, in Georgia, children age fourteen and older are permitted to choose the parent with whom they want to live, whereas in California and most other states, judges do not rely on the child's age but consider the child's maturity. There is a concern that children may not know what is in their best interests and may even pick the less effective parent because he or she has more money or is more permis-

Personal Story: Deciding Who to Live With

Deciding who I would live with was the most difficult part of the divorce process for my parents because neither my mother nor my father wanted to give me up. At the time they separated, I was being taken care of by a lady named Lucia, who lived in our house. My mom could not afford to keep Lucia, though, and she asked my dad to keep me until she got back on her feet. What she meant was that she needed a week or two to find an apartment. Later, in the custody battle, this act of "leaving her baby" was used against her. After a few weeks, when my mom had found an apartment, I began spending equal time with each of my parents. My mom's job continued to take her out of town often, and she needed my dad to take care of me while she was gone. As it happened, though, my mom's new apartment soon became just a cover-up because in reality we were spending most of our time at my mom's new boyfriend's house. After my dad and his family found out that my mom had "their" child living with an older, black man, they decided to take my mom to court to get custody. It was a heated battle. My grandfather was the lawyer for my dad. Friends and family were subpoenaed to testify against my mom. They used her relationship with Pete to portray her as a selfish and unfit mother. My dad's sister accused my mother of not wanting custody of her little girl. "If you really wanted custody of her, you would have taken her from the start," she screamed in the courtroom. The trial tore my parents' families apart, but miraculously, in the end, my mom was awarded custody of me and my dad was granted weekend and holiday visitation. My mom believes that she and my dad could have worked out the arrangement on their own if it had not been for the hostility from both their families. She feels that they were just taking advantage of their position of power and the fact that they had the law, actually a family of lawyers, on their side. Fortunately, the judge was aware of what my mom was up against and this actually worked in her favor. In making his decision, the judge looked beyond each lawyer's case and into who was the more appropriate parent under the circumstances. My mom's extramarital relationship easily made her look like the bad guy, but the judge found out about the problems my dad's gambling had caused and made what I have always thought of as the best judgment possible. At the end of the trial, the judge told my grandfather never to put him in that position again.

sive. A further concern is that letting the child choose which parent to live with will induce later guilt feelings. A related issue is whether children can accurately describe the situation at home; appropriate questioning by specially trained professionals is critical to obtain accurate information from children.[14]

Problems with the Best Interests of the Child Standard

Despite its face value, the best interests of the child standard has drawn an avalanche of criticisms. The key concern is its ambiguity.[15] It sounds good (like apple pie and motherhood), but it does not provide judges with clear, measurable, and definite guidelines. Its inexactness invites judicial bias and arbitrariness.[16] It allows judges to ignore important information, for example, about parents' conflict and to make custody decisions biased by their personal beliefs, attitudes, opinions gender, age, and years of experience.[17] In addition, this standard demands that judges perform the impossible task of predicting what will be best for children in the future.[18] Judges are allowed to consider all, some, or none of the relevant factors, and even if they consider all of them, they may weigh some more heavily than others. Theoretically, law and case precedent should determine judicial decision making; but in reality it is unclear which factors are used.[19] The standard's ambiguity also affects the work of mental-health professionals. Although practicing psychologists are often called upon to conduct child custody evaluations, the best interests standard offers no clear guidelines for their work, and this raises concerns about the validity of their clinical opinions.[20]

Another criticism of the best interests standard is that it encourages protracted conflict between the divorcing parents, as each tries to prove that he or she is the "better" parent in order to "win" custody.[21] The best interests standard may also place mothers at a disadvantage. For one thing, judges may give more weight to socioeconomic factors than mothers' continuity in caretaking.[22] For another, women themselves may make more concessions during negotiations to avoid losing custody or time with their children.[23]

Triggered by the controversies surrounding the best interests of the child standard and in response to ethical claims brought against psychologists who offered expert testimony in child custody evaluations, in 1994, the American Psychological Association released a set of Child Custody Guidelines that outlined the criteria to be used by clinicians working in child custody disputes. Although these guidelines provide a helpful set of criteria for consideration by practitioners, they do not solve the problem. Just like the best interests standard itself, they are neither unambiguous nor binding, and they do not clarify what kind of clinical opinions are ethical and in what situations they are appropriate.[24]

How Many Children Are Involved in Child Custody Allocations?

The precise number of children involved in custody allocations is not known because reporting of child custody cases is not comprehensive or uniform across states. One way of estimating the number of children involved is to extrapolate from the number of divorces. In 2001, there were approximately 1.1 million divorces.[25] At an average rate of 0.9 children per divorce, an estimated one million children were affected.[26] Divorce, however, is not the sole reason for child custody allocations. Currently, one out of three children in the United States is born to unmarried parents.[27] The legal determination of custody is not based on parents' marital status, and thus, the number of children affected by child custody allocations is even larger than the number of children affected by divorce.

Demographics of Single Custodial Parenting

At present, the United States has the highest percentage of single-parent families in any industrialized nation. Of the seventy million children in the country, it is estimated that about twenty-two million live in the primary physical custody of a single parent.[28] It is projected that 50 to 60 percent of children born in the 1990s will live in a single-parent family at some point during their childhood.[29] The majority of custodial parents are mothers (84 percent).[30] About 31 percent of these women have never been married; 44 percent are divorced or separated; and 25 percent are currently married or widowed.[31] More than half of them are European American, about a quarter are African American, and one-seventh are Latina. Custodial fathers are more likely than mothers to be European American (almost three-quarters of them) and less likely to be African American (only one-seventh). They are more likely to be divorced or separated (56 percent) than never married (20 percent) or married or widowed (25 percent).[32] Custodial fathers are also more likely than mothers to be cohabiting with an unmarried partner (33 percent versus 11 percent).[33] The number of father-custody families increased markedly during the 1980s, reflecting the efforts of a growing national fatherhood movement and, perhaps as a result, father-friendlier courts. More than half of all custodial parents have only one child, but custodial mothers are more likely than custodial fathers to have two or more children.[34]

Child Custody in Court

If parents cannot agree on custody and access issues, they may turn to the court system to resolve their dispute. Either party can file a legal motion for custody and related specifics; the other parent then has an opportunity to file a responsive motion and make different or additional requests. Although the majority of custody allocations are, from a legal perspective, agreed upon by the parents, these "agreements" are not without difficulty. Saying that a custody case is "uncontested" does not mean that all is well between the parties involved. The agreement may have come about through calm and rational discussion or after intense and bitter negotiation, or it may have come about because one parent's petition to the court resulted in a default judgment when the other parent did not bother to respond.[35] Most separating parents eventually settle their custody disputes on their own, with the help of a mediator or lawyers or as a result of "bargaining in the shadow of the law"—reaching a last-minute "agreement" as they teeter on the brink of litigation. These settlements occur after the court case is filed when parents realize that they do not have the time, the money, or the emotional stamina to deal with a complex, costly, and lengthy court process.[36] They capitulate, feeling threatened and exhausted. They may fear an unfavorable judgment or they may be unable to keep up with the legal bills.[37] Such settlements seldom represent what parents initially desired or really believe would be best for the child and themselves.

Are Parents Who Litigate Different from Those Who Settle?

The idea that litigating parents must be psychologically different from those who reach an agreement on their own seems commonsensical. We expect "good" parents to be able agree on custody issues and presume that those who can't must be flawed in some way. However, there is no clear evidence to support this belief. Claims that litigating parents are dysfunctional are based on anecdotes, observations of select samples, or clinical theorizing. Moreover, the diagnoses of psychopathologies ascribed to litigating parents vary widely from one clinician to another. Litigating parents have been described as individuals with "personality disorders of unclear origins," whose disturbances are due to losses in childhood or to characterological cognitive distortions, as a result of which they lack empathy and perspective-taking ability, engage in defensiveness and projection of blame, and are self-oriented rather than child-oriented.[38] They have also been described as "perpetually battling" and possessed of a specific character disorder referred to as "relationship disorder."[39] The few studies that have compared litigation and settlement samples have uncovered no meaningful differences between the two groups, however.[40] One recent study comparing sixty parents in child custody litigation with the same number of parents who reached a legal agreement on their own revealed no differences in terms of demographic or personality characteristics such as neuroticism, agreeableness, and hostility.[41] We should remain open to the possibility that parents with custody issues are in a temporary state of crisis and would benefit from a supportive, conciliatory intervention. An adversarial environment that seeks to label, cure, or punish "errant" parents is unlikely to mitigate their conflict or achieve the best possible outcome for the family.

Role and Influence of Lawyers

If a custody dispute proceeds to court, many parents choose to be represented by an attorney. However, it is possible to file *in pro per* and appear without the representation of a lawyer. Judges also may appoint a guardian *ad litem* to represent the child's interests. Guardians *ad litem* may be attorneys, mental-health professionals, or even trained laypeople. They are charged with performing a thorough and objective investigation of the case, and to accomplish this, they solicit the child's views and may interview neighbors, teachers, and friends of the family. They may serve as mediators for the parents and counsel the parents to avoid litigation. Guardians who are attorneys also present and cross-examine witnesses in court. Having a guardian can reduce distortions that may result from the introduction of biased evidence by the two parents or their attorneys.

A lawyer's ability to make a compelling argument for the client can influence the outcome of a custody case, for better or worse. The lawyer's goal—to win the case for the client—is not always easily reconcilable with the American Bar Association's ethical mandate to "treat with consideration all persons involved in the legal process and avoid the infliction of needless harm." Moreover, the consequences of the lawyer's advice can be long-lasting. When researchers in one study followed up individuals who reported that they had been given advice by their attorney to act in ways to encourage the divorce, they found that these individuals adjusted more poorly to the separation that those who had not been given such advice.[42]

Goals of Mediation

■ Protect relationships: facilitate communication and fair negotiation between parties, deescalate conflict, model functional communication, and promote coopera- tion.

■ Increase client control: encourage parties to voice their issues and maintain control over the process of the dispute resolution procedure and its outcome.

■ Satisfy clients: aim for a win-win outcome.

The Mediation Alternative

An alternative to letting lawyers fight out the custody dispute in court is for the divorcing couple to go to mediation to facilitate an agreement about custody issues. Mediators are typically mental-health profes- sionals such as marriage or family counselors. They emphasize negoti- ation and cooperation between the parties with the goal of reaching a mutually acceptable resolution. An effective mediator is neutral and helps parents communicate so they can settle the dispute themselves. Some programs concentrate on child custody issues; others also sort out issues of child support. Divorce and child custody mediation are now available in the private sector in all states, and several states man- date mediation as a first step in resolving custody or visitation disputes.

Mediation versus Litigation

The advantage of mediation over litigation for resolving custody dis- putes has been hotly debated, but these arguments have been guided by ideology rather than scientific evidence.[43] Courts are based on an adversarial system that has its roots in the medieval concept of "trial by combat" in which a dispute was fought out by two combatants and the survivor was deemed right. This adversarial system has been criticized as a way to resolve family disputes; in fact, it has been suggested that its combative atmosphere increases rather than decreases family conflicts. Mediation offers a method of looking for compromises rather than conflicts, and some have recommended that mediation-based processes should replace court-based procedures.[44] However, critics of mediation point out that it is not at all clear that the adversarial system actually has negative effects on families.[45] To this point, neither side has produced conclusive evidence that one procedure is better than the other.

Research on Mediation

Research on mediation has produced some hints of ways that mediation might be superior to litigation:[46]

Child support payments. Participation in mediation programs has been linked to reports of fewer missed child support payments.[47]

Involvement of the nonresidential parent. Mediating non-residential parents have been reported to be more involved with their children than those who litigated.[48]

Compliance. Compliance with custody agreements is reported to be somewhat higher after mediation.[49]

Client satisfaction. Fathers who avail themselves of mediation services have indicated that they are more satisfied than fathers in litigation;[50] however, their satisfaction declines over time. Mothers tend to be equally satisfied with mediation and litigation—in some studies they even indicate that they are more satisfied with litigation.[51]

Reduction in litigation rates. Mediation has been associated with reduced litigation rates; that is, parents who enter mediation are more likely to settle their dispute than parents in litigation.[52] However, *re*litigation rates—after the initial resolution—do not differ for mediation or litigation samples.[53]

Coparenting relationship. Participation in mediation is associated with decreased parental conflict and increased

cooperation—at the time.[54] There is no evidence, however, that mediation contributes to better coparental relations in the years following the dispute. In fact, in one
study, parents who had used mediation reported more conflict with their former spouses after the divorce than those
who had not used mediation.[55] Mediation has, at best, a
limited effect on reducing interparental conflict and increasing interparental cooperation.[56]

Parents' psychological adjustment. There is no evidence
that mediation improves parents' psychological functioning compared with litigation.[57]

Outcomes for children. To date, no studies have established
that children whose custody arrangement was determined
through mediation have a more positive psychological adjustment than children whose custody was determined through
litigation.[58]

In sum, the findings on the benefits of mediation are encouraging, but they are not definitive proof of the advantages of this method
of resolving custody disputes. The problem is that these studies have
not been experiments in which couples were *randomly assigned* to
undergo either mediation or litigation. Thus, we do not know for sure
whether any apparent successes of mediation are a consequence of the
fact that parents who choose to go to mediation are already less liti-
gious, more ready to cooperate, and more committed to staying involved with their children—or that mediation actually has a beneficial
effect.

Problems with Mediation Research

Mediation, as a concept, has great intuitive appeal because it promises
a nonadversarial environment and the help of trained professionals to
facilitate agreements between parents. However, rigorous research to
prove its effectiveness is difficult and costly. Recent studies by Robert
Emery and his colleagues represent the best research on mediation,
and their follow-up evaluations, a decade after the divorce, do offer
limited support for the notion that mediation has more positive effects

than litigation. These researchers improved upon earlier studies by using random assignment, assessing long-term effects, and comparing effects of mediation with effects of litigation, rather than just focusing on mediation.[59] However, even their studies had problems: not everyone agreed to participate; their sample was small and half of the participants could not be located for the follow-up; participants were primarily from low-income families and from a single court district; and some measures of success relied on parents' recollections of events that had taken place nine years earlier. Moreover, the mediation they studied was provided by specially trained *pairs* of mediators, which is not typical of mediation generally.

Applying the findings of research in this area is especially difficult because both mediation and litigation are procedures that vary from setting to setting. The quality and training of mediators differ, and mediation sessions vary in frequency, focus, and duration. Likewise, litigation procedures vary because U.S. courts are decentralized and laws differ from state to state.[60] Even within a single state, there is considerable diversity from county to county.[61] Beyond this, judges differ. As we have already mentioned, judges vary greatly in how they interpret and apply the law, depending on their personal backgrounds, temperaments, and preferences.[62] Thus, it is impossible to know, on the basis of Emery's experimental research, just how the mediation available to a particular couple would compare with litigation. All things considered and notwithstanding its great intuitive appeal, mediation has not been proved to be as effective as hoped.

Negative Consequences of Mediation

There have even been suggestions that mediation is not as good as litigation, at least for some couples. Critics argue that mediation may disadvantage women. They point out that mediation can be used manipulatively to sustain and amplify power imbalances stemming from family violence.[63] It may also make it possible for fathers to trade unwanted custody for lower child support payments in the spirit of "compromising to reach agreement."[64] The observation that men tend to prefer mediation over litigation heightens the concern that men achieve greater benefits from mediation than women.[65] While fathers' rights advocates strongly support mediation, feminist scholars reason that mediation leaves both parties without the procedural protections of the court. Men in this society generally have greater bargaining power than women, and this may be amplified in a setting where the professionals are primarily female.

Evidence from numerous studies demonstrates that mediation is an inappropriate and dangerous alternative to the legal process when domestic violence exists.[66] Unequal power positions and domination-subordination roles of battering husbands and battered wives during marriage are known to continue long after a marriages ends. There is no evidence that mediation produces positive outcomes in violent domestic situations, and it may pressure victims into giving up their rights for the sake of compromising with their batterer. Thus, presumptive statutes favoring fathers' rights, mandated mediation, and joint custody may help sustain unfair financial advantages and continued control over female victims after divorce.[67] Professionals in mental-heath, social service, and legal fields need to understand the potential ramifications of mediation in abusive relationships and help domestic violence victims achieve equitable settlements and safe arrangements.[68]

Mediation has also been criticized because it persuades parents to choose joint custody arrangements when perhaps this is not in every child's best interests.[69] It has been criticized because mediated agreements are more likely to disintegrate than other arrangements.[70] It has also been criticized because, in some studies, individuals who participated in mediation reported more long-term problems and more conflict with their former spouses than individuals who did not use mediation.[71]

Does Mediation or Litigation Really Matter?

The lack of evidence proving that either mediation or litigation is better has been interpreted as an indication that it is not the *type* of procedure per se but the *quality* of the procedure that matters.[72] A recent prospective longitudinal study focused on the effect of variation in the quality of judicial decision making.[73] Parents' perceptions of judicial fairness contributed significantly to their well-being, health, and life

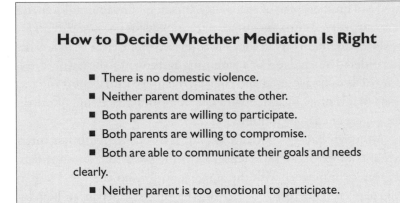

How to Decide Whether Mediation Is Right

- There is no domestic violence.
- Neither parent dominates the other.
- Both parents are willing to participate.
- Both parents are willing to compromise.
- Both are able to communicate their goals and needs clearly.
- Neither parent is too emotional to participate.

satisfaction and, perhaps most importantly, to their relationship with each other. Individuals who felt that the judge had treated them unfairly reported higher rates of depression, stress, conflict, and lack of cooperation from their ex spouse. A follow up with these parents three years after their court appearance indicated that fairness perceptions of the court procedure predicted parents' compliance with court orders and relitigation. Parents who had earlier felt that they were treated unfairly had a 40 percent higher chance of relitigation. These results offer some support to the suggestion that it is the quality of the custody proceedings that increases or decreases family strife.

Parenting Agreements

Court orders usually do not address the details and daily complexities involved in raising children after divorce. Parenting plans are voluntarily negotiated agreements that let parents specify the details of their children's living arrangements and any particular parenting issues that they want spelled out. Common themes include the needs of the child, issues of supervision and discipline, and specific responsibilities such as decision-making authority and transportation. These plans may be worked out on the back of a napkin or with a mediator who tries to help the parents work together on the child's behalf, offering information and encouraging creative solutions. A parenting agreement can be viewed as a business plan of sorts—the business of raising children, to-gether but apart. Courts encourage parenting plans because parents are more likely to follow a plan they have devised themselves than any de-cision ordered by a judge. For a parenting agreement to be legally bind-ing, it needs to be accepted and signed by a judge into a court order, a process that is often included with the filing and processing of the di-vorce papers or custody motions.

Although having a parenting plan is associated with less inter-parental conflict, more satisfaction with the parenting arrangement, and greater compliance with the agreement, it is no cure-all. No par-enting plan can circumvent or remedy the effects of persistent high in-terparental conflict, widely disparate parenting beliefs and practices, and neglectful or abusive parenting. An additional consideration is that parenting plans continually need to be renegotiated and updated as children get older and family circumstances change. As children grow up they often want more input into their visitation schedules or living arrangements. New marriages, changes in jobs or economic con-ditions, changes of schools or activity schedules, or unexpected crises also require adaptations in custody or visitation arrangements.

Child Custody Evaluations

Judges, faced with the difficult task of deciding child custody without clear criteria, have increasingly come to view child custody evaluations as an important component of their decision-making process. In part, this shift may reflect the belief that mental-health professionals are bet-ter equipped than legal professionals to determine family matters; in part, the shift may indicate a readiness to share the burden of decision making in the face of pervasive criticisms of the legal process.

The Role of Child Custody Evaluators

The reason to appoint a child custody evaluator is to have an impartial mental-health professional make a recommendation to the judge about custody and visitation. The custody evaluator's primary objec-tive is not to help the couple work out an optimal arrangement but to make a win-lose recommendation. It is assumed that custody evalua-

tors have more psychological training and will spend more time inter-
viewing and observing the family than a judge possibly could. Unlike a
judge, who is limited to hearing the evidence presented in the courtroom, custody evaluators can assess parents' mental health, parenting
skills, and capacity to care for their children in terms of available time,
emotional support, and money. They can observe the current caretaking arrangement and solicit information about parents' past involvement with the child in order to identify the child's "psychological parent" or "primary caregiver." They can probe into the parents' past and
present lifestyles. To gather information, they may consult with other
people who know the couple, make observations of parent-child interactions, and obtain school and medical records. On the basis of this information, the evaluator then gives an opinion as to the strengths and
weaknesses of each party's position and makes a recommendation to
the judge about who should get custody and how much visitation
should be allowed. Although the evaluator's opinion is not binding,
judges typically use it as a basis for their order.

     This is clearly helpful for the judge's decision making, but there is
no evidence that custody evaluations improve the final outcome for
children or that parents are more satisfied with this process. Furthermore, serious concerns have been expressed about the qualifications of
child custody evaluators, the adequacy of the evaluation process, and
the validity of the measures used in child custody evaluations.

The Adequacy of Evaluators' Qualifications

Grave concerns about the scientific basis of child custody evaluations
were expressed as early as the 1970s and 1980s.[74] The theoretical basis
for developing standards for child custody evaluations was questioned.[75] It was further pointed out that evaluations did not meet the
standards for admissibility in court because it could not be shown that
they were more than mere speculation.[76] Some researchers suggested
that personal biases influence the type of custody arrangement the
evaluator suggested—just as personal biases affected the decisions
judges made.[77] Evaluators' biases were a particular concern when the
evaluator was paid for his or her services by one of the parties.[78] Evaluators may also be biased in favor of the parent who talks more convinc-

ingly or who has an attorney who provides the evaluator with more clients. Thus, child custody evaluations are deemed only as good as the evaluator.

In a recent study in Virginia, researchers assessed the current standard of practice for child custody evaluation among psychologists seen as highly credible by family law attorneys.[79] Self-teaching was reported to be the primary method of training; measures of psychopathology, which have no demonstrated link to parenting, were a primary source of information about parents. Only a few evaluators used home observations or surprise visits to gather information about family functioning. The researchers concluded that better training of custody evaluators and better standardization of custody evaluations are needed to ensure high-quality assessments. Some improvement in the quality of forensic assessments has been observed over the past decade, thanks to efforts to develop professional standards for the field.[80] These standards include guidelines for practice and a proliferation of training, credentialing, and certification procedures for forensic examiners. Nevertheless, the level of practice still falls far short of professional aspirations for the field.

Because the qualifications of child custody evaluators are dubious, a recent article in the *Journal of Psychiatry and Law* offered guidance to attorneys preparing to cross-examine mental-health experts in child custody litigation. Evaluators' adherence to professional standards, procedures used in evaluations, use of collateral source information, selection of assessment instruments, and the degree to which opinions offered are supported by the data were discussed as possible targets for cross-examination. Particular emphasis was placed on determining whether an evaluator had specialized training for the task and was board certified.[81]

The Adequacy of Evaluation Methods

Critics of child custody evaluations point to the lack of clear criteria for *what* to evaluate and *how* to evaluate it. There are also concerns that evaluations are not sufficiently thorough. Specific limitations of the evaluation process include evaluators not spending sufficient time on the evaluation, not making behavioral observations of parents and children, and not having adequate training to conduct such observations and interpret them according to established criteria. For example, even if criteria exist for certain behavioral assessments, as is the case for assessing young children's attachment to their parents, most evaluators are not trained to conduct or interpret these assessments. Moreover, even if evaluators interview and observe parents on several occasions, their time is limited, and the amount of time they spend may be influenced by the couple's ability to pay for the evaluation. There are further concerns about inadequate or conflicting data sources; third-party data typically rely on information volunteered from family and friends of each party and thus lack objectivity.

The absence of accepted criteria for assessment is another factor undermining scientific credibility. For example, evaluators often speak about the psychological "bonding" between parents and their children. Although most would agree that bonding is an important element in a custody evaluation, there is no widely accepted definition of this term.[82] Nevertheless, parents are often compared with each other on the basis of the presumed strength of their bond with their children.

Additional criticisms center on the assessment tools used. Evaluators often give psychological tests to parents and children, for example, the Minnesota Multiphasic Personality Inventory (MMPI-2). Although personality testing may screen for serious mental or personality disorders, it does not assess parenting ability or child adjustment. In recent years, a number of tests designed specifically for use in the context of child custody evaluations have been developed; however, some of these tests do not meet basic professional standards.[83]

Not surprisingly, an analysis of the reliability and validity of assessment methods evaluators use indicated that there is little evidence to support the methods on which professionals base their recommendations to the court.[84] A comprehensive review of legal and psychological research pertaining to child custody determinations concluded that current evidence does not support most of the expert testimony proffered by mental-health practitioners.[85] As the reviewer summed it up, "There is no reason to assume that so-called scientific expert clinical testimony . . . is scientific or expert."[86]

A final concern is that the routine ordering of child custody evaluations poses a financial hardship for many parents. In a recent survey of 338 child custody evaluators, the average cost of an evaluation was $2,646—three times what it was a decade earlier. Nearly all of the evaluators (95 percent) required at least some of the fee to be paid by the parents in advance; 50 percent required the entire fee up front, and 83 percent required full payment before testifying in court.[87]

Before child custody evaluations can fulfill their purpose and promise, mental-health professionals must demonstrate that these evaluations validly assess areas of concern deemed relevant by the judiciary.[88] A key challenge is to be able to predict long-term outcomes for children—a daunting task because of children's changing needs and parents' changing circumstances. To date, there is no evidence that mental-health professionals can perform this feat. Judges should review child custody evaluations carefully and consider their recommendations with a large grain of salt.

Assessing Child Custody Arrangements

Parents often want to know whether one custodial arrangement is best. Because of the great diversity among parents, children, and their circumstances, there is no single best solution to the custody dilemma; we cannot say that any *one* type of arrangement is better for all children or all parents. However, researchers have spent many hours trying to pin down the relative advantages and disadvantages of each.

Joint Custody

Joint custody has received most attention in the past two decades. It has become the preference in many states and is permitted in all states. Although the first joint custody statute was enacted in 1957 in North Carolina,[89] a presumptive attitude toward joint custody emerged in other states only two decades later. Three factors contributed to the increasing popularity of joint custody. First, psychologists pointed to the importance of a child's continuing relationship and involvement with *both* parents after a divorce.[90] They further suggested that the sharing of custody would lessen the burden on each parent and thus increase parents' satisfaction with the custody arrangement.[91] Second, a steadily growing national father's rights movement set the stage for fathers

to demand that they be given equal consideration in custody decisions—the solution, joint custody. Third, judges who, under the best
interests of the child standard, had little direction on how to determine
custody responded to the advice of psychologists and the demands of
fathers.

States with a Presumption for Joint Custody

There is still diversity among states regarding the ordering of joint custody. Some states have a presumption that joint custody is best, which
means that it is ordered unless it is demonstrated that it is not in the
best interests of the child; some states have a preference for joint custody as long as the parents agree; and some states remain silent on the
issue but allow it. Eleven states have a presumption for joint custody
(Florida, Idaho, Iowa, Kansas, Louisiana, Minnesota, Missouri, New
Hampshire, New Mexico, Texas, Wisconsin). Washington, D.C., also
has a presumption for joint custody. Twelve states indicate a preference
for joint custody if the parties agree (Alabama, California, Connecti-
cut, Maine, Michigan, Mississippi, Nebraska, Nevada, Pennsylvania,
Tennessee, Vermont, Washington).[92]

Is Joint Custody Truly "Shared" Custody?

Joint custody is not a single, fixed type of arrangement but is quite het-
erogeneous, with the actual time sharing varying tremendously.[93] A
joint physical custody order may reflect a fifty-fifty division or a forty-
sixty division—or any other arrangement that parents agree upon that
involves the child spending time with each of them. Moreover, court
orders do not equate to actual living arrangements. Although a legal
agreement may stipulate forty-sixty time-sharing, parents may gradually shift to a thirty-seventy schedule in response to daily practicalities
and children's wishes. Thus, it is not uncommon for a joint physical
custody arrangement to be *in reality* functionally indistinguishable
from a sole physical custody arrangement with visitation. Sharing time
and access to children also does not imply sharing child-rearing tasks
evenly or coordinating parenting efforts; even if parents share equal
time with their children, they may be parenting independently rather

than cooperating and communicating with each other about their children's needs and child-care tasks.

The number of cases of actual joint physical custody is undoubtedly overstated in court documents.[94] Parents may demand joint custody for strategic reasons—for example, to lower child support payments[95]—or they may simply realize after the fact that, despite their initial intentions, true time-sharing is impossible. Joint custody is presumed to assure children a continuing relationship with both their parents. In practice, however, a joint custody order cannot truly ensure that both parents stay involved with the child in a meaningful way. One or the other parent may not live up to the initial commitment, the frequent shifting between parents may not work for the children, or parents' individual circumstance may change and they agree to adjust their custody arrangement without returning to court. Research indicates that joint physical custody is relatively unstable over time.[96] Furthermore, people tend to develop arrangements that are best suited for their individual family.[97] It has been estimated that the proportion of truly shared joint custody is as low as 10 percent.[98]

Advantages of Joint Custody

Real joint physical custody has the advantage of assuring children continuing contact with both parents. It alleviates the sense of loss that a noncustodial parent feels and relieves a custodial parent of some of the burdens of sole care and responsibility for children.[99] A functioning joint custody arrangement provides parents with a better balance of time with and without children; it may also alleviate stress caused by changes in family structure or function.[100] Not surprisingly, joint custody has been linked to higher satisfaction with the custody arrangement in parents.[101] It has also been linked to better adjustment in children *if* the parents—not the courts—choose joint custody and cooperate.[102] In these self-selected arrangements, joint custody translates into more paternal involvement and more positive attitudes about the ex-spouse's parenting.[103] Fathers with joint physical custody, compared with noncustodial fathers, have been reported to be more likely to share in decision making about their children, to see them more frequently, and to be more satisfied with the arrangement.[104] Mothers are not necessarily so pleased with joint custody.[105] A functioning joint custody arrangement may give children a greater sense of security and lessen their sense of abandonment by one parent. Joint custody has also been linked to lower rates of relitigation, again, when joint custody was freely chosen by parents rather than imposed by the court.[106] Court-imposed joint custody has not been found to reduce relitigation.[107]

After a recent meta-analytic review of thirty-three studies of custody, one researcher reported that children in joint physical or joint legal custody were better adjusted than children in sole custody.[108] Children were reported to show fewer behavior and emotional problems and have higher self-esteem and better family relations and school performance than children in sole custody arrangements; their parents had fewer conflicts with each other. Although these positive outcomes have been described as a consequence of joint custody,[109] such a causal relationship has not been proved. Joint custody parents also reported less conflict *before* they got divorced.[110] They described their prior relationships in more positive terms and were more agreeable and cooperative.[111] They were also more affluent and well educated than parents with sole custody.[112] These findings, therefore, do not indicate that joint custody by itself *causes* less parental conflict or better child outcomes.[113] The more likely explanation is that more agreeable and cooperative parents choose joint custody and their cooperation and parental commitment contribute to less conflict and better child outcomes.

Disadvantages of Joint Custody

Even if joint custody has advantages for parents and children, there are costs to this arrangement. For one thing, joint custody poses problems for a parent who wants to move to a different area. For another, even if parents stay in the same area, joint custody leads to less stability for children, who must be shuttled between their parents, encountering differences in household rules, parental expectations, and sometimes even socioeconomic status as they move from one household to the other. Children who moved more frequently between their parents were at risk for emotional and behavioral problems in one study of

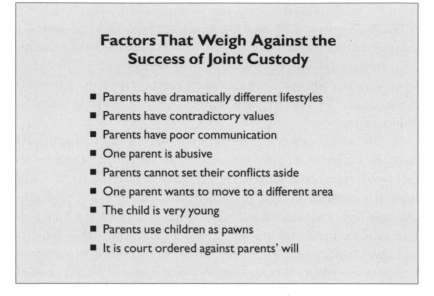

Factors That Weigh Against the Success of Joint Custody

- Parents have dramatically different lifestyles
- Parents have contradictory values
- Parents have poor communication
- One parent is abusive
- Parents cannot set their conflicts aside
- One parent wants to move to a different area
- The child is very young
- Parents use children as pawns
- It is court ordered against parents' will

high-conflict parents, probably because frequent access created more opportunities for disagreements between the parents.[114]

Most critically, joint custody ties parents together—even if they hate each other. Joint custody is a painful yoke when parents are in conflict or didn't want joint custody in the first place.[115] Studies have shown that parents with court-ordered joint custody are less satisfied with the arrangement than parents who voluntarily agree to joint custody.[116] Parents whose marital relationships were full of intense conflict, anger, resentment, and bitterness also don't like shared parenting as much as sole custody.[117] As a general rule, research suggests that joint custody is not a good idea for parents and children in high-conflict families.[118] Because joint custody typically fosters more contact between parents, these arrangements can maintain highly dysfunctional parental relationships.[119] Children who feel caught in the middle when their parents fight face particularly negative outcomes.[120] If both parents have an equal say in any decision making pertaining to their children, disagreements and open conflict between parents can set off confusion, loyalty conflicts, and maladjustment in children. Any benefits derived from frequent access to both parents are diminished by the strain of continued exposure to parents' conflict.[121]

Another possible disadvantage of joint custody is that, despite its

Personal Story: Always Thinking about How to Divide Myself

It was 4:30 a.m. and the light from the hallway crept under my bedroom door. It wouldn't be long till Daddy cracked the door open and picked me up from my warm bed to carry me to the cold van. Then it would be my sister's turn. He would lay each of us down in the bed he had made for us in the back of the van. Then he would make one last trip into the house to get our overnight bags full of clothes, homework for school, and, once a month, a child support check in an envelope for Mom. The donut shop was next. Daddy would stop there every morning to get himself a donut and coffee. Once a week he would surprise us and leave us a white paper bag crumpled at the top with two sprinkled donuts inside. At about 5:00 a.m. we would arrive at Mom's house. Daddy would once again put each of us over his shoulder and carry us in. My sister and I would walk to our bunk beds and try to go back to sleep until 6:30 a.m., when it was time to get up for school. Mom packed our lunches and delivered us to school. Then Daddy would be back to pick us up from school when he got off work at 3:30. We would have dinner with him, finish our homework, pack our bags, go to bed, and then the routine would be repeated. This happened five days a week, from the time I was six until I was fourteen. On the weekend, we would spend one and a half days with Mom and one and a half days with Dad. I don't remember ever being asked if I liked this way of splitting our time exactly down the middle. The one time I questioned it my dad told me I was selfish. I felt horrible afterwards, but I just wanted to sleep through the night in one bed like any other child. After that, I never spoke about it again. The only positive thing about this custody arrangement was that I knew I had two parents who really cared about me. Otherwise, everything was extra difficult because it had to be divided—where we went for holidays, who we sat with at school banquets, how school picture packages were divided up, who we went with to school open houses, who congratulated us first after a school performance, where we had birthday parties, and at whose house we kept our souvenirs and awards. The stress was terrible because I was so worried about hurting one parent's feelings and because I was always thinking about how I was going to divide myself.

theoretical ideal of shared parenting, this arrangement may increase a woman's dependence on her former spouse and on the court.[122] Also, in a joint legal custody arrangement, women, who in most cases are the custodial physical parents, may be limited in their day-to-day parenting efficacy because of their obligation to obtain their ex-husband's agreement on any major decision.

Effects of Father Custody versus Mother Custody

Does it matter whether children in sole custody are in father custody or mother custody? Are there advantages to one or the other arrangement for boys or for girls? We know that there are differences in mothers' and fathers' parenting behavior.[123] Therefore, in the context of custody allocations, the question arises whether these differences are related to differences in children's development. In early research in this area, researchers reported more positive outcomes when children were with a custodial parent of the same sex. Boys in father-custody homes were more socially competent than father-custody girls, and father-son pairs had better relationships than father-daughter pairs; the same gender effects were found in mother-daughter pairs. Moreover, children living with the same-sex parent were better adjusted than children living with the opposite-sex parent in terms of maturity, sociability, and independence.[124]

More recent research, however, has not provided unequivocal support for this same-sex advantage. In the Stanford Custody Project, an advantage of living with the same-sex parent was found—but only for girls.[125] Four years after the divorce, adolescent girls who were living with their mothers were doing better than girls who were living with their fathers; for boys, it did not matter whether the custodial parent was the mother or father. Girls living with their fathers were more emotionally alienated from their fathers and had more conflicts with their mothers; their fathers were less involved and interested in their activities. It should be noted, however, that the majority (76 percent) of these girls had moved in with their fathers sometime after the divorce, and moves into father custody were likely to be the result of family conflicts. Undoubtedly, many of these girls had been sent to live with their fathers because they had discipline problems beyond their mother's control.

In contrast to the results of this study, in a study in southern California, a same-sex advantage was found—but only for boys.[126] This study sampled school-age children and revealed that across a variety of assessments of psychological well-being (self-esteem, anxiety, depression, behavior problems), boys in the custody of their fathers were doing significantly better than boys with their mothers. They also had the advantage of maintaining a more positive relationship with their mother. No same-sex advantage was found for girls in mother custody. In fact, although the advantage of being in father custody was most clear and consistent for boys, it was only slightly less significant for girls. The differences in children's well-being were not eliminated by statistically controlling for the custodial parent's psychological well-being and adequate income or the child's contact with the nonresidential parent. Thus, the conclusion from this study was that children do better in father custody, rather than with the same-sex parent. This finding is consistent with results of other studies as well.[127]

If there is an advantage of father custody—at least for children who aren't sent to live there because they can't get along with their mothers—why might that be? Custodial fathers in the southern California study had advantages over custodial mothers: their incomes were higher and they had fewer children to take care of; they were less likely to require or receive child support and more likely to have emotional support from friends and family. Yet another advantage was that mothers stayed involved with the children in father custody, even though they were no longer living together, so that children continued to think of their mothers as part of the family. This finding of a continued emotional closeness with Mom has appeared in other research: in a national sample of fourteen hundred children, researchers found that children in father custody had a better chance of having good relationships with both their parents than children in mother custody.[128] Only one-third of the twelve- to sixteen-year-olds in that study maintained a positive relationship with an absent (noncustodial) father, compared with more than half of the children who maintained a good relationship with their absent mother.

Thus, there are a number of ways in which living with Dad may have advantages for children's well-being. Before concluding that all children should be placed in father custody after a divorce, however, there are several important cautions. First, there is the tired but true cliché that correlations do not prove causation; the fathers with custody in this study were not randomly assigned by the courts or their wives to take on the burdens and joys of child rearing. Custodial fathers who seek custody, rather than just assenting to it, have been found to be more emotionally invested in their children and to be more effective parents.[129] Second, although children in father custody as a group were doing better than children in mother custody, they were not doing better than the children in mother custody who had high levels of contact with their fathers. Third, not every study indicates that children do better in father custody; a number of studies (albeit with small samples of children in father custody) have not found differences in children's adjustment related to the gender of their custodial parent.[130] Moreover, in the Stanford study there were those girls who had adjustment problems despite being in father custody. As we have already stated, there is no one best custody arrangement for all children. Custody determinations must be made on a case-by-case basis.

Fluidity of Custody Arrangements

The need for making custody decisions does not end when the divorce is final. Until the children are independent adults, shifts in custody are common.[131] Families are fluid environments, and changes can occur even after months and years of a stable custodial arrangement. These may be the result of changes in the parents' status—unemployment, remarriage, or a move to a different area; they may be responses to children's changing needs and desires; or they can be the result of a continuing tug-of-war between competing and conflicted parents.

The courts prefer to place young children in the primary physical custody of one parent rather than in an arrangement that requires frequent switching between parents.[132] Overnight or extended visits with the nonresidential parent are viewed as undermining the stability young children need. In contrast, adolescents have been described as doing as well in joint physical custody as when living primarily with one parent.[133]

A recent longitudinal study traced the evolution of three types of residential custody arrangements over a two-year period: sole father custody, sole mother custody, and joint custody.[134] Results showed that almost half the children in joint custody changed custody arrangements. Changes in custody arrangements were especially common for young children and girls. Girls who changed custody usually went to their mothers. Over time there was also a polarization toward sole custody, indicating, perhaps, a greater need for more stability. In the Stanford study, as well, shifts in residence were common. Nearly one-third of the adolescents had moved during the four-year period since their parents separated, and 13 percent had moved more than once. They were more likely to move out of a dual-residence arrangement than into one, most often into the mother's household. The most common reason for the shift in residence given by the adolescents was that a parent had moved and they wanted to remain near their friends or finish high school where they were.

Sometimes children in one family decide that they want to live with different parents and their custody arrangement is "split." A recent study in Australia indicates that children's wishes contributed to such an arrangement in most families. There was no indication that split custody weakens sibling or parent-child relationships, leads to parent-child alliances, or impairs children's self-esteem.[135] The author concluded that split custody works well in many families for both parents and children.

In sum, child custody arrangements vary considerably across different families; they can be complex and changing over time. At this point there is no evidence that any one custodial arrangement is better than another or that one type of arrangement works for all families.

Child Support

The moral obligation of parents to provide for their children is unquestionable. Not surprisingly, all states require that parents support their children financially until they reach the age of majority, and in some instances even longer if the child has special needs. Noncustodial parents are typically required to pay child support, whereas custodial parents are presumed to fulfill their financial obligation through the daily care of the child. If parents share physical custody, child support is based on the percentage of time the child lives with each parent and each parent's income in relation to their combined incomes. The Child Support Enforcement Office (CSE) reports that in 2003 the agency collected $21.2 billion in child support and had a caseload of 15.9 million.[136] CSE is a federal/state/local partnership to help families locate noncustodial parents, establish paternity when necessary, establish orders for support, and collect child support payments. States must have guidelines to determine how much a parent should pay for child support. Child support orders can be established by a court or by an administrative hearing process. Provisions for health insurance coverage must be included in the support order. CSE's services are available to custodial parents whose coparent is living outside of the home. Families receiving assistance under the Temporary Assistance for Needy Families (TANF) program receive services automatically. Collected child support reimburses the state and federal governments for TANF payments made to the family. Those not receiving public assistance can apply for child support services, and any payments will be forwarded to them.[137]

Enforcement of child support has become a national concern, and many new enforcement mechanisms exist to compel so-called "dead-beat parents" to pay child support. Enforcement may include seizure of real property and tax refunds; credit bureau reporting; suspension of driver's, professional, and recreational licenses; withholding of passports; seizure of bank accounts; freezing of assets; and imprisonment, fines, or both. The most widely used (60 percent) and effective enforcement tool is withholding of wages by employers.

Child Support Statistics and Trends

The most comprehensive and up-to-date information on child support comes from the regularly updated report on *Custodial Mothers and Fathers and Their Child Support* by the U.S. Census Bureau. It indicates that about 60 percent of the 13.4 million custodial parents in this country had child support agreements in 2002.[138] About three-quarters of them received at least some child support payments—a proportion that is unchanged since 1993, although the proportion of custodial parents receiving *full* payments has increased. About one-quarter claimed that their former spouse paid what he (or, more rarely,

she) could; about one-quarter felt that the other parent could not afford to pay. They reported receiving about 60 percent of the child support due them in 2001 (twenty-two billion dollars). The average annual amount of child support received by parents who received at least
some support was forty-three hundred dollars; parents who received
every child support payment received on average fifty-eight hundred
dollars. These amounts did not differ for mothers and fathers.

Awards varied according to demographic characteristics: awards
were lower for ethnic minority mothers, mothers who had less than a
high school education, mothers who had never married or were separated, and mothers who were younger and below the poverty level.[139]
Of the one and a half million custodial parents below the poverty line
who received any payments, the average annual amount of three thousand dollars accounted for 40 percent of their total family income.
Custodial parents receiving full payment of child support had higher
incomes and were more likely to have custody and visitation agreements (77 percent, compared with 56 percent of those who had no
such arrangements). Child support enforcement offices, state depart-
ments, and welfare offices report that the number of requests for assistance relating to child support declined between 1994 and 2002 by
nearly 16 percent.[140] Apparently, greater public awareness of child support obligations and more rigorous enforcement mechanisms are ef-
fecting a positive change.

Who Pays? Predictors of Child Support Payments

Most research on compliance with child support orders has focused on
fathers because they are most often the paying parent. Only about 70
percent of all fathers who are required to pay child support actually
do.[141] More of them *think* or *say* they do, though. Fathers tend to over-
estimate their contributions. They are more likely to report that they
comply with child support orders than their former wives corrobo-
rate.[142] Their reports of the amounts they paid were up to 30 percent
higher than mothers reported.[143]

In a recent study conducted in six Illinois counties, researchers
examined the responses of noncustodial fathers who appeared before
the court to respond to a summons for nonpayment. The primary rea-

sons they gave for not paying were lack of money, lack of access to the child, lack of control over how the money was spent, and the belief that they were not the child's father.[144] Although child support payments are indeed related to fathers' ability to pay, nonpayers are generally not so poor that they could not afford to pay at least some support.[145] Fathers' noncompliance has been related to psychopathic deviance and alcohol use.[146] It has also been linked to personality characteristics like vengefulness, egocentrism, and irresponsibility.[147]

Fathers are more likely to comply with child support orders if enforcement is more stringent, for example, if the payment is withheld by their employer; if they believe the support order is fair; and if they believe that their children are well cared for.[148] Fathers are more likely to pay child support if they have more contact with their children.[149] However, exceptions to this pattern have been observed.[150] It is reasonable that fathers who are more committed to their children would both pay support and visit more.[151]

To Pay or Not to Pay: The Impact of Child Support Payments

A recent meta-analytic study that pooled the information from about sixty studies demonstrated that fathers' payment of child support was positively associated with measures of children's well-being.[152] The receipt of child support has been linked positively to greater attainment of educational goals and reductions in children's behavior problems.[153] More than other income, child support is also related to higher cognitive test scores for children and adolescents.[154] These positive outcomes reflect not only direct effects of receiving child support but also greater parental commitment and involvement. Researchers have found that when reluctant payers were *forced* to pay, the magnitude of the beneficial effect of support on children's educational attainment declined.[155]

Summary

The allocation of child custody rights and responsibilities has varied dramatically at different times in our history. Throughout much of our history fathers were favored in custody decisions and mothers had no rights. Social changes brought about by the Industrial Revolution and the emergence of the discipline of psychology influenced social and legal thinking and gave mothers a prominent role in child custody decisions. The preference for mother custody began to erode in the 1970s when the "tender years" doctrine was abandoned because it violated the equal protection clause of the Fourteenth Amendment for both sexes. Despite this legal change, the majority of custodial parents today are mothers.

If parents cannot agree on a child custody arrangement, a judge may decide custody on the basis of the best interests of the child. Going to court, however, is fraught with challenges as parents need to invest the time, money, and effort to work within the legal procedures. Mediation has been touted as a better alternative to the adversarial method of child custody dispute resolution; however, there is no consistent evidence that mediation procedures are inherently superior to the adversarial procedure. Similarly, the courts' frequent reliance on child custody evaluations conducted by mental-health professionals is not warranted, given the lack of evidence that the conclusions of these evaluations are accurate and that heeding the recommendations leads to positive child outcomes. Three decades of research on child custody evaluations have raised concerns about the qualifications and biases of evaluators, the methods used in evaluations, and the absence of accepted criteria for assessment. Contrary to popular belief, there is no consistent empirical evidence that parents who seek the help of the courts to determine child custody are different from those who work out child custody issues themselves.

Much research has addressed the question of which custody arrangement is best. Joint custody arrangements have received most attention and have become the legal preference in many states. However, assessment of the effectiveness of this type of custody is made difficult by the tremendous variability in the actual time-sharing. Joint custody has the advantage of increasing the likelihood that both parents spend substantial time with their children and that the children are better adjusted. If joint custody is imposed by the court, however, these positive outcomes are not found. Moreover, in high-conflict families, parents and children do not benefit from joint custody. At this point there is no evidence that any custody type is better than another or works for all families. Child custody arrangements often change over time as parents' and children's circumstances change.

The enforcement of child support payments has become a national concern. All states require that parents support their children, and all states have put in place mechanisms to enforce such payments. It is generally accepted that when parents pay, this is linked to more positive child outcomes.

9

Remarriage and Stepfamilies

Basic Facts about Remarriage

High divorce rates create a large pool of experienced candidates for re-marriage.[1] So it is no surprise that most people who divorce remarry.[2] About three-quarters of divorced people remarry, and, of these, about half do so within three years of their divorce.[3] Remarriage is so com-mon that it has become a relatively normal life-course event.[4] Nearly half of the marriages in the United States are remarriages for one or both spouses.[5] The likelihood that people marry twice before their for-tieth birthday doubled, from about 10 percent to about 20 percent, in one generation, at the same time as the divorce rate doubled.[6] But now that the divorce rate has stabilized, remarriage is no longer on the rise.[7] This downtrend in the rate of remarriages in the United States parallels developments in Canada and Western Europe.[8] One explanation is the rising rate of cohabitation. Many couples now live together before remarriage.[9] Not only does cohabitation often precede remarriage, it frequently replaces it altogether.[10]

"Serial marriages"—in which people marry more than twice—are more common than they used to be, but they are still unusual: in 1996, 54 percent of men and 60 percent of women had married once, 13 percent of men and women had married twice, and only 3 percent had

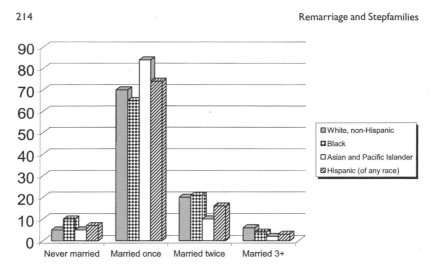

Figure 9-1. Number of marriages by ethnicity in the United States: 1996. Source: Kreider and Fields, 2001.

married three or more times.[11] Apparently, most people learn from their first marriage (and divorce) and don't keep on making the same mistakes. As Figure 9–1 indicates, these distributions differ somewhat by race and ethnicity in the United States, with European Americans and African Americans having a slightly higher probability than other ethnic groups of marrying more than once. However, no more than 6 percent in any ethnic group marries more than twice.[12]

Who Remarries?

What affects the chances for remarriage? Age, for one thing. Young people are more likely to remarry than older people: women who divorced before age twenty-five have an 80 percent chance of remarrying within ten years, compared with 68 percent of women who divorced at age twenty-five or older.[13] This is when young age is an advantage: the median age of remarriage is only thirty-two years for women and thirty-four years for men.[14] Because of increased longevity and better health, the remarriage rate for older adults is increasing.[15] But as people get older, the interval between divorce and remarriage also increases.[16]

Remarriage Statistics at a Glance

■ Nearly half of the marriages in the United States are remarriages.

■ Three-quarters of divorced people remarry; half of them within three years.

■ Rates of remarriage have decreased since the 1980s, partly because of increased cohabitation.

■ Only 3 percent of remarriages are serial marriages, that is, third, fourth, or fifth . . . marriages.

■ Women in rural communities and communities with less male unemployment and poverty are more likely to remarry.

■ Women younger than twenty-five are more likely to remarry than women older than twenty-five.

■ When women younger than twenty-five remarry, their second marriage is more likely to end in divorce.

What about having children? It is interesting to note that in a national sample the presence of children did not significantly affect chances for remarriage. This finding may appear counterintuitive, and it is not entirely consistent with prior research.[17] Single people without "baggage" are presumed to be more attractive marriage partners than those who bring children into the relationship. It may be, however, that individuals with children are more family oriented and are marrying a partner with similar needs. This assumption is supported by a study that examined patterns of marriage and divorce, remarriage and "redivorce" in England, Canada, and the United States. Divorced men without children tended to marry women who had never been married, whereas divorced men with children married divorcees.[18]

Another factor that makes a difference in the chances of remarriage is gender: men are more likely to remarry than women.[19] They tend to marry women who are younger than they are, and the woman's children are likely to be younger than theirs.[20] In a national sample that assessed couples from 1960 through 1989, both husbands and wives in second marriages were about twice as likely (40 percent) to have at least a five-year age gap as people in their first marriage (less than 20 percent).[21]

The characteristics of the community also influence the likelihood of remarriage.[22] Women are more likely to remarry if they live in a rural area than a city. Women who live in the central cities of metropolitan areas are least likely to remarry. This difference is quite large. Women's chance of remarrying is about 45 percent higher in rural areas than in central cities. Minority women are more likely to remarry if they live in more affluent communities—with less male unemployment, less poverty, and lower rates of public assistance. Nonminority women are also more likely to remarry in communities that have fewer never-married women, which suggests that there is more competition for the pool of marriageable males. There are also regional differences: women living in the South are most likely to remarry.

It is not clear whether education benefits or hurts chances for remarriage. In one national sample, education did not clearly contribute to women's chance of remarrying.[23] In another study, however, women's chances for remarriage were lower if they were more educated and were employed. In contrast, education increased the likelihood of remarriage for men.[24]

Race is another relevant factor. African American women are the least likely to remarry (Figure 9–2); they wait longer between divorce and remarriage; they are more likely to experience the breakup of their second marriage; and their remarriages disrupt faster.[25]

"Redivorce" after Remarriage

The probability that a second marriage will break up has risen over past decades.[26] Fifteen percent of remarriages end within three years, and

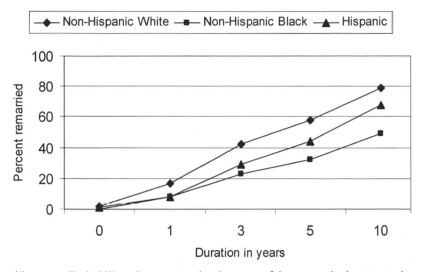

Figure 9-2. Probability of remarriage by duration of divorce and ethnicity in the United States, 1995. Source: Bramlett and Mosher, 2002.

almost a quarter end within five years. This means that at both the three- and five-year marks, second marriages are 5 percent more likely than first marriages to have ended. Second marriages also end more quickly than first marriages.[27] The median length of second marriages is seven years, compared with eight years for first marriages.[28] Apparently, people who have gone through one marital breakdown know the signs and don't wait to drag out the inevitable. As spouses age, the divorce rates of first marriages and second marriages converge.[29]

Risk Factors for Redivorce

Risk factors for a second divorce are similar to those for a first divorce. Table 9–1 shows the probability of a redivorce by the length of marriage and selected characteristics. Age is again a primary risk factor.[30] Although younger women are more likely and quicker to remarry, they are also more likely to redivorce. After ten years of marriage, younger women are about 15 percent more likely to have their second marriage end in divorce than women who were at least age

Table 9-1. Probability of second divorce by duration of marriage and selected characteristics

	Probability of Divorce	
	After 5 Years	After 10 Years
Total divorces	23%	39%
Race/ethnicity		
European American	23%	39%
African American	32%	48%
Latino	17%	29%
Age at remarriage		
Younger than 25	25%	47%
25 and older	22%	34%
Education		
Less than high school	27%	46%
High school	23%	38%
More than high school	20%	37%
Religious affiliation		
Any	22%	39%
None	29%	40%
Family of origin		
Intact two-parent	20%	33%
Other	27%	49%
Ever had forced sex		
No	20%	36%
Yes	29%	45%
Had children at remarriage		
None	18%	32%
One or more wanted	22%	40%
One or more unwanted	27%	44%
Ever had anxiety disorder		
No	20%	34%
Yes	29%	50%

Source: Bramlett and Mosher, 2002.

twenty-five when they remarried. This means that the divorce risk for women who remarry after age twenty-five is approximately equal to the divorce risk for first marriages; about a third have divorced before their tenth anniversary—whereas for younger women the risk is nearly 50 percent.

Redivorce—like divorce the first time around—is also more common for individuals whose parents divorced, who live in poor communities, who have low family incomes and limited education, who suffer from an anxiety disorder, and for women who have been raped. In contrast to first divorces, however, cohabitation before remarriage is not associated with an increased risk of a second divorce.[31]

The presence of children at the time of remarriage is associated with a slightly increased risk of divorce.[32] Stepfamily members must get to know each other and clarify their roles and relationships. The resulting uncertainties and stresses pose a risk for destabilizing the new marital relationship. In fact, whereas in first marriages the most frequent source of conflict is money, in second marriages the most common source of conflict is children.[33] Stepparents and parents fight about how the children should be disciplined, how family resources should be distributed, and how each parent gets along with the other's children.[34] However, although there is bickering and battling, these fights do not inevitably end in divorce. In fact, recent research has found that children in first marriages lower the quality of their parents' marriage and increase their risk of divorce more than stepchildren do.[35] It has been suggested that remarried people are more ready to leave an unsatisfying marriage than people who have married just once. They are experienced divorcers and see divorce as an acceptable—if painful—solution to marital problems.[36] Remarried people also may lack social norms for their roles; they tend to be poorly integrated with parents and in-laws. Remarriages usually lack the ritual joining of two families that the first big white wedding represents. Furthermore, people in remarriages, compared with people in first marriages, may have more of the personality characteristics that lead to divorce, such as neuroticism and impulsiveness.[37] Without change, these characteristics, which contributed to their first divorce, contribute to their second divorce as well.

Challenges and Strengths of Remarriages

Despite the fact that not all remarriages succeed, remarriage does offer a second chance for love, companionship, and a stable family life. So

Personal Story: Adjusting to New Circumstances and Relationships

I was seven when my mother remarried—and how lucky I was. My new stepdad was a wonderful man and best of all he brought along a brother and a sister who were my age. We moved into his big house with a pool. I instantly became best friends with my stepbrother. My new family also came along with a dog, "Jumper." I loved our life. It made me feel good that my stepdad said he would always be there to take care of me. This lasted until the night my stepsister blurted out that my stepdad had had an affair the week before he married my mom. The result was that my mom ended her second marriage five months after it began. The unraveling of her first marriage to my dad had been traumatic, and she was not going to live through another string of disappointments with my stepdad. I never saw my stepbrother again. This hurt. For a long time I kept asking to see him, but my stepdad did not want his kids to have contact with me after my mom divorced him. When I saw my stepdad, he was cold and distant. I tried to hold his hand the way I used to, but he shook it off and walked away, pulling a resistant Jumper along on the leash. I had also lost the privilege of petting the dog.

And then my father remarried. I thought it was a little weird that my stepmom was twenty years younger than my dad, but soon I discovered that her age had certain advantages. She was a lot more fun than my dad. We would go to the movies together (all the movies my dad didn't want to see) and she took me to the video arcades. She also often protected me from my dad's crankiness. So it was nice to have my stepmom in the house as an ally and a playmate. This lasted six whole years. Then my stepmom left my dad. She had found a nicer and younger boyfriend. When she left, she assured me that her differences with my father had nothing to do with me and that she would always keep in touch with me. I have never seen her again.

Now both my parents are on their third marriages, and there is another round of stepsiblings. My stepbrother on my stepfather's side is a year older than I am and really nice but nerdy. My two younger sisters from my stepmother's side are straight out of Cinderella. They wreck my room in my father's house when I am not there and are so noisy and demanding when I am there that I don't get much time with my dad.

My mother seems to be happy. In fact, she just announced that she is going to have a baby. That took my breath away. I don't know why. I have always wanted a brother or sister but now the thought stirs up tremendous anxiety. I think I should be happy but it feels like a blow to the gut. I have always had to adjust to whatever circumstances and characters were in my life. It wasn't just the stepparents and stepsiblings; I also had four sets of step grandparents and too many step uncles and aunts to count. None of them were chosen by me; I just got them. In my short life I have experienced many demands from strangers who descended on my life in a flash and instantly became intimately involved in it. I have experienced so many losses and betrayals, that the thought of one more new relationship is numbing.

are people in remarriages happier? Does remarriage solve problems of poverty and loneliness? Research on the psychological benefits of remarriage suggests that remarriage, by itself, does not make people happy. Some researchers have found that remarried people are less distressed than divorced single people.[38] Others have observed that remarriage is not related to psychological well-being.[39] Apparently, remarriage per se does not improve individuals' adjustment.

But perhaps *some* second marriages are better than first marriages. Just how are second marriages different? A potential strength of remarriage is that remarried adults may be wiser and more mature when they choose their second spouse. Research indicates that many people learn valuable lessons from their failed marriages and apply these insights in new relationships. They are more cautious in selecting a new partner and have more realistic expectations of marriage.[40] They may be more willing to compromise and more determined to succeed in their second marriage.[41]

Remarried couples are more likely to express negative emotions than couples in first marriages, and they report higher levels of disagreement and tension.[42] However, marital quality also improves some in remarriages. Both spouses tend to view their marital roles differently: men are less traditional in their gender roles the second time around, more willing to support their wife's interests, and more likely to share family responsibilities.[43] Couples in second marriages report that they share decision making and household labor more equally and that remarried husbands contribute more to housework than first husbands. They do more cooking, shopping, laundry, and cleaning.[44] Wives in their second marriages are more assertive and tend to seek more power than in their first marriages.[45] Several reasons have been suggested for this difference. Women's experiences in their first marriage and in their subsequent life as a single person give them more psychological resources and independence. Women also tend to bring more material resources to a second marriage, which increases their bargaining power.[46] Because financial independence is important to both spouses in second marriages, it is common for each one to maintain control over some of the resources they bring to the marriage.[47] Men are also more likely to make concessions during conflicts than they were in their first marriage. It appears that the distress men experienced during and after their first divorce raises their awareness of their own and their wife's emotional needs. This, in turn, appears to give wives more leverage in remarriages as compared with first marriages.[48] Women's power is further strengthened if they expressed a reluctance to get remarried and if they selected a husband who expressed more love than they returned.[49]

Perhaps the most frequently mentioned benefit of remarriage is the improvement in economic resources for women and their children. Although it is unclear whether men or women benefit more from remarriage in terms of psychological adjustment, it is clear that women benefit more financially.[50] Divorce has been consistently linked to postdivorce downward mobility and poverty for women; remarriage reverses this problem.[51] But one does not have to be poor to benefit financially: the positive economic effect of remarriage is even greater for high-income individuals than low-income ones.[52] Remarriage is not an unmitigated blessing in terms of finances; demands on the family purse are increased if the marriage brings with it both stepchildren and child support agreements from a previous marriage. Several states have passed laws that oblige stepparents to provide economic support for their stepchildren.

Stepfamilies

Stepfamily Demographics

According to a special report issued by the U.S. Census Bureau, 5 percent (3.3 million) of the approximately sixty-five million children younger than eighteen who live in the United States are stepchildren.[53] However, this underestimates the full count of stepchildren: children who live in single-parent families but have a remarried noncustodial parent are also stepchildren, and so (unofficially) are children living in cohabiting families; about a quarter of cohabiting couples in U.S. households have stepchildren.[54] Stepfamilies are diverse in their composition. One or both spouses may bring one or more children into the marriage, and some remarriages produce additional children, resulting in "his," "hers," and "their" children. Noncustodial parents on either or both sides add to the complexity, as do potential new spouses and their children. A stepfamily may be as simple as a unit of three—a widowed single mother with one child and a stepfather—or, more likely, given that most remarriages occur after a divorce rather than the death of a spouse, as complex as a clan of spouses, ex-spouses, children, stepchildren, siblings, and half siblings.

Societal Views of Stepfamilies

Throughout history and across cultures, stepfamilies have been maligned. Biological parents benefit from a positive bias regarding their intentions toward and investment in their children; stepparents, however, are more likely to be perceived negatively. We all know the stories—in fairy tales and our friends' accountings—of "wicked stepmothers" and "cruel stepfathers." Beliefs about unloved, mistreated, and neglected stepchildren permeate our culture and offer stepfamilies no positive guidance or social support for their roles.[55] The view that stepfamilies are deviant and potentially harmful for children is not only common in popular tales, negative stereotypes of stepparents also influence the attitudes and behaviors of helping professionals.[56]

Role Ambiguity

The lack of a social script for the stepparent role is compounded by an absence of legal protections.[57] For example, stepparents have no legal rights regarding their stepchildren after the remarriage ends through divorce or death.[58] This lack of a social and legal standing may lead stepparents to avoid close attachments and unreserved material investments in their stepchildren. Many stepparents feel that they have all the burdens of parenting without any rights. This feeling is likely to be aggravated if the children continue to maintain contact with their biological, nonresidential parents. Stepparents may take on parenting tasks—feeding, fetching, supervising homework—but their full participation may be thwarted. Policies and practices of schools are oriented toward biological parents and limit stepparent participation.[59] For example, although a stepmother may be a child's primary caretaker, she has no legal right to talk with the child's teacher about the child's performance or to see a child's report card. The stigma attached to stepparents may lead some to present themselves as biological parents.[60] Even within the stepfamily, members do not necessarily agree about what role a stepparent should play.[61] Expectations of parental love and caring may be high without the stepparent having the same decision-making rights as the biological parent. When both parents agree about the stepparent's role, stepfamily adjustment is enhanced and marital and parenting satisfaction is greater.[62]

Intricate Relationships

Not all remarriages include children from prior relationships, of course, and for the approximately 35 percent that do not, adjusting to a remarriage is pretty much the same as adjusting to a first marriage. But when children are involved, remarriage creates intricate challenges for the

Personal Story: Instant Family

My parents were divorced when I was two and my brother was one, and because we were so young we naturally stayed with our mother. But when I was nine and my brother was eight, our father remarried and our parents decided that it would be good for my brother and me to go to live with him and my stepmom. We became this little instant family. We got a cat and a dog, joined Scouts, and went to church. We looked like a family, but we didn't feel like a family. We did things together and had "family fun," but it wasn't "real." I always felt uneasy. I felt as if I had to ask if I could take a shower or get a snack from the fridge. It was as if I was out of place, a guest in what was supposed to be my own home. I had a part to play but I didn't know what it was. My brother and I were confused and out of control. This father person was very scary, and my stepmom, a huge threat. We hated her. Before the year was over, we were back with our mother.

family system. Stepfamily life is complicated by multiple roles and relationships, a variety of household structures, and new family rules that everyone has to learn.[63] As "outsiders" try to join with "insiders," alliances of parents and children may get in the way and impede the formation of new family bonds. Both adults and children must cope with constant transitions as children come and go between households.[64] In addition, as stepsiblings, step-aunts, step-grandparents, and step-friends join the family circle, parents and children must adapt to these new relatives and relationships while, at the same time, maintaining their relationships with existing kin.

A stepfamily is not like a "natural" family that grows gradually over the years. It is an "instant family"—yet it is often accompanied by the same high expectations as if it were a natural family, without the history of growing up together. Unrealistic expectations, hopes for instant love between stepparents and stepchildren, and fantasies of salvation from the losses and pain of the divorce create a hotbed of dissatis-

faction and disagreements.[65] Loyalty conflicts are frequent.[66] Adults
may find their loyalties divided between their children and their new
spouse, and children struggle to balance their loyalties between their
biological parents and their stepparents.

Being a stepparent is a difficult role. The original term "stepparent" referred to a parent who *stepped* into the place of a deceased parent. Nowadays, most stepfamilies are created by divorce, and there is
no vacant place to step into. This makes the stepparent an extra or
"spare" parent.[67] When two parents vie for the same role as either
mother or father, loyalty conflicts are increased, especially if there is
hostility between the two ex-spouses.[68] Stepfamily dynamics may also
negatively affect the relationship between children and their biological
parents. Not only loyalty issues, but also loss of the biological parent's
time and attention, resentment of the remarriage, problems around
discipline, and interparental conflict all add to problems in the child's
relationship with the residential parent.[69] In one study, when adult
children were asked to describe their experiences in their stepfamilies,
they focused particularly on the lack of parental attention and loyalty
issues. Contact with the noncustodial parent has been observed to diminish after the formation of a stepfamily, so this relationship is at risk
as well.[70] These problems in children's relationships with their biological parents are unfortunate because, no matter how many stepparents
are in the equation and no matter how wonderful they are, children's
relationships with their parents are more important for their wellbeing than their relationships with their stepparents.[71]

Stepparent-Stepchild Dynamics

Unlike parenting, stepparenting is not an institutionalized role or a
role to which people aspire.[72] As a result, many stepparents are poorly
prepared. Moreover, once they become stepparents, the role does not
become the core of their identity; they are more likely to find satisfaction in work, marriage, and raising their own children than in relating
to their stepchildren.[73] Not surprisingly, then, some stepparents are
more successful than others: some stepparent-stepchild relationships
grow closer over time, others grow more distant, and yet others become more negative.[74] Stepchildren tend to reject stepparents who

discipline and try to control them early on.[75] They are more affectionate toward stepparents who are supportive and persist in their efforts
to achieve closeness.[76] But like all social relationships, stepparent-
stepchild relationships are a two-way street. If stepchildren ignore the
overtures of their stepparents or treat them with disdain and resentment, stepparents are more likely to withdraw—an outcome that does
not promote stepfamily adjustment over time.[77] Persistent rejection of
the stepparent may lead to an unhealthy alliance between the biological parent and the child, emphasizing the stepparent's role as an in-
truder and undermining both the marriage and family functioning.[78]
Younger children are more likely than older ones to accept and adjust
to the presence of a stepparent.[79] Preadolescent and adolescent children typically have more independence and power in the family, and a
newcomer who interferes with their routines and their relationship to
the biological parent is more likely to be challenged. But regardless of
age, a pattern of hostile and resistant behavior when the stepparent
tries to connect with the child or assert some authority is associated
with stepfamily dysfunction.[80]

Stepfathers

Because, after a divorce, most children live with their mother, there are
more stepfather families than stepmother families, and, not surprisingly, most of the research on stepparents has focused on these men.
Stepfathers tend to see themselves as friends rather than parents, especially if the stepchildren are not living with them.[81] Compared with
biological fathers, stepfathers tend to be less involved; less nurturing,
affectionate, and warm; and less positive about their stepchildren, and
they engage in less supervision of them.[82] Evolutionary psychologists
have suggested that stepparents are less attached, protective, and involved with their stepchildren because they are not genetically related
to them; thus any investment in them would yield no biological pay-
off.[83] It is also plausible, however, that persistent opposition from
stepchildren is the key reason for stepfathers' lack of involvement. Either way, most stepfathers remain disengaged. Only about a third
gradually become more active and involved parents, and their stepchildren, especially their stepsons, benefit from this involvement.[84] Some

stepfathers withdraw from the disciplinarian role but develop a warm, friendly relationship with their stepchildren. They remain supportive of the mother's parenting efforts and leave the primary responsibility for disciplining to her.[85] Children have been found to adjust well to this limited but supportive and positive involvement.[86] This model may be best when full authoritative engagement is not possible.[87]

Stepmothers

Residential stepmothers represent only about 8 percent of all step-mothers.[88] In contrast to stepfathers, however, residential stepmothers are more likely to become the primary caretaker of their stepchildren. To the extent that traditional gender norms persist, women, more than men, feel compelled to take on responsibilities for the home, family caretaking, and their spouse's children. Stepmothers also face family and social pressures to perform as mothers. They are often expected to demonstrate loving and selfless caring toward their stepchildren but are simultaneously viewed as inferior to "real" mothers.[89] As one author poignantly said, "a stepmother must be exceptional before she is considered acceptable."[90] Not surprisingly, stepmothers are more stressed than biological mothers and stepfathers and less likely to assume a parental role.[91]

In a recent study, researchers examined how stepmothers defined their roles, the kinds of relationships to which they aspired in the step-family, and some of the conflicts they experienced as stepmothers.[92] Most stepmothers found themselves in one of three family types: "nu-clear," "extended," or "couple." The "couple" families were the most common and the most successful. These women placed their relation-ship with their husband first and their relationship with the stepchil-dren second. They believed that a strong and stable marriage would ul-timately benefit the children. They accepted the involvement of the biological mother in the children's lives, and left major decision mak-ing and discipline to the biological parents. They expected to be sup-portive toward their stepchildren as they built their friendships with them. In contrast, stepmothers in a "nuclear" type of family emulated the nondivorced nuclear family and tried to restrict children's contact with their biological mother. To foster their ideal of the nuclear family, they engaged fully in the parenting role and acted as full-service care-givers and disciplinarians. Stepmothers in an "extended" type of family focused their energies on the family system and on nurturing relations to extended kin. They did not seek to replace the biological mother but wanted to act as a coparent with her. Mothers in both the nuclear and extended families placed the marital relationship second and reported stress and tension if their families did not fully appreciate their efforts. Apparently, the well-intentioned efforts of stepmothers in nuclear and extended families were not enough to keep them, or their families, happy.

Recommendations for Stepparents

The challenges for stepfathers and stepmothers are quite similar and so are the ways that researchers recommend that they try to achieve func-tional stepfamily relationships. To ease the transition into stepfamily life and decrease tensions and promote positive relationships, re-searchers suggest, stepparents should tread lightly but consistently in their attempts to connect with their stepchildren; they should not withdraw when they experience rejection.[93] Many stepchildren be-lieve that stepparents should not act as parents; therefore, rushing in as a disciplinarian, expecting instant love, trying to replace the biological parent, or acting as the biological parent's equal, will not be well re-ceived.[94] Stepparents need to develop realistic expectations and offer positive and persistent involvement while steering clear of meddling and demanding. An affectionate bond untainted by discipline also re-duces the risk of competing with actively involved nonresidential par-ents and reduces sources of tension and loyalty conflicts for children.[95] Children fare better and remarriages are stronger when spouses focus on establishing a strong, supportive, and positive marriage.[96] Like-wise, stepfathers report greater marital satisfaction if they are not ex-pected to immediately bond with their stepchildren.[97] The steppar-enting role is challenging, but when it works, the successful adjustment of stepfamilies contains three lessons that are valuable for all families: how to deal productively with losses and changes, how to accept and appreciate differences, and how to promote positive rela-tionships by increasing efforts.[98]

Children's Well-Being in Stepfamilies

Research on stepfamilies has long been guided by a search for problems rather than a quest for strengths, and life in a stepfamily has been viewed as inherently problematic for children.[99] But are children in stepfamilies worse off than children in first marriages—or with divorced, single parents? Evidence is mixed.[100] Researchers have discovered that there is indeed an increased risk of behavioral problems and adjustment difficulties among children of stepfamilies compared with children in intact nuclear families; even a comparison with children in single-parent families yields some less favorable outcomes for stepchildren.[101] Stepchildren tend to leave home to establish independent households at younger ages than children from intact families. They are also more likely to have emotional problems such as depression. They get lower grades in school and lower scores on achievement tests, and they are less likely to complete school grades and more likely to drop out of school.[102] However, the differences between stepchildren and children in intact families—like the differences between children from divorced and intact families we discussed in Chapter 5—are small.[103] In fact, most stepchildren do well in school and do not suffer from emotional or behavioral problems.[104] These small effects indicate that there is a great deal of overlap between children in stepfamilies and children in nuclear families; indeed, the overlap is greater than the difference.[105] This means that a substantial number of stepchildren actually score higher on adjustment measures than the average child in an intact biological family.[106] Moreover, although the majority of stepchildren exhibit problems during a transition period immediately after their parent's remarriage, most show considerable resilience, and three-quarters have no long-term problems.[107]

Children's reactions to remarriage and stepfamily life vary depending on a number of factors, including the child's characteristics, the parents' behavior, and external stressors.[108] Children's age is particularly relevant for the adjustment process. Two-thirds of stepchildren are twelve years of age or older at the time of their parents' remarriage; fewer than 8 percent are younger than six.[109] These younger children, however, adjust more easily to their parents' remarriage. The stepparent-stepchild relationship is more challenging when children are tweens or teens. Adolescent stepchildren are at particular risk for externalizing problems, such as alcohol use, delinquency, premature sexual intercourse, and teenage childbearing. They also report more conflict with their stepparents than adolescents in intact families do with their parents.[110]

Gender differences in children's adjustment in stepfamilies are not entirely consistent. In some studies, boys have been found to have more problems than girls.[111] In others, the opposite is true.[112] However, the most consistent finding seems to be that remarriage is more difficult for girls. Because single mothers tend to be poorer monitors of sons' behaviors, which often results in a tense relationship between them, boys may gain from a relationship with a caring and involved stepfather. Daughters, however, may view the stepfather as an intrusion into their close and confiding relationship with their mother.[113] In adolescence, stepdaughters have more extended conflicts with stepfathers than stepsons do and are more likely to withdraw from them or reject them.[114] If a remarried father has a good relationship with his new wife, adolescent girls have poorer adjustment and less positive relationships with their stepmothers than adolescent boys do.[115]

Psychologists have speculated about the reasons for any adverse effects of growing up in a stepfamily. The most common explanations center on the stresses related to remarriage and stepfamily life; when parents remarry, it is stressful for both the adults and the children.[116] Many changes are involved, such as moving to a new residence, adapting to new household members, and learning new household routines and activities. These changes increase stress for children, which in turn leads to poorer performance in school and more emotional and behavior problems.[117] Furthermore, parental competencies may be compromised when forming a stepfamily and negotiating boundaries and roles.[118] Parents invest time and energy in their new spouse, and stepparents may need to attend to their children from prior marriages, thus reducing parental warmth, attention, and monitoring.[119] For younger children, maternal monitoring and control problems improve by about two years after the remarriage. For children who are adolescents at the time of remarriage, however, the situation is more difficult—perhaps because they are already coping with the transitions and stresses that accompany puberty—and they are at greater risk for long-

Personal Story: Afraid of Losing Mother

Five years after the divorce, my mother sat me down to tell me that she was getting married again. I got very upset and started to cry. I tried to talk her out of it, but she said that she had made up her mind. I am still not sure to this day why I got mad at her about getting re-married. I had known her boyfriend for four years and we always got along fine. I used to think that it was because he was trying to take my father's place. Now, I think it was because I was afraid of losing my mother. I had lost everybody else and I was just getting used to there being just the two of us. I did not want to have to share her with any-one else. I did not want anyone to steal my mother.

term problems in the mother-child relationship.[120] Eventually, the relationships of remarried mothers with their children tend to stabilize and return to a pattern similar to that of nondivorced mothers.[121]

Conflicts between divorced parents and among the members of the stepfamily contribute to adverse outcomes for stepchildren.[122] The reason that children from stepfamilies tend to leave home at earlier ages than other children is most likely the higher levels of stress and conflict they experience.[123] Stepchildren also are likely to withdraw as a way to keep peace in the family and for the sake of their own well-being.[124] Another explanation for the problems children in stepfamilies exhibit is the adverse experiences they encountered even before the remarriage, during the divorce and life in a single-parent family.[125] By the time they enter a stepfamily, they already have more adjustment problems, and these contribute to further problems.[126]

Summary

Most people remarry after divorce, and nearly half of all marriages are remarriages for one or the other spouse. Younger people are more likely to remarry than older ones, and men are more likely to remarry than women. Remarriage and stepfamily formation bring with them good news and bad news. The good news is that remarriage offers adults a second chance for marital happiness and a ladder out of poverty. Husbands in second marriages are more helpful around the house and more sensitive to their wife's emotional needs than they were in their first marriages; wives are more independent—psychologically and financially. The bad news is that remarriage is not a guarantee of happiness or affluence and it does not solve children's emotional or academic problems. Remarriage brings challenges and conflicts, especially when children are involved, and stepparents must assume roles that have no positive social scripts and that receive little support and respect. They have a fine line to walk in relating to their stepchildren, offering support and friendship but not parental demands—at least for a while.

Remarriages fail and sometimes dissolve, just as first marriages do—in fact, they end more quickly—and children bring into their stepfamilies problems and expectations that continue their legacy of divorce. Research that simply compares stepfamilies with intact families offers little guidance to individuals for making decisions about remarriage. Although remarriage poses a risk under certain circumstances, it also offers a substantive possibility of success. A more informative research approach would be to focus on examining the diversity of children's responses to parental remarriage and stepfamily life and outlining how risk and protective factors combine to influence child adjustment.

10

Divorce: The Future

What Psychologists Know

Public discussions of "what psychologists know" often pit extreme views against each other. The area of divorce is no exception.[1] Here, two debates have dominated. The first pits the view that divorce does irreparable damage to adults and children against the view that it doesn't really matter at all. In the first corner of this debate, are Wallerstein's clinically based claims of pervasive and permanent harm caused by divorce.[2] In the other corner is Judith Rich Harris's dismissal of divorce effects.[3] It is heredity, Harris claims, not experience in divorced families, that leads to problems.

The second debate is not *whether* divorce is damaging, but *how significant* the damage is. In this debate the opposite corners are represented by Wallerstein, who emphasizes negative outcomes of divorce, and Hetherington, who emphasizes resilience. Each of these important figures in the field of divorce research has spent the past three decades studying families that broke apart in the early 1970s. Wallerstein studied sixty families intensively over the course of her twenty-five-year study and compared them with adults who had grown up in intact families in the same neighborhoods. Hetherington looked at more than fourteen hundred families, of which more than one hundred participated in a twenty-five-year longitudinal study. Hetherington uses numbers and statistical analyses to support her conclusions; Wallerstein relies on probing clinical interviews. Hetherington concludes that most children and adults are able to adapt to divorce over a period of time, and, what is more, some of them even become stronger and able to cope with challenges because divorce has a steeling effect. Wallerstein concludes that even when they are capable and functional, individuals from divorced families are troubled. She focuses on how the children struggle with loneliness and anxiety and end up ill prepared to form their own intimate relationships. In her stories, children of divorce come to adulthood burdened, frightened, and worried about failure; they want love and commitment, but they're afraid they'll never get it.

Our own reading of "what psychologists know" leads us to reject the extremes of both of these debates. As far as the first debate goes, it is clear that some of the problems children and adults from divorced families end up with are not caused by the divorce; they reflect personal characteristics and family dysfunctions that are not part of the divorce process and indeed are most likely partly genetic. At the same time, some problems that children and adults develop are undeniably the direct result of divorce. As for the second debate, we see compelling evidence that the majority of children and adults survive the divorce and end up functioning in the normal range. But, at the same time, a sizable minority remain disadvantaged, and even those who are "in the normal range" typically have lingering regrets about the divorce. We have tried to be balanced in reporting the results of this enormous body of research, but in the end we conclude that divorce is not a good thing and its effects are large and pervasive enough that we should be concerned. At the same time, we believe that divorce can be the best possible alternative if it relieves both children and adults from pervasive and ongoing dysfunction.

On the basis of our reading of this literature, we suggest that the following are some important truths about divorce:

- One thing rarely causes a divorce; many factors lead to the marriage breakup. These factors—which include youth, lack of education, a troubled upbringing, and heavy demands from work and child care—heighten stress and overwhelm the couple's emotional and psychological resources.

Unrealistic expectations about marriage and family life, lack of preparation for parenting, and inadequate communication and negotiation skills amplify these risks. An attractive alternative to the marriage may provide the last straw.

- Effects of divorce are complex; divorce is neither universal panacea nor global disaster. Divorce does not have just two outcomes: winning or losing. There's winning, losing, and everything in between. The diversity of events precipitated by divorce and of people's reactions to those events is striking and suggests that factors other than divorce itself contribute to postdivorce adjustment or dysfunction.

- Both men and women suffer: it's a myth that men are the big winners in divorce. Although they may have fewer economic problems than women, they often have more severe emotional and physical reactions after the separation.

- Children may suffer more in the long run than either of their parents.

- Adjustment takes time. At first, people experience acute psychological symptoms, and these symptoms do not disappear overnight. For most people, they are still at peak levels a year or two after the separation, and even after these acute symptoms have subsided, some people have residual, long-term problems.

- The most critical factor for children's adjustment is the custodial parent's ability to provide consistent positive parenting, discipline, and nurturing. An involved, supportive, firm custodial mother can counter adverse effects of poverty and father absence.

- Developing a child custody arrangement is one of the most important tasks of divorce. Custody profoundly affects both children's and parents' lives, yet few divorcing parents appreciate its importance or are aware of how it will continue to be an issue for many years as their own and their children's needs change. There is no single type of custodial arrangement that is best for all families.

- Remarriage offers a second chance for marital happiness. If children are involved, however, the blending of families is a challenge for which parents and stepparents are ill prepared. Second marriages end in divorce even more quickly than first ones.

Research as a Basis for Policy

Divorce is a controversial social issue. On the one hand, conservatives want to focus efforts on finding ways to save marriages at any cost. They argue for policies that would make it more difficult for individuals to divorce.[4] On the other hand, liberals advocate a plurality of family forms—nuclear families, divorced and single parents, cohabiting unions. . . . When we extrapolate from the research "truths" that psychologists have discovered, we come up with two goals for policy that would please both conservatives and liberals: first, to reduce the incidence of divorce and, second, to diminish the detrimental effects of divorce on adults and children. What kinds of policies might achieve these goals?

Policies to Reduce Divorce

First, certain policies could strengthen marriages and reduce the risk of divorce. Without turning back the clock and making divorce more difficult to obtain, one can think of a variety of *workplace reforms* that could have this effect. Reducing workplace demands and increasing workplace flexibility would allow married people to give more attention to the needs of their families. Paid family leaves would reduce stress and help avoid crises when a child is born or a family member is ill. Flex time and part-time work—especially part-time work with benefits—would allow married couples to coordinate their schedules and free up time to take care of things at home. Affordable, good-quality child care would relieve some of the parents' child-rearing burden. Alternatively, social security and tax benefits for parents who want to stay home and care for young children would give couples more choice about whether they both need to work.

In addition to such external supports, there are *workshops, books, programs, and speakers* whose aim is to strengthen and repair marriage. For example, in Seattle, the Gottman Institute offers weekend workshops, video workshops, and numerous books on the "Art and Science of Love" based on three decades of marriage therapy research.

Policies to *help people prepare for marriage* also might achieve the goal of reducing divorce. Some such policies are already in place. In Oklahoma, couples get a discount when they buy a marriage license if they take a premarital relationship enhancement program (PREP) first, and those who take advantage of the offer, it seems, develop communication skills, experience greater marital satisfaction, and have lower divorce rates.[5] In Modesto, California, and Kansas City, Kansas, as part of the Community Marriage Policy, clergy won't perform marriage ceremonies unless the couple has undergone extensive premarital counseling; divorce rates have dropped 60 percent in those cities.[6] Most significantly, in 2004, the Bush administration announced plans to funnel a billion and a half dollars into training programs to promote healthy marriages. State and local government agencies, community organizations, and religious groups will be funded to develop marriage-promotion programs, especially for low-income couples, high school students, young adults interested in marriage, engaged couples, and married couples after a child is born.

Waiting periods have been proposed as an option to slow the marriage process and foster more deliberation because hasty marriages are at risk for divorce—consider Britney Spears's fifty-five-hour marriage.[7] If the law did not permit hasty marriages, couples might mull over their decision longer and then either just say "no" or take their vows more seriously. A waiting period would give the couple time to participate in a premarital program on the responsibilities of marriage and positive communication strategies. These proposals have been rejected as governmental infringement on an individual's right to make a personal decision; however, since governments infringe on individuals' right to divorce by having waiting periods for divorce, this is not a compelling argument.

"Covenant marriage" is a harder-to-get-into, harder-to-end form of marriage that couples can choose. It is intended to strengthen marriage by encouraging couples to consider their marital commitments more seriously before they tie the knot and restricting the grounds for

divorce thereafter. To obtain a covenant-marriage license, couples must have premarital counseling and agree that they will seek marriage counseling should problems arise. They can divorce, but it takes longer (at least two years, if they have children, instead of six months) and divorces are granted only if there has been abuse, adultery, imprisonment, abandonment, or two years' separation. Louisiana was the first state to allow citizens to choose covenant marriage, in 1997. Arkansas and Arizona have followed suit. Although fewer than 5 percent of Louisiana couples have actually gotten covenant marriages since 1997, there is considerable interest in the idea. One in five people—mostly women—who got married in standard ceremonies say that they would prefer to have gotten a covenant marriage.[8]

Another way of increasing the likelihood that couples will stay together is to *teach them about the difficulties they and their children will face if they get divorced.* Couples who are not in high conflict should be made aware that it may be better for their children if they can stay together.

Policies to Reduce Divorce Effects

If divorce is inevitable, then policies to help people deal with the breakup should be implemented. Divorcing couples need *support, advice, and information* to help them (and their children) deal with the complexities associated with separation. Families most at risk for problems—where conflict is high, children are young, and money is scarce—should be first in line to receive these services. For people with independent resources, "certified divorce planners," such as those trained by the Institute for Divorce Financial Analysts in Southfield, Michigan, are available to assist with the "exit process." To make the breakup as free of conflict as possible, couples can also choose to hire their own teams of child psychologists, counselors, lawyers, and personal divorce coaches—for example, those trained at the Collaborative Divorce Training Institute in Cupertino, California. Some couples hold clergy-attended divorce ceremonies to return their wedding rings and vow "to respect you as an individual," sometimes followed by a "divorce shower" in which friends and family bring gifts to replenish the newly single person's bare shelves. Any of these services could help couples through the separation.

Policies should not contribute to couples' conflicts. Couples who are in conflict should be offered *guidance to help them make decisions* as they go through the process of divorce. Certainly they should not be forced by the court into a custody arrangement that they don't want and won't be able to honor. In a few court systems in the United States, judges appoint "parenting coordinators," usually psychologists or social workers, to help divorcing parents resolve conflicts on day-to-day issues—from drop-off times to who washes the soccer uniforms—and teach parents communication skills so they can eventually work through such issues on their own.[9]

Parents need to *know the likely negative consequences of their divorce for their children*—which they inevitably underestimate. They need information about how to prepare their children for the breakup. They need to know what will help their children adjust and what will exacerbate their problems.

After divorce, policies that facilitate *long-term support for custodial parents* are essential. Divorced parents as well as married parents would be helped by family-friendly workplace reforms. In addition, custodial parents with money problems would benefit from health-care coverage for their children and any other kinds of financial assistance. All divorced parents would benefit from some psychological help, from places like The Center for Divorce Recovery in Northbrook, Illinois, or divorce recovery workshops offered in many communities and churches. *Divorce Magazine* and DivorceMagazine.com are also sources of help for "generation 'ex.'"

Policies to encourage *meaningful father involvement and financial support* after the divorce are important. This means more than giving dads visitation rights on Wednesday nights and alternate weekends. It means informing men—and their wives—about the kinds of contact and support that are most beneficial for children so that they can work out schedules and arrangements that facilitate them. As long as fathers are able to offer their children good-quality care, they should be encouraged to stay involved with them either by taking on custody or by providing "full-service" parental contact when they are together rather than limiting their activities to sporadic "Disneyland" encounters.

Policies should focus on *children's needs*. Children need to be considered in every divorce case—not just when the parents can't agree on custody arrangements and the court has to step in. The "best interests of the child" may not be served by just any custody arrangement. An "expert" should evaluate every custody plan. In the best of all worlds, courts, clinics, or a new agency just for this purpose would provide a place for divorcing parents to come together and make long-term plans for their children. The place would be staffed by knowledgeable people with psychological and mediation skills. Moreover, courts (or this new agency) would follow up later to review the effect of their decisions and orders.

Directions for Future Research

Although the library of divorce research books and articles is enormous and the array of possible divorce-related policies is vast, questions still remain that need to be answered by further research. Psychologists can follow a variety of approaches to answer these questions in the future.

Studies of Family Breakdown and Divorce Adjustment

The first approach is to study families in the real world as they deal with the disintegration of their marriages and the consequences that follow. In these naturalistic studies, it is important to investigate the processes going on in the family before the divorce, the changes in the family environment set in motion by the divorce, and the processes by which these events affect the children.

We need studies that are prospective and longitudinal, that begin before divorce and continue until children reach adulthood. We need studies that include multiple measures—measures of positive as well as negative outcomes, measures based on qualitative methods like clinical interviews as well as on surveys, and measures that tap multiple informants, not just mothers or children.

We need samples that are broad and representative. Previous research on the processes and effects of divorce has been "embarrassingly white and affluent."[10] We need to incorporate minorities—ethnic minorities and custody minorities, such as custodial fathers or children who end up with neither parent after divorce and have to live with a grandparent or in a foster home. We need to define groups carefully, not throwing intact and remarried families into the same group to compare with divorced families, for example.

We need to focus research efforts on examining the diversity of children's responses to parental remarriage and stepfamily life and outlining how risk and protective factors combine to influence children's adjustment.[11] Parents and stepparents will benefit from information that highlights the risk factors and describes the behaviors they should engage in to promote positive outcomes.

We need analyses that take account of diverse trajectories and patterns of outcomes, not just averages. We need analyses that include the total configuration of resources and stressors after a divorce, not just the presence or absence of particular factors. Understanding the contingencies under which divorce leads to diverse outcomes is a priority for future research. If we can identify those children who will experience difficulties, rather than assuming that divorce is damaging to all children, we can provide appropriate assistance and better use limited resources.

Studies of Different Kinds of Marriage and Divorce

Changes in the way we do marriage and divorce can offer researchers "natural experiments" that will help them understand divorce processes. One clear example of a natural experiment is afforded by covenant marriages. Does a covenant-marriage license actually translate into a stronger marriage? According to one study, after two years, the divorce rate among covenant couples in Louisiana was slightly less than half that of standard marriage couples.[12] The problem is, though, that certain people are attracted to covenant marriages; they are better educated, more affluent, and more traditional, with firmly held religious beliefs and no cohabiting or childbearing before marriage—just the kind of people who are less likely to divorce in the first place.[13] Because covenant marriage is "self-selected," comparing these couples will be no more elucidating than the typical correlational studies of marriage and divorce. What is needed is a way to simulate "random" assignment—by comparing covenant couples with comparable couples in other states that do not offer covenant licenses, for example. This would increase our understanding of how structural factors such as the ease or difficulty of obtaining a divorce affect the probability of divorce.

Studies of Mediation

To justify the time and effort of studying the effects of divorce mediation, it is critical to determine which aspects of the mediation process produce positive client outcomes. Rather than simply comparing mediation with litigation, therefore, it would be valuable to study variability *within* mediation procedures. In some programs, for example, mediation means one or two sessions; in other programs it means as many sessions as are needed until all issues are resolved. Some programs focus on child custody only; others offer guidance related to other issues of divorce and financial settlements. Training of mediators also varies from program to program. Before any general conclusions about the benefits of mediation can be drawn, it is necessary to assess and evaluate these variations.

A further consideration is the cultural diversity of mediation clients. The ethnic breakdown of mediation clients increasingly corresponds to the diversity found in the general population.[14] Such diversity highlights the importance of offering mediation programs that serve a multicultural clientele in a culturally sensitive manner. It is likely that different ethnic groups differ in their divorce experience and their needs for services; therefore, research to evaluate these needs would be helpful for the development of effective services for minority groups.

Studies of Marriage and Divorce Adjustment Programs

We cannot randomly assign people to get a divorce or to have joint custody, but we can assign them to programs designed to promote stronger marriages or to ease adjustment to divorce. Studies of the effectiveness of such programs hold great promise for the future—if they include careful assessments, control groups, and long-term follow-up evaluations. Although marriage and divorce programs are becoming more common, there is still a need for more careful studies.

The "Becoming a Family Project" is one of the few instances of a marriage promotion effort that has been rigorously evaluated. It was designed to support communication between partners as they made the transition to becoming parents—a period during which marital satisfaction often declines. Results showed that couples who took part, compared with couples who did not, reported less decline in marital satisfaction in the first two years of parenthood and were less likely to get separated or divorced in the first three years.[15] By the time the children had completed kindergarten, the divorce rate of program participants had caught up, but perhaps the positive effects of the program might have been maintained longer with periodic booster shots. Marriage promotion programs, thus, deserve and require further research.

Programs to promote divorced and divorcing parents' sensitivities and abilities also need further study. Although there are more than five hundred parenting programs for divorced individuals nationwide, few have been systematically evaluated.[16] Most are brief and court mandated. These programs range in length and intensity. One of the simplest is a pamphlet distributed to divorcing parents by the government in the United Kingdom.[17] The pamphlet has the following message:

- Conflict should be kept to a minimum.
- Children need the love, support, and reassurance of both parents.
- Children need clear information about what is happening and why and about what is being planned for their future.
- Children's wishes and anxieties need to be heard and acknowledged.
- Children do best if their parents can cooperate and if they can retain a relationship with both parents.

Both mothers and fathers who received the pamphlet said the information made them rethink how they were handling their divorce, and nearly three-quarters favored some kind of mandatory parenting advice or education.

A comparable effort in the United States is a newsletter for divorced parents.[18] Although this newsletter did not have much effect on divorced mothers' psychological well-being, there are reasons to continue to develop and evaluate such interventions: 47 percent of the mothers reported that they would use a newsletter, whereas only 16 percent indicated that they would participate in a meeting. Thus newsletters, and perhaps electronic communications, have the possibility of reaching many people and conveying useful information about the consequences of divorce.

Education programs for divorcing parents, which also present information about the effects of parental conflict and the benefits of cooperation, are available, too, and might be more effective.[19] Although these programs began less than a decade ago, they have already been mandated in a number of states. The early findings are encouraging and suggest that these programs may reduce levels of parental conflict, raise levels of cooperation, and lower relitigation rates.[20] The programs can be very brief. For example, the PEACE program (Parents' Education about Children's Emotions) involves only a single session, yet it appears to improve parents' ability to empathize with their children.[21] Participants in divorce education programs express a high level of satisfaction and believe that the programs are beneficial.[22] Most programs have not been evaluated, however, and when they are evaluated, most evaluations have not included control groups of divorced individuals who have not participated in the program. In one of the rare studies with a control group, a two-session program called "Children First," which used videotaped scenarios to facilitate discussion of how parents' behavior affects children, had limited success.[23] There was no difference in the likelihood of relitigation between couples who attended the program and those in the control group, but there was some suggestion that the program helped in families in which the risk of children being dragged into postdivorce conflict was high. Given the emotional complexities of divorce, we should not expect brief educational programs to make substantial differences. We need to investigate more extensive programs if we hope to achieve significant benefits.

More comprehensive postdivorce programs, with repeated sessions and more direct parent training, have a better chance of success. In one such program in Arizona, researchers evaluated a program for families with nine- to twelve-year-old children. The program focused on improving mother-child relationship quality and effective discipline, increasing fathers' access to the child, reducing interparental conflict, and improving children's coping skills. Compared with families in the control group, participants improved in relationship quality, parental discipline, attitudes toward father-child contact, and psychological adjustment.[24] Six years later, the adolescents who had participated in the program were less likely to be diagnosed with a mental disorder, had less severe psychological symptoms and behavior problems, and were less likely to use drugs and alcohol and to be sexually promiscuous.[25] These researchers have now conducted five such programs. Still, they recognize that additional research is needed to develop the most effective program, to extend the program to an ethnically diverse population, and to figure out how to deliver programs within existing community institutions.[26]

To lay readers who are searching for clear information that can be translated into usable strategies for the real world, the endless magazine articles and books on divorce, the reams of research, and the frequently inconsistent pronouncements of divorce experts must be bewildering. They may even question whether these authors are so heavily invested in their opinions and positions that "being right" takes the place of "getting it right." To prevent another decade of contradictions and uncertainties about critical issues like the effects of divorce on children and adults, child custody decision making, and the effectiveness of various child custody types, researchers should focus on processes rather than positions. They owe it to the vast audience of concerned citizens to measure, weigh, and evaluate the phenomenon of divorce carefully and objectively. If conscientious scientists conduct such research in the next decade, it will advance our knowledge of divorce and divorce consequences far beyond what psychologists know about divorce today.

Notes

Chapter 1. The Social Context of Divorce

1. The history of divorce is described in Day and Hook, 1987, and Einhorn, 1986.
2. As cited in Simmons, 1998.
3. Cherlin, 1983.
4. Thornton, 1989.
5. Parsons and Bales, 1955.
6. U.S. Census Bureau (2003b). Unfortunately, the numbers reported by the governmental agencies are incomplete. Not all states submit complete data. Most recently, California, Hawaii, Indiana, Louisiana, and Oklahoma were excluded from the statistics reported by the U.S. Census Bureau.
7. 5.3.
8. Goldstein, 1999.
9. Heaton, 2002.
10. 3.8; Sutton and Munson, 2004.
11. U.S. Bureau of the Census, 1992.
12. 2.2; U.S. Bureau of the Census, 1998.
13. 8.1.
14. Simmons and O'Neill, 2001.
15. U.S. Bureau of the Census, 1998.
16. Kreider and Fields, 2001.
17. Bramlett and Mosher, 2002.
18. U.S. Bureau of the Census, 1998.
19. Clarke, 1995.
20. Bramlett and Mosher, 2002.
21. Clarke, 1995.
22. Bramlett and Mosher, 2002.
23. Goode, 1993.
24. U.K. Census, 2001.
25. Homans, 1961.
26. Levinger, 1976; Sabatelli and Shehan, 1993; Thibaut and Kelley, 1959.
27. Thibaut and Kelley, 1959.
28. For example, Amato and Rogers, 1999; Braver, Wolchik, Sandler, and Sheets, 1993; Donovan and Jackson, 1990.
29. Bohannon, 1970.
30. Wiseman, 1975.
31. Wiseman, 1975.
32. Luthar and Cicchetti, 2000.
33. Dryden et al., 1998.
34. Brooks, 1994; Cicchetti and Rogosch, 1997; Werner and Smith, 2001.

35. Brooks, 1994; Dryden et al., 1998; Kirby and Fraser, 1997; Masten et al., 1999; Rutter, 1999; Werner and Smith, 2001.

36. Rutter, 1999; Kirby and Fraser, 1997.

37. Masten, 2001; Rutter, 1979; Luthar and Cicchetti, 2000.

38. Long-term consequences of parental divorce on children's development: Amato, 1999; children's ability to cope with divorce: Emery and Coiro, 1997; familial and extrafamilial factors associated with adolescent well-being in different family structures: Rodgers and Rose, 2002.

39. Bowlby, 1969, 1973, 1989.

40. Ainsworth, 1979.

41. Cassidy and Shaver, 1999; Paley, Cox, and Burchinal, 1999; Ryff and Singer, 2000.

42. Sperling and Berman; 1994; Hazan and Shaver, 1994.

43. Based on responses to the Adult Attachment Interview (AAI); George, Kaplan, and Main, 1984/1985/1996.

44. Bartholomew, 1997.

45. Hendrick and Hendrick, 1989.

46. Bartholomew, 1997.

47. Insecure attachment represents a risk factor for healthy development: Sroufe, 1988; insecure attachment may allow an adult to tolerate the loss of a relationship and feel comfortable without a significant relationship for an extended period: Bartholomew, 1997.

48. Ceglian and Gardner, 1999.

49. Berman, 1988; Birnbaum et al., 1997.

50. Donovan and Jackson, 1990.

Chapter 2. At Risk for Divorce

1. Nimkoff and Ogburn, 1934, p. 6.

2. Burgess, Locke, and Thomas, 1971, p. 7.

3. Aldous and Dumon, 1990, p. 1137.

4. Goode, 1993.

5. Cherlin, 1992; Kitson and Holmes, 1992; Popenoe, 1994.

6. The number of unmarried-couple households increased sevenfold between 1970 and 1994: Saluter, 1996; between 1990 and 2000, households composed of two or more unrelated people increased faster than family households: Simmons and O'Neill, 2001.

7. Spain and Bianchi, 1996.

8. Becker, 1981; Bumpass, 1990.

9. Bramlett and Mosher, 2002; Teachman, Tedrow, and Crowder, 2000; White and Rogers, 2000.

10. Sayer and Bianchi, 2000.

11. Becker, 1981.

12. Sayer and Bianchi, 2000.

13. Sen, 2002.

14. Ono, 1998; see also White and Rogers, 2000.

15. White and Rogers, 2000.

16. Bumpass, 1990.

17. Rogers and Amato, 1997.

18. Bramlett and Mosher, 2002.

19. Bramlett and Mosher, 2002; Bumpass, Martin, and Sweet, 1991; Feng et al., 1999; Martin and Bumpass, 1989.

20. Forthofer et al., 1996.

21. Clarke, 1995.

22. Kreider and Fields, 2001.

23. White and Rogers, 2000.

24. Conger et al., 1990.

25. Bramlett and Mosher, 2002; White and Rogers, 2000.

26. Korman and Leslie, 1985.

27. Cherlin, 1998.

28. Kreider and Fields, 2001.

29. Dillaway and Broman, 2001.

30. Bramlett and Mosher, 2002.

31. Amato, 2000a.

32. Cherlin, 1998.

33. Bennett, Bloom, and Craig, 1989; Bramlett and Mosher, 2002; Teachman, Tedrow, and Crowder, 2000; Schoen, 1995.

34. Oropesa and Gorman, 2000; Tucker, 2000, as cited in Bramlett and Mosher, 2002.

35. Dillaway and Broman, 2001.

36. Bramlett and Mosher, 2002.

37. Bramlett and Mosher, 2002; Shaw, Winslow, and Flanagan, 1999.

38. Bramlett and Mosher, 2002; South and Lloyd, 1995; Teachman, Tedrow, and Crowder, 2000.

39. Bramlett and Mosher, 2002.

40. *Elle*, 2004.

41. Call and Heaton, 1997.

42. Glenn and Supancic, 1984.

43. The influence of the Catholic Church on family life has declined since the 1960s: Thornton, 1985; Catholic women are less likely to divorce than non-Catholics: Bramlett and Mosher, 2002, for European American women.

44. Mahoney et al., 2001.

45. Adults who are affiliated with a religion are also less likely to engage in premarital sex and more likely to see marriage as a lifetime commitment: Treas and Giesen, 2000; and more likely to marry someone if they move in together: Bramlett and Mosher, 2002.

46. Call and Heaton, 1997.

47. Amato and Rogers, 1997.

48. Reiss and Lee, 1988.

49. Booth et al., 1995.

50. Call and Heaton, 1997.

51. Call and Heaton, 1997.

52. Chan and Heaton, 1989; Goode, 1956; Heaton, 2002.

53. Waite and Lillard, 1991.

54. Clarke, 1995.

55. Belsky and Pensky, 1989.

56. Bramlett and Mosher, 2002; White, 1990.

57. Amato, 1996; Wallerstein and Blakeslee, 1989.

58. Amato and Booth, 2001.

59. Terling-Watt, 2001.

60. Bramlett and Mosher, 2002; Keith and Finlay, 1988; Kunz, 2000; Terling-Watt, 2001; Wadsby and Svedin, 1992.

61. Amato and DeBoer, 2001.

62. Bramlett and Mosher, 2002.

63. Nelson et al., 2002.

64. Amato and Rogers, 1997.

65. Kitson and Holmes, 1992.

66. Dolan and Hoffman, 1998; Kitson and Holmes, 1992.

67. Terling-Watt, 2001.

68. Frisco and Williams, 2003.

69. Amato and Rogers, 1997; Betzig, 1989; Kitson and Holmes, 1992; South and Lloyd, 1995.

70. Ambert, 1989.

71. Cano and O'Leary, 2000.

72. Stanley, Markman, and Whitton, 2002.

73. Wadsby and Svedin, 1992

74. Gottman, 1994b; Gottman and Carrere, 1994; Carrere and Gottman, 1999.

75. Roloff and Johnson, 2002.

76. Carrere and Gottman, 1999.

77. Christensen and Shenk, 1991.

78. Gottman, 1998.

79. Gottman et al., 1998.

80. Hooley et al., 1987.

81. 115 studies; Karney and Bradbury, 1995.

82. Research converges on certain personality characteristics as risk factors for divorce: neuroticism and hostility in both husbands and wives: Kelly and Conley, 1987; Kurdek, 1993a; an inability to control impulses, especially in husbands: Kelly and Conley, 1987; Tucker et al., 1998; lack of conscientiousness: Kurdek, 1993a; Tucker et al., 1998; limited perseverance, and a propensity to get angry: Tucker et al., 1998.

83. Tucker et al., 1998.

84. Tucker et al., 1998.

85. Ryckman et al., 2002.

86. Whisman, Sheldon, and Goering, 2000.

87. Bramlett and Mosher, 2002.

88. Ceglian and Gardner, 1999.

89. Jocklin, McGue, and Lykken, 1996.

90. Prescott and Kendler, 2001.

91. Mazur and Michalek, 1998.

92. Kiecolt-Glaser et al., 2003.

93. Prescott and Kendler, 2001; Terling-Watt, 2001.

94. Paolino, McCrady, and Diamond, 1979.

95. Lester, 1997.

96. Power, Rodgers, and Hope, 1999.

97. Bloom, Niles, and Tatcher, 1985.

98. Booth, Johnson, and Edwards, 1983.

99. Joesch and Smith, 1997.

100. Lester, 1996.

Chapter 3. A Marriage Ends

1. Amato and Booth, 1996.

2. Hopper, 1993.

3. Braver, Whitley, and Ng, 1993; Braver and O'Connell, 1998; Furstenberg and Cherlin, 1991; Wadsby and Svedin, 1992.

4. Braver, Whitley, and Ng, 1993.

5. Wadsby and Svedin, 1992; Furstenberg and Cherlin, 1991.

6. Myers, 1989.

7. Blaisure and Allen, 1995; Gottman, 1994b.

8. See Weiss, 1975.

9. See Wiseman, 1975.

10. Wineberg, 1994.

11. Bloom, Hodges, and Caldwell, 1983; Booth and Amato, 1991; Hope, Rodgers, and Power, 1999; Richards, Hardy, and Wadsworth, 1997; Wertlieb et al., 1984.

12. McKenry and Price, 1991.

13. Bloom, Hodges, and Caldwell, 1983.

14. Spanier and Thompson, 1984.

15. Spanier and Thompson, 1984.

16. Neff and Schluter, 1993.

17. Power, Rodgers, and Hope, 1999; Richards, Hardy, and Wadsworth, 1997.

18. Power, Rodgers, and Hope, 1999.

19. Bloom, Hodges, and Caldwell, 1983.

20. Spanier and Thompson, 1983.

21. For similar distinctions, see Bohannon, 1970; Maccoby et al., 1992; Wiseman, 1975.

22. Vaughan, 1986.

23. Emery and Dillon, 1994.

24. See Weiss, 1975.

25. Continued attachment is related to increased emotional and psychological distress: Berman, 1988; Brown et al., 1980; Kitson and Holmes, 1992; and feelings of guilt: Walters-Chapman, Price, and Serovich, 1995.

26. Spanier and Casto, 1979.

27. See Weiss, 1975.

28. See Emery and Dillon, 1994.

29. See Emery and Dillon, 1994.

30. Emery and Dillon, 1994.

31. Maccoby et al., 1992

32. Pruett, Kline, and Jackson, 2001.

33. Perceived inequities in the court process lead people to be less satisfied with the final divorce decree: Sheets and Braver, 1996; and the child custody order: Brentano, 2001.

34. Arendell, 1986.

35. Braver, Cookston, and Cohen, 2002.

36. Spanier and Anderson, 1979.

Chapter 4. Adults in the Aftermath of Divorce

1. Weitzman, 1985.

2. Arendell, 1986, 1995; Cherlin, 1992; Day and Bahr, 1986; Kitson and Holmes, 1992; Lorenz et al., 1997; Peterson, 1996; Pollock and Stroup, 1996; Smock 1994; Stroup and Pollock, 1995.

3. Duncan and Hoffman, 1985; Furstenberg, 1990; Hoffman and Duncan, 1988; Holden and Smock, 1991.

4. Bianchi, Subaiya, and Kahn, 1999; Day and Bahr, 1986; Smock 1994.

5. Pollock and Stroup, 1996; Stroup and Pollock, 1995.

6. U.S. Bureau of the Census, 1998.

7. White and Rogers, 2000.

8. Booth and Amato, 1992; South, Crowder, and Trent, 1998.

9. Sun and Li, 2002.

10. Arendell, 1995; Weiss, 1984.

11. Serovich, Price, and Chapman, 1991.

12. McKenry and Price, 1991.

13. Nelson, 1995.

14. Hughes, Good, and Candell, 1993; McKenry and Price, 1991; Nelson, 1995; Albeck and Kaydar, 2002; Spanier and Thompson, 1984.

15. Hughes, Good, and Candell, 1993.

16. Simons, Johnson, and Lorenz, 1996; Gerstel, 1987.

17. Kitson and Holmes, 1992.

18. Albrecht, 1980; McKenry and Price, 1991.

19. Nelson, 1995.

20. Gerstel, Riessman, and Rosenfield, 1985; Wallerstein and Kelly, 1980b.

21. Spanier and Thompson, 1984.

22. McKenry and Price, 1991.

23. Spanier and Thompson, 1984.

24. Albeck and Kaydar, 2002.

25. Simons, Johnson, and Lorenz, 1996.

26. Hughes, Good, and Candell, 1993.

27. Bloom, Hodges, and Caldwell, 1983; Nelson, 1995.

28. Wallerstein and Kelly, 1980b.

29. Hetherington and Kelly, 2002.

30. McKenry and Price, 1991.

31. Wallerstein and Kelly, 1980b.

32. Anderson-Kheif, 1982; Norton and Glick, 1986; Fassinger, 1989.

33. Fassinger, 1989.

34. Huddleston and Hawkings, 1991b.

35. Cohen, 1995; Hetherington and Kelly, 2002; Hetherington and Stanley-Hagan, 2002.

36. Huddleston and Hawkings, 1991b; Wynn and Bowering, 1990.

37. Colletta, 1983; Hetherington, 1993; Hetherington, Cox, and Cox, 1982; Simons and Associates, 1996; Stolberg et al., 1987.

38. Hetherington and Kelly, 2002.

39. Amato and Gilbreth, 1999; Furstenberg and Cherlin, 1991; Hetherington and Kelly, 2002; Stephens, 1996.

40. Seltzer, 1991; Furstenberg and Cherlin, 1991.

41. Hetherington and Jodl, 1994.

42. Hetherington and Kelly, 2002.

43. Amato, 2000b.

44. Davies, Avison, and McAlpine, 1997; Hope, Rodgers, and Power, 1999; Kim and McKenry, 2002; Mastekaasa, 1994a; Rodgers, Power, and Hope, 1997; Simon and Marcussen, 1999; Thabes, 1997; Wu and Hart, 2002.

45. Hope, Power, and Rodgers, 1999.

46. Thabes, 1997.

47. Garvin, Kalter, and Hansell, 1993b; Weitoft et al., 2002.

48. Brockington, 2001; Cantor and Slater, 1995; Kposowa, 2000; Lester, 1994; Weitoft et al., 2002.

49. Cantor and Slater, 1995.

50. Spanier and Thompson, 1984.

51. Weitoft et al., 2002.

52. Magura and Shapiro, 1988; Power, Rodgers, and Hope, 1999; Proudfoot and Teesson, 2002; Weitoft et al., 2002.

53. Power, Rodgers, and Hope, 1999.

54. Amato, 2000b; Mastekaasa, 1994a; Wade and Cairney, 2000; Hope, Rodgers, and Power, 1999; Rodgers, Power, and Hope, 1997; Lucas et al., 2003.

55. Davies, Avison, and McAlpine, 1997; Johnson and Wu, 2002; Lorenz et al., 1997.

56. Cargan and Whitehurst, 1990; Kurdek, 1991.

57. Cargan and Whitehurst, 1990.

58. Hope, Rodgers, and Power, 1999; Johnson and Wu, 2002; Lorenz et al., 1997; Mastekaasa, 1994b, 1997; Rodgers, Power, and Hope, 1997; Wade and Cairney, 2000.

59. Johnson and Wu, 2002.

60. Lorenz et al., 1997.

61. They were twice as likely to have a friend move away, twice as likely to have a child involved with alcohol, six times as likely to move to a different residence, and six times as likely to be physically attacked or sexually assaulted; in the second and third years after the divorce, the number of stressful events dropped, but only slightly, to five.

62. Amato, 2000b; Tucker et al., 1996.

63. Weitoft et al., 2002.

64. Spanier and Thompson, 1984.

65. Bloom, Hodges, and Caldwell, 1983.

66. Kiecolt-Glaser et al., 1987, 1988.

67. Gallo et al., 2003.

68. Riessman, 1990.

69. Kitson and Holmes, 1992; Molina, 1999.

70. Arendell, 1986; Molina, 1999; Riessman, 1990.

71. Chiriboga and Catron, 1991.

72. Hetherington, 2003.

73. Amato, 2000b.

74. Chiriboga, 1982; Hetherington, 2003; Kitson and Holmes, 1992; Wang and Amato, 2000.

75. Wallerstein, 1986.

76. Chiriboga and Catron, 1991.

77. Kitson and Holmes, 1992; Hetherington and Kelly, 2002; Lorenz et al., 1997.

78. Amato, 2000b; Wallerstein and Kelly, 1980b.

79. Hetherington and Kelly, 2002; Kurdek and Blisk, 1983; Thomas, 1982.

80. Zavoina, 1997.

81. Chiriboga and Catron, 1991.

82. Chiriboga and Catron, 1991; Cohen, 1995; Richmond and Christensen, 2000.

83. DeGarmo and Kitson, 1996; Bloom and Clement, 1984.

84. Brown and Manela, 1978; Cohen, 1995; Kurdek and Blisk, 1983.

85. Wang and Amato, 2000.

86. Booth and Amato, 1991; Simon and Marcussen, 1999.

87. Kitson and Holmes, 1992.

88. Johnson and Wu, 2002.

89. Aseltine and Kessler, 1993; Wheaton, 1990; Kim and McKenry, 2002.

90. Thabes, 1997.

91. Kitson and Holmes, 1992.

92. Chiriboga and Catron, 1991.

93. Amato, 2000b.

94. Spanier and Thompson, 1983; Thiriot and Buckner, 1991; Waldron, Ching, and Fair, 1986; Wang and Amato, 2000.

95. Kiecolt-Glaser et al., 1988.

96. Sakraida, 2002.

97. Walters-Chapman, Price, and Serovich, 1995; Kitson and Holmes, 1992.

98. Hetherington and Kelly, 2002.

99. Johnson and Wu, 2002; Kitson and Holmes, 1992.

100. Chiriboga and Catron, 1991; DeGarmo and Kitson, 1996; Lorenz et al., 1997; Miller et al., 1998; O'Connor et al., 1998.

101. Thabes, 1997.

102. Chiriboga and Catron, 1991; Garvin, Kalter, and Hansell, 1993a, 1993b; Hetherington and Kelly, 2002; Waggener and Galassi, 1993; Zavoina, 1997.

103. Clarke-Stewart and Bailey, 1989; Burrell, 2002; Richmond and Christensen, 2000; Vaux, 1985.

104. Kitson and Holmes, 1992; Smerglia, Miller, and Kort-Butler, 1999.

105. Ginsberg, 1986.

106. Brown, 1982.

107. Spanier and Thompson, 1984.

108. Pett, 1982; Plummer and Koch-Hattem, 1986, for men; Thiriot and Buckner, 1991, for women; see Amato, 2000b; Hughes, Good, and Candell, 1993.

109. Hughes, Good, and Candell, 1993.

110. Bursik, 1991a, 1991b; Thabes, 1997.

111. Daniels-Mohring and Berger, 1984; Hughes, Good, and Candell, 1993; Thiriot and Buckner, 1991.

112. Spanier and Thompson, 1984.

113. Spanier and Thompson, 1983, 1984; Thabes, 1997.

114. Leslie and Grady, 1988.

115. Thabes, 1997.

116. Picard, Lee, and Hunsley, 1997.

117. Ginsberg, 1986; Isaacs and Leon, 1986; Picard, Lee, and Hunsley, 1997; Spanier and Thompson, 1984.

118. Isaacs and Leon, 1986; Picard, Lee, and Hunsley, 1997.

119. Anderson-Kheif, 1982.

120. Halem, 1982.

121. Contact with in-laws is infrequent: Picard, Lee, and Hunsley, 1997; contact with in-laws predicts adjustment: Gander and Jorgensen, 1990; Spanier and Thompson, 1984; Stone, 2002.

122. Chiriboga and Catron, 1991; Menaghan and Lieberman, 1986.

123. Sansom and Farnill, 1997.

124. See Amato 2000b; Hetherington and Kelly, 2002.

125. Ginsberg, 1986; McKenry and Price, 1991.

126. Facchino and Aron, 1990.

127. Spanier and Thompson, 1984; Tschann, Johnston, and Wallerstein, 1989.

128. Hetherington and Kelly, 2002.

129. Wang and Amato, 2000; see Amato, 2000b; Stone, 2002.

130. Results concerning cohabitation: Kurdek, 1991; Mastekaasa, 1994b; Thabes, 1997; results concerning remarriage: Johnson and Wu, 2002; Wang and Amato, 2000.

131. Results concerning support groups: Colburn, Lin, and Moore, 1992; psychotherapy: Thabes, 1997; newsletter: Hughes et al., 1994.

132. Kitson and Holmes, 1992; White and Bloom, 1981.

133. Byrne, 1990; Goethal et al., 1983; Lee and Hett, 1990; Lee, Picard, and Blain, 1994.

134. Palamattathil, 2002.

135. Hetherington and Kelly, 2002; Kitson and Holmes, 1992.

136. Clarke-Stewart and Bailey, 1989; Duffy, Thomas, and Trayner, 2002; Greif, 1985.

137. See Amato, 2000b; Booth and Amato, 1991; Garvin, Kalter, and Hansell, 1993b; Kitson and Holmes, 1992; Shapiro, 1996; Simons, Johnson, and Lorenz, 1996; Thabes, 1997; Wang and Amato, 2000; Zavoina, 1997.

138. Belle, 1990.

139. Plummer and Koch-Hattem, 1986.

140. Braver et al., 1989; Menaghan and Lieberman, 1986; Tschann, Johnston, and Wallerstein, 1989.

141. Booth and Amato, 1992.

142. Hetherington and Kelly, 2002.

143. Thiriot and Buckner, 1991.

144. Kitson and Holmes, 1992; Weitoft et al., 2002.

145. Clarke-Stewart and Bailey, 1989.

146. Anderson-Kheif, 1982.

147. Pett and Vaughan-Cole, 1986.

148. Greif, 1985.

149. Spanier and Thompson, 1984.

150. Hemstroem, 1996; Johnson and Wu, 2002; Lorenz et al., 1997.

151. Wadsby and Svedin, 1992.

152. See Amato, 2000b; Clarke-Stewart and Bailey, 1989; Thiriot and Buckner, 1991.

153. Waldron, Ching, and Fair, 1986.

154. Mauldin, 1991.

155. Stone, 2002.

156. Hetherington and Kelly, 2002.

157. Wallerstein, 1986.

158. Wang and Amato, 2000.

159. Kurdek and Blisk, 1983.

160. Kitson and Holmes, 1992; Masheter, 1991.

161. Ahrons, 1986; Goodman 1993.

162. Maccoby, Depner, and Mnookin, 1990.

163. Ahrons, 1986.

164. Hardesty, 2002.

165. Shalansky, Ericksen, and Henderson, 1999.

166. Arendell, 1995.

167. Toews, McKenry, and Catlett, 2003.

168. Isaacs and Leon, 1988.

169. Thabes, 1997.

170. Ehrenberg, 1996; Ahrons and Rodgers, 1987; Bursik, 1991a, 1991b; Stone, 2002; Thiriot and Buckner, 1991.

171. Madden-Derdich, Leonard, and Christopher, 1999; Emery, 1994.

172. Masheter, 1997.

173. Goodman, 1993.

174. Tschann, Johnson, and Wallerstein, 1989; Masheter, 1991.

175. Masheter, 1997.

176. Hetherington, Cox, and Cox, 1978.

177. Isaacs and Leon, 1988.

178. Arendell, 1995.

179. See Amato, 2000b; Maciejewski, Prigerson, and Mazure, 2001; Kim and McKenry, 2002.

180. Riessman, 1990; Chase-Lansdale and Hetherington, 1990.

181. Zeiss, Zeiss, and Johnson, 1980.

182. Cantor and Slater, 1995; Kposowa, 2000; Lester, 1994.

183. Wu and Hart, 2002; Riessman and Gerstel, 1985; Bloom and Caldwell, 1981.

184. Divorced men had excess mortality compared with married men of 143 percent versus 63 percent for women: Hemstroem, 1996.

185. Hetherington, 2003.

186. Chiriboga and Catron, 1991; Braver, Whitley, and Ng, 1993; Colburn, Lin, and Moore, 1992; Wallerstein, 1986.

187. Colburn, Lin, and Moore, 1992; Wadsby and Svedin, 1992; Spanier and Thompson, 1984.

188. Kitson and Holmes, 1992; Riessman and Gerstel, 1985.

189. Gander and Jorgensen, 1990; Kurdek, 1991.

190. Kessler and McRae, 1984; Strickland, 1992.

191. Aseltine and Kessler, 1993; Marks and Lambert, 1998; Simon and Marcussen, 1999.

192. Clarke-Stewart and Bailey, 1989.

193. Chiriboga and Catron, 1991.

194. Wallerstein, 1985.

195. Bevvino, 2000; Bloom and Hodges, 1981; Caldwell, Bloom, and Hodges, 1983; Wadsby and Svedin, 1992.

196. Colburn, Lin, and Moore, 1992.

197. Hetherington, 2003.

198. Wadsby and Svedin, 1992.

199. Wallerstein, 1986.

200. Arendell, 1995; Vaux, 1985.

201. Men lose their confidant: Gerstel, Riessman, and Rosenfield, 1985; Riessman and Gerstel, 1985; women's friendships become more intense: Albeck and Kaydar, 2002.

202. Hetherington and Kelly 2002; Vaux, 1985; Wadsby and Svedin, 1992.

203. Wadsby and Svedin, 1992.

204. Women maintain old relationships: Gerstel, 1988; Wadsby and Svedin, 1992; men move and suffer: Asher and Bloom, 1983.

205. Burrell, 2002.

206. McKenry and Price, 1991.

207. Gerstel, 1987.

208. Gerstel, 1988.

209. Burrell, 2002.

210. Hetherington and Kelly, 2002.

211. Plummer and Koch-Hattem, 1986.

212. Plummer and Koch-Hattem, 1986.

213. Spanier and Thompson, 1984.

214. O'Brien, 1987; Riessman and Gerstel, 1985.

215. Men date more often: Petronio and Endres, 1986; men have more partners: Neff and Mantz, 1998.

216. McKenry and Price, 1991.

217. Spanier and Thompson, 1984.

218. Hetherington and Kelly, 2002.

219. National Center for Health Statistics, 1992; U.S. Bureau of the Census, 1992.

220. On average, men receive 22 percent more support than women; Burrell, 2002.

221. Colburn, Lin, and Moore, 1992.

222. Seltzer and Brandreth, 1995.

223. The proportion of father custody has increased: Furstenberg and Cherlin, 1991; fewer than 12 percent of fathers have custody: U.S. Bureau of the Census, 1998.

224. Shapiro, 2003.

225. Anderson-Kheif, 1982.

226. Baum, 2003.

227. Dudley, 1996; Kitson and Holmes, 1992.

228. Weitzman, 1985.

229. Prengle, 1999.

230. Dudley, 1996.

231. Anderson-Kheif, 1982.

232. Anderson-Kheif, 1982; Leite and McKenry, 2003.

233. Arendell, 1995; Lehr and MacMillan, 2001.

234. Umberson and Williams, 1993.

235. Hemstroem, 1996.

236. Hetherington and Kelly, 2002.

237. Hetherington, 1993; Hetherington and Kelly, 2002; Simons and Associates, 1996.

238. Hetherington and Kelly, 2002.

239. Mothers make less progress up the ladder: Airsman and Sharda, 1993; are less likely to move out of poverty: Mauldin, 1991.

240. Spanier and Thompson, 1984; Wallerstein, 1986.

241. Gasser and Taylor, 1976.

242. Hetherington, 1993; Simons and Associates, 1996; Cohen, 1995; Shapiro and Lambert, 1999.

243. Hammond and Muller, 1992.

244. Amato, 2000b; Garrison, 1994; Norton and Glick, 1986.

245. Wallerstein and Kelly, 1980b.

246. Hetherington and Kelly, 2002.

247. Bianchi, Subaiya, and Kahn, 1999.

248. Bloom, Hodges, and Caldwell, 1983; Weitzman, 1985.

249. Clarke-Stewart and Bailey, 1989.

250. Furstenberg and Cherlin, 1991.

251. U.S. Bureau of the Census, 1992.

252. Arendell, 1995.

253. Arendell, 1986.

254. Wallerstein and Kelly, 1980b; Weitzman, 1985.

255. Coney and Mackey, 1989.

256. Sheets and Braver, 1996.

257. Anderson-Kheif, 1982.

258. Cohen, 1995; Gelles, 1989; Gerstel, Riessman, and Rosenfield, 1985; Hilton and Desrochers, 2000; Hope, Power, and Rodgers, 1999; Hope, Rodgers, and Power, 1999; Johnson and Wu, 2002; Madden-Derdich, Leonard, and Christopher, 1999; Menaghan and Lieberman, 1986; Shapiro, 1996.

259. Kolevzon and Gottlieb, 1983; Lindsay and Scherman, 1987.

260. Lamb, Sternberg, and Thompson, 1999; Plummer and Koch-Hattem, 1986; Spanier and Thompson, 1983.

261. Hetherington, 2003; Wallerstein, 1985.

262. Booth and Amato, 1991; Chiriboga and Catron, 1991; Lorenz et al., 1997; Spivey and Scherman, 1980.

263. Kitson and Holmes, 1992; Lorenz et al., 1997; Spivey and Scherman, 1980.

264. Chiriboga and Catron, 1991.

265. Kitson and Holmes, 1992; Lorenz et al., 1997.

266. Aseltine and Kessler, 1993; DeGarmo and Kitson, 1996; Gray and Silver, 1990; Mastekaasa, 1995; Wang and Amato, 2000; Woody et al., 1984.

267. Johnson and Wu, 2002.

268. Amato, 2000a.

269. Kitson and Holmes, 1992.

270. Huddleston and Hawkings, 1991a, p. 204.

271. Duffy, Thomas, and Trayner, 2002.

272. Lamb, Sternberg, and Thompson, 1999.

273. Wallerstein, 1986; Wallerstein and Blakeslee, 1989; Wallerstein, Lewis, and Blakeslee, 2000.

274. Hetherington, 2003.

Chapter 5. Effects of Divorce on Children

1. Ahlburg and DeVita, 1992; Bumpass, 1984; Wolchik, Sandler et al., 2002.

2. Amato, 1994a, 2000b, 2001.

3. Amato and Keith, 1991b.

4. Amato, 2001.

5. National Longitudinal Survey of Youth: Emery et al., 1999; National Study of Families and Households: Hanson, 1999; High School and Beyond Study: Astone and McLanahan, 1991; British National Longitudinal Study: Cherlin et al., 1991.

6. Hetherington and Clingempeel, 1992.

7. Parent reports: Guidubaldi and Cleminshaw, 1985; child reports: Walczak and Burns, 1984.

8. Leaverton, 1977.

9. Emery, 1999b.

10. Francke, 1983.

11. Laumann-Billings and Emery, 2000.

12. Solomon and George, 1999.

13. Clarke-Stewart et al., 2000.

14. Walczak and Burns, 1984.

15. Mazur, 1993.

16. Pruett et al., 2003.

17. Arendell, 1986.

18. Wallerstein and Kelly, 1980b.

19. Herman and Bretherton, 2001.

20. Pruett and Pruett, 1999.

21. Kurdek and Siesky, 1979.

22. Hetherington, Cox, and Cox, 1982; Peretti and di Vitorrio, 1993; Wallerstein, 1983; Wallerstein and Kelly, 1980b.

23. Pett et al., 1999; Hodges, Tierney, and Buchsbaum, 1984.

24. Peretti and di Vitorrio, 1993; Pruett et al., 2003; Wallerstein, 1983; Wallerstein and Kelly, 1980b.

25. Neal, 1983.

26. Hingst, 1981.

27. Drapeau, Samson, and Saint-Jacques, 1999.

28. Hoyt et al., 1990.

29. Wallerstein, 1984; Hingst, 1981.

30. Hingst, 1984; Wallerstein, 1983; Wallerstein and Kelly, 1980b.

31. Bonkowski, Boomhower, and Bequette, 1985.

32. Drapeau, Samson, and Saint-Jacques, 1999.

33. Weyer and Sandler 1998.

34. Amato 2001; Amato and Keith 1991b. See also Call, Beer, and Beer, 1994; Downey, 1994.

35. Guidubaldi, Perry, and Nastasi, 1987b; Guidubaldi and Duckworth, 2001.

36. Allison and Furstenberg, 1989; Hetherington and Clingempeel, 1992; Hoyt et al., 1990.

37. Hetherington and Clingempeel, 1992.

38. Bergman, El-Khouri, and Magnusson, 1987.

39. Springer and Wallerstein, 1983.

40. Burns and Dunlop, 1999.

41. Springer and Wallerstein, 1983; Workman and Beer, 1992.

42. Walczak and Burns, 1984.

43. Reinhard, 1977.

44. Wallerstein, 1983.

45. Springer and Wallerstein, 1983.

46. Wallerstein and Kelly, 1980b.

47. Brubeck and Beer, 1992; Jeynes, 1998; Sun and Li, 2002.

48. Simons and Associates, 1996.

49. McLanahan, 1999.

50. Forehand, Middleton, and Long, 1987; Forehand et al., 1991; Hetherington and Clingempeel, 1992.

51. Peterson and Zill, 1986.

52. Hetherington and Clingempeel, 1992; Workman and Beer, 1992.

53. Kirby, 2002; Simons and Associates, 1996.

54. Simons and Associates, 1996.

55. Kirby, 2002; Turner, Irwin, and Millstein, 1991.

56. Brubeck and Beer, 1992; Forehand et al., 1991; Hetherington and Clingempeel, 1992; Peterson and Zill, 1986; Kirby, 2002; Simons and Associates, 1996; Simons et al., 1999.

57. Brubeck and Beer, 1992; Kirby, 2002; Sun and Li, 2002.

58. Simons and Associates, 1996; Simons et al., 1999.

59. Bonkowski, 1989.

60. Pryor, 1999.

61. Rodgers, Power, and Hope, 1997.

62. Rodgers, 1994.

63. Furstenberg and Kiernan, 2001.

64. Amato, 2001.

65. Amato and Keith, 1991a.

66. Amato, 2001.

67. Emery, 1999b.

68. Results concerning psychological help: Zill, Morrison, and Coiro, 1993; skipping school, getting suspended, getting in trouble with the police: Hanson, 1999; dropping out of high school, getting pregnant, being out of work: McLanahan and Sandefur, 1994; getting a divorce: Amato and DeBoer, 2001; distress and depression in childhood: Harland et al., 2002; distress and depression in adulthood: Rodgers, Power, and Hope, 1997.

69. Harland et al., 2002.

70. Weitoft et al., 2003.

71. Hanson, 1999.

72. Wallerstein and Kelly, 1980b; Lewis and Wallerstein, 1987; Wallerstein, Lewis, and Blakeslee, 2000.

73. Isaacs, Leon, and Donohue, 1986.

74. Amato and Keith, 1991a.

75. Results concerning behavior problems: Morrison and Cherlin, 1995; adjustment problems, physical symptoms, social relationships: Walczak and Burns, 1984; adjustment problems: Wolchik, Sandler et al., 2002; school dropout: Zill, Morrison, and Coiro, 1993; school dropout, teen childbirth: McLanahan, 1999.

76. Hetherington and Kelly, 2002.

77. Hetherington and Kelly, 2002; McLanahan, 1999; Zill, Morrison, and Coiro, 1993.

78. Amato, 2003.

79. Lamb, Sternberg, and Thompson, 1999.

80. Allison and Furstenberg, 1989; Harland et al., 2002.

81. Quinlivan et al., 2004.

82. Hetherington and Kelly, 2002.

83. Amato, 2000b.

84. Burns and Dunlop, 1999; Wallerstein and Kelly, 1980b; Wallerstein and Blakeslee, 1989.

85. Harland et al., 2002; Wallerstein and Blakeslee, 1989.

86. Harland et al., 2002.

87. Amato and Keith, 1991b.

88. Burns and Dunlop, 1999.

89. Amato and Keith, 1991b; Forehand et al., 1991.

90. Kaye, 1988–89; Sun and Li, 2002.

91. McLanahan and Sandefur, 1994.

92. Amato and Keith, 1991b; Forehand et al., 1991; Pagani et al., 1997.

93. Wallerstein, 1984; Wallerstein and Kelly, 1980b.

94. Wallerstein and Corbin, 1989.

95. Guidubaldi, Perry, and Nastasi, 1987b.

96. Wallerstein and Lewis, 1998.

97. Fergusson, Horwood, and Lynskey, 1994; Furstenberg and Teitler, 1994; Wallerstein and Lewis, 1998; Kiernan and Hobcraft, 1997; McLanahan, 1999.

98. Hetherington, 2003; Hetherington and Kelly, 2002.

99. McLanahan, 1999.

100. Fergusson, Horwood, and Lynskey, 1994.

101. Wolchik, Sandler et al., 2002.

102. Fergusson, Horwood, and Lynskey, 1994; Furstenberg and Teitler, 1994; Hetherington, 2003; Hetherington and Kelly, 2002; Wallerstein and Lewis, 1998; Neher and Short, 1998.

103. Furstenberg and Teitler, 1994; McLanahan, 1999.

104. Amato, 1999.

105. Amato and Keith, 1991b. See also Amato, 1999; Amato and Booth, 1991; Amato and Keith, 1991a.

106. Brennan and Shaver, 1998; Chase-Lansdale, Cherlin, and Kiernan, 1995; Cherlin, Chase-Lansdale, and McRae, 1998; Rodgers, Power, and Hope, 1997.

107. They are troubled, impulsive, and irresponsible: Hetherington and Kelly, 2002; more likely to be aggressive and commit crimes: Amato and Keith, 1991b; Dixon, Charles, and Craddock, 1998; Furstenberg and Teitler, 1994; Juby and Farrington, 2001;

more likely to abuse substances: Furstenberg and Teitler, 1994; Hope, Power, and Rodgers, 1998.

108. Zill, Morrison, and Coiro, 1993.

109. For example, Wallerstein and Lewis, 1998.

110. Amato, 1999; Amato and Keith, 1991b; Ross and Mirowsky, 1999; Feng et al., 1999; Furstenberg and Teitler, 1994; McLanahan, 1999.

111. Ross and Mirowsky, 1999; Jacquet and Surra, 2001.

112. Brennan and Shaver, 1998; Summers et al., 1998; Walker and Ehrenberg, 1998; Hetherington, 2003; Ross and Mirowsky, 1999.

113. Walker and Ehrenberg, 1998. It is particularly problematic for a relationship if the woman's parents are divorced. Women with divorced parents are less satisfied with their romantic relationships, and this dissatisfaction may show up in nagging and criticizing: Jacquet and Surra, 2001. In one study, engaged couples were videotaped discussing two areas of conflict. Couples in which the woman's parents were divorced were more negative in their communication (it didn't seem to matter if the man's parents were divorced): Sanders, Halford, and Behrens, 1999.

114. Wallerstein, Lewis, and Blakeslee, 2000.

115. Amato, 1999; Amato and Keith, 1991a; Ross and Mirowsky, 1999. This is especially so when the wife (or both spouses) has experienced the dissolution of her parents' marriage: Amato, 1996.

116. Amato and DeBoer, 2001.

117. Amato and Keith, 1991a.

118. Amato and Booth, 1991; Amato, 1999; Hetherington, 2003.

119. Amato and Keith 1991a; Luecken and Fabricius, 2003.

120. Tucker et al., 1997.

121. Hetherington and Kelly, 2002.

Chapter 6. What Causes Children's Problems?

1. Lamb, Sternberg, and Thompson, 1999, p. 127.
2. Wallerstein and Kelly, 1980; Jacobson, 1978a.
3. Ducibella, 1995; Waldron, Ching, and Fair, 1986.
4. Walker, 2003.
5. Wallerstein and Kelly, 1980b.
6. Mitchell, 1985; Jacobson, 1978a; Walczak and Burns, 1984.
7. Kurdek and Siesky, 1979.
8. Hingst, 1984;. Mazur, 1993; Pruett and Pruett, 1999; Walczak and Burns, 1984.
9. Mazur, 1993; Kalter and Plunkett, 1984.
10. Hoffman and Avila, 1998.
11. Kalter and Plunkett, 1984.
12. Kurdek and Siesky, 1979.
13. Wallerstein and Kelly, 1980b.
14. Children are confused: Copeland, 1985; kept in the dark: Duran-Aydintug, 1997; see no reason for the divorce: Amato, 2001; Grych and Fincham, 1990; fear abandonment: Kurdek and Berg, 1987; Wolchik, Tein et al., 2002.
15. Kim, Sandler, and Tein, 1997.

16. McLanahan, 1999.

17. Emery, 1999b; McLanahan, 1999.

18. Drapeau, Samson, and Saint-Jacques, 1999.

19. Anthony, 1997.

20. Drapeau, Samson, and Saint-Jacques, 1999.

21. Wallerstein and Kelly, 1980b.

22. South, Crowder, and Trent, 1998.

23. McLanahan, 1999.

24. Bumpass, 1984; McLanahan, 1999; Morrison and Cherlin, 1995.

25. U.S. Census Bureau, 2003a.

26. McLanahan, 1999.

27. See Amato, 2000; Booth and Amato, 1991; Garvin, Kalter, and Hansell, 1993b; Kitson and Holmes, 1992; Shapiro, 1996; Simons, Johnson, and Lorenz, 1996; Thabes, 1997; Wang and Amato, 2000; Zavoina, 1997; Hilton and Desrochers, 2000.

28. That is, lack of economic resources statistically "mediates" the effect of divorce on these outcomes: behavior problems: Carlson and Corcoran, 2001; depressed mood: Aseltine, 1996; test scores in math, science, reading, and social studies, less self-esteem: Sun and Li, 2002; school performance: Downey, 1994.

29. Downey, 1994.

30. Guidubaldi, Perry, and Nastasi, 1987b.

31. McLanahan, 1999.

32. Sun and Li, 2002.

33. Furstenberg and Nord, 1985; Furstenberg et al., 1983; Stephens, 1996.

34. Furstenberg and Cherlin, 1991.

35. Seltzer, 1991.

36. Braver and O'Connell, 1998.

37. Furstenberg and Cherlin, 1991; Umberson and Williams, 1993; Seltzer and Bianchi, 1988; Slater, 1999; Stephen, Freedman, and Hess, 1993; Stephens, 1996.

38. Stewart, 1999b.

39. Furstenberg et al., 1983.

40. Baker and McMurray, 1998; Stewart, 1999a.

41. Maccoby et al., 1993.

42. Furstenberg and Nord, 1985.

43. Mitchell, 1985.

44. Dunlop, Burns, and Bermingham, 2001.

45. Zill, Morrison, and Coiro, 1993.

46. Wells and Johnson, 2001.

47. Results concerning problems in childhood: Amato and Keith, 1991b; symptoms in adulthood: Rodgers, Power, and Hope, 1997; Rodgers, 1994.

48. Videon, 2002.

49. Simons et al., 1999.

50. Emery, 1999b.

51. Hingst, 1981; Kitson and Holmes, 1992; Mitchell, 1985.

52. Goetting, 1983; Hetherington, Cox, and Cox, 1982; Hetherington and Kelly, 2002.

53. Wynn and Bowering, 1990.

54. Goetting, 1983; Conyers, 1977.

55. Hetherington and Kelly, 2002.

56. Hetherington and Stanley-Hagan, 2002.

57. Hetherington, Cox, and Cox, 1982; Simons et al., 1999; Simons, Johnson, and Lorenz, 1996.

58. Avenevoli, Sessa, and Steinberg, 1999; Hetherington, Bridges, and Insabella, 1998.

59. Hetherington, 2003.

60. Simons, Johnson, and Lorenz, 1996.

61. Hetherington and Stanley-Hagan, 2002; Pett et al., 1999.

62. Hodgson, Dienhart, and Daly, 2001.

63. McLanahan, 1999.

64. Hilton and Devall, 1998; Karr and Easley, 1986; MacKinnon, Brody, and Stoneman, 1982, 1986; Poehlmann and Fiese, 1994.

65. Pett et al., 1999.

66. Karr and Easley, 1986; MacKinnon, Brody, and Stoneman, 1982, 1986; Poehlmann and Fiese, 1994.

67. Simons, Johnson, and Lorenz, 1996.

68. Demo and Acock, 1996; McLanahan, 1999.

69. Hetherington, Bridges, and Insabella, 1998.

70. Kurdek and Siesky, 1979.

71. Wallerstein, 1985.

72. Hetherington and Stanley-Hagan, 2002; MacKinnon, 1988–89.

73. Dornbusch et al., 1985.

74. Wallerstein, 1985; Devall, Stoneman, and Brody, 1986; Hetherington and Stanley-Hagan, 2002.

75. Jurkovic, Thirkield, and Morrell, 2001.

76. Hetherington and Stanley-Hagan, 2002.

77. Hetherington, Bridges, and Insabella, 1998.

78. Amato, 1993; Astone and McLanahan, 1991; Carlson and Corcoran, 2001.

79. Pett et al., 1999.

80. Downey, 1994.

81. McLanahan, 1999.

82. Simons et al., 1999.

83. Simons, Johnson, and Lorenz, 1996.

84. Emery, 1999b; McLanahan, 1999.

85. Buchanan and Heiges, 2001.

86. Anderson-Kheif, 1982; Buchanan and Heiges, 2001.

87. Arendell, 1995.

88. Buchanan and Heiges, 2001.

89. Buchanan, Maccoby, and Dornbusch, 1991; Maccoby et al., 1992, 1993.

90. Hetherington, Law, and O'Connor, 1993.

91. Patterson and Forgatch, 1990.

92. Amato, 2000b; Buchanan and Heiges, 2001; Simons et al., 1999.

93. For example, Dixon, Charles, and Craddock, 1998.

94. Block, Block, and Gjerde, 1986.

95. Doherty and Needle, 1991; Elliot and Richards, 1991; Hetherington, 1999; Jenkins and Smith, 1993; Shaw, Winslow, and Flanagan, 1999; Sun, 2001; Sun and Li, 2002.

96. Amato and Booth, 1996.

97. Allison and Furstenberg, 1989; Forehand, Armistead, and David, 1997; Morrison and Cherlin, 1995; Hetherington, 1999; Jenkins and Smith, 1993.

98. Videon, 2002.

99. Cherlin et al., 1991; Hanson, 1999; Morrison and Coiro, 1999; Sun and Li, 2002.

100. Emery et al., 1999.

101. Gohm et al., 1998; Brodzinsky, Hitt, and Smith, 1993; Kendler et al., 1992.

102. Block, Block, and Gjerde, 1988; Hanson, 1999; Kiernan and Mueller, 1999; Shaw, Winslow, and Flanagan, 1999; Katz and Gottman, 1993.

103. In the top third of the sample, Hanson, 1999.

104. Krishnakumar and Buehler, 2000.

105. Block, Block, and Gjerde, 1988; Sun, 2001; Sun and Li, 2001, 2002.

106. Kiernan and Mueller, 1999; Shaw, Emery, and Tuer, 1993—for boys.

107. Cherlin et al., 1991; Shaw, Winslow, and Flanagan, 1999.

108. Papp, Cummings, and Goeke-Morey, 2002.

109. Amato, 1993; Amato and Keith, 1991b; Buehler et al., 1998; Depner, Leino, and Chun, 1992; Ernest, Murphy, and O'Leary, 1989; Jenkins and Smith, 1991; Kelly, 2000; Reid and Crisafulli, 1990; Harold et al., 1997; Katz and Gottman, 1993; Rogers and Holmbeck, 1997.

110. Results concerning internalizing and externalizing problems, trouble with peers: Vandewater and Lansford, 1998; performance in school, trouble with police: Hanson, 1999; happiness, well-being: Gohm et al., 1998; Hanson, 1999.

111. Amato and Booth, 2001.

112. McNeal and Amato, 1998.

113. Davies and Cummings, 1994.

114. Cummings, 1994.

115. Cummings, 1987; Cummings, Iannotti, and Zahn-Waxler, 1985.

116. Harger and El-Sheikh, 2003.

117. Amato and Keith, 1991b.

118. Results concerning behavior problems: Morrison and Coiro, 1999; Vandewater and Lansford, 1998; well-being: Amato, 1993; achievement: Long et al., 1987; adult life satisfaction: Amato and Booth, 1991.

119. Results concerning perceived competence: Long et al., 1987; problem behavior and psychological distress: Allison and Furstenberg, 1989; marital and relationship instability: Hetherington, 2003; relationships with father, educational attainment: Amato, in press.

120. Hanson, 1999.

121. Results concerning behavior problems: Morrison and Coiro, 1999; education: McLanahan, 1999.

122. Heinicke, Guthrie, and Ruth, 1997.

123. Morrison and Coiro, 1999.

124. Jekielek, 1998.

125. Hanson, 1999.

126. Amato, Loomis, and Booth, 1995.

127. Hetherington, 1999.

128. Booth, 1999.

129. Morrison and Coiro, 1999.

130. Hanson, 1999.
131. Hetherington, 1999.
132. Amato, 2001.
133. Amato, Rezac, and Booth, 1995.
134. Booth and Amato, 2001; Amato and DeBoer, 2001.
135. Amato, 2001; Amato and Booth, 1997.
136. Amato, 2000b.
137. Amato, 1993.

Chapter 7. What Helps Children Adjust?

1. Amato, 1994a, 2000b.
2. Woodward, Fergusson, and Belsky, 2000; Zill, Morrison, and Coiro, 1993.
3. Wallerstein, Lewis, and Blakeslee, 2000.
4. Furstenberg and Kiernan, 2001; Hope, Power, and Rodgers, 1998.
5. Amato and Booth, 1991.
6. Age is unrelated to finishing high school, attending college, steady job, teen motherhood: McLanahan, 1999; arrests, substance abuse: Furstenberg and Teitler, 1994; mental health problems: Amato and Booth, 1991; Chase-Lansdale, Cherlin, and Kiernan, 1995; Rodgers, Power, and Hope, 1997.
7. Tidwell, Reis, and Shaver, 1996.
8. Hetherington, 1989; Hetherington, Cox, and Cox, 1979, 1982.
9. Wallerstein and Kelly, 1980b; Kline et al., 1989.
10. Guidubaldi and Perry, 1985; Guidubaldi, Perry, and Nastasi, 1987a, 1987b.
11. Hetherington and Kelly, 2002.
12. Lewis and Wallerstein, 1987; Allison and Furstenberg, 1989; Fergusson, Lynskey, and Horwood, 1994; Sun and Li, 2002; Amato, 2001; Amato and Keith, 1991b.
13. Amato and Keith, 1991a; Furstenberg and Teitler, 1994; Gohm et al., 1998; Rodgers, Power, and Hope, 1997; McLanahan, 1999.
14. Amato, 2001; Amato and Keith, 1991b.
15. Cherlin et al., 1991; Morrison and Cherlin, 1995; Mott, Kowaleski-Jones, and Meneghan, 1997; Simons and Associates, 1996.
16. For contrary evidence, however, see Vandervalk et al., 2004.
17. Bonkowski, Boomhower, and Bequette, 1985.
18. Boys had more fights: Brach, Camara, and Houser, 2000; larger effect size: Amato, 2001.
19. Lengua, Wolchik, and Braver, 1995.
20. Dixon, Charles, and Craddock, 1998; Feng et al., 1999; McCabe, 1997; Rodgers, Power, and Hope, 1997.
21. Amato, 2001; Simons et al., 1999.
22. Girls showed negative effects prior to separation: Doherty and Needle, 1991; simulation study: Cummings, Iannotti, and Zahn-Waxler, 1985.
23. Tschann et al., 1990.
24. Hetherington, 1989, 1991.
25. Hetherington, 1989; Wallerstein and Kelly, 1980b.
26. Guidubaldi and Duckworth, 2001; Kraynak, 1997.

27. Katz and Gottman, 1997.

28. Guidubaldi and Duckworth, 2001; Katz and Gottman, 1997; Kraynak, 1997.

29. Hetherington, 1989.

30. Katz and Gottman, 1997; Lengua et al., 1999.

31. Guidubaldi, Perry, and Nastasi, 1987b; Mazur et al., 1999; Farber, Felner, and Primavera, 1985; Healy, Stewart, and Copeland, 1993; Sandler, Tein, and West, 1994; Sandler et al., 2000.

32. Results concerning outcomes in childhood: Guidubaldi, Perry, and Nastasi, 1987b; Mazur et al., 1999; in adulthood: Walker and Ehrenberg, 1998.

33. Lamb, Sternberg, and Thompson, 1999.

34. DeSimone-Luis, O'Mahoney, and Hunt, 1979; Goldberg et al., 1992; Hodges, Wechsler, and Ballantine, 1979; Wallerstein and Kelly, 1980b.

35. DeSimone-Luis, O'Mahoney, and Hunt, 1979.

36. Clarke-Stewart and Hayward, 1996; Hodges, Tierney, and Buchsbaum, 1984; Lengua, Wolchik, and Braver, 1995.

37. Buchanan, Maccoby, and Dornbusch, 1996; Kalter et al., 1989.

38. Clarke-Stewart and Hayward, 1996; Guidubaldi and Perry, 1985; Kalter et al., 1989; Hetherington, Cox, and Cox, 1982; Kurdek and Berg, 1983; Kurdek, Blisk, and Siesky, 1981; Silitsky, 1996; Wallerstein and Kelly, 1980b.

39. Results for preschoolers: Clarke-Stewart et al., 2000; Deater-Deckard and Dunn, 1999; Dunn et al., 1998; school-age children: Kline et al., 1989; Mednick et al., 1990; adolescents: Forehand et al., 1987.

40. Guidubaldi and Cleminshaw, 1985.

41. Buchanan, Maccoby, and Dornbusch, 1996.

42. Koerner et al., 2002.

43. Wallerstein, Lewis, and Blakeslee, 2000.

44. Emery, Kitzmann, and Waldron, 1999.

45. Hetherington, Cox, and Cox, 1982; Wallerstein and Kelly, 1980b; Kalter et al., 1989; Peterson and Zill, 1986; Walsh and Stolberg, 1988–89.

46. Guidubaldi, Perry, and Nastasi, 1987a, 1987b.

47. Avenevoli, Sessa, and Steinberg, 1999; Buchanan, Maccoby, and Dornbusch, 1996; Maccoby et al., 1993; Rodgers and Rose, 2002.

48. Avenevoli, Sessa, and Steinberg, 1999; Hetherington and Clingempeel, 1992; Wallerstein and Corbin, 1989; Wolchik, Wilcox et al., 2000.

49. Hetherington and Kelly, 2002.

50. Avenevoli, Sessa, and Steinberg, 1999; Deater-Deckard and Dunn, 1999; Guidubaldi, Perry, and Nastasi, 1987a, 1987b. They also have a poor self-image: Dunlop, Burns, and Bermingham, 2001.

51. Katz and Gottman, 1997; Wolchik, Wilcox et al., 2000.

52. Evaluations after separation: Tschann et al., 1990; years after divorce: Wallerstein and Corbin, 1989; of young children: Deater-Deckard and Dunn, 1999; of older children: Buchanan, Maccoby, and Dornbusch, 1996; Peterson and Zill, 1986.

53. Deater-Deckard and Dunn, 1999.

54. Wierson et al., 1989.

55. Forgatch and DeGarmo, 1999; Martinez and Forgatch, 2001.

56. Haine et al., 2003.

57. Wallerstein and Tanke, 1996.

58. Braver, Ellman, and Fabricius, 2003.

59. Jacobson, 1978b.

60. Laumann-Billings and Emery, 2000.

61. Meta-analyses: Amato and Gilbreth, 1999; Amato and Keith, 1991b; literature review: Amato, 1998.

62. Hess and Camara, 1979; Isaacs, 1988; Wallerstein and Kelly, 1980b.

63. Lund, 1987; Pagani-Kurtz and Derevensky, 1997.

64. Wallerstein and Kelly, 1980a.

65. Arditti, 1992.

66. King and Heard, 1999.

67. Lamb, Sternberg, and Thompson, 1999; Amato and Rezac, 1994; Hetherington, 1999; Hetherington, Bridges and Insabella, 1998; Johnston, 1994; Maccoby et al., 1992.

68. Amato, 1998.

69. Arendell, 1986; Furstenberg and Nord, 1985; Hetherington, Cox, and Cox, 1976.

70. Lamb, Sternberg, and Thompson, 1999; Hetherington, Bridges, and Insabella, 1998; Simons and Associates, 1996; Clarke-Stewart and Hayward, 1996.

71. Pruett et al., 2003.

72. Struss et al., 2001.

73. Barber, 1994.

74. Amato and Gilbreth, 1999.

75. Simons, Johnson, and Lorenz, 1996.

76. Hingst, 1984.

77. Results in childhood: Amato and Gilbreth, 1999; Pruett et al., 2003; Whiteside and Becker, 2000; adolescence: Amato and Gilbreth, 1999; Buchanan and Maccoby, 1993; adulthood: Summers et al., 1998.

78. Amato and Gilbreth, 1999; Amato and Booth 1991.

79. Drill, 1986.

80. Wallerstein and Blakeslee, 1989; Wallerstein, Lewis, and Blakeslee, 2000.

81. Buchanan and Maccoby, 1993; Buchanan, Maccoby, and Dornbusch, 1996.

82. See Amato and Keith, 1991b; Buchanan and Heiges, 2001; Silitsky, 1996; Vandewater and Lansford, 1998.

83. Solomon and George, 1999.

84. Johnston, 1994; Johnston, Kline, and Tschann, 1989; Hetherington, 1999; Johnston and Roseby, 1997; Lee, 1997.

85. Buchanan, Maccoby, and Dornbusch, 1991, 1996; Hetherington, 1999; Johnston, Kline, and Tschann, 1989.

86. Maccoby et al., 1993.

87. Brown et al., 1991; Kitzmann and Emery, 1994; Long et al., 1988.

88. Long et al., 1988.

89. Ahrons and Rodgers, 1987; Hetherington, 1999; Maccoby et al., 1992.

90. Bonach and Sales, 2002.

91. Camara and Resnick, 1988; Guidubaldi, Perry, and Nastasi, 1987a; Heath and MacKinnon, 1988; Linker, Stolberg, and Green, 1999; Lund, 1987.

92. Camara and Resnick, 1989.

93. Aseltine, 1996; Buchanan, Maccoby, and Dornbusch, 1996; Forehand, Biggar, and Kotchick, 1998; Linker, Stolberg, and Green, 1999; Sandler et al., 1991; Sheets, Sandler, and West, 1996; Silitsky, 1996; Short, 1998a, 1998b.

94. Sandler et al., 1991.

95. Cowen, Pedro-Carroll, and Alpert-Gillis, 1990; Kurdek, 1988; Silitsky, 1996.

96. Rodgers and Rose, 2002.

97. Kurdek, 1988; Teja and Stolberg, 1993; Kurdek and Siesky, 1980.

98. Hetherington and Kelly, 2002.

99. Lengua, Wolchik, and Braver, 1995.

100. Guidubaldi, Perry, and Nastasi, 1987a.

101. Isaacs and Leon, 1986; Lussier et al., 2002.

102. Amato and Keith, 1991c; DelCarmen and Virgo, 1993; McLanahan, 1999.

103. McLanahan, 1999.

104. Gohm et al., 1998.

105. Lamb, Sternberg, and Thompson, 1999.

106. Wolchik et al., 1989.

107. Emery, Kitzmann, and Waldron, 1999.

108. Burroughs, Wagner, and Johnson, 1997.

109. Emery, Kitzmann, and Waldron, 1999.

110. Stolberg and Mahler, 1994.

111. Alpert-Gillis, Pedro-Carroll, and Cowen, 1989.

112. Crosbie-Burnett and Newcomer, 1990; Garvin, Leber, and Kalter, 1991; Stolberg and Garrison, 1985; Stolberg and Mahler, 1994.

113. Lee, Picard, and Blain, 1994; Skitka and Frazier, 1995.

114. Emery, Kitzmann, and Waldron, 1999.

115. Pedro-Carroll, Sutton, and Wyman, 1999.

116. Dawson-McClure et al., 2004.

117. Lengua, Wolchik, and Braver, 1995.

118. Emery, 1999b.

119. Hetherington, Bridges, and Insabella, 1998.

120. Ash and Guyer, 1987.

121. Chase-Lansdale and Hetherington, 1990; Ehrenberg, 1996; King, 1994; Lund, 1987; Leite and McKenry, 2003; Pruett et al., 2003; Whiteside and Becker, 2000.

122. Stephen, Freedman, and Hess, 1993.

123. Buchanan, Maccoby, and Dornbusch, 1991.

124. Fauber et al., 1990.

125. Forehand et al., 1991; Tschann et al., 1990.

126. DeGarmo, Forgatch, and Martinez, 1999; Ge et al., 1992, 1994.

127. Lengua, Wolchik, and Braver, 1995.

128. Hetherington, Bridges, and Insabella, 1998.

Chapter 8. Child Custody and Child Support

1. Arditti and Madden-Derdich, 1997.

2. Grossberg, 1985.

3. Bowlby, 1958, 1969.

4. Harlow and Zimmerman, 1959.

5. Bettelheim, 1956.

6. Ginott, 1975.

7. For example, *Orr vs. Orr,* 1979; *Reed vs. Reed,* 1971.

8. Sorensen and Goldman, 1990.

9. California Civil Code, § 4607 (West 1981), later repealed and added, without substantive change, to California Family Code §§ 3170–3177 (West 1994).

10. Rheinstein, 1972.

11. Elkin, 1973; Wallerstein and Kelly, 1980b.

12. Maccoby et al., 1992.

13. Maccoby, 1999.

14. Crossman et al., 2002.

15. Kelly, 1997.

16. Mnookin, 1975; Schneider, 1991; Scott, 1992.

17. The best interests of the child standard allows judges to ignore information about parents' conflict: Sorensen et al., 1997; to make custody decisions biased by personal beliefs, attitudes, and opinions: Stamps, Kunen, and Rock-Faucheux, 1997; gender: Chesler, 1986; Grillo, 1991; Maryland Special Joint Committee on Gender Bias in the Courts, 1989; Polikoff, 1982; Utsumi, 1991; age and years of experience: Ellis, 1991; Pearson and Luchesi Ring, 1982; Stamps, Kunen, and Rock-Faucheux, 1997; Weinberg, 1999.

18. Fineman, 1988; Houlgate, 1987.

19. Emery, 1999b; Settle and Lowery, 1982.

20. Melton et al., 1987; Krauss and Sales, 2000; Lavin and Sales, 1998.

21. Fineman, 1988.

22. Fineman, 1988.

23. Scott, 1992.

24. Ackerman, 1995.

25. National Center for Health Statistics, 2002.

26. Clarke, 1995.

27. National Center for Health Statistics, 2002.

28. Grall, 2003.

29. Bumpass and Sweet, 1989; Bumpass and Raley, 1995; Furstenberg and Cherlin, 1991.

30. Grall, 2003. This distribution of mother and father custody has been stable since 1994.

31. Grall, 2003.

32. Grall, 2003.

33. Casper and Bianchi, 2002; Grall, 2003.

34. Grall, 2003.

35. Maccoby et al., 1992.

36. Mnookin and Kornhauser, 1979.

37. Maccoby et al., 1992.

38. Ellis, 2000.

39. Hoppe, 1997.

40. Brentano, 2001; Emery, 2001.

41. Brentano, 2001.

42. Anderson, 1989.

43. Margulies and Luchow, 1992; Rosenberg, 1991.

44. McKenry, 1979; Saayman and Saayman, 1988–89.

45. Grillo, 1991; Fineman, 1988; Melton and Lind, 1982.

46. Benjamin and Irving, 1995; Dillon and Emery, 1996; Emery, 1999a; Emery et al., 2001; Kelly, 1990, 1996. Positive results are not always found: see Kressel et al., 1989; Pearson, 1991.

47. Bautz and Hill, 1991; Emery, Matthews, and Kitzmann, 1994.

48. Emery et al., 2001.

49. Emery, Matthews, and Kitzmann, 1994; Irving and Benjamin, 1992.

50. Emery et al., 2001.

51. Emery, Matthews, and Kitzmann, 1994.

52. Emery, Matthews, and Kitzmann, 1994.

53. Emery, Matthews, and Kitzmann, 1994.

54. Emery et al., 2001.

55. Toews and McKenry, 2001.

56. Emery, 2001.

57. Emery et al., 2001; Kelly, 1996.

58. Dillon and Emery, 1996; Emery, 1999a; Emery et al., 2001; Krauss and Sales, 2000.

59. Dillon and Emery, 1996; Emery et al., 2001.

60. Guttman, 1993.

61. Goerdt, 1992.

62. Pearson and Luchesi Ring, 1982; Weinberg, 1999.

63. Brinig, 1995.

64. Fineman, 1988; Hester, 1992.

65. Fineman, 1988, 1989; Grillo, 1991.

66. Hart, 1990.

67. Austin and Jaffe, 1990; Pagelow, 1993.

68. Geffner, 1992; Geffner and Pagelow, 1990.

69. Bautz and Hill, 1991; Bohmer and Ray, 1994.

70. Bohmer and Ray, 1994.

71. Individuals who participated in mediation reported more long-term problems: Dillon and Emery, 1996; Emery et al., 2001; and more conflict with their former spouses than individuals who did not use mediation: Toews and McKenry, 2001.

72. See Kitzmann and Emery, 1994; Kelly, 1996.

73. Brentano, 2001.

74. Grisso, 1986; Melton et al., 1987; Okpaku, 1976; Ziskin, 1981.

75. Davis and Dudley, 1985.

76. Ziskin, 1981.

77. Karras and Berry, 1985.

78. Duquette, 1978.

79. Gourley and Stolberg, 2000.

80. Nicholson and Norwood, 2000.

81. Martindale, 2001.

82. Gardner, 1999.

83. Otto, Edens, and Barcus, 2000; Otto, Buffington-Vollum, and Edens, 2003.

84. Hysjulien et al., 1994.

85. Krauss and Sales, 2000.

86. Krauss and Sales, 2000, p. 864.

87. Ackerman and Ackerman, 1997.

88. Otto, Edens, and Barcus, 2000; Otto, Buffington-Vollum, and Edens, 2003.

89. Folberg, 1991.

90. Roman and Haddad, 1978; Wallerstein and Kelly, 1980b.

91. Hetherington, Cox, and Cox, 1985; Kelly, 1988.

92. National Conference of State Legislatures, 2003.

93. Maccoby, Depner, and Mnookin, 1990.

94. Emery, 1999b; Maccoby et al., 1992.

95. Emery, 1999b.

96. Buchanan, Maccoby, and Dornbusch, 1996.

97. Johnston, 1995.

98. Emery, 1999b; Little, 1992.

99. Pearson and Thoennes, 1990.

100. Lowery and Settle, 1985; Twaite and Luchow, 1996.

101. Benjamin and Irving, 1990; Greif, 1995; Kelly, 1993; Shrier et al. 1991.

102. Gunnoe and Braver, 2001; Kelly, 1993; Maccoby et al.,1992.

103. Pearson and Thoennes, 1990.

104. Fathers with joint physical custody, compared with noncustodial fathers, have been reported to be more likely to share in decision making about their children, to see them more frequently: Gunnoe and Braver, 2001; and to be more satisfied with the arrangement: Arditti, 1992; Little, 1992; Shrier et al., 1991.

105. Shrier et al., 1991.

106. Emery and Wyer, 1987; Emery, Matthews, and Wyer, 1991.

107. Kuehl, 1989; Phear et al., 1984.

108. Bauserman, 2002.

109. Bender, 1994; Sales, Manber, and Rohman, 1992; Wolchik, Braver, and Sandler, 1985.

110. Bauserman, 2002.

111. Brotsky, Steinman, and Zemmelman, 1991.

112. Compared with parents with sole custody, parents with joint custody were more affluent: Pearson and Thoennes, 1990; Shrier et al., 1991; and well educated: Arditti, 1992; Shrier et al., 1991.

113. As has been suggested by Bauserman, 2002.

114. Johnston, Kline, and Tschann, 1989.

115. Benjamin and Irving, 1990.

116. Kelly, 1993; Maccoby, Depner, and Mnookin, 1990.

117. Parents whose marital relationships were full of intense conflict, anger, resentment, and bitterness don't like shared parenting: Benjamin and Irving, 1990; as much as sole custody: Arditti and Madden-Derdich, 1997.

118. Austin and Jaffe, 1990; Brown, 1994; Geffner, 1992; Geffner and Pagelow, 1990; Hart, 1990; Johnston, Kline, and Tschann, 1989; Johnston, Kline, and Tschann, 1991; Johnston, 1994; Wallerstein, 1987; Kline et al., 1989.

119. More contact: Nelson, 1989; more dysfunction: Opie, 1993.

120. Johnston, Kline, and Tschann, 1989; Kelly, 1993.

121. Hetherington, Cox, and Cox, 1978; Lee, 2002.

122. Bartlett and Stack, 1991.

123. Cowan and Cowan, 1992.

124. Santrock and Warshak, 1979; Warshak and Santrock, 1983.

125. Buchanan, Maccoby, and Dornbusch, 1996.

126. Clarke-Stewart and Hayward, 1996.

127. Amato and Keith, 1991b, meta-analysis of studies of adolescents.

128. Peterson and Zill, 1986.

129. DeMaris and Greif, 1992; Risman, 1986.

130. Bisnaire, Firestone, and Rynard, 1990; DeSimone-Luis, O'Mahoney, and Hunt, 1979; Guttmann and Lazar, 1998; Johnston, Kline, and Tschann, 1989; Lowenstein and Koopman, 1978; Luepnitz, 1982, 1986; Rosen, 1979; Schnayer and Orr, 1988–89. The average number of children in father custody in these studies was only fourteen.

131. Dillon and Emery, 1996; Emery et al., 2001.

132. Garrity and Baris, 1994; Goldstein, Freud, and Solnit, 1973; Goldstein et al., 1986; Hodges, 1991.

133. Maccoby et al., 1993.

134. Cloutier and Jacques, 1997.

135. Hawthorne, 2000.

136. U.S. Dept. of Health and Human Services, Administration for Children and Families, 2002.

137. U.S. Dept. of Health and Human Services, Administration for Children and Families, 2002.

138. Grall, 2003.

139. Grall, 2003.

140. Grall, 2003.

141. U.S. Bureau of the Census, 1999.

142. Braver, Fitzpatrick, and Bay, 1991.

143. Sonenstein and Calhoun, 1990.

144. Dubey, 1996.

145. Child support payments are related to fathers' ability to pay: Braver, Fitzpatrick, and Bay, 1991; and nonpayers are generally not so poor that they could not afford to pay at least some support: Meyer and Bartfeld, 1996.

146. Dion et al., 1997.

147. Nuta, 1986.

148. Fathers are more likely to comply with child support orders if enforcement is more stringent, for example, if the payment is withheld by their employer: Meyer and Bartfeld, 1996; if they believe the support order is fair: Lin, 2000; and if they believe that their children are well cared for: Aughinbaugh, 2001.

149. Arditti and Keith, 1993; Grall, 2003.

150. Gunnoe and Braver, 2001.

151. Veum, 1993.

152. Amato and Gilbreth, 1999.

153. Argys et al., 1996.

154. More than other income, child support is also related to higher cognitive test scores for children: Argys et al., 1998; and adolescents: Peters and Mullis, 1997.

155. Hernandez, Beller, and Graham, 1995, 1996.

Chapter 9. Remarriage and Stepfamilies

1. U.S. Bureau of the Census, 1992.

2. U.S. Bureau of the Census, 1992.

3. About three-quarters of divorced people remarry: Furstenberg and Cherlin, 1991; of these about half do so within three years of their divorce: Kreider and Fields, 2001.

4. U.S. Bureau of the Census, 1992.

5. Bumpass, Sweet, and Castro-Martin, 1990.

6. The likelihood that people marry twice before their fortieth birthday doubled, from about 10 percent to about 20 percent, in one generation: Kreider and Fields, 2001 (comparing two birth cohorts: 1925–34 and 1945–54); at the same time as the divorce rate doubled: Kreider and Fields, 2001.

7. U.S. Bureau of the Census, 1992.

8. Zheng and Balakrishnan, 1994.

9. Cherlin and Furstenberg, 1994.

10. Bumpass, Raley, and Sweet, 1995.

11. Kreider and Fields, 2001.

12. Kreider and Fields, 2001.

13. Bramlett and Mosher, 2002.

14. Kreider and Fields, 2001.

15. Holden and Kuo, 1996.

16. Wilson and Clarke, 1992.

17. Buckle, Gallup, and Rodd, 1996.

18. Buckle, Gallup, and Rodd, 1996.

19. South, 1991.

20. Wilson and Clarke, 1992.

21. Kreider and Fields, 2001.

22. Bramlett and Mosher, 2002.

23. Bramlett and Mosher, 2002.

24. Montalto and Gerner, 1998.

25. Bramlett and Mosher, 2002.

26. Bramlett and Mosher, 2002.

27. Castro-Martin and Bumpass, 1989.

28. Kreider and Fields, 2001.

29. Clarke and Wilson, 1994.

30. Bramlett and Mosher, 2002; Wu and Penning, 1997.

31. Bramlett and Mosher, 2002.

32. Bramlett and Mosher, 2002.

33. Stanley, Markman, and Whitton, 2002.

34. Clingempeel, Colyar, and Hetherington, 1994; Hobart, 1991; Pasley, Koch, and Ihinger-Tallman, 1993.

35. Kurdek, 1993b; Bramlett and Mosher, 2002.

36. Furstenberg and Spanier, 1984.

37. Booth and Edwards, 1992; Capaldi and Patterson, 1991.

38. Shapiro, 1996.

39. Richards, Hardy, and Wadsworth, 1997; Spanier and Furstenberg, 1982.

40. Smith et al., 1991.

41. Benokraitis, 1993.

42. Remarried couples are more likely to express negative emotions than couples in first marriages: Bray and Kelly, 1998; Hetherington, 1993; and they report higher levels of disagreement and tension: Hobart, 1991.

43. Smith et al., 1991.

44. Couples in second marriages report that they share decision making and house-hold labor more equally: Pyke and Coltrane, 1996; remarried husbands contribute more to housework than first husbands: Deal, Stanley-Hagan, and Anderson, 1992; they do more cooking, shopping, laundry, and cleaning: Ishii-Kuntz and Coltrane, 1992.

45. Pyke, 1994.

46. Pyke and Coltrane, 1996.

47. Burgoyne and Morison, 1997.

48. Hobart, 1991.

49. Pyke, 1994.

50. Results related to psychological adjustment: Marks, 1995; Pasley and Ihinger-Tallman, 1990.

51. Garrison, 1994.

52. Ozawa and Yoon, 2002.

53. Kreider, 2003.

54. Bumpass, Sweet, and Cherlin, 1991.

55. Coleman, Ganong, and Goodwin, 1994.

56. Ganong and Coleman, 1997.

57. Coleman, Ganong, and Fine, 2000; Fine and Fine, 1992.

58. Fine and Fine, 1992.

59. Crosbie-Burnett, 1994.

60. Stover and Hope, 1993.

61. Fine, Ganong, and Coleman, 1997.

62. Fine, Ganong, and Coleman, 1997; Kurdek and Fine, 1991.

63. Benokraitis, 1993; Lamanna and Riedmann, 1994.

64. Visher, 1994.

65. Papernow, 1993; Visher and Visher, 1988.

66. Ganong and Coleman, 1994; Maccoby et al., 1992.

67. Lamanna and Riedmann, 1994.

68. Crosbie-Burnett, 1991.

69. Cartwright, 2003.

70. McKenry et al. 1996.

71. Cartwright and Seymour, 2002.

72. See Cherlin, 1978.

73. Thoits, 1992.

74. Not surprisingly, then, some stepparents are more successful than others: some stepparent-stepchild relationships grow closer over time, others grow more distant: Coleman, Ganong, and Fine, 2000; Ganong and Coleman, 1994; and yet others become more negative: Bray and Kelly, 1998; Hetherington, 1993.

75. Ganong et al., 1999.

76. Bray and Kelly, 1998; Ganong et al., 1999.

77. Coleman, Ganong, and Fine, 2000; Hetherington, 1993; Hetherington and Clingempeel, 1992; Ganong et al., 1999.

78. See Bray, 1999; Hetherington and Stanley-Hagan, 2002.

79. Marsiglio, 1992.

80. Anderson et al., 1999; Bray, 1999.

81. Church, 1999.

82. In comparison with biological fathers, stepfathers tend to be less involved; less nurturing, affectionate, and warm; and less positive about their stepchildren: Amato, 1987; Fine, Coleman, and Ganong, 1999; Hetherington and Clingempeel, 1992; Hetherington and Stanley-Hagan, 2002; they engage in less supervision of them: Hetherington and Clingempeel, 1992; Kurdek and Fine, 1995.

83. Daly and Wilson, 1996.

84. Bray, 1999; Hetherington and Clingempeel, 1992; Hetherington and Stanley-Hagan, 2002.

85. Hetherington and Stanley-Hagan, 2002.

86. Bray, 1999; Hetherington and Clingempeel, 1992; Hetherington and Stanley-Hagan, 2002.

87. Hetherington and Stanley-Hagan, 2002.

88. Cherlin and Furstenberg, 1994.

89. Nielsen, 1999.

90. Duberman, 1975, p. 50.

91. Church, 1999; Pasley and Ihinger-Tallman, 1988; Santrock and Sitterle, 1987.

92. Church, 1999.

93. Fine, Coleman, and Ganong, 1999.

94. Hetherington and Kelly, 2002.

95. Cherlin and Furstenberg, 1994; Hetherington and Stanley-Hagan, 2002.

96. Bray, 1999; Cherlin and Furstenberg, 1994; Hetherington and Clingempeel, 1992; Hetherington and Stanley-Hagan, 2002.

97. Bray, 1999.

98. Visher, 1994.

99. Research on stepfamilies has long been guided by a search for problems rather than a quest for strengths: Coleman, 1994; Coleman, Ganong, and Goodwin, 1994; life in a stepfamily has been viewed as inherently problematic for children: Popenoe, 1994.

100. Coleman, 1994; Coleman, Ganong, and Fine, 2000; Hetherington and Jodl, 1994.

101. Cherlin and Furstenberg, 1994; Hetherington, Bridges, and Insabella, 1998.

102. Findings for stepchildren: they tend to leave home to establish independent households at younger ages than children from intact families: Kiernan, 1992; they are more likely to have emotional problems such as depression: Hanson, McLanahan, and Thomson, 1996; Zill, Morrison, and Coiro, 1993; they get lower grades in school: Bogenscheider, 1997; and lower scores on achievement tests: Pong, 1997; they are less likely to complete school grades: Teachman, Paasch, and Carver, 1996; and more likely to drop out of school: Astone and McLanahan, 1991.

103. Amato, 1994b.

104. Most stepchildren do well in school: Chase-Lansdale, Cherlin, and Kiernan, 1995; Rodgers, Power, and Hope, 1997; Pong, 1997; and do not suffer from emotional or behavioral problems: Lissau and Sorenson, 1994.

105. Amato, 1994b.

106. Amato, 1994b.

107. Hetherington and Jodl, 1994.

108. Hetherington, Bridges, and Insabella, 1998.

109. Kreider, 2003.

110. Adolescent stepchildren are at risk for externalizing problems, such as alcohol use: Hoffmann and Johnson, 1998; delinquency: Coughlin and Vuchinich, 1996; premature sexual intercourse: Day, 1992; and teenage childbearing: Astone and Washington, 1994. They also report more conflict with their stepparents than adolescents in intact families do with their parents: Barber and Lyons, 1994; Kurdek and Fine, 1993a.

111. Coley, 1998; Dunn et al., 1998.

112. Needle, Su, and Doherty, 1990.

113. Bray, 1999; Bray and Berger, 1993; Hetherington and Clingempeel, 1992; Hetherington and Jodl, 1994.

114. Vuchinich et al., 1991.

115. Brand and Clingempeel, 1987.

116. Henry and Lovelace, 1995.

117. Menaghan, Kowaleski-Jones, and Mott, 1997.

118. Hoffmann and Johnson, 1998.

119. Parents invest time and energy in their new spouse, and stepparents may need to attend to their children from prior marriages: Bogenscheider, 1997; Teachman, Paasch, and Carver, 1996; Pong, 1997; thus reducing parental warmth, attention, and monitoring: Hetherington, 1993.

120. Hetherington, 1993.

121. Bray, 1999; Hethcrington and Clingempeel, 1992.

122. Hanson, McLanahan, and Thomson, 1996; Kurdek and Fine, 1993b.

123. Kiernan, 1992.

124. Hanson, McLanahan, and Thomson, 1996.

125. Anderson et al., 1999.

126. Hetherington and Clingempeel, 1992; Hethcrington and Kelly, 2002.

Chapter 10. Divorce: The Future

1. Cherlin, 1999.

2. Wallerstein, Lewis, and Blakcslee, 2000.

3. Harris, 1998, p. 308.

4. For example, the Council on Families in America.

5. Markman et al., 1988; Stanley et al., 1995; Stanley et al., 2001.

6. Wetzstein, 2004.

7. Stanley, 2001; Kurdek, 1993a.

8. Wetzstein, 2004.

9. Bailey, 2004.

10. Lamb, Sternberg, and Thompson, 1999.

11. See Hetherington and Stanley-Hagan, 2002; Hetherington, Bridges, and Insabella, 1998.

12. Nock, 2002.

13. Hawkins et al., 2002; Wilson et al., 2003.

14. Judicial Council of California, Center for Families, Children and the Courts, 2000.

15. Schultz and Cowan, 2001.

16. Emery, Kitzmann, and Waldron, 1999.

17. Walker, 2003.

18. Hughes et al., 1994.

19. Emery, 2001.

20. Arbuthnot and Gordon, 1996, 1997; Arbuthnot, Kramer, and Gordon, 1997; Kramer et al., 1998; Toews and McKenry, 2001.

21. Arbuthnot and Gordon, 1996.

22. For example, McKenry, Clark, and Stone, 1999.

23. Kramer et al., 1998; Kramer and Kowal, 1998.

24. Wolchik, West et al., 2000.

25. Wolchik, Sandler et al., 2002.

26. Haine et al., 2003.

References

Ackerman, M. J. (1995). *A clinician's guide to child custody evaluations.* Oxford, England: Wiley.

Ackerman, M. J., and Ackerman, M. C. (1997). Custody evaluation practices: A survey of experienced professionals (revisited). *Professional Psychology: Research and Practice, 28,* 137–145.

Ahlburg, D. A., and DeVita, C. J. (1992). New realities of the American family. *Population Bulletin, 47*(2), 2–45.

Ahrons, C. (1986). The continuing coparental relationship between divorced spouses. *American Journal of Orthopsychiatry, 51,* 415–428.

Ahrons, C. R., and Rodgers, R. H. (1987). *Divorced families: A multidisciplinary developmental view.* New York: Norton.

Ainsworth, M. S. (1979). Infant-mother attachment. *American Psychologist, 34,* 932–937.

Airsman, L. A., and Sharda, B. D. (1993). A comparative study of the occupational attainment processes of white men and women in the United States: The effects of having ever married, spousal education, children and having ever divorced. *Journal of Comparative Family Studies, 24,* 171–187.

Albeck, S., and Kaydar, D. (2002). Divorced mothers: Their network of friends pre- and post-divorce. *Journal of Divorce and Remarriage, 36(3–4),* 111–138.

Albrecht, S. L. (1980). Reactions and adjustments to divorce: Differences in the experiences of males and females. *Family Relations, 29,* 59–68.

Aldous, J., and Dumon, W. (1990). Family policy in the 1980s: Controversy and consensus. *Journal of Marriage and the Family, 52,* 1136–1151.

Allison, P. D., and Furstenberg, F. F., Jr. (1989). How marital dissolution affects children: Variations by age and sex. *Developmental Psychology, 25,* 540–549.

Alpert-Gillis, L. J., Pedro-Carroll, J. A., and Cowen, E. L. (1989). The Children of Divorce Intervention Program: Development, implementation, and evaluation of a program for young urban children. *Journal of Consulting and Clinical Psychology, 57,* 583–589.

Amato, P. R. (1987). Family processes in one-parent, stepparent, and intact families: The child's point of view. *Journal of Marriage and Family, 49,* 327–337.

Amato, P. R. (1993). Children's adjustment to divorce: Theories, hypotheses, and empirical support. *Journal of Marriage and Family, 55,* 23–38.

Amato, P. R. (1994a). Life-span adjustment of children to their parents' divorce. *Future of Children, 4,* 143–164.

Amato, P. R. (1994b). The implications of research findings on children in step-families. In A. Booth and J. Dunn (eds.), *Stepfamilies: Who benefits? Who does not?* (pp. 81–87). Hillsdale, N.J.: Erlbaum.

Amato, P. R. (1996). Explaining the intergenerational transmission of divorce. *Journal of Marriage and Family, 58,* 628–640.

Amato, P. R. (1998). More than money? Men's contributions to their children's lives. In A. Booth and A. C. Crouter (eds.), *Men in families: When do they get involved? What difference does it make?* (pp. 241–278). Mahwah, N.J.: Erlbaum.

Amato, P. R. (1999). Children of divorced parents as young adults. In E. M. Hetherington (ed.), *Coping with divorce, single parenting, and remarriage: A risk and resiliency perspective* (pp. 147–163). Mahwah, N.J.: Erlbaum.

Amato, P. R. (2000a). Diversity within single-parent families. In D. Demo, K. R. Allen, and M. A. Fine (eds.), *Handbook of Family Diversity* (pp. 149–172). New York: Oxford University Press.

Amato, P. R. (2000b). The consequences of divorce for adults and children. *Journal of Marriage and Family, 62,* 1269–1287.

Amato, P. R. (2001). Children of divorce in the 1990s: An update of the Amato and Keith (1991) meta-analysis. *Journal of Family Psychology, 15,* 355–370.

Amato, P. R. (2003). Reconciling divergent perspectives: Judith Wallerstein, quantitative family research, and children of divorce. *Family Relations, 52,* 332–339.

Amato, P. R. (in press). Marital discord, divorce, and children's well-being: Results from a 20-year longitudinal study of two generations. In K. A. Clarke-Stewart and J. Dunn (eds.), *Families count: Effects on child and adolescent development.* London: Cambridge University Press.

Amato, P. R., and Booth, A. (1991). Consequences of parental divorce and marital unhappiness for adult well-being. *Social Forces, 69,* 895–914.

Amato, P. R., and Booth, A. (1996). A prospective study of divorce and parent-child relationships. *Journal of Marriage and Family, 58,* 356–365.

Amato, P. R., and Booth, A. (1997). *A generation at risk: Growing up in an era of family upheaval.* Cambridge, Mass.: Harvard University Press.

Amato, P. R., and Booth, A. (2001). The legacy of parents' marital discord: Consequences for children's marital quality. *Journal of Personality and Social Psychology, 81,* 627–638.

Amato, P. R., and DeBoer, D. D. (2001). The transmission of marital instability across generations: Relationship skills or commitment to marriage? *Journal of Marriage and Family, 63,* 1038–1051.

Amato, P. R., and Gilbreth, J. G. (1999). Nonresident fathers and children's well-being: A meta-analysis. *Journal of Marriage and Family, 61,* 557–573.

Amato, P. R., and Keith, B. (1991a). Parental divorce and adult well-being: A meta-analysis. *Journal of Marriage and Family, 53,* 43–58.

Amato, P. R., and Keith, B. (1991b). Parental divorce and the well-being of children: A meta-analysis. *Psychological Bulletin, 110,* 26–46.

Amato, P. R., and Keith, B. (1991c). Separation from a parent during childhood and adult socioeconomic attainment. *Social Forces, 70,* 187–206.

Amato, P. R., Loomis, L. S., and Booth, A. (1995). Parental divorce, marital conflict, and offspring well-being during early adulthood. *Social Forces, 73,* 895–915.

Amato, P. R., and Rezac, S. J. (1994). Contact with nonresidential parents, interparental conflict, and children's behavior. *Journal of Family Issues, 15,* 191–207.

Amato, P. R., Rezac, S. J., and Booth, A. (1995). Helping between parents and young adult offspring: The role of parental marital quality, divorce, and remarriage. *Journal of Marriage and Family, 57,* 363–374.

Amato, P. R., and Rogers, S. J. (1997). A longitudinal study of marital problems and subsequent divorce. *Journal of Marriage and Family, 59,* 612–624.

Amato, P. R., and Rogers, S. J. (1999). Do attitudes toward divorce affect marital quality? *Journal of Family Issues, 20,* 69–86.

Ambert, A.-M. (1989). *Ex-spouses and new spouses: A study of relationships.* Greenwich, Conn.: JAI Press.

Anderson, F. A. (1989). An exploration of a divorce statute: Implications for future policy development. *Journal of Divorce, 12*(4), 1–18.

Anderson, E. R., Greene, S. M., Hetherington, E. M., and Clingempeel, W. G. (1999). The dynamics of parental remarriage: Adolescent, parent, and sibling influences. In E. M. Hetherington (ed.), *Coping with divorce, single parenting, and remarriage: A risk and resiliency perspective* (pp. 295–319). Mahwah, N.J.: Erlbaum.

Anderson-Kheif, S. (1982). *Divorced but not disastrous.* Englewood Cliffs, N.J.: Prentice Hall.

Anthony, K. H. (1997). Bitter homes and gardens: The meanings of home to families of divorce. *Journal of Architectural and Planning Research, 14,* 1–19.

Arbuthnot, J., and Gordon, D. A. (1996). Does mandatory divorce education for parents work? A six-month outcome evaluation. *Family and Conciliation Courts Review, 34,* 60–81.

Arbuthnot, J., Kramer, K. M., and Gordon, D. A. (1997). Patterns of relitigation following divorce education. *Family and Conciliation Courts Review, 35,* 269–279.

Arditti, J. A. (1992). Differences between fathers with joint custody and noncustodial fathers. *American Journal of Orthopsychiatry, 62,* 186–195.

Arditti, J. A., and Keith, T. Z. (1993). Visitation frequency, child support pay ment, and the father-child relationship postdivorce. *Journal of Marriage and Family, 55,* 699–712.

Arditti, J. A., and Madden-Derdich, D. (1997). Joint and sole custody mothers: Implications for research and practice. *Families in Society, 78,* 36–45.

Arendell, T. (1986). *Mothers and divorce: Legal, economic, and social dilemmas.* Berkeley: University of California Press.

Arendell, T. (1995). *Father and divorce.* Thousand Oaks, Calif.: Sage Publications.

Argys, L. M., Peters, H. E., Brooks-Gunn, J., and Smith, J. R. (1996, October). Contributions of absent fathers to child well-being: The impact of child support dollars and father-child contact. Paper presented at the Conference on Father Involvement, Bethesda, Md.

Argys, L. M., Peters, H. E., Brooks-Gunn, J., and Smith, J. R. (1998). The impact of child support on cognitive outcomes of young children. *Demography, 35,* 159–173.

Aseltine, R. H., Jr. (1996). Pathways linking parental divorce with adolescent depression. *Journal of Health and Social Behavior, 37,* 133–148.

Aseltine, R. H., Jr., and Kessler, R. C. (1993). Marital disruption and depression in a community sample. *Journal of Health and Social Behavior, 34,* 237–251.

Ash, P., and Guyer, M. J. (1987). The functions of psychiatric evaluations in contested child custody visitation cases. *Journal of the American Academy of Child Psychiatry, 25,* 554–561.

Asher, S. J., and Bloom, B. L. (1983). Geographic mobility as a factor in adjustment to divorce. *Journal of Divorce, 6*(4), 69–84.

Astone, N. M., and McLanahan, S. S., (1991). Family structure, parental practices and high school completion. *American Sociological Review, 56*(3), 309–321.

Astone, N. M., and Washington, M. L. (1994). The association between grandparental co-residence and adolescent childbearing. *Journal of Family Issues, 15,* 574–589.

Aughinbaugh, A. (2001). Signals of child achievement as determinants of child support. *American Economic Review, 91,* 140–144.

Austin, G. W., and Jaffe, P. G. (1990). Follow-up study of parents in custody and access disputes. *Canadian Psychology, 31,* 172–179.

Avenevoli, S., Sessa, F. M., and Steinberg, L. (1999). Family structure, parenting practices, and adolescent adjustment: An ecological examination. In E. M. Hetherington (ed.), *Coping with divorce, single parenting, and remarriage: A risk and resiliency perspective* (pp. 65–90). Mahwah, N.J.: Erlbaum.

Bailey, D. S. (2004). Reconceptualizing custody. *Monitor on Psychology,* September, 44–45.

Baker, R. J., and McMurray, A. M. (1998). Contact fathers' loss of school in-
    volvement. *Journal of Family Studies, 4,* 201–214.

Barber, B. L. (1994). Support and advice from married and divorced fathers:
    Linkages to adolescent adjustment. *Family Relations, 43,* 433–438.

Barber, B. L., and Lyons, J. M. (1994). Family processes and adolescent adjust-
    ment in intact and remarried families. *Journal of Youth and Adolescence,
    23,* 421–436.

Bartholomew, K. (1997). Adult attachment processes: Individual and couple
    perspectives. *British Journal of Medical Psychology, 70,* 249–263.

Bartlett, K. T., and Stack, C. B. (1991). Joint custody, feminism, and the depen-
    dency dilemma. In J. Folberg (ed.), *Joint custody and shared parenting* (2nd
    ed., pp. 63–87). New York: Guilford.

Baum, N. (2003). The male way of mourning divorce: When, what, and how.
    Clinical Social Work Journal, 31, 37–50.

Bauserman, M. R. (2002). Child adjustment in joint-custody versus sole-cus-
    tody arrangements: A meta-analytic review. *Journal of Family Psychology,
    16,* 91–102.

Bautz, B. J., and Hill, R. M. (1991). Mediating the breakup: Do children win?
    Mediation Quarterly, 8, 199–210.

Becker, G. S. (1981). *A Treatise on the Family.* Cambridge, Mass.: Harvard Uni-
    versity Press.

Beer, J., and Beer, J. (1992). Aggression of youth as related to parental divorce
    and eye color. *Perceptual and Motor Skills, 75* (3, Pt. 2), 1066.

Belle, D. (1990). Poverty and women's mental health. *American Psychologist, 45,*
    385–389.

Belsky, J., and Pensky, E. (1989). Marital change across the transition to parent-
    hood. *Marriage and Family Review, 12* (3–4), 133–156.

Bender, W. N. (1994). Joint custody: The option of choice. *Journal of Divorce
    and Remarriage. 21* (3–4), 115–131.

Benjamin, M., and Irving, H. H. (1990). Comparison of the experience of satis-
    fied and dissatisfied shared parents. *Journal of Divorce and Remarriage,
    14* (1), 43–61.

Benjamin, M., and Irving, H. H. (1995). Research in family mediation: Review
    and implications. *Mediation Quarterly, 13,* 53–82.

Bennett, N. G., Bloom, D. E., and Craig, P. H. (1989). The divergence of Black
    and White marriage patterns. *American Journal of Sociology, 95,* 692–722.

Benokraitis, N. V. (1993). *Marriages and families: Changes, choices, and con-
    straints* (3rd ed.). Englewood Cliffs, N.J.: Prentice Hall.

Bergman, L. R., El-Khouri, B., and Magnusson, D. (1987). Reactions to separa-
    tion: Separated children's adjustment at age 13. Individual development
    and adjustment (Report No. 68. Department of Psychology). Stockholm:
    University of Stockholm.

Berman, W. H. (1988). The role of attachment in the post-divorce experience. *Journal of Personality and Social Psychology, 54,* 496–503.

Bettelheim, B. (1956). Fathers shouldn't try to be mothers. *Parents' Magazine, 10,* 124–125.

Betzig, L. (1989). Causes of conjugal dissolution: A cross-cultural study. *Current Anthropology, 30,* 654–676.

Bevvino, D. L. (2000). Divorce adjustment as a function of gender, education level, personality, length of separation, disentanglement, initiator status and meaning. *Dissertation Abstracts International: Section B: The Sciences and Engineering, 60*(12-B), 6353.

Bianchi, S. M., Subaiya, L., and Kahn, J. R. (1999). The gender gap in the economic well-being of nonresident fathers and custodial mothers. *Demography, 36,* 195–203.

Birnbaum, G. E., Orr, I., Mikulincer, M., and Florian, V. (1997). When marriage breaks up: Does attachment style contribute to coping and mental health? *Journal of Social and Personal Relationships, 14,* 643–654.

Bisnaire, L. M. C., Firestone, P., and Rynard, D. (1990). Factors associated with academic achievement in children following parental separation. *American Journal of Orthopsychiatry, 60,* 66–76.

Blaisure, K. R., and Allen, K. R. (1995). Feminists and the ideology and practice of marital equality. *Journal of Marriage and Family, 57,* 5–19.

Block, J., Block, J. H., and Gjerde, P. F. (1988). Parental functioning and the home environment in families of divorce: Prospective and concurrent analyses. *Journal of the American Academy of Child and Adolescent Psychiatry, 27,* 207–213.

Block, J. H., Block, J., and Gjerde, P. F. (1986). The personality of children prior to divorce: A prospective study. *Child Development, 57,* 827–840.

Bloom, B. L., and Caldwell, R. A. (1981). Sex differences in adjustment during the process of marital separation. *Journal of Marriage and Family, 43,* 693–701.

Bloom, B. L., and Clement, C. (1984). Marital sex role orientation and adjustment to separation and divorce. *Journal of Divorce, 7*(3), 87–98.

Bloom, B. L., and Hodges, W. F. (1981). The predicament of the newly separated. *Community Mental Health Journal, 17,* 277–293.

Bloom, B. L., Hodges, W. F., and Caldwell, R. A. (1983). Marital separation: The first eight months. In E. J. Callahan and K. A. McCluskey (eds.), *Life-span developmental psychology: Nonnormative life events* (pp. 217–239). New York: Academic Press.

Bloom, B. L., Niles, R. L., and Tatcher, A. M. (1985). Sources of marriage dissatisfaction among newly separated persons. *Journal of Family Issues, 6*(3), 359–374.

Bogenscheider, K. (1997). Parental involvement in adolescent schooling: A proximal process with transcontextual validity. *Journal of Marriage and Family, 59,* 718–733.

Bohannon, P. (1970). The six stations of divorce. In P. Bohannon (ed.), *Divorce and after: An analysis of the emotional and social problems of divorce* (pp. 29–55). New York: Doubleday.

Bohmer, C., and Ray, M. L. (1994). Effects of different dispute resolution methods on women and children after divorce. *Family Law Quarterly, 28,* 223–245.

Bonach, K., and Sales, E. (2002). Forgiveness as a mediator between post divorce cognitive processes and coparenting quality. *Journal of Divorce and Remarriage, 38*(1–2), 17–38.

Bonkowski, S. E. (1989). Lingering sadness: Young adults' response to parental divorce. *Social Casework, 70,* 219–223.

Bonkowski, S. E., Boomhower, S. J., and Bequette, S. Q. (1985). What you don't know can hurt you: Unexpressed fears and feelings of children from divorcing families. *Journal of Divorce, 9*(1), 33–45.

Booth, A. (1999). Causes and consequences of divorce: Reflections on recent research. In R. A. Thompson and P. R. Amato (eds.), *The postdivorce family: Children, parenting, and society* (pp. 29–48). Thousand Oaks, Calif.: Sage Publications.

Booth, A., and Amato, P. R. (1991). Divorce and psychological stress. *Journal of Health and Social Behavior, 32,* 396–407.

Booth, A., and Amato, P. R. (1992). Divorce, residential change, and stress. *Journal of Divorce and Remarriage, 18*(2), 205–213.

Booth, A., and Amato, P. R. (2001). Parental predivorce relations and offspring postdivorce well-being. *Journal of Marriage and Family, 63,* 197–212.

Booth, A., and Edwards, J. N. (1992). Starting over: Why remarriages are more unstable. *Journal of Family Issues, 13,* 179–194.

Booth, A., Johnson D. R., Branaman, A., and Sica, A. (1995). Belief and behavior: Does religion matter in today's marriage? *Journal of Marriage and Family, 57,* 661–671.

Booth, A., Johnson, D. R., and Edwards, J. N. (1983). Measuring marital instability. *Journal of Marriage and Family, 45*(2), 387–395.

Bowlby, J. (1958). The nature of the child's tie to the mother. *International Journal of Psycho-Analysis, 39,* 350–373.

Bowlby, J. (1969). *Attachment and loss: Vol. 1. Attachment.* New York: Basic Books.

Bowlby, J. (1973). *Attachment and loss: Vol. 2. Separation: Anxiety and anger.* New York: Basic Books.

Bowlby, J. (1989). The role of attachment in personality development and psychopathology. In S. I. Greenspan and G. H. Pollock (eds.), *The course of life: Vol. 1. Infancy* (pp. 229–270). Madison, Conn.: International Universities Press.

Brach, E. L., Camara, K. A., and Houser, R. F., Jr. (2000). Patterns of interaction in divorced and non-divorced families: Conflict in dinnertime conversation. *Journal of Divorce and Remarriage, 33*(1–2), 75–89.

Bramlett, M. D., and Mosher, W. D. (2002). Cohabitation, marriage, divorce and remarriage in the United States. *National Center for Health Statistics: Vital Health Statistics, 23*(22).

Brand, E., and Clingempeel, W. G. (1987). Interdependencies of marital and step-parent-stepchild relationships and children's psychological adjustment: Research findings and clinical implications. *Family Relations, 36,* 140–145.

Braver, S. L., Cookston, J. T., and Cohen, B. R. (2002). Experiences of family law attorneys with current issues in divorce practice. *Family Relations, 51,* 325–334.

Braver, S. L., Ellman, I. M., and Fabricius, W. V. (2003). Relocation of children after divorce and children's best interests: New evidence and legal considerations. *Journal of Family Psychology, 12,* 206–219.

Braver, S. L., Fitzpatrick, P. J., and Bay, R. C. (1991). Noncustodial parent's report of child support payments. *Family Relations, 40,* 180–185.

Braver, S. L., Gonzalez, N., Wolchik, S. A., and Sandler, I. N. (1989). Economic hardship and psychological distress in custodial mothers. *Journal of Divorce, 12*(4), 19–34.

Braver, S. L., and O'Connell, D. (1998). *Divorced dads: Shattering the myths.* New York: Putnam.

Braver, S. L., Whitley, M., and Ng, C. (1993). Who divorced whom? Methodological and theoretical issues. *Journal of Divorce and Remarriage, 20*(1–2), 1–20.

Braver, S. L., Wolchik, S. A., Sandler, I. N., and Sheets, V. L. (1993). A social exchange model of nonresidential parent involvement. In C. E. Depner and J. H. Bray (eds.), *Nonresidential parenting: New vistas in family living* (pp. 87–108). Thousand Oaks, Calif.: Sage Publications.

Bray, J. H. (1999). From marriage to remarriage and beyond: Findings from the Developmental Issues in Stepfamilies Research Project. In M. E. Hetherington (ed.), *Coping with divorce, single parenting, and remarriage: A risk and resiliency perspective* (pp. 253–271). Mahwah, N.J.: Erlbaum.

Bray, J. H., and Berger, S. H. (1993). Developmental Issues in Stepfamilies Research Project: Family relationships and parent-child interactions. *Journal of Family Psychology, 7,* 76–90.

Bray, J., and Kelly, J. (1998). *Stepfamilies.* New York: Broadway.

Brennan, K. A., and Shaver, P. R. (1998). Attachment styles and personality disorders: Their connections to each other and to parental divorce, parental death, and perceptions of parental caregiving. *Journal of Personality, 66,* 835–878.

Brentano, C. (2001). Child custody litigation and family adjustment: The role of procedural and distributive justice. *Dissertation Abstracts International, 62*(3-B), 1613.

Brinig, M. F. (1995). Does mediation systematically disadvantage women? *William and Mary Journal of Women and the Law, 2,* 1–34.

Brockington, I. (2001). Suicide in women. *International Clinical Psychopharmacology, 16* (Suppl. 2), S7—S19.

Brodzinsky, D., Hitt, J. C., and Smith, D. (1993). Impact of parental separation and divorce on adopted and nonadopted children. *American Journal of Orthopsychiatry, 63,* 451–461.

Brooks, R. B. (1994). Children at risk: Fostering resilience and hope. *American Journal of Orthopsychiatry, 64*(4), 545–553.

Brotsky, M., Steinman, S., and Zemmelman, S. (1991). Joint custody through mediation: A longitudinal assessment of the children. In J. Folberg (ed.), *Joint custody and shared parenting* (2nd ed., pp. 167–176). New York: Guilford.

Brown, B. F. (1982). Divorce adjustment and social support: A study of their relationship through a divorce adjustment group approach designed to facilitate the building of social support. *Dissertation Abstracts International, 43*(1-B), 242.

Brown, C. (1994). The impact of divorce on families: The Australian experience. *Family and Conciliation Courts Review, 32,* 149–167.

Brown, J. H., Eichenberger, S. A., Portes, P. R., and Christensen, D. N. (1991). Family functioning factors associated with the adjustment of children of divorce. *Journal of Divorce and Remarriage, 17*(1–2), 81–96.

Brown, P., Felton, B. J., Whiteman, V., and Manela, R. (1980). Attachment and distress following marital separation. *Journal of Divorce, 3,* 303–317.

Brown, P., and Manela, R. (1978). Changing family roles: Women and divorce. *Journal of Divorce, 1,* 325–328.

Brubeck, D., and Beer, J. (1992). Depression, self-esteem, suicide ideation, death anxiety, and GPA in high school students of divorced and nondivorced parents. *Psychological Reports, 71*(3, Pt. 1), 755–763.

Buchanan, C. M, and Heiges, K. L. (2001). When conflict continues after the marriage ends: Effects of postdivorce conflict on children. In J. H. Grych and F. D. Fincham (eds.), *Interparental conflict and child development: Theory, research, and applications* (pp. 337–362). New York: Cambridge University Press.

Buchanan, C. M., and Maccoby, E. E. (1993, March). Relationships between adolescents and their nonresidential parents: A comparison of nonresidential mothers and fathers. Paper presented at the biennial meeting of the Society for Research in Child Development, New Orleans.

Buchanan, C. M., Maccoby, E. E., and Dornbusch, S. M. (1991). Caught between parents: Adolescents' experience in divorced homes. *Child Development, 62,* 1008–1029.

Buchanan, C. M., Maccoby, E. E., and Dornbusch, S. M. (1996). *Adolescents after divorce.* Cambridge, Mass.: Harvard University Press.

Buckle, L., Gallup, G. G., and Rodd, Z. A. (1996). Marriage as a reproductive contract: Patterns of marriage, divorce, and remarriage. *Ethology and Sociobiology, 17,* 363–377.

Buehler, C. A., Krishnakumar, A., Stone, G., Anthony, C., Pemberton, S., Gerard, J., and Barber, B. (1998). Interparental conflict styles and youth problem behaviors: A two-sample replication study. *Journal of Marriage and Family, 60,* 119–133.

Bumpass, L. L. (1984). Children and marital disruption: A replication and update. *Demography, 21,* 71–82.

Bumpass, L. L. (1990). What's happening to the family? Interactions between demographics and institutional change. *Demography, 27*(4), 483–498.

Bumpass, L. L., Martin, T. C., and Sweet, J. A. (1991). The impact of family background and early marital factors on marital disruption. *Journal of Family Issues, 12,* 22–42.

Bumpass, L. L., and Raley, R. K. (1995). Redefining single-parent families: Cohabitation and changing family reality. *Demography, 32,* 97–109.

Bumpass, L. L., Raley, R. K., and Sweet, J. A. (1995). The changing character of stepfamilies: Implications of cohabitation and nonmarital childbearing. *Demography, 32,* 425–436.

Bumpass, L. L., and Sweet, J. A. (1989). Children's experience in single-parent families: Implications of cohabitation and marital transitions. *Family Planning Perspectives, 21,* 256–260.

Bumpass, L. L., Sweet, J. A., and Castro-Martin, T. (1990). Changing patterns of remarriage. *Journal of Marriage and Family, 52,* 747–756.

Bumpass, L. L., Sweet, J. A., and Cherlin, A. (1991). The role of cohabitation in declining rates of marriage. *Journal of Marriage and Family, 53,* 913–927.

Burns, A., and Dunlop, R. (1998). Parental divorce, parent-child relations, and early adult relationships: A longitudinal Australian study. *Personal Relationships, 5,* 393–407.

Burns, A., and Dunlop, R. (1999). How did you feel about it? Children's feelings about their parents' divorce at the time and three and ten years later. *Journal of Divorce and Remarriage, 31*(3–4), 19–35.

Burgess, E. W., Locke, H. J., and Thomas, M. M. (1971). *The family, from traditional to companionship.* New York: Van Nostrand Reinhold.

Burgoyne, C. B., and Morison, V. (1997). Money in remarriage: Keeping things simple and separate. *Sociological Review, 45,* 363–395.

Burrell, N. A. (2002). Divorce: How spouses seek social support. In M. Allen, R. W. Preiss, B. M. Gayle, and N. A. Burrell (eds.), *Interpersonal communication research: Advances through meta-analysis* (pp. 247–262). Mahwah, N.J.: Erlbaum.

Burroughs, M. S., Wagner, W. W., and Johnson, J. T. (1997). Treatment with children of divorce: A comparison of two types of therapy. *Journal of Divorce and Remarriage, 27*(3–4), 83–99.

Bursik, K. (1991a). Adaptation to divorce and ego development in adult women. *Journal of Personality and Social Psychology, 60,* 300–306.

Bursik, K. (1991b). Correlates of women's adjustment during the separation and divorce process. *Journal of Divorce, 14*(3–4), 137–162.

Byrne, R. C. (1990). The effectiveness of the Beginning Experience Workshop: A paraprofessional group marathon workshop for divorce adjustment. *Journal of Divorce, 13*(4), 101–120.

Caldwell, R. A., Bloom, B. L., and Hodges, W. F. (1983). Sex differences in separation and divorce: A longitudinal perspective. *Issues in Mental Health Nursing, 5,* 103–120.

California Civil Code, § 4607 (West 1981).Call, G., Beer, J., and Beer, J. (1994). General and test anxiety, shyness, and grade point average of elementary school children of divorced and nondivorced parents. *Psychological Reports, 74,* 512–514.

Call, V. R. A., and Heaton T. B. (1997). Religious influence on marital stability. *Journal for the Scientific Study of Religion, 36,* 382–392.

Camara, K. A., and Resnick, G. (1988). Interparental conflict and cooperation: Factors moderating children's post-divorce adjustment. In E. M. Hetherington and J. D. Arastch (eds.), *Impact of divorce, single parenting, and stepparenting on children* (pp. 169–195). Hillsdale, N.J.: Erlbaum.

Camara, K. A., and Resnick, G. (1989). Styles of conflict resolution and cooperation between divorced parents: Effects on child behavior and adjustment. *American Journal of Orthopsychiatry, 59,* 560 575.

Cano, A., and O'Leary, D. K. (2000). Infidelity and separations precipitate major depressive episodes and symptoms of nonspecific depression and anxiety. *Journal of Consulting and Clinical Psychology, 68,* 774–781.

Cantor, C. H., and Slater, P. J. (1995). Marital breakdown, parenthood, and suicide. *Journal of Family Studies, 1,* 91–102.

Capaldi, D. M., and Patterson, G. R. (1991). Relation of parental transitions to boys' adjustment problems: I. A linear hypotheses. II. Mothers at risk for transitions and unskilled parenting. *Developmental Psychology, 27,* 489–504.

Cargan, L., and Whitehurst, R. N. (1990). Adjustment differences in the divorced and the redivorced. *Journal of Divorce and Remarriage, 14*(2), 49–78.

Carlson, M. J., and Corcoran, M. E. (2001). Family structure and children's behavioral and cognitive outcomes. *Journal of Marriage and Family, 63,* 779–792.

Carrere, S., and Gottman, J. M. (1999). Predicting the future of marriages. In E. M. Hetherington (ed.), *Coping with divorce, single parenting, and remarriage: A risk and resiliency perspective* (pp. 3–22). Mahwah, N.J.: Erlbaum.

Cartwright, C. (2003). Therapists' perceptions of bioparent-child relationships in stepfamilies: What hurts? What helps? *Journal of Divorce and Remarriage, 38*(3–4), 147–166.

Cartwright, C., and Seymour, F. (2002). Young adults' perceptions of parents' response in stepfamilies: What hurts? What helps? *Journal of Divorce and Remarriage, 37*(3–4), 123–141.

Casper, L. M., and Bianchi, S. M. (2002). *Continuity and change in the American family.* Thousand Oaks, Calif.: Sage Publications.

Cassidy, J., and Shaver, P. R. (eds.). (1999). *Handbook of attachment: Theory, research, and clinical applications.* New York: Guilford Press.

Castro-Martin, T., and Bumpass, L. (1989). Recent trends and differentials in marital disruption. *Demography, 26,* 37–51.

Ceglian, C. P., and Gardner, S. (1999). Attachment style: A risk for multiple marriages? *Journal of Divorce and Remarriage, 31*(1–2), 125–139.

Chan, L. Y., and Heaton, T. B. (1989). Demographic determinants of delayed divorce. *Journal of Divorce, 13*(1), 97–112.

Chase-Lansdale, P. L., Cherlin, A. J., and Kiernan, K. E. (1995). The long-term effects of parental divorce on the mental health of young adults: A developmental perspective. *Child Development, 66,* 1614–1634.

Chase-Lansdale, P. L., and Hetherington, E. M. (1990). The impact of divorce on life-span development: Short and long term effects. In P. B. Baltes, D. L. Featherman, and R. M. Lerner (eds.), *Life-span development and behavior,* Vol. 10 (pp. 105–150). Hillsdale, N.J.: Erlbaum.

Cherlin, A. J. (1978). Remarriage as an incomplete institution. *American Journal of Sociology, 84,* 634–650.Cherlin, A. J. (1983). Changing family and household: Contemporary lessons from historical research. *Annual Review of Sociology, 9,* 51–66.

Cherlin, A. J. (1992). *Marriage, divorce, remarriage.* Cambridge, Mass.: Harvard University Press.

Cherlin, A. J. (1998). Marriage and marital dissolution among Black Americans. *Journal of Comparative Family, 29,* 147–158.

Cherlin, A. J. (1999). Going to extremes: Family structure, children's well-being, and social science. *Demography, 36,* 421–428.

Cherlin, A. J., Chase-Lansdale, P. L., and McRae, C. (1998). Effects of parental divorce on mental health throughout the life course. *American Sociological Review, 63,* 239–249.

Cherlin, A. J., and Furstenberg, F. F. (1994). Stepfamilies in the United States: A reconsideration. *Annual Review of Sociology, 20,* 359–381.

Cherlin, A. J., Furstenberg, F. F., Jr., Chase-Lansdale, P. L., Kiernan, K. E., Robins, P. K., Morrison, D. R., and Teitler, J. O. (1991). Longitudinal studies of effects of divorce on children in Great Britain and the United States. *Science, 252,* 1386–1389.

Chesler, P. (1986). *Mothers on trial: The battle for children and custody.* New York: McGraw-Hill.

Chiriboga, D. A. (1982). Adaptation to marital separation in later and earlier life. *Journal of Gerontology, 37,* 109–114.

Chiriboga, D. A., and Catron, L. S. (1991). *Divorce: Crisis, challenge or relief?* New York: New York University Press.

Christensen, A., and Shenk, J. L. (1991). Communication, conflict, and psychological distance in nondistressed, clinic, and divorcing couples. *Journal of Consulting and Clinical Psychology, 59,* 458–463.

Church, E. (1999). Who are the people in your family? Stepmothers' diverse notions of kinship. *Journal of Divorce and Remarriage, 31,* 83–105.

Cicchetti, D., and Rogosch, F. A. (1997). The role of self-organization in the promotion of resilience in maltreated children. *Development and Psychopathology, 9*(4), 799–817.

Clarke, S. C. (1995). Advance report of final divorce statistics, 1989 and 1990. *Monthly Vital Statistics Report, 43*(8), Hyattsville, Md.: National Center for Health Statistics.

Clarke, S. C., and Wilson, B. F. (1994). The relative stability of remarriages: A cohort approach using vital statistics. *Family Relations, 43,* 305–310.

Clarke-Stewart, K. A., and Bailey, B. L. (1989). Adjusting to divorce: Why do men have it easier? *Journal of Divorce, 13*(2), 75–94.

Clarke-Stewart, K. A., and Hayward, C. (1996). Advantages of father custody and contact for the psychological well-being of school-age children. *Journal of Applied Developmental Psychology, 17,* 239–270.

Clarke-Stewart, K. A., Vandell, D. L., McCartney, K., Owen, M. T., and Booth, C. (2000). Effects of parental separation and divorce on very young children. *Journal of Family Psychology, 14,* 304–326.

Clingempeel, G., Colyar, J., and Hetherington, E. M. (1994). Toward a cognitive dissonance conceptualization of stepchildren and biological children loyalty conflicts: A construct validity study. In K. Pasley and M. Ihinger-Tallman (eds.), *Stepparenting: Issues in theory, research, and practice* (pp. 151–174). Westport, Conn.: Greenwood.

Cloutier, R., and Jacques, C. (1997). Evolution of residential custody arrangements in separated families: A longitudinal study. *Journal of Divorce and Remarriage, 28*(1–2), 17–33.

Cohen, O. (1995). Divorced fathers raise their children by themselves. *Journal of Divorce and Remarriage, 23*(1–2), 55–73.

Colburn, K., Lin, P. L., and Moore, M. C. (1992). Gender and the divorce experience. *Journal of Divorce and Remarriage, 17*(3–4), 87–108.

Coleman, M. (1994). Stepfamilies in the United States: Challenging biased assumptions. In A. Booth and J. Dunn (eds.), *Stepfamilies: Who benefits? Who does not?* (pp. 29–35). Hillsdale, N.J.: Erlbaum.

Coleman, M., Ganong, L., and Fine, M. (2000). Reinvestigating remarriage: Another decade of progress. *Journal of Marriage and Family, 62,* 1288–1307.

Coleman, M., Ganong, L., and Goodwin, C. (1994). The presentation of stepfamilies in marriage and family textbooks: A reexamination. *Family Relations, 43,* 289–297.

Coley, R. L. (1998). Children's socialization experiences and functioning in single-mother households: The importance of fathers and other men. *Child Development, 69,* 219–230.

Colletta, N. D. (1983). Stressful lives: The situation of divorced mothers and their children. *Journal of Divorce, 6*(3), 19–32.

Coney, N. S., and Mackey, W. C. (1989). Perceptions of the problems of the divorced father. *Journal of Divorce, 13*(1), 81–96.

Conger, R. D., Elder, G. H., Lorenz, F. O., Conger, K. J., Simons, R. L., Whitbeck, L. B., Huck, S., Melby, J. N. (1990). Linking economic hardship to marital quality and instability. *Journal of Marriage and Family, 52,* 643–656.

Conyers, J. G. (1977). Comparing school success of students from conventional and broken homes. *Phi Delta Kappan, 58,* 647.

Copeland, A. P. (1985). Individual differences in children's reactions to divorce. *Journal of Clinical Child Psychology, 14,* 11–19.

Cowan, C. P., and Cowan, P. A. (1992). *When partners become parents.* New York: Basic.

Cowen, E. L., Pedro-Carroll, J. L., and Alpert-Gillis, L. J. (1990). Relationship between support and adjustment among children of divorce. *Journal of Child Psychology and Psychiatry, 31,* 727–735.

Coughlin, C., and Vuchinich, S. (1996). Family experience in preadolescence and the development of male delinquency. *Journal of Marriage and Family, 58,* 491–501.

Crosbie-Burnett, M. (1991). Impact of joint versus sole custody and quality of co-parental relationship on adjustment of adolescents in remarried families. *Behavioral Sciences and the Law, 9,* 439–449.

Crosbie-Burnett, M. (1994). The interface between stepparent families and schools: Research, theory, policy, and practice. In K. Pasley and M. Ihinger-Tallman (eds.), *Stepparenting: Issues in theory, research, and practice* (pp. 199–216). Westport, Conn.: Greenwood.

Crosbie-Burnett, M., and Newcomer, L. L. (1990). Group counseling children of divorce: The effects of a multimodal intervention. *Journal of Divorce, 13*(3), 69–78.

Crossman, A. M., Powell, M. B., Principe, G. F., and Ceci, S. J. (2002). Child testimony in custody cases: A review. *Journal of Forensic Psychology Practice, 2,* 1–32.

Cummings, E. M. (1987). Coping with background anger in early childhood. *Child Development, 58,* 976–984.

Cummings, E. M. (1994). Marital conflict and children's functioning. *Social Development, 3,* 16–36.

Cummings, E. M., Iannotti, R. J., and Zahn-Waxler, C. (1985). Influence of conflict between adults on the emotions and aggression of young children. *Developmental Psychology, 21,* 495–507.

Daly, M., and Wilson, M. I. (1996). Violence against stepchildren. *Current Directions in Psychological Science, 5,* 77–80.

Daniels-Mohring, D., and Berger, M. (1984). Social network changes and the adjustment to divorce. *Journal of Divorce, 8*(1), 17–32.

Davies, L., Avison, W. R., and McAlpine, D. D. (1997). Significant life experiences and depression among single and married mothers. *Journal of Marriage and Family, 59,* 294–308.

Davies, P. T., and Cummings, E. M. (1994). Marital conflict and child adjustment: An emotional security hypothesis. *Psychological Bulletin, 116,* 387–411.

Davis, P., and Dudley, R. (1985). Family evaluations and the development of standards for child custody determinations. *Columbia Journal of Law and Social Problems, 19,* 505–515.

Dawson-McClure, S. R., Sandler, I. N., Wolchik, S. A., and Millsap, R. E. (2004). Risk as a moderator of the effects of prevention programs for children from divorced families: A six-year longitudinal study. *Journal of Abnormal Child Psychology, 32,* 175–190.

Day, R. D. (1992). The transition to first intercourse among racially and culturally diverse youth. *Journal of Marriage and Family, 54,* 749–762.

Day, R. D., and Bahr, S. J. (1986). Income changes following divorce and remarriage. *Journal of Divorce, 9*(3), 75–88.

Day, R. D., and Hook, D. (1987). A short history of divorce: Jumping the broom—and back again. *Journal of Divorce, 10*(3–4), 57–73.

Deal, J. E., Stanley-Hagan, M., and Anderson, J. C. (1992). The marital relationships in remarried families. *Monographs of the Society for Research in Child Development, 57*(2–3), Serial No. 227.

Deater-Deckard, K., and Dunn, J. (1999). Multiple risks and adjustment in young children growing up in different family settings: A British community study of stepparent, single mother, and nondivorced families. In E. M. Hetherington (ed.), *Coping with divorce, single parenting, and remarriage: A risk and resiliency perspective* (pp. 47–64). Mahwah, N.J.: Erlbaum.

DeGarmo, D. S., Forgatch, M. S., and Martinez, C. R., Jr. (1999). Parenting of divorced mothers as a link between social status and boys' academic outcomes: Unpacking the effects of socioeconomic status. *Child Development, 70,* 1231–1245.

DeGarmo, D. S., and Kitson, G. C. (1996). Identity relevance and disruption as predictors of psychological distress for widowed and divorced women. *Journal of Marriage and Family, 58,* 983–997.

DelCarmen, R., and Virgo, G. N. (1993). Marital disruption and nonresidential parenting: A multicultural perspective. In C. E. Depner, and J. H. Bray (eds.), *Nonresidential parenting: New vistas in family living* (pp. 13–36). Thousand Oaks, Calif.: Sage Publications.

DeMaris, A., and Greif, G. L. (1992). The relationship between family structure and parent-child relationship problems in single father households. *Journal of Divorce and Remarriage, 18*(1–2), 55–78.

Demo, D. H., and Acock, A. C. (1996). Family structure, family process, and adolescent well-being. *Journal of Research on Adolescence, 6,* 457–488.

Depner, C. E., Leino, E. V., and Chun, A. (1992). Interparental conflict and child adjustment: A decade review and meta-analysis. *Family and Conciliation Courts Review, 30,* 323–341.

DeSimone-Luis, J., O'Mahoney, K., and Hunt, D. (1979). Children of separation and divorce: Factors influencing adjustment. *Journal of Divorce, 3*(1), 37–42.

Devall, E., Stoneman, Z., and Brody, G. (1986). The impact of divorce and maternal employment on 60 pre-adolescent children. *Family Relations, 35,* 153–159.

Dillaway, H., and Broman, C. (2001). Race, class and gender differences in marital satisfaction and divisions of household labor among dual-earner couples. *Journal of Family Issues, 22*(3), 309–327.

Dillon, P. A., and Emery, R. E. (1996). Divorce mediation and resolution of child custody disputes: Longterm effects. *American Journal of Orthopsychiatry, 66,* 131–140.

Dion, M. R., Braver, S. L., Wolchik, S., and Sandler, I. N. (1997). Alcohol abuse and psychopathic deviance in noncustodial parents as predictors of child-support payment and visitation. *American Journal of Orthopsychiatry, 67,* 70–79.

Dixon, C. S., Charles, M. A., and Craddock, A. A. (1998). The impact of experiences of parental divorce and parental conflict on young Australian adult men and women. *Journal of Family Studies, 4,* 21–34.

Doherty, W. J., and Needle, R. H. (1991). Psychological adjustment and substance use among adolescents before and after a parental divorce. *Child Development, 62,* 328–337.

Dolan, M. A., and Hoffman, C. D. (1998). Determinants of divorce among women: A reexamination of critical influences. *Journal of Divorce and Remarriage, 28*(3–4), 97–106.

Donovan, R. L., and Jackson, B. L. (1990). Deciding to divorce: A process guided by social exchange, attachment and cognitive dissonance theories. *Journal of Divorce, 13*(4), 23–35.

Dornbusch, S. M., Carlsmith, J. M., Bushwall, S. J., Ritter, P. L., Leiderman, H., Hastorf, A. H., and Gross, R. T. (1985). Single parents, extended households, and the control of adolescents. *Child Development, 56,* 326–341.

Downey, D. B. (1994). The school performance of children from single-mother and single-father families: Economic or interpersonal deprivation? *Journal of Family Issues, 15,* 129–147.

Drapeau, S., Samson, C., and Saint-Jacques, M.-C. (1999). The coping process among children of separated parents. *Journal of Divorce and Remarriage, 31*(1–2), 15–37.

Drill, R. L. (1986). Young adult children of divorced parents: Depression and the perception of loss. *Journal of Divorce, 10*(1–2), 169–187.

Dryden, J., Johnson, B. R., Howard, S., and McGuire, A. (1998, April). Resiliency: A comparison of construct definitions arising from conversations with 9 year old—12 year old children and their teachers. Paper presented at the Annual Meeting of the American Educational Research Association, San Diego, Calif.

Duberman, L. (1975). *The reconstituted family: A study of remarried couples and their children.* Chicago: Nelson-Hall.

Dubey, S. (1996). *A study of reasons for nonpayment of child support by noncustodial parents.* U.S. Department of Health and Human Services, Office of Child Support Enforcement. Retrieved May 7, 2004, from http://www.acf.dhhs.gov/programs/cse/new/csr9701.htm.

Ducibella, J. S. (1995). Consideration of the impact of how children are informed of their parents' divorce decision: A review of the literature. *Journal of Divorce and Remarriage, 2*(3–4), 121–142.

Dudley, J. R. (1996). Noncustodial fathers speak about their parental role. *Family and Conciliation Courts Review, 34,* 410–426.

Duffy, M. E., Thomas, C., and Trayner, C. (2002). Women's reflections on divorce: 10 years later. *Health Care for Women International, 23,* 550–560.

Duncan, G. J., and Hoffman, S. D. (1985). Economic consequences of marital instability. In M. David and T. Smeeding (eds.), *Horizontal equity, uncertainty, and economic well-being* (pp. 427–467). Chicago: University of Chicago Press.

Dunlop, R., Burns, A., and Bermingham, S. (2001). Parent-child relations and adolescent self-image following divorce: A 10 year study. *Journal of Youth and Adolescence, 30,* 117–134.

Dunn, J., Deater-Deckard, K., Pickering, K., O'Connor, T. G., Golding, J., and ALSPAC Study Team. (1998). Children's adjustment and prosocial behavior in step-, single, and nonstep-family settings: Findings from a community study. *Journal of Child Psychology and Psychiatry, 39,* 1083–1095.

Duquette, D. N. (1978). Child custody decision-making: The lawyer-behavioral scientist interface. *Journal of Clinical Child Psychology, 55,* 192–195.

Duran-Aydintug, C. (1997). Adult children of divorce revisited: When they speak up. *Journal of Divorce and Remarriage, 27*(1–2), 71–83.

Ehrenberg, M. F. (1996). Cooperative parenting arrangements after marital separation: Former couples who make it work. *Journal of Divorce and Remarriage, 26*(1–2), 93–115.

Einhorn, J. (1986). Child custody in historical perspective: A study of changing social perceptions of divorce and child custody in Anglo-American law. *Behavioral Sciences and the Law, 4,* 119–135.

Elkin, M. (1973). Conciliation courts: The reintegration of disintegrating families. *Family Coordinator, 63,* 64–70.

Elle (2004). Girls gone wild: 1000+ women tell how they found romance online, June.

Elliot, B. J., and Richards, M. P. M. (1991). Children and divorce: Educational performance and behavior before and after separation. *International Journal of Law and the Family, 5,* 258–287.

Ellis, E. M. (2000). *Divorce wars: Interventions with families in conflict.* Washington, D.C.: American Psychological Association.

Ellis, W. L. (1991). *The effects of background characteristics of attorneys and judges on decision-making in domestic relations court: An analysis of child support awards.* New York: Haworth Press.

Emery, R. E. (1994). *Renegotiating family relationships: Divorce, child custody, and mediation.* New York: Guilford.

Emery, R. E. (1999a). *Marriage, divorce, and children's adjustment* (2nd ed.). Newbury Park, Calif.: Sage Publications.

Emery, R. E. (1999b). Postdivorce family life for children: An overview of research and some implications for policy. In R. A. Thompson and P. R. Amato (eds.), *The postdivorce family: Children, parenting, and society* (pp. 3–27). Thousand Oaks, Calif.: Sage Publications.

Emery, R. E. (2001). Interparental conflict and social policy. In J. H. Grych and F. D. Fincham (eds.), *Interparental conflict and child development: Theory, research, and applications* (pp. 417–439). New York: Cambridge University Press.

Emery, R. E., and Coiro, M. J. (1997). Some costs of coping: Stress and distress among children from divorced families. In D. Cicchetti and S. L. Toth (eds.), *Developmental perspectives on trauma: Theory, research, and intervention. Rochester symposium on developmental psychology,* Vol. 8 (pp. 435–462). Rochester, N.Y.: University of Rochester Press.

Emery, R. E., and Dillon, P. (1994). Conceptualizing the divorce process: Renegotiating boundaries of intimacy and power in the divorced family system. *Family Relations, 43,* 374–379.

Emery, R. E., Kitzmann, K. M., and Waldron, M. (1999). Psychological interventions for separated and divorced families. In E. M. Hetherington (ed.), *Coping with divorce, single parenting, and remarriage: A risk and resiliency perspective* (pp. 323–344). Mahwah, N.J.: Erlbaum.

Emery, R. E., Laumann-Billings, L., Waldron, M. C., Sbarra, D. A., and Dillon, P. (2001). Child custody mediation and litigation: Custody, contact, and coparenting 12 years after initial dispute resolution. *Journal of Consulting and Clinical Psychology, 69,* 323–332.

Emery, R. E., Matthews, S. G., and Kitzmann, K. M. (1994). Child custody mediation and litigation: Parents' satisfaction and functioning one year after settlement. *Journal of Consulting and Clinical Psychology, 62,* 124–129.

Emery, R. E., Matthews, S. G., and Wyer, M. M. (1991). Child custody mediation and litigation: Further evidence on the differing views of mothers and fathers. *Journal of Consulting and Clinical Psychology, 59*(3), 410–418.

Emery, R. E., Waldron, M., Kitzmann, K. M., and Aaron, J. (1999). Delinquent behavior, future divorce or nonmarital childbearing, and externalizing behavior among offspring: A 14-year prospective study. *Journal of Family Psychology, 13,* 568–579.

Emery, R. E., and Wyer, M. M. (1987). Child custody mediation and litigation: An experimental evaluation of the experience of parents. *Journal of Consulting and Clinical Psychology, 55*(2), 179–186.

Ernest, N., Murphy, C. M., and O'Leary, K. D. (1989). Interspousal aggression, marital discord, and child problems. *Journal of Consulting and Clinical Psychology, 57,* 453–455.

Facchino, D., and Aron, A. (1990). Divorced fathers with custody: Method of obtaining custody and divorce adjustment. *Journal of Divorce, 13*(3), 45–56.

Farber, S. S., Felner, R. D., and Primavera, J. (1985). Parental separation/divorce and adolescents. An examination of factors mediating adaptation. *American Journal of Community Psychology, 13,* 171–185.

Fassinger, P. A. (1989). Becoming the breadwinner: Single mothers' reactions to changes in their paid work lives. *Family Relations, 38,* 404–411.

Fauber, R., Forehand, R., Thomas, A. M., and Wierson, M. (1990). A mediational model of the impact of marital conflict on adolescent adjustment in intact and divorced families: The role of disrupted parenting. *Child Development, 61,* 1112–1123.

Feng, D., Giarrusso, R., Bengtson, V. L., and Frye, N. (1999). Intergenerational transmission of marital quality and marital instability. *Journal of Marriage and Family, 61,* 451–463.

Fergusson, D. M., Horwood, L. J., and Lynskey, M. T. (1994). Parental separation, adolescent psychopathology, and problem behaviors. *Journal of the American Academy of Child and Adolescent Psychiatry, 33,* 1122–1131.

Fergusson, D. M., Lynskey, M. T., and Horwood, L. J. (1994). The effects of parental separation, the timing of separation and gender on children's performance on cognitive tests. *Journal of Child Psychology and Psychiatry and Allied Disciplines, 35,* 1077–1092.

Fine, M. A., Coleman, M., and Ganong, L. (1999). A social constructionist multi-method approach to understanding the stepparent role. In E. M. Hetherington (ed.), *Coping with divorce, single parenting, and remarriage: A risk and resiliency perspective* (pp. 273–294). Mahwah, N.J.: Erlbaum.

Fine, M. A., and Fine, D. R. (1992). Recent changes in laws affecting stepfamilies: Suggestions for legal reform. *Family Relations, 41,* 334–340.

Fine, M. A., Ganong, L., and Coleman, M. (1997). The relation between role constructions and adjustment among stepparents. *Journal of Family Issues, 18,* 503–525.

Fineman, M. (1988). Dominant discourse, professional language, and legal change in child custody decision making. *Harvard Law Review, 101,* 727–774.

Fineman, M. (1989). The politics of custody and gender: Child advocacy and the transformation of custody decision making in the USA. In C. Smart and S. Sevenhuijsen (eds.), *Child custody and the politics of gender* (pp. 27–50). New York: Routledge Press.

Folberg, J. (1991). Custody overview. In J. Folberg (ed.), *Joint custody and shared parenting* (2nd ed., pp. 3–10). New York: Guilford Press.

Forehand, R., Armistead, L., and David, C. (1997). Is adolescent adjustment following parental divorce a function of predivorce adjustment? *Journal of Abnormal Child Psychology, 25,* 157–164.

Forehand, R., Biggar, H., and Kotchick, B. A. (1998). Cumulative risk across family stressors: Short- and long-term effects for adolescents. *Journal of Abnormal Child Psychology, 26,* 119–128.

Forehand, R., Fauber, R., Long, N., Brody, G. H., and Slotkin, J. (1987). Maternal depressive mood following divorce: An examination of predictors and adolescent adjustment from a stress model perspective. In J. P. Vincent (ed.), *Advances in family intervention, assessment and theory,* Vol. 4 (pp. 71–98). Greenwich, Conn.: JAI Press.

Forehand, R., Middleton, K., and Long, N. (1987). Adolescent functioning as a consequence of recent parental divorce and the parent-adolescent relationship. *Journal of Applied Developmental Psychology, 8,* 305–315.

Forehand, R., Wierson, M., Thomas, A. M., Fauber, R., Armistead, L., Kemptom, T., and Long, N. (1991). A short-term longitudinal examination of young adolescent functioning following divorce: The role of family factors. *Journal of Abnormal Child Psychology, 19,* 97–111.

Forgatch, M. S., and DeGarmo, D. S. (1999). Parenting through change: An effective prevention program for single mothers. *Journal of Consulting and Clinical Psychology, 67,* 711–724.

Forthofer, M. S., Kessler, R. C., Story, A. L., and Gotlib, I. H. (1996). The effect of psychiatric disorder on the probability and timing of first marriage. *Journal of Health and Social Behavior, 37,* 121–132.

Francke, L. B. (1983). *Growing up divorced.* New York: Linden Press/Simon and Schuster.

Frisco, M. L., and Williams, K. (2003). Perceived housework equity, marital happiness, and divorce in dual-earner households. *Journal of Family Issues, 24,* 51–73.

Furstenberg, F. F., Jr. (1990). Divorce and the American family. *Annual Review of Sociology, 16,* 379–403.

Furstenberg, F. F., Jr., and Cherlin, A. J. (1991). *Divided families: What happens to children when parents part.* Cambridge, Mass.: Harvard University Press.

Furstenberg, F. F., and Kiernan, K. E. (2001). Delayed parental divorce: How much do children benefit? *Journal of Marriage and Family, 63,* 446–457.

Furstenberg, F. F., Jr., and Nord, C. W. (1985): Parenting apart: Patterns of childrearing after marital disruption. *Journal of Marriage and Family, 47,* 893–904.

Furstenberg, F. F., Jr., Peterson, J. L., Nord, C. W., and Zill, N. (1983). The life course of children of divorce: Marital disruption and parental contact. *American Sociological Review, 48,* 656–668.

Furstenberg, F. F., Jr., and Spanier, G. B. (1984). The risk of dissolution in remarriage: An examination of Cherlin's hypothesis of incomplete institutionalization. *Family Relations, 33,* 433–441.

Furstenberg, F. F., and Teitler, J. O. (1994). Reconsidering the effects of marital disruption: What happens to children of divorce in early adulthood? *Journal of Family Issues, 15,* 173–190.

Gallo, L. C., Troxel, W. M., Matthews, K. A., and Kuller, L. H. (2003). Marital status and quality in middle-aged women: Associations with levels and trajectories of cardiovascular risk factors. *Health Psychology, 22,* 453–463.

Gander, A. M., and Jorgensen, L. A. B. (1990). Postdivorce adjustment: Social support among older divorced persons. *Journal of Divorce, 13*(4), 37–56.

Ganong, L., and Coleman, M. (1994). Adolescent stepchild-stepparent relationships: Changes over time. In K. Pasley and M. Ihinger-Tallman (eds.), *Stepparenting: Issues in theory, research, and practice* (pp. 87–106). New York: Greenwood.

Ganong, L., and Coleman, M. (1997). How society views stepfamilies. *Marriage and Family Review, 26,* 85–106.

Ganong, L., Coleman, M., Fine, M., and Martin, P. (1999). Stepparents' affinity-seeking and affinity maintaining strategies with stepchildren. *Journal of Family Issues, 20,* 299–327.

Gardner, R. A. (1999). Assessment for the stronger, healthier psychological bond in child-custody evaluations. *Journal of Divorce and Remarriage, 31*(1–2), 1–14.

Garrison, M. (1994). The economic consequences of divorce. *Family and Conciliation Courts Review, 32,* 10–26.

Garrity, C. B., and Baris, M. A. (1994). *Caught in the middle.* New York: Lexington Books.

Garvin, V., Kalter, N., and Hansell, J. (1993a). Divorced women: Factors contributing to resiliency and vulnerability. *Journal of Divorce and Remarriage, 21*(1–2), 21–39.

Garvin, V., Kalter, N., and Hansell, J. (1993b) Divorced women: Individual differences in stressors, mediating factors, and adjustment outcome. *American Journal of Orthopsychiatry, 63*(2), 232–240.

Garvin, V., Leber, D., and Kalter, N. (1991). Children of divorce: Predictors of change following preventive intervention. *American Journal of Orthopsy-chiatry, 61,* 438–447.

Gasser, R. D., and Taylor, C. M. (1976). Role adjustment of single parent fathers with dependent children. *The Family Coordinator, 25,* 397–401.

Ge, X., Conger, R. D., Lorenz, F. O., Elder, G. H., and Simons, R. L. (1992). Linking family economic hardship to adolescent distress. *Journal of Research on Adolescence, 2,* 351–378.

Ge, X., Lorenz, F. O., Conger, R. D., Elder, G. H., and Simons, R. L. (1994). Trajectories of stressful life events and depressive symptoms during adolescence. *Developmental Psychology, 30,* 467–483.

Geffner, R. (1992). Guidelines for using mediation with abusive couples. *Psychotherapy in Private Practice, 10*(1–2), 77–92.

Geffner, R., and Pagelow, M. D. (1990). Mediation and child custody issues in abusive relationships. *Behavioral Sciences and the Law, 8,* 151–159.

Gelles, R. J. (1989). Child abuse and violence in single-parent families: Parent absence and economic deprivation. *American Journal of Orthopsychiatry, 59,* 492–501.

George, C., Kaplan, N., and Main, M. (1984/1985/1996). *The adult attachment interview* (3rd ed.). Unpublished manuscript, Department of Psychology, University of California, Berkeley.

Gerstel, N. (1987). Divorce and stigma. *Social Problems, 34,* 172–186.

Gerstel, N. (1988). Divorce, gender, and social integration. *Gender and Society, 2,* 343–367.

Gerstel, N., Riessman, C. K., and Rosenfield, S. (1985). Explaining the symptomatology of separated and divorced women and men: The role of material conditions and social networks. *Social Forces, 64,* 84–101.

Ginott, H. (1975). *Between parent and child.* New York: Macmillan.

Ginsberg, D. (1986). Friendship and postdivorce adjustment. In J. M. Gottman and J. G. Parker (eds.), *Conversations of friends: Speculations on affective development. Studies in emotion and social interaction* (pp. 346–376). New York: Cambridge University Press.

Glenn, N. D., and Supancic, M. (1984). The social and demographic correlates of divorce and separation in the U.S.: An update and reconsideration. *Journal of Marriage and Family, 46*(3), 563–585.

Goerdt, John A. (1992). *Divorce courts: Case management, case characteristics, and the pace of litigation in 16 urban jurisdiction.* Williamsburg, Va.: National Center for State Courts, Publication Number R-141.

Goethal, K. G., Thiessen, J. D., Henton, J., Avery, A. W., and Joanning, H. (1983). Facilitating postdivorce adjustment among women: A one-month follow-up. *Family Therapy, 10,* 61–68.

Goetting, A. (1983). Divorce outcome research: Issues and perspectives. In A. S. Skolnick and J. H. Skolnick (eds.), *The family in transition* (pp. 367–386). Boston: Little, Brown.

Gohm, C. L., Oishi, S., Darlington, J., and Diener, E. (1998). Culture, parental conflict, parental marital status, and the subjective well-being of young adults. *Journal of Marriage and Family, 60,* 319–334.

Goldberg, W. A., Greenberger, E., Hamill, S., and O'Neil, R. (1992). Role demands in the lives of employed single mothers with preschoolers. *Journal of Family Issues, 13,* 312–333.

Goldstein, J., Freud, A., and Solnit, A. J. (1973). *Beyond the best interests of the child.* New York: Free Press.

Goldstein, J., Freud, A., Solnit, A. J., and Goldstein, S. (1986). *In the best interests of the child.* New York: Free Press.

Goldstein, J. R. (1999). The leveling of divorce in the United States. *Demography, 36,* 409–414.

Goode, W. (1956). *After divorce.* Glencoe, Ill.: Free Press.

Goode, W. J. (1993). *World changes in divorce patterns.* New Haven, Conn.: Yale University Press.

Goodman, C. C. (1993). Divorce after long term marriages: Former spouse relationships. *Journal of Divorce and Remarriage, 20*(1–2), 43–62.

Gottman, J. M. (1994a). An agenda for marital therapy. In S. M. Johnson and L. S. Greenberg (eds.), *The heart of the matter: Perspectives on emotion in marital therapy* (pp. 256–293). Philadelphia: Brunner/Mazel.

Gottman, J. M. (1994b). *What predicts divorce? The relationship between marital processes and marital outcomes.* Hillsdale, N.J.: Erlbaum.

Gottman, J. M. (1998). Toward a process model of men in marriages and families. In A. Booth and A. C. Crouter (eds.), *Men in families: When do they get involved? What difference does it make?* (pp. 149–192). New York: Russell Sage.

Gottman, J. M., and Carrere, S. (1994). Why can't men and women get along? Developmental roots and marital inequities. In D. J. Canary and L. Stafford (eds.), *Communication and relational maintenance.* (pp. 203–229). New York: Greenwood.

Gottman, J. M., Coan, J., Carrere, S., and Swanson, C. (1998). Predicting marital happiness and stability from newlywed interactions. *Journal of Marriage and Family, 60,* 5–22.

Gourley, E. V. III, and Stolberg, A. L. (2000). An empirical investigation of psychologists' custody evaluation procedures. *Journal of Divorce and Remarriage, 33*(1–2), 1–29.

Grall, T. (2003). Custodial mothers and fathers and their child support: 2001. *Current Population Reports,* P60–225. U.S. Bureau of the Census. Washington, D.C.: U.S. Government Printing Office.

Gray, J. D., and Silver, R. C. (1990). Opposite sides of the same coin: Former spouses' divergent perspectives in coping with their divorce. *Journal of Personality and Social Psychology, 59,* 1180–1191.

Greif, G. L. (1985). *Single fathers.* Lexington, Mass.: Lexington Books.

Greif, G. L. (1995). Single fathers with custody following separation and divorce. *Marriage and Family Review, I. 20,* 213–231.

Grillo, T. (1991). The mediation alternative: Process dangers for women. *The Yale Law Journal, 100,* 1545–1610.

Grisso, T. (1986). *Evaluating competencies: Forensic assessments and instruments.* New York: Plenum.

Grossberg, M. (1985). *Governing the hearth: Law and family in nineteenth-century America.* Chapel Hill: University of North Carolina Press.

Grych, J. H., and Fincham, F. D. (1990). Marital conflict and children's adjustment: A cognitive-contextual framework. *Psychological Bulletin, 108,* 267–290.

Guidubaldi, J., and Cleminshaw, H. (1985). Divorce, family health, and child adjustment. *Family Relations, 34,* 35–41.

Guidubaldi, J., and Duckworth, J. (2001). Divorce and children's cognitive ability. In E. L. Grigorenko and R. J. Sternberg (eds.), *Family environment and intellectual functioning: A life-span perspective* (pp. 97–118). Mahwah, N.J.: Erlbaum.

Guidubaldi, J., and Perry, J. D. (1985). Divorce and mental health sequelae for children: A two-year follow-up of a nationwide sample. *Journal of the American Academy of Child Psychiatry, 24,* 531–537.

Guidubaldi, J., Perry, J. D., and Nastasi, B. K. (1987a). Assessment and intervention for children of divorce: Implication of the NASP-KSU Nationwide Study. In J. P. Vincent (ed.), *Advances in family intervention, assessment and theory,* Vol. 4 (pp. 33–70). Greenwich, Conn.: JAI Press.

Guidubaldi, J., Perry, J. D., and Nastasi, B. K. (1987b). Growing up in a divorced family: Initial and long-term perspective on children's adjustment. In S. Oskamp (ed.), *Annual Review of Applied Social Psychology,* Vol. 7 (pp. 202–237). Beverly Hills, Calif.: Sage Publications.

Gunnoe, M. L., and Braver, S. L. (2001). The effects of joint legal custody on mothers, fathers, and children controlling for factors that predispose a sole maternal versus joint legal award. *Law and Human Behavior, 25,* 25–43.

Guttmann, J. (1993). *Divorce in psychosocial perspective: Theory and research.* Hillsdale, N.J.: Erlbaum.

Guttmann, J., and Lazar, A. (1998). Mother's or father's custody: Does it matter for social adjustment? *Educational Psychology, 18,* 225–234.

Haine, R. A., Sandler, I. N., Wolchik, S. A., Tein, J.-Y., and Dawson-McClure, S. R. (2003). Changing the legacy of divorce: Evidence from prevention programs and future directions. *Family Relations, 52,* 397–405.

Halem, L. C. (1982). *Separated and divorced women.* Westport, Conn.: Greenwood.

Hammond, R. J., and Muller, G. O. (1992). The late-life divorced: Another look. *Journal of Divorce and Remarriage, 17*(3–4), 135–150.

Hanson, T. L. (1999). Does parental conflict explain why divorce is negatively associated with child welfare? *Social Forces, 77*, 1283–1316.

Hanson, T. L., McLanahan, S. S., and Thomson, E. (1996). Double jeopardy: Parental conflict and stepfamily outcomes for children. *Journal of Marriage and Family, 58*, 141–154.

Hardesty, J. L. (2002). Separation assault in the context of postdivorce parenting: An integrative review of the literature. *Violence against Women, 8*, 597–625.

Harger, J., and El-Sheikh, M. (2003). Are children more angered and distress by man-child than woman-child arguments and by interadult versus adult-child disputes? *Social Development, 12*, 162–181.

Harland, P., Reijneveld, S. A., Brugman, E., Verloove-Vanhorick, S. P., and Verhulst, F. C. (2002). Family factors and life events as risk factors for behavioral and emotional problems in children. *European Child and Adolescent Psychiatry, 11*(4), 176–184.

Harlow, H. F., and Zimmerman, R. R. (1959). Affectional responses in the infant monkey. *Science, 130*, 421–432.

Harold, G. T., Fincham, F. D., Osborne, L. N., and Conger, R. D. (1997). Mom and Dad are at it again: Adolescent perceptions of marital conflict and adolescent psychological distress. *Developmental Psychology, 33*, 333–350.

Harris, J. R. (1998). *The nurture assumption: Why children turn out the way they do.* New York: Free Press.

Hart, B. J. (1990). Gentle jeopardy: The further endangerment of battered women and children in custody mediation. *Mediation Quarterly, 7*, 317–330.

Hawkins, A. J., Nock, S. L., Wilson, J. C., Sanchez, L., and Wright, J. D. (2002). Attitudes about covenant marriage and divorce: Policy implication from a three-state comparison. *Family Relations, 51*, 166–175.

Hawthorne, B. (2000). Split custody as a viable post-divorce option. *Journal of Divorce and Remarriage, 33*(3–4), 1–19.

Hazan, C., and Shaver, P. R. (1994). Attachment as an organizational framework for research on close relationships. *Psychological Inquiry, 5*(1), 1–22.

Healy, J. M., Stewart, A. J., and Copeland, A. P. (1993). The role of self-blame in children's adjustment to parental separation. *Personality and Social Psychology Bulletin, 19*, 279–289.

Heath, P. A., and MacKinnon, C. (1988). Factors related to the social competence of children in single-parent families. *Journal of Divorce, 11*(3–4), 49–66.

Heaton, T. B. (2002). Factors contributing to increasing marital stability in the U.S. *Journal of Family Issues, 23*, 392–409.

Heinicke, C. M., Guthrie, D., and Ruth, G. (1997). Marital adaptation, divorce, and parent-infant development: A prospective study. *Infant Mental Health Journal, 18*, 282–299.

Hemstroem, O. (1996). Is marriage dissolution linked to differences in mortality risks for men and women? *Journal of Marriage and Family, 58,* 366–378.

Hendrick, C., and Hendrick, S. S. (1989). Research on love: Does it measure up? *Journal of Personality and Social Psychology, 56,* 784–794.

Henry, C. S., and Lovelace, S. G. (1995). Family resources and adolescent family life satisfaction in remarried family households. *Journal of Family Issues, 16,* 765–786.

Herman, P., and Bretherton, I. (2001). "He was the best daddy": Postdivorce preschoolers' representations of loss and family life. In A. Goencue and E. L. Klein (eds.), *Children in play, story, and school* (pp. 177–203). New York: Guilford.

Hernandez, P., Beller, A. H., and Graham, J. W. (1995). Changes in the relationship between child support payments and educational attainment of offspring, 1979–1988. *Demography, 32,* 249–260.

Hernandez, P., Beller, A. H., and Graham, J. W. (1996). The child support enforcement amendments of 1984 and educational attainment of young adults in the United States. *Review of Labour Economics and Industrial Relations, 10,* 538–558.

Hess, R. D., and Camara, K. A. (1979). Post-divorce family relationships as mediating factors in the consequences of divorce for children. *Journal of Social Issues, 35*(4), 79–96.

Hester, T. (1992). The mental health professional in child custody determinations incident to divorce. *Women's Rights Law Reporter, 14,* 109–137.

Hetherington, E. M. (1989). Coping with family transitions: Winners, losers, and survivors. *Child Development, 60,* 1–14.

Hetherington, E. M. (1991). Coping with family transitions: Winners, losers, and survivors. In S. Chess, and M. E. Hertzig (eds.), *Annual Progress in Child Psychiatry and Child Development, 1990* (pp. 221–241). Philadelphia: Brunner/Mazel.

Hetherington, E. M. (1993). An overview of the Virginia Longitudinal Study of Divorce and Remarriage with a focus on early adolescence. *Journal of Family Psychology, 7,* 39–56.

Hetherington, E. M. (1999). Should we stay together for the sake of the children? In E. M. Hetherington (ed.), *Coping with divorce, single parenting, and remarriage: A risk and resiliency perspective* (pp. 93–116). Mahwah, N.J.: Erlbaum.

Hetherington, E. M. (2003). Intimate pathways: Changing patterns in close personal relationships across time. *Family Relations, 52,* 318–331.

Hetherington, E. M., Bridges, M., and Insabella, G. M. (1998). What matters? What does not? Five perspectives on the association between marital transitions and children's adjustment. *American Psychologist, 53,* 167–184.

Hetherington, E. M., and Clingempeel, W. G. (1992). Coping with marital transitions: A family systems perspective. *Monographs of the Society for Research in Child Development, 57*(2–3), Serial No. 227, 1–242.

Hetherington, E. M., Cox, M., and Cox, R. (1976). Divorced fathers. *Family Coordinator, 25,* 417–428.

Hetherington, E. M., Cox, M., and Cox, R. (1978). The aftermath of divorce. In J. H. Stevens, Jr., and M. Mathews (eds.), *Mother/child, father/child relationships* (pp. 149–176). Washington, D.C.: National Association for the Education of Young Children.

Hetherington, E. M., Cox, M., and Cox, R. (1979). Play and social interaction in children following divorce. *Journal of Social Issues, 35,* 26–49.

Hetherington, E. M., Cox, M., and Cox, R.(1982). Effects of divorce on parents and children. In M. E. Lamb (ed.), *Nontraditional families: Parenting and child development* (pp. 233–288). Hillsdale, N.J.: Erlbaum.

Hetherington, E. M., Cox, M., and Cox, R. (1985). Long-term effects of divorce and remarriage on the adjustment of children. *Journal of the American Academy of Child Psychiatry, 24,* 518–530.

Hetherington, E. M., and Jodl, K. M. (1994). Stepfamilies as settings for child development. In A. Booth and J. Dunn (eds.), *Stepfamilies: Who benefits? Who does not?* (pp. 55–79). Hillsdale, N.J.: Erlbaum.

Hetherington, E. M., and Kelly, J. (2002). *For better or for worse: Divorce reconsidered.* New York: W. W. Norton.

Hetherington, E. M., Law, T. C., and O'Connor, T. G. (1993). Divorce: Challenges, changes, and new chances. In F. Walsh (ed.), *Normal family processes* (2nd ed., pp. 208–234). New York: Guilford.

Hetherington, E. M., and Stanley-Hagan, M. (1999). The adjustment of children with divorced parents: A risk and resiliency perspective. *Journal of Child Psychology and Psychiatry and Allied Disciplines, 40,* 129–140.

Hetherington, E. M., and Stanley-Hagan, M. (2002). Parenting in divorced and remarried families. In M. H. Bornstein (ed.), *Handbook of parenting: Vol. 3. Being and becoming a parent* (2nd ed., pp. 287–315). Mahwah, N.J.: Erlbaum.

Hilton, J. M., and Desrochers, S. (2000). The influence of economic strain, coping with roles, and parental control on the parenting of custodial single mothers and custodial single fathers. *Journal of Divorce and Remarriage, 33*(3–4), 55–76.

Hilton, J. M., and Devall, E. L. (1998). Comparison of parenting and children's behavior in single-mother, single-father, and intact families. *Journal of Divorce and Remarriage, 29*(3–4), 23–54.

Hingst, A. G. (1981). Child and divorce: The child's view. *Journal of Clinical Child Psychology, 3,* 161–164.

Hingst, A. G. (1984). Children and divorce: The parent's view. *Conciliation Courts Review, 22,* 89–95.

Hobart, C. (1991). Conflict in remarriages. *Journal of Divorce and Remarriage,* *15,* 69–86.

Hodges, W. F. (1991). *Interventions for children of divorce: Custody, access, and psychotherapy* (2nd ed.). New York: Wiley.

Hodges, W. F., Tierney, C. W., and Buchsbaum, H. K. (1984). The cumulative effect of stress on preschool children of divorce and intact families. *Journal of Marriage and Family, 46,* 611–617.

Hodges, W. F., Wechsler, R. C., and Ballantine, C. (1979). Divorce and the preschool child: Cumulative stress. *Journal of Divorce, 3*(1), 55–67.

Hodgson, J., Dienhart, A., and Daly, K. (2001). Time juggling: Single mothers' experience of time-press following divorce. *Journal of Divorce and Remarriage, 35*(1–2), 1–28.

Hoffman, C. D., and Avila, A. M. (1998). Young children's negative stereotyping of peers from divorced families. *Journal of Divorce and Remarriage, 29*(1–2), 67–78.

Hoffman, S. D., and Duncan, G. J. (1988). What are the economic consequences of divorce? *Demography, 25,* 641–645.

Hoffmann, J. P., and Johnson, R. A. (1998). A national portrait of family structure and adolescent drug use. *Journal of Marriage and Family, 60,* 633–645.

Holden, K. C., and Kuo, H. D. (1996). Complex marital histories and economic well-being: The continuing legacy of divorce and widowhood as the HRS cohort approaches retirement. *Gerontologist, 36,* 383–390.

Holden, K. C., and Smock, P. J. (1991). The economic costs of marital dissolution: Why do women bear a disproportionate cost? *Annual Review of Sociology, 17,* 51–78.

Homans, G. (1961). *Social behavior: Its elementary forms.* New York: Harcourt, Brace, and World.

Hooley, J. M., Richters, J. E., Weintraub, S., and Neale, J. M. (1987). Psychopathology and marital distress: The positive side of positive symptoms. *Journal of Abnormal Psychology, 96,* 27–33.

Hope, S., Power, C., and Rodgers, B. (1998). The relationship between parental separation in childhood and problem drinking in adulthood. *Addiction, 93,* 505–514.

Hope, S., Power, C., and Rodgers, B. (1999). Does financial hardship account for elevated psychological distress in lone mothers? *Social Science and Medicine, 49,* 1637–1649.

Hope, S., Rodgers, B., and Power, C. (1999). Marital status transitions and psychological distress: Longitudinal evidence from a national population sample. *Psychological Medicine, 29,* 381–389.

Hoppe, C. F. (1997). Perpetually battling parents. In B. S. Mark and J. A. Incorvaia, (eds.), *The handbook of infant, child, and adolescent psychotherapy: Vol. 2. New directions in integrative treatment* (pp. 485–501). Northvale, N.J.: Jason Aronson.

Hopper, J. (1993). The rhetoric of motives in divorce. *Journal of Divorce and Re-marriage, 14*(3–4), 33–60.

Houlgate, L. D. (1987). Divorce child custody disputes. *Journal of Divorce, 10*(3–4), 15–26.

Hoyt, L. A., Cowen, E. L., Pedro-Carroll, J. L., and Alpert-Gillis, L. J. (1990). Anxiety and depression in young children of divorce. *Journal of Clinical Child Psychology, 19*, 26–32.

Huddleston, R. J., and Hawkings, L. D. (1991a). A comparison of physical and emotional health after divorce in a Canadian and United States' sample. *Journal of Divorce and Remarriage, 15*(1–2), 193–207.

Huddleston, R. J., and Hawkings, L. D. (1991b). The effect of divorce on daily routine. *Family and Conciliation Courts Review, 29*, 150–159.

Hughes, R., Jr., Clark, C. D., Schaefer-Hernan, P., and Good, E. S. (1994). An evaluation of a newsletter intervention for divorced mothers. *Family Relations, 43*, 298–304.

Hughes, R., Jr., Good, E. S., and Candell, K. A. (1993). Longitudinal study of the effects of social support on the psychological adjustment of divorced mothers. *Journal of Divorce and Remarriage, 19*(1–2), 37–56.

Hysjulien, C., Wood, B., Benjamin, G., and Andrew, H. (1994). Child custody evaluations: A review of methods used in litigation and alternative dispute resolution. *Family and Conciliation Courts Review, 32*, 466–489.

Irving, H. H., and Benjamin, M. (1992). An evaluation of process and outcome in a private family mediation service. *Mediation Quarterly, 10*, 35–55.

Isaacs, M. B. (1988). The visitation schedule and child adjustment: A three-year study. *Family Process, 27*, 251–256.

Isaacs, M. B., and Leon, G. H. (1986). Social networks, divorce, and adjustment: A tale of three generations. *Journal of Divorce, 9*(4), 1–15.

Isaacs, M. B., and Leon, G. (1988). Divorce, disputation, and discussion: Communicational styles among recently separated spouses. *Journal of Family Psychology, 1*, 298–311.

Isaacs, M. B., Leon, G., and Donohue, A. M. (1986). Who are the "normal" children of divorce? On the need to specify population. *Journal of Divorce, 10*(1–2), 107–119.

Ishii-Kuntz, M., and Coltrane, S. (1992). Remarriage, stepparenting, and household labor. *Journal of Family Issues, 13*, 215–233. Jacobson, D. S. (1978a). The impact of marital separation/divorce on children: III. Parent-child communication and child adjustment, and regression analysis of findings from overall study. *Journal of Divorce, 2*, 175–194.

Jacobson, D. S. (1978b). The impact of marital separation/divorce on children: I. Parent-child separation and child adjustment. *Journal of Divorce, 1*, 341–359.

Jacquet, S. E., and Surra, C. A. (2001). Parental divorce and premarital couples:

Commitment and other relationship characteristics. *Journal of Marriage and Family, 63,* 627–638.

Jekielek, S. M. (1998). Parental conflict, marital disruption and children's emotional well-being. *Social Forces, 76,* 905–936.

Jenkins, J. M., and Smith, M. A. (1991). Marital disharmony and children's behavior problems: Aspects of a poor marriage that affect children adversely. *Journal of Child Psychology and Psychiatry, 32,* 793–810.

Jenkins, J. M., and Smith, M. A. (1993). A prospective study of behavioural disturbance in children who subsequently experience parental divorce: A research note. *Journal of Divorce and Remarriage, 19*(1–2), 143–160.

Jeynes, W. H. (1998). Examining the effects of divorce on the academic achievement of children: How should we control for SES? *Journal of Divorce and Remarriage, 29*(3–4), 1–21.

Jocklin, V., McGue, M., and Lykken, D. T. (1996). Personality and divorce: A genetic analysis. *Journal of Personality and Social Psychology, 71,* 288–299.

Joesch, J. M., and Smith, K. R. (1997). Children's health and their mothers' risk of divorce or separation. *Social Biology, 44*(3–4), 159–169.

Johnson, D. R., and Wu, J. (2002). An empirical test of crisis, social selection, and role explanations of the relationship between marital disruption and psychological distress: A pooled time-series analysis of four-wave panel data. *Journal of Marriage and Family, 64,* 211–224.

Johnston, J. R. (1994). High-conflict divorce. *The Future of Children, 4*(1), 165–182.

Johnston, J. R. (1995). Children's adjustment in sole custody compared to joint custody families and principles for custody decision making. *Family and Conciliation Courts Review, 33,* 415–425.

Johnston, J. R., Kline, M., and Tschann, J. M. (1989). Ongoing postdivorce conflict: Effects on children of joint custody and frequent access. *American Journal of Orthopsychiatry, 59,* 576–592.

Johnston, J. R., Kline, M., and Tschann, J. M. (1991). Ongoing post-divorce conflict in families contesting custody: Do joint custody and frequent access help? In. J. Folberg (ed). *Joint custody and shared parenting* (2nd ed.), pp. 177–184. New York: Guilford Press.

Johnston, J. R., and Roseby, V. (1997). *In the name of the child: A developmental approach to understanding and helping children of conflicted and violent divorce.* New York: Free Press.

Juby, H., and Farrington, D. P. (2001). Disentangling the link between disrupted families and delinquency. *British Journal of Criminology, 41,* 22–40.

Judicial Council of California, Center for Families, Children and the Courts (2000). *Report 12: Preparing court-based child custody mediation services for the future.* Statewide Uniform Statistical Reporting System: The 1996 Client Baseline Study, 2000.

Jurkovic, G. J, Thirkield, A., and Morrell, R. (2001). Parentification of adult children of divorce: A multidimensional analysis. *Journal of Youth and Adolescence, 30,* 245–257.

Kalter, N., Kloner, A., Schreier, S., and Okla, K. (1989). Predictors of children's postdivorce adjustment. *American Journal of Orthopsychiatry, 59,* 605–618.

Kalter, H., and Plunkett, J. W. (1984). Children's perceptions of the causes and consequences of divorce. *Journal of the American Academy of Child Psychiatry, 23,* 326–334.

Karney, B. R., and Bradbury, T. N. (1995). The longitudinal course of marital quality and stability: A review of theory, method, and research. *Psychological Bulletin, 118,* 3–34.

Karr, S. K., and Easley, B. (1986). Exploration of effects of divorce on the preschool HOME inventory. *Psychological Reports, 59,* 659–662.

Karras, D., and Berry, K. K. (1985). Custody evaluations: A critical review. *Professional Psychology—Research and Practice, 16*(1), 76–85.

Katz, L. F., and Gottman, J. M. (1993). Patterns of marital conflict predict children's internalizing and externalizing behaviors. *Developmental Psychology, 29,* 940–950.

Katz, L. F., and Gottman, J. M. (1997). Buffering children from marital conflict and dissolution. *Journal of Clinical Child Psychology, 26,* 157–171.

Kaye, S. H. (1988–89). The impact of divorce on children's academic performance. *Journal of Divorce, 12*(2–3), 283–298.

Keith, V. M., and Finlay, B. (1988). The impact of parental divorce on children's education attainment, marital timing, and likelihood of divorce. *Journal of Marriage and Family, 50,* 797–809.

Kelly, E. L., and Conley, J. J. (1987). Personality and compatibility: A prospective analysis of marital stability and marital satisfaction. *Journal of Personality and Social Psychology, 52,* 27–40.

Kelly, J. B. (1988). Longer-term adjustment in children of divorce: Converging findings and implications for practice. *Journal of Family Psychology, 2,* 119–140. Kelly, J. B. (1990). Is mediation less expensive? Comparison of mediated and adversarial divorce costs. *Mediation Quarterly, 8,* 15–26.

Kelly, J. B. (1993). Current research on children's postdivorce adjustment: No simple answers. *Family and Conciliation Courts Review, 31,* 29–49.

Kelly, J. B. (1996). A decade of divorce mediation research: Some answers and questions. *Family and Conciliation Courts Review, 34,* 373–385.

Kelly, J. B. (1997). The best interests of the child: A concept in search of meaning. *Family and Conciliation Courts Review, 35,* 377–387.

Kelly, J. B. (2000). Children's adjustment in conflicted marriage and divorce: A decade review of research. *Journal of the American Academy of Child and Adolescent Psychiatry, 39,* 963–973.

Kendler, K. S., Neale, M. C., Kessler, R. C., Heath, A. C., and Eaves, J. J. (1992).

Childhood parental loss and adult psychopathology in women: A study perspective. *Archives of General Psychiatry, 49,* 109–116.

Kessler, R. C., and McRae, J. A., Jr. (1984). A note on the relationships of sex and marital status to psychological stress. In J. R. Greenley (ed.), *Research in Community and Mental Health,* Vol. 4 (pp. 109–130). Greenwich, Conn.: JAI press.

Kiecolt-Glaser, J. K., Bane, C., Glaser, R., and Malarkey, W. B. (2003). Love, marriage, and divorce: Newlyweds' stress hormones foreshadow relationship changes. *Journal of Consulting and Clinical Psychology, 71,* 176–188.

Kiecolt-Glaser, J. K., Fisher, L. D., Ogrocki, P., and Stout, J. C. (1987). Marital quality, marital disruption, and immune function. *Psychosomatic Medicine, 49,* 13–34.

Kiecolt-Glaser, J. K., Kennedy, S., Malkoff, S., Fisher, L., Speicher, C. E., and Glaser, R. (1988). Marital discord and immunity in males. *Psychosomatic Medicine, 50,* 213–229.

Kiernan, K. E. (1992). The impact of family disruption in childhood on transitions made in young adult life. *Population Studies, 46,* 213–234.

Kiernan, K. E., and Hobcraft, J. (1997). Parental divorce during childhood: Age at first intercourse, partnership and parenthood. *Population Studies, 51*(1), 41–55.

Kiernan, K. E., and Mueller, G. (1999). Who divorces? In S. McRae (ed.), *Population and household change in Britain* (pp. 377–403). Oxford, England: Oxford University Press.

Kim, H. K., and McKenry, P. C. (2002). The relationship between marriage and psychological well-being: A longitudinal analysis. *Journal of Family Issues, 23,* 885–911.

Kim, L. S., Sandler, I. N., and Tein, J.-Y. (1997). Locus of control as a stress moderator and mediator in children of divorce. *Journal of Abnormal Child Psychology, 25,* 145–155.

King, V. (1994). Nonresident father involvement and child well-being: Can dads make a difference? *Journal of Family Issues, 15,* 78–96.

King, V., and Heard, H. E. (1999). Nonresident father visitation, parental conflict, and mother's satisfaction: What's best for child well-being? *Journal of Marriage and Family, 61,* 385–396.

Kirby, J. B. (2002). The influence of parental separation on smoking initiation in adolescents. *Journal of Health and Social Behavior, 43,* 56–71.

Kirby, L., and Fraser, M. (1997). Risk and resilience in childhood. In Mark Fraser (ed.), *Risk and resilience in childhood: An ecological perspective* (pp. 10–33). Washington, D.C.: NASW Press.

Kitson, G. C., and Holmes, W. M. (1992). *Portrait of divorce: Adjustment to marital breakdown. Perspectives on marriage and the family.* New York: Guilford Press.

Kitzmann, K. M., and Emery, R. E. (1994). Child and family coping one year after mediated and litigated child custody disputes. *Journal of Family Psychology, 8,* 150–159.

Kline, M., Tschann, J. M., Johnston, J. R., and Wallerstein, J. S. (1989). Children's adjustment in joint and sole physical custody families. *Developmental Psychology, 25,* 430–438.

Koerner, S. S., Wallace, S., Lehman, S. J., and Raymond, M. (2002). Mother-to-daughter disclosure after divorce: Are there costs and benefits? *Journal of Child and Family Studies, 11,* 469–483.

Kolevzon, M. S., and Gottlieb, S. J. (1983). The impact of divorce: A multivariate study. *Journal of Divorce, 7*(2), 89–98.

Korman, S. K., and Leslie, G. R. (1985). *The family in social context* (6th ed.). Toronto, Canada: Oxford University Press.

Kposowa, A. J. (2000). Marital status and suicide in the National Longitudinal Mortality Study. *Journal of Epidemiology and Community Health, 54*(4), 254–261.

Kramer, K. M., Arbuthnot, J., Gordon, D. A., Rousis, N. J., and Hoza, J. (1998). Effects of skill-based versus information based divorce education programs on domestic violence and parental communication. *Family and Conciliation Courts Review, 36,* 9–31.

Kramer, L., and Kowal, A. (1998). Long-term follow-up of a court-based intervention for divorcing parents. *Family and Conciliation Courts Review, 36,* 452–465.

Krauss, D., and Sales, B. D. (2000). Legal standards, expertise, and experts in the resolution of contested child custody cases. *Psychology, Public Policy, and Law, 6*(4), 843–879.

Kraynak, A. R. (1997). The relationship of children's intellectual ability and adjustment to parental divorce. *Dissertation Abstracts International: Section B: The Sciences and Engineering, 57*(12-B), 7758.

Kreider, R. M. (2003). *Adopted children and stepchildren: 2000. Census 2000 special reports,* CENSR-6RV. Washington, D.C.: U.S. Government Printing Office.

Kreider, R. M., and Fields, J. M. (2001). Number, timing, and duration of marriages and divorces: Fall 1996. *Current Population Reports,* P70–80. U.S. Census Bureau. Washington, D.C.: U.S. Government Printing Office.

Kressel, K., Butler-DeFreitas, F., Forlenza, S. G., and Wilcox, C. (1989). Research in contested custody mediations: An illustration of the case study method. *Mediation Quarterly, 24,* 55–70.

Krishnakumar, A., and Buehler, C. (2000). Interparental conflict and parenting behaviors: A meta-analytic review. *Family Relations, 49,* 25–44.

Kuehl, S. J. (1989). Against joint custody: A dissent to the General Bullmoose theory. *Family and Conciliation Courts Review, 30*(2), 37–45.

Kunz, J. (2000). The intergenerational transmission of divorce: A nine generation study. *Journal of Divorce and Remarriage, 34*(1–2), 169–175.

Kurdek, L. A. (1988). Social support of divorced single mothers and their children. *Journal of Divorce, 11*(3–4), 167–188.

Kurdek, L. A. (1991). The relations between reported well-being and divorce history, availability of a proximate adult, and gender. *Journal of Marriage and Family, 53,* 71–78.

Kurdek, L. A. (1993a). Predicting marital dissolution: A 5-year prospective longitudinal study of newlywed couples. *Journal of Personality and Social Psychology, 64,* 221–242.

Kurdek, L. A. (1993b). Issues in proposing a general model of the effects of divorce on children. *Journal of Marriage and Family, 55,* 39–41.

Kurdek, L. A., and Berg, B. (1983). Correlates of children's adjustment to their parents' divorces. In L. A. Kurdek (ed.), *Children and divorce* (pp. 47–60). San Francisco: Jossey-Bass.

Kurdek, L. A., and Berg, B. (1987). Children's beliefs about parental divorce scale: Psychometric characteristics and concurrent validity. *Journal of Consulting and Clinical Psychology, 55,* 712–718.

Kurdek, L. A., and Blisk, D. (1983). Dimensions and correlates of mothers' divorce experiences. *Journal of Divorce, 6*(4), 1–24.

Kurdek, L. A., Blisk, D., and Siesky, A. E. (1981). Correlates of children's long-term adjustment to their parents' divorce. *Developmental Psychology, 17,* 565–579.

Kurdek, L. A., and Fine, M. A., (1991). Cognitive correlates of satisfaction for mothers and stepfathers in stepfather families. *Journal of Marriage and the Family, 53*(3), 565–572.

Kurdek, L., and Fine, M. (1993a). Parent and nonparent residential family members as providers of warmth and supervision to young adolescents. *Journal of Family Psychology, 7,* 245–249.

Kurdek, L., and Fine, M. (1993b). The relation between family structure and young adolescents' appraisals of family climate and parenting behavior. *Journal of Family Issues, 14,* 279–290.

Kurdek, L. A., and Fine, M. A. (1995). Mothers, fathers, stepfathers, and siblings as providers of supervision, acceptance, and autonomy to young adolescents. *Journal of Family Psychology, 9,* 95–99.

Kurdek, L. A., and Siesky, A. E. (1979). An interview study of parents' perceptions of their children's reactions and adjustment to divorce. *Journal of Divorce, 3*(1), 5–17.

Kurdek, L. A., and Siesky, A. E. (1980). Effects of divorce on children: The relationship between parent and child perspectives. *Journal of Divorce, 4*(2), 85–99.

Lamanna, M. A., and Riedmann, A. (1994). *Marriages and families: Making choices and facing change* (5th ed.) Belmont, Calif.: Wadsworth Publishing.

Lamb, M. E., Sternberg, K. J., and Thompson, R. A. (1999). The effects of divorce and custody arrangements on children's behavior, development, and adjustment. In M. E. Lamb (ed.), *Parenting and child development in "nontraditional" families* (pp. 125–135). Mahwah, N.J.: Erlbaum.

Laumann-Billings, L., and Emery, R. E. (2000). Distress among young adults from divorced families. *Journal of Family Psychology, 14*, 671–687.

Lavin, M., and Sales, B. (1998). Moral justifications of limit on expert testimony. In S. Ceci and H. Hembrook (eds.), *Expert witnesses in child abuse cases: What can and should be said in court?* (pp. 59–81). Washington, D.C.: American Psychological Association.

Leaverton, D. (1977). Diabetes via divorce. *Human Behavior, 6*, 55.

Lee, C. M., Picard, M., and Blain, M. D. (1994). A methodological and substantive review of intervention outcome studies for families undergoing divorce. *Journal of Family Psychology, 8*, 3–15.

Lee, J. M., and Hett, G. G. (1990). Post-divorce adjustment: An assessment of a group intervention. *Canadian Journal of Counselling, 24*, 199–209.

Lee, M. (1997). Post-divorce interparental conflict, children's contact with both parents, children's emotional processes, and children's behavioral adjustment. *Journal of Divorce and Remarriage, 27*(3–4), 61–82.

Lee, M. (2002). A model of children's postdivorce behavioral adjustment in maternal- and dual-residence arrangements. *Journal of Family Issues, 23*, 672–697.

Lehr, R., and MacMillan, P. (2001). The psychological and emotional impact of divorce: The noncustodial fathers' perspective. *Families in Society, 82*, 373–382.

Leite, R. W., and McKenry, P. (2003). Aspects of father status and postdivorce father involvement with children. *Journal of Family Issues, 23*, 601–623.

Lengua, L. J., Sandler, I. N., West, S. G., Wolchik, S. A., and Curran, P. J. (1999). Emotionality and self-regulation, threat appraisal, and coping in children of divorce. *Development and Psychopathology, 11*, 15–37.

Lengua, L. J., Wolchik, S. A., and Braver, S. L. (1995). Understanding children's divorce adjustment from an ecological perspective. *Journal of Divorce and Remarriage, 22*(3–4), 25–53.

Leslie, L. A., and Grady, K. (1988). Social support for divorcing mothers: What seems to help? *Journal of Divorce, 11*(3–4), 147–165.

Lester, D. (1994). The protective effect of marriage for suicide in men and women. *Giornale Italiano di Suicidologia, 4*(2), 83–85.

Lester, D. (1996). The impact of unemployment on marriage and divorce. *Journal of Divorce and Remarriage, 25*(3–4), 151–153.

Lester, D. (1997). The effect of alcohol consumption on marriage and divorce at the national level. *Journal of Divorce and Remarriage, 27*(3–4), 159–161.

Levinger, G. (1976). A social psychological perspective on marital dissolution. *Journal of Social Issues, 32*(1), 21–47.

Lewis, J. M., and Wallerstein, J. S. (1987). Family profile variables and long-term outcome in divorce research: Issues at a ten-year follow-up. In J. M. Vincent (ed.), *Advances in family intervention, assessment and theory,* Vol. 4 (pp. 121–142). Greenwich, Conn.: JAI Press.

Lin, I. (2000). Perceived fairness and compliance with child support obligations. *Journal of Marriage and Family, 62,* 388–398.

Lindsay, G. R., and Scherman, A. (1987). The impact of children and time lapse since divorce on women's postdivorce adjustment. *Journal of Mental Health Counseling, 9,* 174–183.

Linker, J. S., Stolberg, A. L., and Green, R. G. (1999). Family communication as a mediator of child adjustment to divorce. *Journal of Divorce and Remarriage, 30*(1–2), 83–97.

Lissau, I., and Sorensen, T. I. A. (1994). Parental neglect during childhood and increased risk of obesity in young adulthood. *Lancet, 343,* 324–327.

Little, M. A. (1992). The impact of the custody plan on the family: A five-year follow-up: Executive summary. *Family and Conciliation Courts Review, 30,* 243–251.

Long, N., Forehand, R., Fauber, R., and Brody, G. H. (1987). Self-perceived and independently observed competence of young adolescents as a function of parental marital conflict and recent divorce. *Journal of Abnormal Child Psychology, 15,* 15–27.

Long, N., Slater, E., Forehand, R., and Fauber, R. (1988). Continued high or reduced interparental conflict following divorce: Relation to young adolescent adjustment. *Journal of Consulting and Clinical Psychology, 56,* 467–469.

Lorenz, F. O., Simons, R. L., Conger, R. D., Elder, G. H., Jr., Johnson, C., and Chao, W. (1997). Married and recently divorced mothers' stressful events and distress: Tracing change across time. *Journal of Marriage and Family, 59,* 219–232.

Lowenstein, J. S., and Koopman, E. J. (1978). A comparison of the self-esteem between boys living with single-parent mothers and single-parent fathers. *Journal of Divorce, 2*(2), 195–208.

Lowery, C. R., and Settle, S. A. (1985). Effects of divorce on children: Differential impact of custody and visitation patterns. *Family Relations, 34,* 455–463.

Lucas, R. E., Clark, A. E., Georgellis, Y., and Diener, E. (2003). Reexamining adaptation and the set point model of happiness: Reactions to changes in marital status. *Journal of Personality and Social Psychology, 84,* 527–539.

Luecken, L. J., and Fabricius, W. V. (2003). Physical health vulnerability in adult children from divorced and intact families. *Journal of Psychosomatic Research, 55,* 221–228.

Luepnitz, D. A. (1982). *Child custody: A study of families after divorce.* Lexington, Mass.: Lexington Books.

Luepnitz, D. A. (1986). A comparison of maternal, paternal, and joint custody:

Understanding the varieties of post divorce family life. *Journal of Divorce, 9*(3), 1–12.

Lund, M. (1987). The non-custodial father: Common challenges in parenting after divorce. In C. Lewis and M. O'Brien (eds.), *Reassessing fatherhood* (pp. 212–224). London: Sage Publications.

Lussier, G., Deater-Deckard, K., Dunn, J., and Davies, L. (2002). Support across two generations: Children's closeness to grandparents following parental divorce and remarriage. *Journal of Family Psychology, 16,* 363–376.

Luthar, S., and Cicchetti, D. (2000). The construct of resilience: Implications for interventions and social policies. *Development and Psychopathology, 12,* 857–885.

Maccoby, E. E. (1999). The custody of children of divorcing families: Weighing the alternatives. In R. A. Thompson and P. R. Amato (eds.). *The postdivorce family: Children, parenting, and society* (pp. 51–70). Thousand Oaks, Calif.: Sage Publications.

Maccoby, E. E., Buchanan, C. M., Mnookin, R. H., and Dornbusch, S. M. (1993). Postdivorce roles of mothers and fathers in the lives of their children. *Journal of Family Psychology, 7,* 24–38.

Maccoby, E. E., Depner, C. E., and Mnookin, R. H. (1990). Coparenting in the second year after divorce. *Journal of Marriage and Family, 52,* 141–155.

Maccoby, E. E., Mnookin R. H., Depner C. E., and Peters, H. E. (1992). *Dividing the child: Social and legal dilemmas of custody.* Cambridge, Mass.: Harvard University Press.

Maciejewski, P. K., Prigerson, H. G., and Mazure, C. M. (2001). Sex differences in event-related risk for major depression. *Psychological Medicine, 31,* 593–604.

MacKinnon, C. E. (1988–89). Sibling interactions in married and divorced families: Influence of ordinal position, socioeconomic status, and play context. *Journal of Divorce, 12*(2–3), 221–234.

MacKinnon, C. E., Brody, G. H., and Stoneman, Z. (1982). The effects of divorce and maternal employment on the home environments of preschool children. *Child Development, 53,* 1392–1399.

MacKinnon, C. E., Brody, G. H., and Stoneman, Z. (1986). The longitudinal effects of divorce and maternal employment on the home environments of preschool children. *Journal of Divorce, 9*(4), 65–78.

Madden-Derdich, D. A., Leonard, S. A., and Christopher, F. S. (1999). Boundary ambiguity and coparental conflict after divorce: An empirical test of a family systems model of the divorce process. *Journal of Marriage and Family, 61,* 588–598.

Magura, M., and Shapiro, E. (1988). Alcohol consumption and divorce: Which causes which? *Journal of Divorce, 12*(1), 127–136.

Mahoney, A., Pargament, K. I., Tarakeshwar, N., and Swank, A. B. (2001). Religion in the home in the 1980s and 1990s: A meta-analytic review and conceptual analysis of links between religion, marriage, and parenting. *Journal of Family Psychology, 15,* 559–596.

Margulies, S., and Luchow, A. (1992). Litigation, mediation and the psychology of divorce. *The Journal of Psychiatry and Law, 20,* 483–504.

Markman, H., Floyd, F., Stanley, S., and Storaasli, R. (1988). Prevention of marital distress: A longitudinal investigation. *Journal of Consulting and Clinical Psychology, 56,* 210–217.

Marks, N. F. (1995). Midlife marital status differences in social support relationships with adult children and psychological well-being. *Journal of Family Issues 16,* 5–28.

Marks, N. F., and Lambert, J. D. (1998). Marital status continuity and change among young and midlife adults. *Journal of Family Issues, 19,* 652–686.

Marsiglio, W. (1992). Stepfathers with minor children living at home: Parenting perceptions and relationship quality. *Journal of Family Issues, 13,* 195–214.

Martin, T. C., and Bumpass, L. L. (1989). Recent trends in marital disruption. *Demography, 26,* 37–51.

Martindale, D. (2001). Cross-examining mental health professionals in child custody litigation. *Journal of Psychiatry and Law, 29,* 483–511.Martinez, C. R., Jr., and Forgatch, M. (2001). Preventing problems with boys' noncompliance: Effects of a parent training intervention for divorcing mothers. *Journal of Consulting and Clinical Psychology, 69,* 416–428.

Maryland Special Joint Committee on Gender Bias in the Courts (1989). Domestic violence and the courts. *Response, 12,* 3–6.

Masheter, C. (1991). Postdivorce relationships between ex-spouses: The roles of attachment and interpersonal conflict. *Journal of Marriage and Family, 53,* 103–110.

Masheter, C. (1997). Healthy and unhealthy friendship and hostility between ex-spouses. *Journal of Marriage and Family, 59,* 463–475.

Mastekaasa, A. (1994a). Marital status, distress, and well-being: An international comparison. *Journal of Comparative Family Studies, 25*(2), 183–205.

Mastekaasa, A. (1994b). Psychological well-being and marital dissolution: Selection effects? *Journal of Family Issues, 15,* 208–228.

Mastekaasa, A. (1995). Age variations in the suicide rates and self-reported subjective well-being of married and never married persons. *Journal of Community and Applied Social Psychology, 5,* 21–39.

Masten, A. S. (2001). Ordinary magic: Resilience processes in development. *American Psychologist, 56*(3), 227–238.

Masten, A. S., Hubbard, J. J., Gest, S. D., Tellegen, A., Garmezy, N., and Ramirez, M. (1999). Competence in the context of adversity: Pathways to resilience and maladaptation from childhood to late adolescence. *Development and Psychopathology, 11*(1), 143–169.

Mauldin, T. A. (1991). Economic consequences of divorce or separation among women in poverty. *Journal of Divorce and Remarriage, 14*(3–4), 163–178.

Mazur, A., and Michalek, J. (1998). Marriage, divorce, and male testosterone. *Social Forces, 77,* 315–330.

Mazur, E. (1993). Developmental differences in children's understanding of marriage, divorce, and remarriage. *Journal of Applied Developmental Psychology, 14,* 191–212.

Mazur, E., Wolchik, S. A., Virdin, L., Sandler, I. N., and West, S. G. (1999). Cognitive moderators of children's adjustment to stressful divorce events: The role of negative cognitive errors and positive illusions. *Child Development, 70,* 231–245.

McCabe, K. M. (1997). Sex differences in the long term effects of divorce on children: Depression and heterosexual relationship difficulties in the young adult years. *Journal of Divorce and Remarriage, 27*(1–2), 123–135.

McKenry, P. C. (1979). Mediation eases the split. *Practitioners Digest, 3,* 8–16.

McKenry, P. C., Clark, K. A., and Stone, G. (1999). Evaluation of a parent education program for divorcing parents. *Family Relations, 48,* 129–137.

McKenry, P., McKelvey, M., Leigh, D., and Wark, L. (1996). Nonresidential father involvement: A comparison of divorced, separated, never married, and remarried fathers. *Journal of Divorce and Remarriage, 25,* 1–13.

McKenry, P. C., and Price, S. J. (1991). Alternatives for support: Life after divorce: A literature review. *Journal of Divorce and Remarriage, 15*(3–4), 1–19.

McLanahan, S. S. (1999). Father absence and the welfare of children. In E. M. Hetherington (ed.), *Coping with divorce, single parenting, and remarriage: A risk and resiliency perspective* (pp. 117–145). Mahwah, N.J.: Erlbaum.

McLanahan, S., and Sandefur, G. (1994). *Growing up with a single parent: What hurts, what helps.* Cambridge, Mass.: Harvard University Press.

McNeal, C., and Amato, P. R. (1998). Parents' marital violence: Long-term consequences for children. *Journal of Family Issues, 19*(2), 123–139.

Mednick, B. R., Baker, R. L., Reznick, C., and Hocevar, D. (1990). Long-term effects of divorce on adolescent academic achievement. *Journal of Divorce, 13*(4), 69–88.

Melton, G. B., and Lind, E. A. (1982). Procedural justice in family court: Does the adversary model make sense? *Child and Youth Services, 5,* 63–81.

Melton, G. B., Petrila, J., Poythress, N. G., and Slobogin, C. (1987). *Psychological evaluations for the courts: A handbook for mental health professionals and lawyers.* New York: Guilford.

Menaghan, E. G., Kowaleski-Jones, L., and Mott, F. L. (1997). The intergenerational costs of parental social stressors: Academic and social difficulties in early adolescence for children of young mothers. *Journal of Health and Social Behavior, 38,* 72–86.

Menaghan, E. G., and Lieberman, M. A. (1986). Changes in depression following divorce: A panel study. *Journal of Marriage and Family, 48,* 319–328.

Meyer, D. R., and Bartfeld, Judi. (1996). Compliance with child support orders in divorce cases. *Journal of Marriage and Family, 58,* 201–212.

Miller, N. B., Smerglia, V. L., Gaudet, D. S., and Kitson, G. C. (1998). Stressful life events, social support, and the distress of widowed and divorced women: A counteractive model. *Journal of Family Issues, 19,* 181–203.

Mitchell, A. K. (1985). *Children in the middle: Living through divorce.* London: Tavistock.

Mnookin, R. H. (1975). Child custody adjudication: Judicial functions in the face of indeterminacy. *Law and Contemporary Problems, 39,* 226–293.

Mnookin, R. H., and Kornhauser, L. (1979). Bargaining in the shadow of the law: The case of divorce. *Yale Law Journal, 88,* 8950–8997.

Molina, O. (1999). The effect of divorce on African American working women. *Journal of Divorce and Remarriage, 32*(1–2), 1–15.

Montalto, C. P., and Gerner, J. L. (1998). The effect of expected changes in marital status on labor supply decisions of women and men. *Journal of Divorce and Remarriage, 28*(3–4), 25–51.

Morrison, D. R., and Cherlin, A. J. (1995). The divorce process and young children's well-being: A prospective analysis. *Journal of Marriage and Family, 57,* 800–812.

Morrison, D. R., and Coiro, M. J. (1999). Parental conflict and marital disruption: Do children benefit when high-conflict marriages are dissolved? *Journal of Marriage and Family, 61,* 626–637.

Mott, F. L., Kowaleski-Jones, L., and Meneghan, E. G. (1997). Paternal absence and child behavior: Does a child's gender make a difference? *Journal of Marriage and Family, 59,* 103–118.

Myers, M. F. (1989). *Men and divorce.* New York: Guilford Press.

National Center for Health Statistics. (1992). *Monthly vital statistics report.* Washington, D.C.: U.S. Department of Health and Human Services.

National Center for Health Statistics. (2002). *Births, marriages, divorces, and deaths: Provisional data for 2001, 50*(14), Table 1.

National Conference of State Legislatures (2003). Presumption/preference for joint custody. Retrieved May 7, 2004, from http://www.ncsl.org/programs/cyf/jointcustody.htm.

Neal, J. H. (1983). Children's understanding of their parents' divorces. In L. A. Kurdek (ed.), *Children and divorce* (pp. 3–14). San Francisco: Jossey Bass.

Needle, R., Su, S., and Doherty, W. (1990). Divorce, remarriage, and adolescent substance use: A prospective longitudinal study. *Journal of Marriage and Family, 52,* 157–169.

Neff, J. A., and Mantz, R. J. (1998). Marital status transition, alcohol consumption, and number of sex partners over time in a tri-ethnic sample. *Journal of Divorce and Remarriage, 29*(1–2), 19–42.

Neff, J. A., and Schluter, T D. (1993). Marital status and depressive symptoms:

The role of race/ethnicity and sex. *Journal of Divorce and Remarriage, 20,* 137–160.

Neher, L. S., and Short, J. L. (1998). Risk and protective factors for children's substance use and antisocial behavior following parental divorce. *American Journal of Orthopsychiatry, 68,* 154–161.

Nelson, E. C., Heath, A. C., Madden, P. A. F., Cooper, L., Dinwiddie, S. H., Bucholz, K. K., Glowinski, A., McLaughlin, T., Dunne, M. P., Statham, D. J., and Martin, N. G. (2002). Association between self-reported childhood sexual abuse and adverse psychosocial outcomes: Results from a twin study. *Archives of General Psychiatry, 59,* 139–145.

Nelson, G. (1995). Women's social networks and social support following marital separation: A controlled prospective study. *Journal of Divorce and Remarriage, 23*(1–2), 149–171.

Nelson, R. (1989). Parental hostility, conflict and communication in joint and sole custody families. *Journal of Divorce, 13*(20), 145–157.

Nicholson, R. A., and Norwood, S. (2000). The quality of forensic psychological assessments, reports, and testimony: Acknowledging the gap between promise and practice. *Law and Human Behavior, 24,* 9–44.

Nielsen, L. (1999). Demeaning, demoralizing, and disenfranchising divorced dads: A review of the literature. *Journal of Divorce and Remarriage, 31*(3–4), 139–177.

Nimkoff, M. F., and Ogburn, W. F. (1934). *The family.* Boston: Houghton Mifflin.

Nock, S., described by Perina, K. (2002). Covenant marriage: A new marital contract. *Psychology Today,* March-April, p. 18.

Norton, A. J., and Glick, P. C. (1986). One parent families: A social and economic profile. *Family Relations, 35,* 9–17.

Nuta, V. R. (1986). Emotional aspects of child support enforcement. *Family Relations, 35,* 177–181.

O'Brien, M. (1987). Patterns of kinship and friendship among lone fathers. In C. Lewis and M. O'Brien (eds.), *Reassessing fatherhood* (pp. 225–245). London: Sage Publications.

O'Connor, T. G., Hawkins, N., Dunn, J., Thorpe, K., Golding, J., and the ALSPAC Study Team (1998). Family type and depression in pregnancy: Factors mediating risk in a community sample. *Journal of Marriage and Family, 60,* 757–770.

Okpaku, S. (1976). Psychology: Impediment or aid in child custody cases? *Rutgers Law Review, 29,* 1117–1153.

Ono, H. (1998). Husbands' and wives' resources and marital dissolution. *Journal of Marriage and Family, 60,* 674–689.

Opie, A. (1993). Ideologies of joint custody. *Family and Conciliation Courts Review, 31,* 313–326.

Oropesa, R. S., and Gorman B. K. (2000). Ethnicity, immigration, and beliefs about marriage as a "tie that binds." In L. J. Waite, C. Bachrach, M. Hindin, E. Thomson, and A. Thornton (eds.), *The ties that bind: Perspectives on marriage and cohabitation* (pp. 118–211). New York: Aldine de Gruyter.

Orr vs. Orr (1979). U.S. Supreme Court case, 440 U.S. 268.

Otto, R. K., Buffington-Vollum, J. K., and Edens, J. F. (2003). Child custody evaluation. In A. M. Goldstein (ed.), *Handbook of psychology: Vol. 11. Forensic psychology* (pp. 179–208). New York: Wiley.

Otto, R. K., Edens, J. F., and Barcus, E. H. (2000). The use of psychological testing in child custody evaluations. *Family and Conciliation Courts Review, 38,* 312–340.

Ozawa, M. N., and Yoon, H. (2002). The economic benefit of remarriage: Gender and income class. *Journal of Divorce and Remarriage, 36*(3–4), 21–39.

Pagani, L., Boulerice, B., Tremblay, R. E., and Vitaro, F. (1997). Behavioural development in children of divorce and remarriage. *Journal of Child Psychology and Psychiatry and Allied Disciplines, 38,* 769–781.

Pagani-Kurtz, L., and Derevensky, J. L. (1997). Access by noncustodial parents: Effects upon children's postdivorce coping resources. *Journal of Divorce and Remarriage, 27*(1–2), 43–55.

Pagelow, M. D. (1993). Justice for victims of spouse abuse in divorce and child custody cases. *Violence and Victims, 8,* 69–83.

Palamattathil, G. V. (2002). The impact of an integrated forgiveness intervention in enhancing the psychological well-being among recently divorced adults. *Dissertation Abstracts International, 62*(10-B), 4799.

Paley, B., Cox, M. J., and Burchinal, M., R. (1999). Attachment and marital functioning: Comparison of spouses with continuous-secure, earned-secure, dismissing, and preoccupied attachment stances. *Journal of Family Psychology, 13*(4), 580–597.

Paolino, T. J., McCrady, B. S., and Diamond, S. (1979). Statistics on alcoholic marriages: An overview. *International Journal of the Addictions, 13,* 1285–1293.

Papernow, P. (1993). *Becoming a stepfamily: Patterns of development in remarried families.* New York: Gardner Press.

Papp, L. M., Cummings, E. M., and Goeke-Morey, M. C. (2002). Marital conflicts in the home when children are present versus absent. *Developmental Psychology, 38,* 774–783.

Parsons, T., and Bales, R. (1955). *Family, socialization and interaction process.* Glencoe, Ill.: The Free Press.

Pasley, K., and Ihinger-Tallman, M. (1988). Remarriage and stepfamilies. In C. S. Chilman, E. W. Nunnally, and F. M. Cox (eds.), *Families in trouble* (pp. 24–221). Newbury Park, Calif.: Sage Publications.

Pasley, K., and Ihinger-Tallman, M. (1990). Remarriage in later adulthood: Correlates of perceptions of family adjustment. *Family Perspectives, 24,* 263–274.

Pasley, K., Koch, M., and Ihinger-Tallman, M. (1993). Problems in remarriage: An exploratory study of intact and terminated remarriages. *Journal of Divorce and Remarriage, 20,* 63–83.

Patterson, G. R., and Forgatch, M. S. (1990). Initiation and maintenance of process disrupting single-mother families. In G. R. Patterson (ed.), *Depression and aggression in family interaction* (pp. 209–245). Hillsdale, N.J.: Erlbaum.

Pearson, J. (1991). The equity of mediated divorce agreements. *Mediation Quarterly, 9,* 179–197.

Pearson, J., and Luchesi Ring, M. A. (1982). Judicial decision-making in contested custody cases. *Journal of Family Law, 21,* 703–724.

Pearson, J., and Thoennes, N. (1990). Custody after divorce: Demographic and attitudinal patterns. *American Journal of Orthopsychiatry, 60,* 233–249.

Pedro-Carroll, J. L., Sutton, S. E., and Wyman, P. A. (1999). A two-year follow-up evaluation of a preventive intervention for young children of divorce. *School Psychology Review, 28,* 467–476.

Peretti, P. O., and di Vitorrio, A. (1993). Effect of loss of father through divorce on personality of the preschool child. *Social Behavior and Personality, 21,* 33–38.

Peters, H. E., and Mullis, N. C. (1997). The role of family income and sources of income in adolescent achievement. In G. Duncan and J. Brooks-Gunn (eds.), *Consequences of growing up poor* (pp. 340–381). New York: Russell Sage Foundation.

Peterson, J. L., and Zill, N. (1986). Marital disruption, parent-child relationships, and behavior problems in children. *Journal of Marriage and Family, 48,* 295–307.

Peterson, R. R. (1996). A re-evaluation of the economic consequences of divorce. *American Sociological Review, 61,* 528–536.

Petronio, S., and Endres, T. (1986): Dating and the single-parent: Communication in the social network. *Journal of Divorce, 9*(2), 83–105.

Pett, M. A., and Vaughan-Cole, B. (1986). The impact of income issues and social status on post-divorce adjustment of custodial parents. *Family Relations, 35,* 103–111.

Pett, M. A., Wampold, B. E., Turner, C. W., and Vaughan-Cole, B. (1999). Paths of influence of divorce on preschool children's psychosocial adjustment. *Journal of Family Psychology, 13,* 145–164.

Pett, M. G. (1982). Predictors of satisfactory social adjustment of divorced single parents. *Journal of Divorce, 5*(3), 1–17.

Phear, W. P., Beck, J. C., Hauser, B. B., Clark, S. C., and Whitney, R. A. (1984). An empirical study of custody agreements: Joint versus sole legal custody. In J. Folberg (ed.), *Joint custody and shared parenting* (pp. 419–441). Washington, D.C.: Bureau of National Affairs.

Picard, M., Lee, C. M., and Hunsley, J. (1997). Social supports received and desired: The experiences of recently divorced parents with their parents and parents-in-law. *Journal of Divorce and Remarriage, 27*(1–2), 57–69.

Plummer, L. P., and Koch-Hattem, A. (1986). Family stress and adjustment to divorce. *Family Relations, 35,* 523–529.

Poehlmann, J. A., and Fiese, B. H. (1994). The effects of divorce, maternal employment, and maternal social support on toddlers' home environment. *Journal of Divorce and Remarriage, 22*(1–2), 121–136.

Polikoff, N. (1982). Why are mothers losing: A brief analysis of criteria used in child custody determination, *Women's Rights Law Reporter, 7,* 235–243.

Pollock, G. E., and Stroup, A. L. (1996). Economic consequences of marital dissolution for Blacks. *Journal of Divorce and Remarriage, 26*(1–2), 49–68.

Popenoe, D. (1994). The evolution of marriage and the problem of stepfamilies. In A. Booth and J. Dunn (eds.), *Stepfamilies: Who benefits? Who does not?* (pp. 3–27). Hillsdale, N.J.: Erlbaum.

Pong, S. L. (1997). Family structure, school context, and eighth grade math and reading achievement. *Journal of Marriage and Family, 59,* 734–746.

Power, C., Rodgers, B., and Hope, S. (1999). Heavy alcohol consumption and marital status: Disentangling the relationship in a national study of young adults. *Addiction, 94,* 1477–1487.

Prengle, S. (1999). *Still a dad.* New York: Mission Creative Energy.

Prescott, C. A., and Kendler, K. S. (2001). Associations between marital status and alcohol consumption in a longitudinal study of female twins. *Journal of Studies on Alcohol, 62,* 589–604.

Proudfoot, H., and Teesson, M. (2002). Who seeks treatment for alcohol dependence? *Social Psychiatry and Psychiatric Epidemiology, 37*(10), 451–456.

Pruett, M., Kline, M., and Jackson, T. D. (2001). Perspectives on the divorce process: Parental perceptions of the legal system and its impact on family relations. *Journal of the American Academy of Psychiatry and the Law, 29,* 18–28.Pruett, K. D., and Pruett, M. K. (1999). "Only God decides": Young children's perception of divorce and the legal system. *Journal of the American Academy of Child and Adolescent Psychiatry, 38,* 1544–1550.

Pruett, M. K., Williams, T. Y., Insabella, G., and Little, T. D. (2003). Family and legal indicators of child adjustment to divorce among families with young children. *Journal of Family Psychology, 17,* 169–180.

Pryor, J. (1999). Waiting until they leave home: The experiences of young adults whose parents separate. *Journal of Divorce and Remarriage, 32,* 47–61.

Pyke, K. D. (1994). Women's employment as a gift or burden? Marital power across marriage, divorce, and remarriage. *Gender and Society, 8,* 73–91.

Pyke, K., and Coltrane, S. (1996). Entitlement, obligation, and gratitude in family work. *Journal of Family Issues, 17,* 60–82.

Quinlivan, J. A., Tan, L. H., Steele, A., and Black, K. (2004). Impact of demographic factors, early family relationships and depressive symptomatology in teenage pregnancy. *Australian and New Zealand Journal of Psychiatry, 38*(4), 197–203.

Reed vs. Reed (1971). U.S. Supreme Court case, 404 U.S. 71.

Reid, W. J., and Crisafulli, A. (1990). Marital discord and child behavior problems: A meta-analysis. *Journal of Abnormal Child Psychology, 18,* 105–117.

Reinhard, D. W. (1977). The reaction of adolescent boys and girls to the divorce of their parents. *Journal of Clinical Child Psychology, 6,* 21–23.

Reiss, I. L., and Lee, G. R. (1988). *Family systems in America* (4th ed.). Fort Worth, Tex.: Harcourt Brace.

Rheinstein, M. (1972). *Marriage stability, divorce, and the law.* Chicago: University of Chicago Press.

Richards, M., Hardy, R., and Wadsworth, M. (1997). The effects of divorce and separation on mental health in a national U.K. birth cohort. *Psychological Medicine, 27,* 1121–1128.

Richmond, L. S., and Christensen, D. H. (2000). Coping strategies and postdivorce health outcomes. *Journal of Divorce and Remarriage, 34*(1–2), 41–59.

Riessman, C. K. (1990). *Divorce talk: Women and men make sense of personal relationships.* New Brunswick, N.J.: Rutgers University Press.

Riessman, C. K., and Gerstel, N. (1985). Marital dissolution and health: Do males or females have greater risk? *Social Science and Medicine, 20,* 627–635.

Risman, B. J. (1986). Can men "mother"? Life as a single father. *Family Relations, 35,* 95–102.

Rodgers, B. (1994). Pathways between parental divorce and adult depression. *Journal of Child Psychology and Psychiatry and Allied Disciplines, 35,* 1289–1308.

Rodgers, B., Power, C., and Hope, S. (1997). Parental divorce and adult psychological distress: Evidence from a national cohort: A research note. *Journal of Child Psychology and Psychiatry and Allied Disciplines, 38,* 867–872.

Rodgers, K. B., and Rose, H. A. (2002). Risk and resiliency factors among adolescents who experience marital transitions. *Journal of Marriage and Family, 64,* 1024–1037.

Rogers, M. J., and Holmbeck, G. N. (1997). Effects of interparental aggression on children's adjustment: The moderating role of cognitive appraisal and coping. *Journal of Family Psychology, 11,* 125–130.

Rogers, S. J., and Amato, P. R. (1997). Is marital quality declining? The evidence from two generations. *Social Forces, 75,* 1089–1100.

Roloff, M. E., and Johnson, K. L. (2002). Serial arguing over the relational life course: Antecedents and consequences. In A. L. Vangelisti, H. T. Reis, and M. A. Fitzpatrick (eds.), *Stability and change in relationships: Advances in personal relationships* (pp. 107–128). New York: Cambridge University Press.

Roman, M., and Haddad, W. (1978). *The disposable parent.* New York: Holt, Rinehart and Winston.

Rosen, R. (1979). Some crucial issues concerning children of divorce. *Journal of Divorce, 3*(1), 19–25.

Rosenberg, J. D. (1991). In defense of mediation. *Family and Conciliation Courts Review, 30,* 422–467.

Ross, C. E., and Mirowsky, J. (1999). Parental divorce, life-course disruption and adult depression. *Journal of Marriage and Family, 61,* 1034–1045.

Rutter, M. (1979). Protective factors in children's responses to stress and disadvantage. In M. W. Kent and J. E. Rolf (eds.), *Primary prevention of psychopathology: Vol. 3. Social competence in children* (pp. 49–74). Hanover, N.H.: University Press of New England.

Rutter, M. (1999). Resilience concepts and findings: Implications for family therapy. *Journal of Family Therapy, 21,* 119–144.

Ryckman, R. M., Thornton, B., Gold, J. A., and Burckle, M. A. (2002). Romantic relationships of hypercompetitive individuals. *Journal of Social and Clinical Psychology, 21*(5), 517–530.

Ryff, C. D., and Singer, B. (2000). Interpersonal flourishing: A positive health agenda for the new millennium. *Personality and Social Psychology Review, 4*(1), 30–44.

Saayman, G. S., and Saayman, R. V. (1988–89). The adversarial legal process and divorce: Negative effects upon the psychological adjustment of children. *Journal of Divorce, 12*(2–3), 329–348.

Sabatelli, R. M., and Shehan, C. L. (1993). Exchange and resource theories. In P. G. Boss and W. J. Doherty (eds.), *Sourcebook of family theories and methods: A contextual approach* (pp. 385–417). New York: Plenum Press.

Sakraida, T. J. (2002). Divorce transition, coping responses, and health-promoting behavior of midlife women. *Dissertation Abstracts International, 62*(12-B), 5646.

Sales, B., Manber, R., and Rohman, L. (1992). Social science research and child-custody decision making. *Applied and Preventive Psychology, 1,* 23–40. New York: Cambridge University Press.

Saluter, A. F. (1996). Marital status and living arrangements: March 1994. *Current Population Reports,* P20–484. U.S. Bureau of the Census. Washington, D.C.: U.S. Government Printing Office.

Sanders, M. R., Halford, W. K., and Behrens, B. C. (1999). Parental divorce and premarital couple communication. *Journal of Family Psychology, 13,* 60–74.

Sandler, I. N., Tein, J.-Y., and West, S. G. (1994). Coping, stress, and the psychological symptoms of children of divorce: A cross-sectional and longitudinal study. *Child Development, 65,* 1744–1763.

Sandler, I. N., Tein, J.-Y., Mehta, P., Wolchik, S., and Ayers, T. (2000). Coping efficacy and psychological problems of children of divorce. *Child Development, 71,* 1099–1118.

Sandler, I., Wolchik, S., Braver, S., and Fogas, B. (1991). Stability and quality of life events and psychological symptomatology in children of divorce. *American Journal of Community Psychology, 19,* 501–520.

Sansom, D., and Farnill, D. (1997). Stress following marriage breakdown: Does social support play a role? *Journal of Divorce and Remarriage, 26*(3–4), 39–49.

Santrock, J. W., and Sitterle, K. A. (1987). Parent-child relationships in step-mother families. In K. Pasley and M. Ihinger-Tallman (eds.), *Remarriage and stepparenting: Current research and theory* (pp. 273–233). New York: Guilford.

Santrock, J. W., and Warshak, R. A. (1979). Father custody and social development in boys and girls. *Journal of Social Issues, 35*(4), 112–125.

Sayer, L. C., and Bianchi, S. M. (2000). Women's economic independence and the probability of divorce: A review and reexamination. *Journal of Family Issues, 21,* 906–943.

Schnayer, R., and Orr, R. R. (1988–89). A comparison of children living in single-mother and single-father families. *Journal of Divorce, 12*(2–3), 171–184.

Schneider, C. (1991). Discretion, rules, and law: Child custody and the UMDA best interest standard. *Michigan Law Review, 89,* 215–246.

Schoen R. (1995). The widening gap between black and white marriage rates: Context and implications. In M. B. Tucker and C. Mitchell-Kernan (eds.), *The decline in marriage among African Americans* (pp. 103–116). New York: Russell Sage.

Schultz, M. S., and Cowan, C. P. (2001, April). Promoting healthy beginnings: Marital quality during the transition to parenthood. Paper presented at the meeting of the Society for Research in Child Development, Minneapolis, Minn.

Scott, E. (1992). Pluralism, parental preference, and child custody. *California Law Review, 80,* 615–672.

Seltzer, J. A. (1991). Relationships between fathers and children who live apart: The father's role after separation. *Journal of Marriage and Family, 53,* 79–101.

Seltzer, J. A., and Bianchi, S. M. (1988). Children's contact with absent parents. *Journal of Marriage and Family, 50,* 663–677.

Seltzer, J. A., and Brandreth, Y. (1995). What fathers say about involvement with children after separation. In W. Marsiglio (ed.), *Fatherhood: Contemporary theory, research, and social policy* (pp. 166–192). Thousand Oaks, Calif.: Sage Publications.

Sen, B. (2002). Does married women's market work affect marital stability adversely? An intercohort analysis using NLS data. *Review of Social Economy, 60,* 71–92.

Serovich, J. M., Price, S. J., and Chapman, S. F. (1991). Former in-laws as a source of support. *Journal of Divorce and Remarriage, 17*(1–2), 17–25.

Settle, S. A., and Lowery, C. R. (1982). Child custody decisions: Content analysis of a judicial survey. *Journal of Divorce, 6*(1–2), 125–138.

Shalansky, C., Ericksen, J., and Henderson, A. D. (1999). Abused women and child custody: The ongoing exposure to abusive ex-partners. *Journal of Advanced Nursing, 29,* 416–426.

Shapiro, A. (2003). Later-life divorce and parent-adult child conduct and proximity: A longitudinal analysis. *Journal of Family Issues, 24,* 264–285.

Shapiro, A. D. (1996). Marital status transitions, father-child relationships, and fathers' psychological well-being. *Dissertation Abstracts International, 57*(6-A), 2692.

Shapiro, A., and Lambert, J. D. (1999). Longitudinal effects of divorce on the quality of the father-child relationship and on fathers' psychological well-being. *Journal of Marriage and Family, 61,* 397–408.

Shaw, D. S., Emery, R. E., and Tuer, M. D. (1993). Parental functioning and children's adjustment in families of divorce: A prospective study. *Journal of Abnormal Child Psychology, 21,* 119–134.

Shaw, D. S., Winslow, E. B., and Flanagan, C. (1999). A prospective study of the effects of marital status and family relations on young children's adjustment among African American and European American families. *Child Development, 70,* 742–755.

Sheets, V. L., and Braver, S. L. (1996). Gender differences in satisfaction with divorce settlements. *Family Relations, 45,* 336–342.

Sheets, V., Sandler, I., and West, S. G. (1996). Appraisals of negative events by preadolescent children of divorce. *Child Development, 67,* 2166–2182.

Short, J. L. (1998a). Evaluation of a substance abuse prevention and mental health promotion program for children of divorce. *Journal of Divorce and Remarriage, 28*(3–4), 139–155.

Short, J. L. (1998b). Predictors of substance use and mental health of children of divorce: A prospective analysis. *Journal of Divorce and Remarriage, 29*(1–2), 147–166.

Shrier, D. K., Simring, S. K., Shapiro, E. T., Greif, J. B., and Lindenthal, J. J. (1991). Level of satisfaction of fathers and mothers with joint or sole custody arrangements: Results of a questionnaire. *Journal of Divorce and Remarriage, 16*(3–4), 163–169.

Silitsky, D. (1996). Correlates of psychological adjustment in adolescents from divorced families. *Journal of Divorce and Remarriage, 26*(1–2), 151–169.

Simmons, C. (1998). *Readings on no-fault divorce.* California Research Bureau, California State Library, CRB-98–004.

Simmons, T., and O'Neill, G. (2001). *Households and families: 2000,* C2KBR/01–8. U.S. Census Bureau. Washington, D.C.: U.S. Government Printing Office.

Simon, R. W., and Marcussen, K. (1999). Marital transitions, marital beliefs, and mental health. *Journal of Health and Social Behavior, 40,* 111–125.

Simons, R. L., and Associates (1996). *Understanding differences between divorced and intact families: Stress, interaction, and child outcome.* Thousand Oaks, Calif.: Sage Publications.

Simons, R. L., Johnson, C., and Lorenz, F. O. (1996). Family structure differences in stress and behavioral predispositions. In R. L. Simons and Associates (eds.), *Understanding differences between divorced and intact families: Stress, interaction, and child outcome* (pp. 45–64). Thousand Oaks, Calif.: Sage Publications.

Simons, R. L., Lin, K. H., Gordon, L. C., Conger, R. D., and Lorenz, F. O. (1999). Explaining the higher incidence of adjustment problems among children of divorce compared with those in two-parent families. *Journal of Marriage and Family, 61,* 1020–1033.

Skitka, L. J., and Frazier, M. (1995). Ameliorating the effects of parental divorce: Do small group interventions work? *Journal of Divorce and Remarriage, 24*(3–4), 159–180.

Slater, L. B. (1999). Attachment and paternal investment in divorced fathers. *Dissertation Abstracts International, 59*(10-A), 3869.

Smerglia, V. L., Miller, N. B., and Kort-Butler, L. (1999). The impact of social support on women's adjustment to divorce: A literature review and analysis. *Journal of Divorce and Remarriage, 32*(1–2), 63–89.

Smith, R. M., Goslen, M. A., Byrd, A. J., and Reece, L. (1991). Self-other orientation and sex-role orientation of men and women who remarry. *Journal of Divorce and Remarriage, 14*(3–4), 3–32.

Smock, P. (1994). Gender and the short-run economic consequences of marital disruption. *Social Forces, 73,* 242–262.

Solomon, J., and George, C. (1999). The development of attachment in separated and divorced families: Effects of overnight visitation, parent and couple variables. *Attachment and Human Development, 1,* 2–33.

Sonenstein, F. L., and Calhoun, C. A. (1990). Determinants of child support: A pilot survey of absent parents. *Contemporary Policy Issues, 8,* 75–94.

Sorensen, E. D., and Goldman, J. (1990). Custody determinations and child development: A review of the current literature. *Journal of Divorce, 13*(4), 53–67.

Sorensen, E., Goldman, J., Sheeber, L., Albanese, I., Ward, M., Williamson, L., and McDanal, C. (1997). Judges' reliance on psychological, sociological, and legal variables in contested custody decisions. *Journal of Divorce and Remarriage, 27,* 1–24.

South, S. J. (1991). Sociodemographic differentials in mate selection preferences. *Journal of Marriage and Family, 53,* 928–940.

South, S. J., Crowder, K. D., and Trent, K. (1998). Children's residential mobility and neighborhood environment following parental divorce and remarriage. *Social Forces, 77,* 667–693.

South, S. J., and Lloyd, K. M. (1995). Spousal alternatives and marital dissolution. *American Sociological Review, 60,* 21–35.

Spain, D., and Bianchi, S. M. (1996). *Balancing act: Motherhood, marriage, and employment among American women.* New York: Russell Sage.

Spanier, G. B., and Anderson, E. A. (1979). The impact of the legal system on adjustment to marital separation. *Journal of Marriage and the Family, 41,* 605–613.Spanier, G. B., and Casto, R. F. (1979). Adjustment to separation and divorce: An analysis of 50 case studies. *Journal of Divorce, 2,* 241–253.

Spanier, G. B., and Furstenberg, F. F. (1982). Remarriage after divorce: A longitudinal analysis of well-being. *Journal of Marriage and Family, 44,* 709–720.

Spanier, G. B., and Thompson, L. (1983). Relief and distress after marital separation. *Journal of Divorce, 7*(1), 31–49.

Spanier, G. B., and Thompson, L. (1984). *Parting: The aftermath of separation and divorce.* Beverly Hills, Calif.: Sage Publications.

Sperling, M. B., and Berman, W. H. (1994). *Attachment in adults: Theory, assessments and treatment.* New York: Guilford.

Spivey, P. B., and Scherman, A. (1980). The effects of time lapse on personality characteristics and stress on divorced women. *Journal of Divorce, 4*(1), 49–59.

Springer, C., and Wallerstein, J. S. (1983). Young adolescents' responses to their parents' divorces. In L. A. Kurdek (ed.), *Children and divorce* (pp. 15–29). San Francisco: Jossey Bass.

Sroufe, L. A. (1988). The role of infant-caregiver attachment in development. In J. Belsky and T. Nezworski (eds.), *Clinical implications of attachment* (pp. 18–40). Hillsdale, N.J.: Erlbaum.

Stamps, L. E., Kunen, S., and Rock-Faucheux, A. (1997). Judges' beliefs dealing with child custody decisions. *Journal of Divorce and Remarriage, 28* (1–2), 3–16.

Stanley, S. M. (2001). Making the case for premarital education. *Family Relations, 50,* 272–280.

Stanley, S. M., Markman, H. J., and Whitton, S. W. (2002). Communication, conflict and commitment: Insights on the foundations of relationship success from a national survey. *Family Process, 41,* 659–675.

Stanley, S. M., Markman, H. J., Peters, St. M., and Leber, B. D. (1995). Strengthening marriages and preventing divorce: New directions in prevention research. *Family Relations, 44,* 392–401.

Stanley, S. M., Markman, H. J., Prado, L. M., Olmos-Gallo, P. A., Tonelli, L., St. Peters, M., Leber, B. D., Bobulinski, M., Cordova, A., and Whitton, S. W. (2001). Community based premarital prevention: Clergy and lay leaders on the front lines. *Family Relations, 50,* 67–76.

Stephen, E. H., Freedman, V. A., and Hess, J. (1993). Near and far: Contact of children with their non-residential fathers. *Journal of Divorce and Remarriage, 20*(3), 171–191.

Stephens, L. S. (1996). Will Johnny see daddy this week?: An empirical test of three theoretical perspectives of postdivorce contact. *Journal of Family Issues, 17,* 466–494.

Stewart, S. D. (1999a). Disneyland dads, Disneyland moms? How nonresident parents spend time with absent children. *Journal of Family Issues, 20,* 539–556.

Stewart, S. D. (1999b). Nonresident mothers' and fathers' social contact with children. *Journal of Marriage and Family, 61,* 894–907.

Stolberg, A. L., Camplair, C. W., Currier, K., and Wells, M. J. (1987). Individual, familial and environmental determinants of children's postdivorce adjustment and maladjustment. *Journal of Divorce, 11*(1), 51–70.

Stolberg, A. L., and Garrison, K. M. (1985). Evaluating a primary prevention program for children of divorce. *American Journal of Community Psychology, 13,* 111–124.

Stolberg, A. L., and Mahler, J. (1994). Enhancing treatment gains in a school-based intervention for children of divorce through skill training, parental involvement, and transfer procedures. *Journal of Consulting and Clinical Psychology, 62*(1), 147–156.

Stone, G. (2002). Nonresidential father postdivorce well-being: The role of social supports. *Journal of Divorce and Remarriage, 36*(3–4), 139–150.

Stover, R., and Hope, C. (1993). *Marriage, family, and intimate relations.* Fort Worth, Tex.: Holt, Rinehart and Winston.

Strickland, B. R. (1992). Women and depression. *Current Directions in Psychological Science, 1*(4), 132–135.

Stroup, A. L., and Pollock, G. F. (1995). Economic consequences of marital dissolution. *Journal of Divorce and Remarriage, 22*(1–2), 37–53.

Struss, M., Pfeiffer, C., Preuss, U., and Felder, W. (2001). Adolescents from divorced families and their perceptions of visitation arrangements and factors influencing parent-child contact. *Journal of Divorce and Remarriage, 35*(1–2), 75–89.

Summers, P., Forehand, R., Armistead, L., and Tannenbaum, L. (1998). Parental divorce during early adolescence in Caucasian families: The role of family process variables in predicting the long-term consequences for early adult psychosocial adjustment. *Journal of Consulting and Clinical Psychology, 66,* 327–336.

Sun, Y. (2001). Family environment and adolescents' well-being before and after parents' marital disruption: A longitudinal analysis. *Journal of Marriage and Family, 63,* 697–713.

Sun, Y., and Li, Y. (2001). Marital disruption, parental investment, and children's academic achievement: A prospective analysis. *Journal of Family Issues, 22,* 27–62.

Sun, Y., and Li, Y. (2002). Children's well-being during parents' marital disruption process: A pooled time-series analysis. *Journal of Marriage and Family, 64,* 472–488.

Sutton, P. D., and Munson, M. L. (2004). Births, marriages, divorces, and deaths: Provisional data for September 2003. *National Vital Statistics Reports, 52*(16). Hyattsville, Md.: National Center for Health Statistics.

Teachman, J. D., Paasch, K., and Carver, K. (1996). Social capital and dropping out of school early. *Journal of Marriage and Family, 58,* 773–783.

Teachman, J. D., Tedrow, L. M., and Crowder K. D. (2000). The changing demography of America's families. *Journal of Marriage and Family, 62,* 1234–1246.

Teja, S., and Stolberg, A. L. (1993). Peer support, divorce, and children's adjustment. *Journal of Divorce and Remarriage, 20*(3–4), 45–64.

Terling-Watt, T. (2001). Explaining divorce: An examination of the relationship between marital characteristics and divorce. *Journal of Divorce and Remarriage, 35*(3–4), 125–145.

Thabes, V. (1997). Survey analysis of women's long-term, postdivorce adjustment. *Journal of Divorce and Remarriage, 27*(3–4), 163–175.

Thibaut, J., and Kelley, H. H. (1959). *The social psychology of groups.* New York: Wiley.

Thiriot, T. L., and Buckner, E. T. (1991). Multiple predictors of satisfactory postdivorce adjustment of single custodial parents. *Journal of Divorce and Remarriage, 17*(1–2), 27–48.

Thoits, P. A. (1992). Identity structures and psychological well-being: Gender and marital status comparisons. *Social Psychology Quarterly, 55,* 236–256.

Thomas, S. P. (1982). After divorce: Personality factors related to the process of adjustment. *Journal of Divorce, 5*(3), 19–36.

Thornton, A. (1985). Reciprocal influences of family and religion in a changing world. *Journal of Marriage and Family, 47*(2), 381–394.

Thornton, A. (1989). Changing attitudes toward family issues in the United States. *Journal of Marriage and Family, 51,* 873–893.

Tidwell, M.-C. O., Reis, H. T., and Shaver, P. R. (1996). Attachment, attractiveness, and social interaction: A diary study. *Journal of Personality and Social Psychology, 71,* 729–745.

Toews, M. L., and McKenry, P. C. (2001). Court-related predictors of parental cooperation and conflict after divorce. *Journal of Divorce and Remarriage, 35*(1–2), 57–73.

Toews, M. L., McKenry, P. C., and Catlett, B. S. (2003). Male-initiated partner abuse during marital separation prior to divorce. *Violence and Victims, 18,* 387–402.

Treas, J., and Giesen, D. (2000). Sexual infidelity among married and cohabiting Americans. *Journal of Marriage and the Family, 62*(1), 48–60.

Tschann, J. M., Johnston, J. R., Kline, M., and Wallerstein, J. D. (1990). Conflict, loss, change and parent-child relationships: Predicting children's adjustment during divorce. *Journal of Divorce, 13*(4), 1–22.

Tschann, J. M., Johnston, J. R., and Wallerstein, J. S. (1989). Resources, stressors, and attachment as predictors of adult adjustment after divorce: A longitudinal study. *Journal of Marriage and Family, 51,* 1033–1046.

Tucker, J. S., Friedman, H. S., Schwartz, J. E., Criqui, M. H., Tomlinson-Keasey, C., Wingard, D. L., and Martin, L. R. (1997). Parental divorce: Effects on individual behavior and longevity. *Journal of Personality and Social Psychology, 73,* 381–391.

Tucker, J. S., Friedman, H. S., Wingard, D. L., and Schwartz, J. E. (1996). Marital history at midlife as a predictor of longevity: Alternative explanations to the protective effect of marriage. *Health Psychology, 15*(2), 94–101.

Tucker, J. S., Kressin, N. R., Spiro, A., and Ruscio, J. (1998). Intrapersonal characteristics and the timing of divorce: A prospective investigation. *Journal of Social and Personal Relationships, 15,* 211–225.

Tucker, M. B. (2000). Marital values and expectations in context: Results from a 21-city survey. In L. J. Waite, C. Bachrach, M. Hindin, E. Thomson, and A. Thornton (eds.), *The ties that bind: Perspectives on marriage and cohabitation* (pp. 166–187). New York: Aldine de Gruyter.

Turner, R. A., Irwin, C. E., Jr., and Millstein, S. G. (1991). Family structure, family processes, and experimenting with substances during adolescence. *Journal of Research on Adolescence, 1,* 93–106.

Twaite, J. A., and Luchow, A. K. (1996). Custodial arrangements and parental conflict following divorce: The impact on children's adjustment. *Journal of Psychiatry and Law, 24,* 53–75.

U.K. Census. (2001). National Statistics: Average age at marriage and divorce: Social trends 33. Retrieved May 5, 2004, from http://www.national-statistics.org.uk/STATBASE/ssdataset.asp?vlnk=6356&More=Y.

United Nations, Department of International Economic and Social Affairs (1992). 1990 Demographic Yearbook/Annuaire Demographique/Sales No. E/F.91.Xiii.1. Renouf Pub. Co. Ltd., Ottawa, Canada.

U.S. Bureau of the Census. (1992). *Current Population Reports,* P23–180, *Marriage, divorce, and remarriage in the 1990's.* Washington, D.C.: U.S. Government Printing Office.

U.S. Bureau of the Census. (1998). *Statistical Abstracts of the United States,* Nos. 159 and 160. Washington, D.C.: U.S. Government Printing Office.

U.S. Bureau of the Census. (1999). Custodial support for custodial mothers and fathers: 1995. *Current Population Reports,* P60. Washington, D.C.: U.S. Government Printing Office.

U.S. Census Bureau. (2003a). Poverty in the United States: 2002. *Current Population Reports.* Washington, D.C.: U.S. Department of Commerce.

U.S. Census Bureau. (2003b). *Statistical Abstract of the United States: Section 2. Vital statistics.* Retrieved May 10, 2004, from http://www.census.gov/prod/2004pubs/03statab/vitstat.pdf.

U.S. Dept. of Health and Human Services, Administration for Children and Families . *Factsheet: Office of Child Support Enforcement*. Retrieved May 11, 2005, from http://www.acf.hhs.gov/opa/fact_sheets/cse_factsheet.html.

Umberson, D., and Williams, C. L. (1993). Divorced fathers: Parental role strain and psychological distress. *Journal of Family Issues, 14*, 378–400.

Utsumi, K. (1991). Inequalities for women in the California divorce law. *Journal of Divorce and Remarriage, 16*, 153–160.

Vandervalk, I., Spruijt, E., De Goede, M., Meeus, W., and Mass, C. (2004). Marital status, marital process, and parental resources in predicting adolescents' emotional adjustment: A multilevel analysis. *Journal of Family Issues, 25*, 291–317.

Vandewater, E. A., and Lansford, J. E. (1998). Influences of family structure and parental conflict on children's well-being. *Family Relations, 47*, 323–330.

Vaughan, D. (1986). *Uncoupling: Turning points in intimate relationship*. New York: Oxford University Press.

Vaux, A. (1985). Variations in social support associated with gender, ethnicity, and age. *Journal of Social Issues, 41*, 89–110.

Veum, J. R. (1993). The relationship between child support and visitation: Evidence from longitudinal data. *Social Science Research, 22*(3), 229–244.

Videon, T. M. (2002). The effects of parent-adolescent relationships and parental separation on adolescent well-being. *Journal of Marriage and Family, 64*, 489–503.

Visher, E. B. (1994). Lessons from remarried families. *American Journal of Family Therapy, 22*, 327–336.

Visher, E. B., and Visher, J. S. (1988). *Old loyalties, new ties: Therapeutic strategies with stepfamilies*. New York: Brunner/Mazel.

Vuchinich, S., Hetherington, E. M., Vuchinich, R., and Clingempeel, G. (1991). Parent-child interaction and gender differences in early adolescents' adaptation to stepfamilies. *Developmental Psychology, 27*, 618–626.

Wade, T. J., and Cairney, J. (2000). Major depressive disorder and marital transition among mothers: Results from a national panel study. *The Journal of Nervous and Mental Diseases, 188*, 741–750.

Wadsby, M., and Svedin, C. G. (1992). Divorce: Different experiences of men and women. *Family Practice, 9*, 451–460.

Waggener, N. M., and Galassi, J. P. (1993). The relation of frequency, satisfaction, and type of socially supportive behaviors to psychological adjustment in marital separation. *Journal of Divorce and Remarriage, 21*(1–2), 139–159.

Waite, L. J., and Lillard, L. A. (1991). Children and marital disruption. *American Journal of Sociology, 96*, 930–953.

Walczak, Y., and Burns, S. (1984). *Divorce: The child's point of view*. London: Harper and Row.

Waldron, J. A., Ching, J. W., and Fair, P. H. (1986). A children's divorce clinic: Analysis of 200 cases in Hawaii. *Journal of Divorce, 9*(3), 111–121.

Walker, J. (2003). Radiating messages: An international perspective. *Family Relations, 52,* 406–417.

Walker, T. R., and Ehrenberg, M. F. (1998). An exploratory study of young persons' attachment styles and perceived reasons for parental divorce. *Journal of Adolescent Research, 13*(3), 320–342

Wallerstein, J. (1983). Children of divorce: Stress and developmental tasks. In N. Garmezy and M. Rutter (eds.), *Stress, coping, and development in children* (pp. 265–302). New York: McGraw-Hill.

Wallerstein, J. S. (1984). Children of divorce: Preliminary report of a ten-year follow-up of young children. *American Journal of Orthopsychiatry, 54,* 444–458.

Wallerstein, J. S. (1985). The overburdened child: Some long-term consequences of divorce. *Social Work, 30,* 116–123.

Wallerstein, J. S. (1986) Women after divorce: Preliminary report from a ten-year follow up. *American Journal of Orthopsychiatry, 56,* 65–77.

Wallerstein, J. S. (1987). Children of divorce: Report of a ten-year follow-up of early latency-age children. *American Journal of Orthopsychiatry, 57,* 199–211.

Wallerstein, J. S., and Blakeslee, S. (1989). *Second chances: Men, women, and children a decade after divorce.* New York: Ticknor and Fields.

Wallerstein, J. S., and Corbin, S. B. (1989). Daughters of divorce: Report from a ten-year follow-up. *American Journal of Orthopsychiatry, 59,* 593–604.

Wallerstein, J. S., and Kelly, J. B. (1980a). Effects of divorce on the visiting father-child relationship. *American Journal of Psychiatry, 137,* 1534–1539.

Wallerstein, J. S., and Kelly, J. B. (1980b). *Surviving the breakup: How children and parents cope with divorce.* New York: Basic Books.

Wallerstein, J. S., and Lewis, J. (1998). The long-term impact of divorce on children: A first report from a 25-year study. *Family and Conciliation Courts Review, 36,* 368–383.

Wallerstein, J. S., Lewis, J. M., and Blakeslee, S. (2000). *The unexpected legacy of divorce: A 25 year landmark study.* New York: Hyperion.

Wallerstein, J. S., and Tanke, T. J. (1996). To move or not to move: Psychological and legal considerations in the relocation of children following divorce. *Family Law Quarterly, 30,* 305–332.

Walsh, P. E., and Stolberg, A. L. (1988–89). Parental and environmental determinants of children's behavioral, affective and cognitive adjustment to divorce. *Journal of Divorce, 12*(2–3), 265–282.

Walters-Chapman, S. F., Price, S. J., and Serovich, J. M. (1995) The effects of guilt on divorce adjustment. *Journal of Divorce and Remarriage, 22*(3–4), 163–177.

Wang, H., and Amato, P. R. (2000). Predictors of divorce adjustment: Stressors, resources, and definitions. *Journal of Marriage and Family, 62,* 655–668.

Warshak, R. A., and Santrock, J. W. (1983) The impact of divorce in father-custody and mother-custody homes: The child perspective. *New Directions for Child Development, 19,* 29–46.

Weinberg, D. C. (1999). The effect of personality upon judicial attitudes and decision-making in contested custody cases. *Dissertation Abstracts International: Section B: The Sciences and Engineering, 60*(1-B), 0404.

Weiss, R. S. (1975). *Marital separation.* New York: Basic Books.

Weiss, R. S. (1984). The impact of marital dissolution on income and consumption in single-parent households. *Journal of Marriage and Family, 46,* 115–127.

Weitoft, G. R., Haglund, B., Hjern, A., and Rosén, M. (2002). Mortality, severe morbidity and injury among long-term lone mothers in Sweden. *International Journal of Epidemiology, 31,* 573–580.

Weitoft, G. R., Hjern, A., Haglund, B., and Rosén, M. (2003). Mortality, severe morbidity, and injury in children living with single parents in Sweden: A population-based study. *Lancet, 361,* 289–295.

Weitzman, L. J. (1985). *The divorce revolution.* New York: The Free Press.

Wells, Y. D., and Johnson, T. M. (2001). Impact of parental divorce on willingness of young adults to provide care for parents in the future. *Journal of Family Studies, 7,* 160–170.

Werner, E., and Smith, R. (2001). *Journeys from childhood to midlife: Risk, resilience, and recovery.* Ithaca, N.Y.: Cornell University Press.

Wertlieb, D., Budman, S., Demby, A., and Randall, M. (1984). Marital separation and health: Stress and intervention. *Journal of Human Stress, 10,* 18–26.

Wetzstein, C. (2004, February 1). Breaking up isn't hard enough to do. *The Washington Times.* http://www.washingtontimes.com/specialreport/2004 0201-011626-9566r.htm.

Weyer, M., and Sandler, I. N. (1998). Stress and coping as predictors of children's divorce-related ruminations. *Journal of Clinical Child Psychology, 27,* 78–86.

Wheaton, B. (1990). Life transitions, role histories, and mental health. *American Sociological Review, 55,* 209–223.

Whisman, M. A., Sheldon, C. T., and Goering, P. (2000). Psychiatric disorders and dissatisfaction with social relationships: Does type of relationship matter? *Journal of Abnormal Psychology, 109,* 803–808.

White, L. K. (1990). Determinants of divorce: A review of research in the eighties. *Journal of Marriage and Family, 52,* 904–912.

White, L., and Rogers, S. J. (2000). Economic circumstances and family outcomes: A review of the 1990s. *Journal of Marriage and Family, 62,* 1035–1051.

White, S. W., and Bloom, B. (1981). Factors relating to the adjustment of divorcing men. *Family Relations, 30*, 349–360.

Whiteside, M. F., and Becker, B. J. (2000). Parental factors and the young child's postdivorce adjustment: A meta-analysis with implications for parenting arrangements. *Journal of Family Psychology, 14*, 5–26.

Wierson, M., Forehand, R., Fauber, R., and McCombs, A. (1989). Buffering young male adolescents against negative parental divorce influences: The role of good parent-adolescent relations. *Child Study Journal, 19*, 101–115.

Wilson, B., and Clarke, S. (1992). Remarriages: A demographic profile. *Journal of Family Issues, 13*, 123–141.

Wilson, J. C., Nock, S. L., Sanchez, L., and Wright, J. D. (2003, April). Covenant marriages: Are they less troubled? Paper presented at the annual meeting of the Southern Sociological Society, New Orleans.

Wineberg, H. (1994). Marital reconciliation in the United States: Which couples are successful? *Journal of Marriage and the Family, 56*, 80–88.

Wiseman, R. S. (1975). Crisis theory and the process of divorce. *Social Casework, 56*, 205–212.

Wolchik, S. A., Braver, S. L., and Sandler, I. N. (1985). Maternal versus joint custody. *Journal of Clinical Child Psychology, 14*(1), 5–10.

Wolchik, S. A., Ruehlman, L. S., Braver, S. L., and Sandler, I. N. (1989). Social support of children of divorce: Direct and stress buffering effects. *American Journal of Community Psychology, 17*, 485–501.

Wolchik, S. A., Sandler, I. N., Millsap, R. E., Plummer, B. A., Greene, S. M., Anderson, E. R., Dawson-McClure, S. R., Hipke, K., and Haine, R. A. (2002). Six-year follow-up of preventive interventions for children of divorce: A randomized controlled trial. *Journal of the American Medical Association, 288*, 1874–1881.

Wolchik, S. A., Tein, J.-Y., Sandler, I. N., and Doyle, K. (2002). Fear of abandonment as a mediator of the relations between divorce stressors and mother-child relationship quality and children's adjustment problems. *Journal of Abnormal Child Psychology, 30*, 401–418.

Wolchik, S. A., West, S. G., Sandler, I. N., Tein, J.-Y., Coatsworth, D., Lengua, L., Weiss, L., Anderson, E. R., Greene, S. M., and Griffin, W. A. (2000). An experimental evaluation of theory-based mother and mother-child programs for children of divorce. *Journal of Consulting and Clinical Psychology, 68*, 843–856.

Wolchik, S. A., Wilcox, K. L., Tein, J.-Y., and Sandler, I. N. (2000). Maternal acceptance and consistency of discipline as buffers of divorce stressors on children's psychological adjustment problems. *Journal of Abnormal Child Psychology, 28*, 87–102.

Woodward, L., Fergusson, D. M., and Belsky, J. (2000). Timing of parental separation and attachment to parents in adolescence: Results of a prospective study from birth to age 16. *Journal of Marriage and Family, 62*, 162–174.

Woody, J. D., Colley, P., Schlegelmilch, J., and Maginn, P. (1984). Parental stress and adjustment following divorce. *Crisis Intervention, 13*(4), 133–147.

Workman, M., and Beer, J. (1992). Aggression, alcohol dependency, and self-consciousness among high school students of divorced and nondivorced parents. *Psychological Reports, 71,* 279–286.

Wu, Z., and Hart, R. (2002). The effects of marital and nonmarital union transition on health. *Journal of Marriage and Family, 64,* 420–432.

Wu, Z., and Penning, M. (1997). Marital instability after midlife. *Journal of Family Issues, 18,* 459–478.

Wynn, R. L., and Bowering, J. (1990). Homemaking practices and evening meals in married and separated families with young children. *Journal of Divorce and Remarriage, 14*(2), 107–124.

Zavoina, R. R. (1997). A study of social support, socioeconomic well-being, attitudes toward women's roles, self-efficacy, and women's psychological adjustment after divorce. *Dissertation Abstracts International: Section B: The Sciences and Engineering, 57*(10-B), 6602.

Zeiss, A. M., Zeiss, R. H., and Johnson, S. M. (1980). Sex differences in initiation and adjustment to divorce. *Journal of Divorce, 4*(2), 21–33.

Zheng, W., and Balakrishnan, T. R. (1994). Cohabitation after marital disruption in Canada. *Journal of Marriage and Family, 55,* 723–734.

Zill, N., Morrison, D. R., and Coiro, M. J. (1993). Long-term effects of parental divorce on parent-child relationships, adjustment, and achievement in young adulthood. *Journal of Family Psychology, 7,* 91–103.

Ziskin, J. (1981). *Coping with psychiatric and psychological testimony.* Venice, Calif.: Law and Psychology Press.

Index

Page numbers in italics indicate figures and tables.

Abandonment, children's feelings of, 110, 111, 113, 131, 137, 160

Abusive marriages, 80, 147

Abusive relationship, between ex-spouses, 87–88, 192

Academic performance, of children of divorce, 114, 117–118, 120, 121, 125

Acceptance and integration stage of divorce, 23–24, 58

Adjustment to divorce, adult, *78,* 236; age and, 77–78; career success and, 86–87; children's adjustment affected by, 157–159; economic factors in, 84–86, 158; gender differences in, 89–99, 104; individual differences in, 100; patterns of, 100–103; personal qualities and, 78–79; professional assistance in, 83–84, 105; quality of marriage related to, 79–80; social support in, 81–83, 104–105; time span for, 99–100. *See also* Ex-spouse relationship

Adjustment to divorce, children's, 128–129; age at time of divorce and, 153–154; coparental cooperation in, 58–59, 165–166, 172, 173; duration of, 124–125, 236; economic factors in, 158; father contact in, 162–165, 172, 173, 174; gender differences in, 154–156; multiple factors in, 171–174, *174;* parental well-being in, 158–159; parenting quality in, 159–160, 164, 172–173, 236; personal qualities in, 156–157; social support in, 168–171; stress limitation in, 166–167

Adjustment to stepfamily, children's, 230–232

Adolescents: delinquent behavior of, 118, 121, 122, 126, 145; divorce adjustment of, 158; emotional reaction of, to divorce, 116–119, 125, 130; family responsibilities of, 140, 141, 158; psychological problems of, 126; remarriage adjustment of, 231–232; school problems

among, 11, 118, 121, 125, 126, 135, 136, 142; sexual activity of, 117, 118, 125–126, 127; shifts in custody arrangement and, 207; social supports for, 168; stepparent relationship with, 227; supervision of, 140, 142, 159

Adult children, long-term effects of divorce on, 119, 121, 126–128

Adultery. *See* Infidelity

Adversarial model of adjudication, 63, 64, 188–189

African Americans: divorce risk of, *35,* 39–40; marriage rate of, 39; redivorce risk of, *218;* remarriage rate of, *214,* 214, 216; in single-parent families, 185; social support in divorce adjustment for, 169

Age: child's wishes in custody decision and, 181; divorce adjustment (adult) and, 77–78, 97–98; divorce adjustment (children's) and, 153–154; divorce rate and, *38;* stepfamily adjustment and, 230–231; of stepparent, 220

Age at marriage: divorce risk and, *35, 36,* 36–38; redivorce risk and, 217–218, *218;* at second marriage, 214, 220

Aggressive behavior, children's: parental conflict and, 147; postdivorce, 115, 118, 124–125; predivorce, 30

Ainsworth, Mary, 25–26

Alabama, joint custody in, 199

Alaska, custody decisions in, 181

Alcohol abuse: among children of divorce, 117, 120, 121, 122; divorce risk and, 49; postdivorce, 74, 75, 100; in separation period, 56

Amato, Paul, 34, 107, 114, 120, 121, 122, 126, 150

American Bar Association, 187

American Psychological Association, 184

Anger, 56, 72, 74; and ambivalence stage of divorce, 23, 54, 55; argument style